ONE MILLION DOLLAR CHALLENGE!

The U.S. Drug Enforcement Administration (DEA) has stated repeatedly and unequivocally that marijuana has no medical value, and consequently has classified it as a Schedule I controlled substance, along with heroin – even though the synthetic drug Marinol, with the same psychoactive ingredient, is classified in Schedule III.

Author David R. Ford offers to pay the DEA *one million dollars*, if, within one year from the publication of this book, the government can prove that marijuana has no medical value, on the condition that if it cannot, the federal government agrees to release all prisoners presently serving time for nonviolent marijuana-related offenses, to cease arresting and charging others with such offenses, and to move marijuana from Schedule I to Schedule III.

Publisher's Note to the Media

A message to media representatives from Good Press:

We are often contacted for interviews with author David R. Ford. While we pass these requests on to him faithfully, you may reach him directly at his email address: dave@DavidRFord.com. For the fastest response, please make "Interview" the first word on the Subject line.

You may also wish to visit his web site at www.DavidRFord.com

---

Author's Note to the Reader

Dave welcomes your comments, by email or old-fashioned letter post:
dave@DavidRFord.com
David R. Ford
c/o Good Press
P. O. Box 1771
Sonoma, California 95476

For a wealth of information on drug policy, especially regarding the medical use of marijuana, visit Dave's web site at www.DavidRFord.com

Good Medicine, Great Sex!

How Marijuana Brought Me Creativity, Passion, and Prosperity

DAVID R. FORD

Edited by Brian & Diane Christeson
Designed by Bookcovers.com

Published by
Good Press
Award-Winning Books
P. O. Box 1771
Sonoma, California 95476

Also, by David R. Ford:
Marijuana: Not Guilty As Charged / David R. Ford; foreword by Tod H. Mikuriya, M.D.
ISBN 0-9655932-5-8

Our books are distributed exclusively by
Bookworld Companies
1941 Whitfield Park Loop
Sarasota, Florida 34243
www.bookworld.com
Fax: 800/777-2525
orders@bookworld.com

Library of Congress Cataloging-in-Publication Data

Ford, David R.
    Good Medicine Great Sex! How Marijuana Brought Me Creativity, Passion, and Prosperity / David R. Ford. Includes references and index.
    p. cm
    ISBN 0-9655932-0-7
    Library of Congress Control Number: 2003104627

    1.Autobiographical—Marijuana—United States. 2. Cannabis—Law and legislation—United States. 3. Marijuana—medical. 4. Propaganda. 5. Sexual behavior.

Manufactured in the United States of America.

Reader's Advisory

This book describes some sexual acts graphically.

Disclaimer

Nothing in this book should be construed as condoning illegal drug use of any kind. To be even clearer: *This book is not written to encourage teens to use any drug, including cannabis.*

The information contained herein is solely for educational purposes and is not to be considered a substitute for medical or legal advice. Readers should consult health-care professionals in all matters regarding their health.

David R. Ford

Dave was prompted to write books about marijuana after spending more than 50 of his 75 years watching scientific research demolish government lies about a benign and beneficial plant over and over again – and then watching the drug warriors pick up the falsehoods, dust them off, repaint them in bright new colors, and trot them out over and over again. In his earlier work, *Marijuana: Not Guilty As Charged*, he cited a wealth of solid scientific evidence that cannabis offers enormous medical benefits, with vastly less risk of harm than many FDA-approved pharmaceuticals.

In *Good Medicine, Great Sex!* he adds to that immense store of proof, and more: He uses his own life story – and the experiences of other happy, successful people – to show that, far from killing initiative, desire, and drive, marijuana can stimulate ingenuity, passion, and dedication. Dave's unique style of writing factual books that read like novels have created a tremendous following, and led to interviews on more than 100 radio stations, and to speaking engagements before audiences both sympathetic and hostile to his message.

Intrepid journalist and broadcaster, irrepressible entrepeneur, globe-trotting adventurer, cheerful cancer survivor, devoted family man, fearless advocate, Dave has lived a life many will envy. In the book in your hands, Ford holds back nothing: exciting sexual adventures, booming business enterprises, and tireless efforts to encourage internationally respected people to open the closet door and acknowledge their own use of cannabis, both medically and for fun.

Dedication

This book is respectfully dedicated to
the former governor of New Mexico, Gary Johnson

From the time I was a teenager I had this fantasy of a politician who had the courage to be completely honest, and not worry about votes. I rejoiced when that fantasy became a reality. Republican Governor Gary Johnson acknowledged trying cocaine and smoking marijuana in his early twenties. As a mature adult he understood that drugs are a fact of life and we must learn to live with them, with *honest* drug education and *harm reduction.*

Governor Johnson is an avid triathlete who doesn't smoke cigarettes and hasn't had a drink of alcohol or used any illegal drugs since 1988. He was elected governor in 1994 and reelected in 1998, becoming the first governor in New Mexico history to win two consecutive four-year terms. In addition to numerous other achievements for his state, on March 21, 2001, Governor Johnson announced the passage of four major drug reform laws in New Mexico. The new legislation restores voting rights to felons after their sentences are completed. As an example of harm reduction, pharmacies in New Mexico are now permitted to sell syringes to drug users without the risk of criminal liability. This one measure prevents thousands of unnecessary deaths annually from AIDS and Hepatitis C contracted from dirty needles. Another new law provides civil and criminal immunity to a person who administers, uses, or possesses a drug to counteract a heroin overdose.

And his good work continues. On March 1, 2002, Governor Johnson signed into law several drug-reform bills, which he called "steps in reducing the harm caused by the failed War on Drugs. I think this legislation will result in less death, disease, and crime." Some highlights of the legislation:

- Granted judges more discretion in sentencing nonviolent habitual offenders. Sponsored by Rep. Ken Martinez, D-Grants, it took effect July 1, 2002.
- Reformed the state's asset forfeiture law to protect innocent property owners in drug-related cases. Sponsored by Senate Majority Leader Manny Aragon, D-Albuquerque, took effect July 1, 2002.
- Allowed convicted felons in drug cases to receive federal assistance, such as food stamps. Sponsored by Rep. Joe Thompson, R-Albuquerque, and Sen. Linda Lopez, D-Albuquerque, it took effect May 15, 2002.
- Created a seven-member commission with the power to consider early release from prison of certain nonviolent drug offenders. Sponsored by Rep. Mimi Stewart, D-Albuquerque, it also took effect May 15, 2002.

Numerous other bills that he attempted to get through the legislature included measures to decriminalize the possession of small amounts of marijuana and to legalize medical marijuana; to reform civil asset forfeiture laws and provide increased funding for probation and drug treatment; to provide treatment, not incarceration, for users of hard drugs; and to eliminate mandatory-minimum sentencing. Two thirds of New Mexicans supported the governor.

Governor Johnson produced the most comprehensive agenda for drug-policy reform ever considered by a state legislature. He cared more about honesty than getting votes. Congratulations, Governor. Perhaps one day we can say, "Congratulations, Mr. President"!

Table of Contents

doctors, and no drug companies, recommend cannabis for pain • Who are these potheads, and why have they wasted their lives? • Cannabis is competition to major cartels • Competition from pot haunts alcohol companies • Is the drug war profitable for those who perpetuate it? • Is marijuana competition to pharmaceutical companies? • Synthetic marijuana compared to the real thing • Are organic cannabis patients treated fairly? • Pot smokers come from all walks of life – but walk a thorny path • Racism in the War on Drugs • Women used, abused, and incarcerated • The Higher Education Act punishes the poor • It isn't enough that you're sick or dying… • DEA terrorizes sick and dying California cannabis patients – why? • What's the alternative? • Who decides? Who should decide? • What must be done • Today's activists will be tomorrow's heroes • Too few users are active in the movement to reform marijuana laws • Are you a NORML person? • The Drug Policy Alliance • Common Sense for Drug Policy • The Marijuana Policy Project • The Internet will be a major factor in ending the War on Drugs • Jurors have more power than they know • Medical-marijuana patients and caregivers winning jury trials • The struggle continues… • Federal court rules that doctors can recommend pot • The Supreme Court ignores marijuana's confirmed medical value • The efficacy of medical marijuana is confirmed – again • Santa Rosa bust drives patients back to the alleys • Santa Cruz bust targets the dying • San Francisco is a winner • Is beautiful Diane Sawyer cannabis-educated? • Federal judge's gag order backfires • Terminal multiple sclerosis patient meets Congressman • Congressman Barney Frank pushes for states' rights to legalize medical marijuana • Attorney General John Ashcroft raids firms selling cannabis equipment • States free inmates to save money • Medical-pot users lose in U.S. court • Poll puts pot on front burner • Vermont Senate passes medical-marijuana bill • Canadian judge stops pot possession trial • Dutch pharmacies start stocking medical marijuana • Cannabis medicine "on sale this year" in Britain • Bush to nominate woman prosecutor to head DEA • Maryland legislature snubs drug czar, okays medical marijuana • GOP leaders pressure Maryland governor to veto medical marijuana • Football star uses cannabis for relaxation and medicine • One final question

Penalties against possession of a drug should not be more damaging to an individual than the drug itself. Therefore, I support legislation amending Federal law to eliminate all Federal penalties for up to one ounce of marijuana.

— President Jimmy Carter: August 2, 1977

All laws which can be violated without doing any one an injury are laughed at ... they direct and incite men's thoughts the more toward those very objects; for we always strive toward what is forbidden and desire the things we are not allowed to have.

— Baruch Spinoza (1630-1677)

Preface: The inside track, including sex

This book is about my life, smoking pot, making money, and enjoying great sex – thanks to the splendor in the grass! The goal of the book is to make my lifetime of cannabis investigation available to legislators who are ready to hear the truth, and to the general public who have been deceived by the legislators who are not. Telling the truth about cannabis can be perilous. Such risks fade, however, in comparison to the costs of imprisonment for being in possession of a plant that is one of the safest therapeutically active substances known to man. Lies about marijuana must stop.

This self-portrayal tells the story of a number of successful business enterprises and a rousing sex life, both enhanced by the use of marijuana (the correct name is cannabis). I will show you how the creativity and sensual effect of this beneficial plant could enrich your life, if it were legal for adults.

Essentially, this book is a story of a long and satisfying life. I'd like you to sit back and enjoy this adventure as I've enjoyed my life. Along the way I'm going to depart from pure storytelling and give you information I've acquired in over a half century of investigation on cannabis. I have interacted with thousands of medical and social users of cannabis, and have interviewed hundreds of them.

I would prefer not to go into my personal sex exploits. However, I will do almost whatever it takes to get the attention of the country. Sex sells and I'm the guy who can give you your money's worth, as you'll soon discover!

I'm just a guy telling you his true-life story. I'll give you some of the facts up front on why cannabis should never have been illegal, especially for those who have medical needs for it. The rest of the book can be mostly just – my story enhanced by grass. You could just go straight to chapter 1 (unless you want to read a preview about how pot enhances sex!) First, though, let's clear up a few important governing factors.

The War on Drugs, and on marijuana in particular, is barbaric, scandalous, and a waste of taxpayers' money. We're told that coming down heavy on pot users is necessary "to save the kids." It's time to change to an approach that really will save them: sensible regulation, *honest* information, and harm reduction – replacing prohibition and punishment with realistic measures that minimize the harmful effects of drug use.

It's certain that what we're doing now isn't keeping drugs away from kids. Teens report they have easier access to pot than they have to either alcohol or tobacco, according to a national survey released August 20, 2002. The survey was conducted by the National Center on Addiction and Substance Abuse (CASA) at Columbia University, and it concludes that "*regulation of cannabis would likely result in reduced teen use.*"[1]

Choosing words: cannabis, marijuana, hemp, ...

Many books, magazine articles, and news stories use the terms marijuana, cannabis, and hemp as if they had identical meanings, frequently in the same story. Generally they all refer to the plant cannabis, which is now called marijuana. Using hemp and cannabis interchangeably can be confusing to a reader who needs to see the difference between a valuable medicine and a useful source of fiber.

Hemp has no medical or intoxicating value, but it's a valuable resource economically and environmentally, providing oil, fuel, fiber, pulp for paper, and biomass for clean methanol fuels. The seeds can be cooked as a nutritious cereal, providing a complete vegetable protein. Its versatility is astonishing, providing fiber for the manufacture of rope, insulating building materials, and clothing fabric. Literally thousands of other articles can be manufactured from hemp. It is estimated that one acre of hemp, which can be grown in three to four months, can save four acres of timberland used for paper.

Hemp's one flaw is that it offers competition to many patented products, such as Nylon and other synthetics manufactured by DuPont and other large companies. For this crime it was indicted and convicted along with marijuana. Politicians, and publishers such as Hearst Newspapers, deliberately blurred the distinction between them, and demonized and outlawed hemp along with marijuana in 1937, for financial gain.

The American Medical Association recognizes the medicinal botanical by the name *cannabis sativa*. The female plant has flowers, sometimes called *buds* or *colas*; and it is these which contain the active ingredient, tetrahydrocannabinol, also referred to as delta-1-THC, delta-9-THC, or merely THC. I will just use the abbreviation, THC.

Hashish, often called hash, is the resin, the sticky material from the female flower of the cannabis plant. The THC level is higher than in the bud, so less is needed to achieve the same effect – whether it's used for medicine or for fun.

I will frequently avoid the word marijuana, because that word has itself been a centerpiece of a decades-long effort to demonize an herb that has been medicine for thousands of years. Generally, I'll use the correct term, cannabis, but I'll also use familiar colloquialisms like grass, happy grass, pot, plant, and joint.

The propaganda begins

Back in the 1930s, the country's first drug czar, Harry J. Anslinger, headed the Federal Bureau of Narcotics. With the end of alcohol prohibition and the onset of the depression, his agency came almost to a shuddering halt. Anslinger was faced with a drastic reduction of his agents. He realized that he needed a new evil to pursue in order to save the Bureau. He picked cannabis. The FBN changed its name to today's Drug Enforcement Administration. (DEA)

Cannabis prohibition was created and is fueled today by ignorance, arrogance, politics, greed, power, money, outright lies, perjury, and racism.

Anslinger began this shameful history of deception with utterly unsupported assertions like "Fifty percent of all violent crimes were committed by Mexicans, Turks, Filipinos, Spaniards, Greeks, Latin-Americans, and Negroes, and those crimes could be traced directly to the use of marijuana."

Exposing the ultimate hypocrisy

Nicotine products cause the deaths of 430,000 Americans each year. It's legal, and our coin-operated politicians are still subsidizing farmers who grow the world's most death-causing drug. We continue to export cigarettes to places where thousands of eight- and nine-year-olds sell them, smoke them, become addicted, and die early. Could Uncle Sam be the world's biggest drug exporter?

The most popular recreational drug and the one most intimately associated with violent behavior is not included in the "enemies list" of the official War on Drugs. It is ignored by the government, no doubt due to media-cultivated acceptance and monumental political contributions. That drug is alcohol, which causes the deaths of 100,000 Americans each year, more than six times more deaths annually than *all illegal drugs combined.* Ninety percent of alcohol drinkers do not abuse alcohol. The same is true of users of other drugs. Alcohol, however, is the number one drug problem.

On April 10, 2002, Knight Ridder Newspapers reported the following sobering assessment: Alcohol-related accidents kill an estimated 1,400 college students each year. Alcohol contributes to 600,000 assaults, 500,000 injuries, and 70,000 sexual assaults every year. In 2001, two million students acknowledged having driven a car after drinking, and 400,000 students between the ages of 18 and 24 reported having unprotected sex while under the influence. Alcohol is abused by 14 million Americans, and kills 100,000 each year.[2]

It's estimated that alcohol is implicated in half of all serious injuries and deaths of young people. Government surveys show that the beer and distilled spirits industry earns an estimated $1 billion nationwide from underage youth.[3]

In 5,000 years of recorded history *cannabis has not caused one toxicity-related death.* If marijuana were legal and alcohol were prohibited, we'd hear the government ranting that alcohol is 100,000 times more dangerous than cannabis!

The government reports (*without* the fanfare that accompanies its marijuana propaganda) that all illegal drugs combined cause 16,000 deaths a year – and many of the hazards associated with these drugs are products of their illegality, rather than of the drugs themselves. The numbers of deaths attributed to overdoses of heroin and other drugs are grossly exaggerated in any case. The relatively small numbers of deaths actually caused by overdose typically result from the impurities and unpredictable dosages inevitable in a black market. Black-market drugs do kill some users – the same way bathtub gin and methanol killed drinkers during alcohol prohibition. Deaths caused by "bad hooch" dropped sharply when the Volsted Act was repealed. What can we expect when drug prohibition follows alcohol prohibition?

As people, we are all connected; we are all one. Empathy and honesty should prevail rather than hysterical press releases. We must challenge anti-marijuana crusaders, including legislators, law officers, judges, publishers, broadcasters, celebrities – everyone who shapes public opinion – to tell the truth. Many times these people open their minds to the medical magic of marijuana when a family member is suffering from AIDS or cancer... but why must a simple lesson demand such a grim price?

After my book *Marijuana: Not Guilty As Charged* became available nationally, I began receiving dozens of emails from people who enjoyed it, and some wanted to meet me.

One was a lady who had just finished the book. I invited her and her husband to my home. Shireen appears to be in her mid-twenties. Husband Dennis is 29, handsome, very mellow and soft-spoken, with a shy smile. He has coal-black hair, a dark complexion, and serious brown eyes. Shireen is the opposite, with blond hair and sapphire eyes. We immediately became friends, and have been close for about three years. I have never met a couple more in love with each other and their two babies. Cede, age four, idolized her daddy. He played piggyback with her and her two-year-old brother, Cayman. Dennis frequently changed Cayman's diapers, helped prepare barbecues, and played with his children and wife in the pool. The children were always immaculate and filled with love and admiration for mother and father. This family could easily adorn the cover of any parents' magazine.

One day while Dennis was playing with the children on the lawn, Shireen confided in me, "I came from a background of divorce and sexual abuse. Dennis has been the only person in my life who has supported me and allowed me to start believing in myself. He has the most amazing outlook on life. He is full of compassion and desire to help people. I have never seen him hesitate to help anyone in need. Dennis is the kind of guy who stops to help an elderly person change a tire on the highway. He is so selfless. I have met no one else like that in today's busy world."

While the children napped, Dennis, Shireen, and I talked about medical marijuana. Dennis grew cannabis and supported medical-cannabis facilities. He frequently donated cannabis to sick and dying patients. I'm convinced that Dennis grew medical cannabis because he knows that it is good medicine, not for the money. He looked forward to the day when cannabis would be legalized for medical use nationally, and sold in pharmacies for around $35 per ounce. Today, medical-quality cannabis costs $400 or more per ounce, which is still less expensive than synthetic pharmaceutical drugs. Dennis loves growing plants and he felt a calling to see that only the finest-quality medical cannabis reached sick and dying patients. His medicine went to dispensaries that have been legalized by voters. Dennis practiced strict quality control and professional management.

I suffer from severe back spasms from injuries earlier in my life, and have a doctor-written recommendation for cannabis. For Christmas 2001, Dennis presented me with a container of his cannabis. I was totally amazed. One puff stopped my muscle spasms in less than three minutes. I have *never* experienced such high quality. The cannabis was so smooth, I hardly knew I had taken a puff. I could imagine how cancer, AIDS and anorexia patients, and those suffering from constant pain and other ailments, must thank God when they use cannabis grown with such love and compassion as Dennis has.

On March 31, 2002, for conducting one of the most professional medical-cannabis growing operations in the country, Dennis Hunter was arrested by the DEA. This was his second arrest for growing medical cannabis. His parents and grandparents, who had worked the soil for generations, put up their properties, worth more than two million dollars, so that Dennis could be with Shireen and the children until his trial begins. Still the court, which frequently allows bail for alleged murderers, refuses to allow Dennis out on bail.

In federal court, an oath is required: "I swear to tell the truth, the whole truth, and nothing but the truth." However, *the truth is absent under prosecution by a federal government that ignores the truth,* that *cannabis is medicine.* It is impermissible to utter the words "medical marijuana" in a court of law, even in one's own defense. The government does not tell the truth, and in federal court refuses to allow medical-marijuana growers to tell the truth! Our justice system thus forces the accused to incriminate themselves:

> Prosecutor: "Did you grow marijuana?"
> Defendant: "Yes, sir."
> Prosecutor: "Were you selling that marijuana?"
> Defendant: "Yes, sir. But,"

This is the Hunter family, as lovely and loving as they appear in this picture. The DEA is tearing this family apart because Dennis Hunter's compassion for sick and dying people led him to provide them with medical marijuana.

Dennis adores his wife and babies. Here he's holding two-year-old Cayman. For the crime of compassion, Dennis faces 20 years to life in prison. This book may be about me, but it's for Dennis, and Dennis's family, and all the other victims of the War on Drugs.

> Judge: "We don't want to hear any buts. Answer the question."
>
> Defendant: "Yes. I sold it."
>
> Prosecutor to jury: "You heard the witness. There is only one choice: you must return a verdict of guilty as charged!"

Dennis is facing *20 years to life in prison* for growing some of the finest-quality medicine in the country. Ten DEA agents handcuffed him in front of his children, in their own home. The children do not understand what is happening and almost constantly cry and fuss. Shireen has lost more than ten pounds and is ill.

Should Dennis Hunter be put in prison, possibly for the rest of his life, for the crime of compassion? Pot *must* be moved from Schedule I to Schedule III, equal to the synthetic pot capsule Marinol, or legalized. Even if you have never used cannabis, please demand a change in the law. Dennis is only one of around 75,000 nonviolent Americans now incarcerated for being in possession of a relatively harmless plant, one of the world's safest medicines and safest highs. How will Shireen, their children, and tens of thousands of other children grow up with a parent, or both parents, in prison? Two-year-old Cayman no longer recognizes his "dada." The DEA turns good Samaritans into criminals.

What drugs are dangerous?

What is a positively dangerous drug? Clearly, one that can cause death.

By that standard, aspirin is dangerous and marijuana is not. Aspirin sometimes causes internal bleeding that, in severe cases, leads to the deaths of more than 2,000 Americans each year.

Another 100,000 Americans lose their lives each year from the toxic effects of prescription medications certified "safe and effective" by the FDA.[4]

In half of all homicides, alcohol is found in either the killer or the victim, according to the National Institute on Alcohol Abuse and Alcoholism.

Tobacco smoking is the #1 cause of preventable premature death in the Unites States, taking as many as 430,000 lives a year.

Yet all these drugs are legal, and marijuana is not.

Death is far from the only dire consequence of the War on Drugs. Otherwise law-abiding people, peacefully growing grass for the ill and dying, too frequently find themselves in that first fatal trip through the criminal "justice" system. If sentenced to prison, they will join the 75,000 citizens who are currently incarcerated. For what? Being in possession of pot. They lose the peaceful, honorable lives they had and find themselves in a school for crime – and ironically, a place where illegal drugs are seldom hard to find. Our "three strikes" laws and heavy mandatory minimum sentences doom hundreds of thousands of otherwise ordinary people to decades, even lifetimes, in prison. For many, possession of a personal amount of pot was a third strike. The drug war, rather than protecting children, is ruining their lives by taking them away from their parents, who have been imprisoned for using and being in possession of an herb less harmful than aspirin.

Now in my seventies, I have seen most of my friends die from alcohol, nicotine, poor diet, or drugs the FDA calls "safe." My pot-using friends are still alive and enjoying life, including sex, well into their eighties. Interacting with thousands of cannabis users for over 50 years, I have learned that cannabis is one of the world's safest medicines and highs.

We would like to believe our government. Can we?

It is understandable that the public is spooked by pot propaganda. We all want to believe our government. The feds maliciously have placed cannabis in Schedule I, along with heroin. In the face of masses of evidence to the contrary, they claim that it is unsafe, highly subject to abuse, too dangerous to prescribe, and has *no medical value.* Even if you're dying, even if cannabis is the only medicine that can keep you alive, *any* marijuana use is criminal. The *synthetic* copy-cat capsule Marinol, however, whose active ingredient is the same as marijuana's, is a Schedule *III* drug, easily prescribed, making pharmaceutical companies even richer. Cocaine and morphine are Schedule II drugs. Those who believe government propaganda will believe that those drugs are less harmful than pot!

Cannabis: no medical value?

Organizations that have endorsed medical use of cannabis include the AIDS Action Council, American Academy of Family Physicians, American Public Health Association, California Medical Association, California Society of Addiction Medicine, Lymphoma Foundation of America, National Association of People With AIDS, National Nurses Society on Addictions, *The New England Journal of Medicine,* and others. To mention just a few of the newspapers whose editorial boards have endorsed access to medical marijuana: the *Boston Globe, Chicago Tribune, Miami Herald, New York Times, Orange County Register,* and *USA Today.*

The gateway theory is government smoke and mirrors

The *gateway theory*, also known as the *stepping-stone hypothesis*, was conjured up by government agencies to scare people off of cannabis. We're told that pot users are 85 times more likely to use cocaine. Follow closely. This claim is superficially clever, but untrue. Approximately 83 million Americans have used pot, a very popular drug compared to cocaine. Divide the proportion of pot users who had ever tried coke (17 percent) by the proportion of cocaine users who had never used pot (0.2 percent). The "risk factor" of 85 percent is large, not because so many pot users experiment with coke, but because very few people try coke without first trying pot.

Using the same Enron-type math, one might say that mother's milk, used frequently, is a stepping stone to drinking milkshakes! Or that ping-pong is a gateway sport for tennis players. Alcohol is also said to be a gateway drug. How many people do you know who have a few drinks, then run to a back alley with their arm out seeking a shot of heroin? If pot did not exist, could any intelligent person say that no one would get high on some other drug? Every unbiased study, national or international, has shown that pot is not a gateway drug.

Why don't more doctors recommend medical marijuana?

If marijuana is safe and effective, why do so few doctors recommend it? One reason is that drug warriors in government pay close attention to those who don't toe the official line very closely. They have – and too often use – the power to restrict or rescind physicians' right to prescribe legal drugs, and thus in effect to prevent them from practicing their profession. How eager would you be to risk the loss of your career after all those years of training? Also, there are no Medical Marijuana 101 classes in universities. Consequently, doctors are subjected to the same government deception about cannabis as the rest of us.

Here's an example of another reason:

Pharmaceutical companies frequently give doctors free trips and arrange paid speaking engagements. Drug manufacturer Purdue Pharma played host to hundreds of doctors at all-expense-paid weekends to discuss pain management. Doctors were then recruited and paid to speak to other doctors at some of the 7,000 pain-management seminars that Purdue sponsored around the country.

What was stressed was prescribing OxyContin, a painkiller produced by Purdue Pharma. In four years this drug's sales amounted to $1 billion, more than Viagra's. (That's enough to make your hair stand on end.) With such bait, what physician is motivated to recommend relatively harmless but non-patentable cannabis?

Yet, according to a report in the Santa Rosa *Press Democrat*, "OxyContin has been a factor in the deaths of at least 120 people, and medical examiners are still counting."[5]

All illegal drugs combined cause less than one sixth as many deaths as government-approved drugs, a fraction that could shrink even further if the drugs' potency were standardized and labeled. And how many deaths has medical marijuana caused again? None.

If politics didn't prevail in our society, alcohol and nicotine, the world's two most deadly drugs, would replace pot on Schedule I, alongside heroin, but they are not included in the official War on Drugs at all, because the drug war is about politics, money, control, and jobs. The alcohol and tobacco lobbies in this country represent enormous revenue to the federal government and huge campaign contributions to parties and individual candidates.

The Partnership for a Drug Free America (PDFA) has been funded by the alcohol and tobacco cartels, and still receives large contributions from pharmaceutical companies. If PDFA's directors have the usual sensitivity to which side of their bread is buttered, it probably isn't necessary for those big companies to whisper in their ears: "Our financial backing will continue just as long as you refrain from mentioning that our legal drugs cause many times more deaths than all illegal drugs combined."

The federal government works closely with large corporations, aiding them in every way possible to market their products. These favors come back to Uncle Sam as tax dollars and campaign contributions. It is as if the federal government is saying, "Mess with our multi-billion-dollar corporations like the pharmaceutical companies by growing your own medicine, or selling it to the sick and dying, and we'll put you in prison for longer than we imprison murderers, rapists, and child molesters."

Whether the government admits it or not, that's exactly what it is doing. Consider the story of William Foster, a 38-year-old computer programmer in Oklahoma who suffers from crippling rheumatoid arthritis and was sentenced to an outrageous 93 years in prison for growing his own medicine. Also reflect on the fate of Todd McCormick, whom I call "the Luther Burbank of medical marijuana," who was researching assorted strains of cannabis to discover which would best treat various illnesses – including his own cancer. He lives in California, and is serving a five-year prison term.

When did war become a domestic policy?

Today, few people are aware that the earliest drug warriors concealed the longtime use of cannabis as a medicine by "re-labeling the product": replacing the traditional name "cannabis" with "marijuana" to make it sound foreign and threatening. When the 1937 Marijuana Tax Act came before the U.S. House of Representatives, a Congressman asked, "What is the bill?" A colleague replied, "It has something to do with something called marihuana. I believe it is a narcotic of some kind." The prohibition bill passed in less than two minutes. If members of the U.S. House of Representatives had known that the Act was about cannabis, the bill probably never would have passed, and the herb would have remained legal for adults. As it was, the Act prohibited only the *non-medical* (recreational) use of marijuana. *Even at that moment, the government implicitly acknowledged that the plant has medical value.*

Prohibition is not only futile, but counterproductive. Publicly attacking various drugs, including some that kids have never heard of, actually stimulates experimentation by calling attention to new drugs to try. Remember that flurry of warnings about glue sniffing? Soon all the stores were sold out of airplane glue! When I was a kid there were two choices: pot or alcohol. Had we been fed the names of other drugs, most teen rebels would have pushed to learn those names and try them. Remember how we thought when we were kids:

> Tommy O'Meara entered the confessional box . "Bless me, Father, for I have sinned. I have been with a loose girl."
>
> "And who was it you were with?"
>
> "I can't be tellin' you, Father. I don't want to ruin her reputation."
>
> "Was it Brenda O'Malley?"
>
> "I cannot say."
>
> "Was it Patricia Kelly?"
>
> "I'll never tell."
>
> "Was it Liz Shannon?"
>
> "I'll not tell her name."
>
> "Was it Cathy McGuiness?"
>
> "Please, Father, I cannot tell you."

"You've sinned, my son, and you must atone."

The confessor finally tired of his interrogation, gave Tommy his penance, and dismissed him. As Tommy slipped back into his pew his friend Sean slid over and whispered, "What'd you get?"

Tommy smiled. "Four good leads!"

A wiser approach

What does the mother of a teenage son do about the prospect that he will soon experiment with drugs – when she is also an honest long-time researcher in the field? If her name is Marsha Rosenbaum, she writes him this letter, published in the San Francisco Chronicle on September 7, 1998:

A MOTHER'S ADVICE ABOUT DRUGS

Dear Johnny,

This fall you will be entering high school, and like most American teenagers, you'll have to navigate drugs. Like most parents, I would prefer that you not use drugs. However, I realize that despite my wishes, you might experiment.

I will not use scare tactics to deter you. Instead, having spent the past 25 years researching drug use, abuse, and policy, I will tell you a little about what I have learned, hoping this will lead you to make wise choices. My only concern is your health and safety. When people talk about "drugs," they are generally referring to illegal substances such as marijuana, cocaine, methamphetamine (speed), psychedelic drugs (LSD, Ecstasy, "shrooms"), and heroin.

These are not the only drugs that make you high. Alcohol, cigarettes, and many other substances (like glue) cause intoxication of some sort. The fact that one drug or another is illegal does not mean one is better or worse for you. All of them temporarily change the way you perceive things and the way you think...

If you are offered drugs, be cautious. Watch how people behave, but understand that everyone responds differently – even to the same substance. If you do decide to experiment, be sure you are surrounded by people you can count on. Plan your transportation and under no circumstances drive or get into a car with anyone else who has been using alcohol or other drugs. Call us or any of our close friends any time, day or night, and we will pick you up, no questions asked and no consequences.

And please, Johnny, use moderation. It is impossible to know what is contained in illegal drugs because they are not regulated. The majority of fatal overdoses occur because young people do not know the strength of the drugs they consume, or how they combine with other drugs. Please do not participate in drinking contests, which have killed too many young people. Whereas marijuana by itself is not fatal, too much can cause you to become disoriented and sometimes paranoid. And of course, smoking can hurt your lungs, later in life and now.

Johnny, as your father and I have always told you about a range of activities (including sex), think about the consequences of your actions before you act. Drugs are no different. Be skeptical, and most of all, be safe.

Love, Mom [6]

You can find more of Marsha's wisdom at the excellent Safety First web site, www.safety1st.org, a project of the Drug Policy Alliance.

A cautionary tale for politicians

California Attorney General Dan Lungren wondered why he lost his 1998 campaign to become Governor. Lungren chose to support the federal prohibition of pot rather than the initiative that was on the ballot that year to legalize the medical use of marijuana – ignoring the majority of Californians who voted for the proposition. Dan, how could you have thought they would vote for you?

"We don't want to send the wrong message"

A politician recently said, "We're still going to win the War on Drugs. It just needs a good shot in the arm!"

Ready for the adventure?

I must admit, I have experimented with pot. But for only 58 years.

I'm but one of millions of successful, hard-working, self-motivated, taxpaying Americans who use pot medically, for creativity, and for the sheer enjoyment of it. And you bet, for great sex! The hypothesis that marijuana makes people stupid and less ambitious is ludicrous. I see that acknowledging my use of cannabis gives me the opportunity to show first-hand documentation of the numerous uses of this herb, and also to confirm that pot is one of the world's safest drugs.

As the author of the hardcover book, *Marijuana: Not Guilty As Charged*, I know that pot, among its other medical gifts, enhances creativity, soothes intolerable pain, boosts mood, and raises sex to an art form. In *Good Medicine, Great Sex!* I will tell you how smoking grass has made me a better businessman, a better journalist, a better lover, and a more sensitive person – and, as a cancer survivor, a better, more relaxed, smiling patient.

Speaking of smiling... one more to put you in the right mood for the road ahead:

Example of how marijuana improves lovemaking

The young queen eagerly anticipated her approaching wedding. The young king, a little more experienced in the ways of the world than his young consort-to-be, planned beyond the pageantry of the royal wedding to the royal wedding night that would follow.

He wanted his virgin queen to begin their married life together with an exquisite, long-lasting orgasm, and knew that cannabis causes time to seem to slow down, and sensations to be more intense. He sent forth his manservant to obtain for him the finest cannabis in the realm.

The long-awaited day – and night – arrived at last. The king showed his bride how to take several puffs of happy grass. Their lovemaking was sensuous, creative, and increasingly intense. In the midst of a mutual superorgasm, the queen cried out, "My liege! My darling! ...Is this... what the commoners call... mari...mari...wwwanaaa?"

"Yyyeesss, my love, my queen!" he replied, "This... is what... the commoners... call mari...mari...wwwanaaa...."

"Oh *darling, darling*... it's too *good* for them!"

Now it's time for the adventure to begin.

Early childhood in Northern California

Dad had immigrated from New Zealand. Like most Americans in those days of innocence, he believed nearly all of what was reported by the press and by those who ran the country. For example, he believed what America's first drug czar, Harry Anslinger, said about marijuana. Dad was convinced that a man in such a high position was honorable and would not lie.

Mother was a poet, and highly educated. Her poems appeared in *Parent's Magazine, The Ladies Home Journal,* and other magazines. There were times that she told us kids that she believed that she was kidnapped at age three from a wealthy family in Vienna where her father was a doctor. Her nanny, whom she called Gody, brought her to America and raised her as her own child. Even when she was dying, Gody wouldn't tell Mother where she came from.

Mother was wonderful. She was beautiful, very intelligent, and highly skilled, a super mom and a great cook. She read stories to us three children: *Heidi, Bambi, Nobody's Boy, Cinderella, Pinocchio.* (Years later whenever I saw our drug czar, I flashed on Pinocchio.)

Early memories

The most terrifying experience of my childhood came in my fourth year: Mother took me to the funeral of a friend of the family. I recall riding to the funeral parlor in a large black car with shades on the windows. When we got to the coffin, seeing a person dead frightened me. I was asked to kiss the dead lady. My stomach began churning; I just couldn't do it. That horror remained with me for years. I never wanted a child of mine to feel such terror. Years later that painful scene from my childhood was repeated.

When I was five it was discovered that I had tuberculosis. Mother had been a nurse during World War I, and she took awesome care of me. I had to remain in bed for one solid year; and during that time Mom taught me to read. Doctors told me never to smoke cigarettes. (They didn't tell me not to smoke pot.) Today, my lungs are perfect. I listened to all the soap operas of the day: *Ma Perkins, Stella Dallas, Jack Armstrong – the All American Boy*, (he didn't smoke pot). I also enjoyed the radio news shows. Those shows later encouraged me to seek a career in broadcasting

My introduction to grass at age eight, 1936

One sunny autumn day our lessons at Red Hill School in Northern California were done. My two older sisters, Margo and Carol, and I watched the leaves flutter to the ground while we waited for Dad or Mom to pick us up. We heard a car's horn sounding, and spotted a shiny new dark blue four-door Ford with white-sidewall tires. Inside were a beaming Mom and Dad. We excitedly clambered into the car and immediately were mesmerized by the exciting fragrance that only a new car offers.

"Is it ours?" we squealed in unison.

"Yep," said Dad, proudly. "Be careful, children, this car cost $600."

Later that afternoon Mother drove us kids into San Rafael, 10 miles from where we lived in Fairfax. She asked me to wait near the car while the girls had their bangs trimmed.

I drifted over to the tobacconist's shop, where I enjoyed the fragrance of the various tobaccos wafting through the door. A Latino youngster ambled over, carrying a large brown paper bag. From it he withdrew a small bag about the size of my hand. "Want some happy grass for your dad and mom? It's only 10 cents."

He put the open bag to my nose. I liked the fresh smell; it reminded me of a sweet newly cut lawn. "Why do you call it happy grass?" I asked.

His big brown eyes looked at me with a condescending smile. "Because it makes you happy!"

"My dad only smokes Camels," I said. "I don't think he'd like to smoke grass. He cuts our grass, and it doesn't make him happy. And he doesn't smoke it."

With rolling eyes the youngster shook his shaggy head of black curly hair, and walked a few feet to a guy sitting on a bench waiting for a bus.

Just then an old guy about 50 with gray hair and silver-rimmed glasses low on his nose walked over to me and said, "Don't ever smoke that stuff the kid had. It will make you crazy and you could kill your parents. It's called marijuana."

"Thanks," I said. A shiver ran down my spine.

I noted the man on the bench handing the kid a coin. The guy was maybe thirty and dressed in coveralls. He took a small paper out of his pocket, put some of that grass stuff on it and rolled a small cigarette. He lit it and inhaled deeply, and an unforgettable expression transformed his face. It was as if he had just eaten a tasty piece of candy. As I walked near him, he blew a ring of smoke my way.

I said, "That stuff will make you crazy."

He laughed and said, "I was watching you, kid. You don't have clue of what it is or what it does, do you?"

"No, I don't," I said.

He continued, "I heard the old guy talk to you. Don't believe all the baloney you hear, kid. This is good stuff, better than whiskey. You feel happy. Fixes pain. No headache. No hangover. No puke on yer shoes. Alcohol people don't like ya t' get a free high. They spread bullshit."

The bus arrived. He winked at me, smiled, and boarded the bus. That was the first time I'd heard the word "marijuana." And the word "bullshit." I could visualize that it would be a large amount.

The news on the radio began talking about drug dealers selling reefers, also called marijuana, to grade-school children during recess or right after school, with the hope of turning them into addicts.

Dad responds to a well-meant suggestion

Once a buddy told me that his parents smoked happy grass; and that when they did they were both really happy. He said, "When they smoke that happy-grass stuff, mom cooks the greatest meals. And you should see them *eat!* Then they play with me. I wish they smoked it all the time, 'cause when they drink liquor they play with me sometimes, but they also fight."

I thought about my own parents. They argued a lot. Maybe I'd found a way for them to be happy together. That night at dinner I said, "Hey, Pop, why don't you and Mom smoke that happy grass stuff? It's called marijuana, too. It will make you like you're in love again. What do you say, Pop?"

Wrong question! Dad's face looked as if it had been broiled, and he was shaking. He had a look of "kill" on his face, like the time he caught a big fish and was about to chop its head off. I thought he was going to spill his glass of bourbon and swallow his cigarette. "Mr. Harry Anslinger heads our Federal Bureau of Narcotics, and he said that marijuana is the most violence-causing drug in the history of mankind. It turns people into criminals, and many marijuana users go insane! Mr. Anslinger not only made that statement before the Congress of the United States; he and his staff also speak to parent-teacher groups, police, judges, and the FBI. Don't ever mention the word marijuana in this house again!"

I trusted my Dad; but why would my school buddy lie? And then one story on the news reported that a youngster who smoked marijuana used an ax and slaughtered his entire family.[7] I was confused. (The story turned out to be pure fiction.)

How The Marijuana Tax Act of 1937 came about

Listening to the radio, reading newspapers, and listening to adults who visited Mom and Pop, I began to learn about the prohibition of drugs. I also began to question the many stories about marijuana being "deadly." Mother told me that before 1914, drugs were legal – with virtually no violence. She said that business in the Bureau of Narcotics was slow during the 1920s, other than for alcohol prohibition, which they saw as coming to a jolting conclusion because citizens refused to accept it any longer. Mother said, "It was terrifying. Alcohol prohibition caused more violence and deaths than the country had ever known. Prohibition never works. It causes hidden use."

I never forgot mother's words: "Prohibition never works. It causes hidden use."

Race fears exploited to outlaw marijuana

Mother was not only my dearest friend, she was also my home teacher. Over the years she encouraged me to research and learn more about cannabis. (I later found that everything she had told me was true.) She said that before 1937, marijuana was used primarily by minority groups such as African- and Mexican-Americans, who had virtually no money. They used marijuana for its medicinal value, for relaxation, for sexual enhancement, and in religious ceremonies, because it cost practically nothing. Other segments of the population used alcohol.

Mexican immigrants were moving into the United States rapidly. In the 20s they, like black Americans, found work because they would work for wages others wouldn't accept. When depression ravaged the American economy and unemployed topped 30%, the few available jobs were now in demand by white Americans. Mexican- and African-Americans and other minorities became the objects of scorn and were often falsely accused of being provoked to violence by "reefers" (marijuana). The government said that blacks would smoke those reefers, then rape white women and make them pregnant.

My parents divorce; Mom moves us to Washington, D.C.

My parents' fights intensified, and before the end of 1937 they were divorced. In the settlement Mom got the house, which she sold for cash. Then she booked reservations for Washington, D.C., on the Southern Pacific Railroad for us three kids and herself.

It was thrilling to board our Pullman car, and what fun and adventure to awake each morning to scenery we'd never imagined. The food was good and the porters were friendly and helpful.

Five days and nights later we arrived in our country's capital. Mother found an apartment for us and got a job. She was a speed typist and took shorthand. Mom managed to take us to the Washington Monument, the Lincoln Memorial, the Smithsonian Institution, and other sites around the Capitol.

Easter Sunday, 1938, Mother took us three children to the White House for the annual Easter egg hunt. The most exciting part was when President Roosevelt came out on the balcony and talked to us kids.

We didn't prosper in Washington. We were constantly moving to different apartments and schools. We moved from D.C. to Maryland, then to Virginia. We three children were frequently boarded out. We attended four or five schools, moving every few months. I was now at my tenth school, and not yet 10 years old.

My magazine of choice was *Popular Mechanics*. The February 1938 issue drew my attention to hemp. The story was entitled, "New Billion-Dollar Crop." Today, with inflated dollars, it would read "New 11-Billion-Dollar Crop." The magazine featured a story relating the hundreds of uses of the fascinating *nonintoxicating* plant. It was indeed eye-opening to learn that hemp, a relative of cannabis, would produce thousands of textile products, food, building materials, rope, and much more. I went to the library, wanting to know more about this plant that the government said was just as dangerous as marijuana.

My eyes widened as I pored over several books in the library about a plant that all evidence pointed to as something we should be saluting rather than suppressing. There was a time in our history when hemp was so valued that both President Washington and President Thomas Jefferson grew it and sold it. The only people who ever died from it were those who wore hemp rope around their necks – at their executions.

Archaeologists have found evidence that people in China used hemp more than 10,000 years ago. As people discovered that twisted strands are far stronger than individual strands, they began spinning and weaving hemp fibers into fabric. Such fabric took the place of animal skins for clothes. In China, people also used hemp for making shoes. The Chinese cherished the mulberry plant because it was the food most preferred by silkworms. Silk, however, was only for the rich; hemp was for everyone. Hemp was so highly respected, along with the mulberry plant, that the Chinese called their country "the land of mulberry and hemp."[8]

By 1630, hemp fiber was in half of the clothing worn by Americans. Ships rigged with hemp cordage and woven hemp sails engaged in worldwide commerce. Did you ever wonder where the word "canvas" came from? "Cannabis" sails made Columbus's trips to the New World possible; other fibers would have decayed somewhere in mid-Atlantic As I learned this history I wondered: Was the hemp plant banished because it still offered unwelcome commercial competition to newer, patented products such as Nylon and other synthetics manufactured by DuPont?

DEA says it can't tell the difference between hemp and marijuana!

The DEA continues to fight the re-legalization of hemp, asserting that pot growers would make its job harder by hiding marijuana plants in rows of hemp. They wouldn't, because the hemp and pot would cross-pollinate and destroy the marijuana's potency. Again, politics, money, and hypocrisy abound.

Hemp contains just 0.3 percent THC, too little to provide either fun or healing. In this sense, it might be compared to a dogwood tree that does not produce dogs, but yields fine wood for the fireplace. At 10 years of age I was dumbfounded by what I'd learned. Clearly the government didn't care about the drunks lying in alleyways, or people getting high from legal medical drugs, but it had the time and energy to worry about an impossibility: that we might get high from a non-intoxicating plant. I concluded there had to be other reasons. Then it came to me: You could grow marijuana or hemp in your backyard, but then the government and its powerful billionaire friends wouldn't make money from it.

Back to the West Coast

It was just a year to the day we left for Washington, D.C., that we headed back to San Francisco. Dad was right outside the window of the train as it screeched to a stop As the door opened, the hiss of the steam and the smell of the oil were almost as exciting as when we had departed. We almost ran down the steps of the train and into Dad's outstretched arms.

Mother found a house in Los Gatos in May 1938. I began writing a newspaper of four pages, called *The Bugle*. It covered local news, including whatever gossip I could dig up, and sold for four cents.

Mother encouraged my cannabis education!

I was folding papers ready to deliver them when I heard mother laughing. "David, come read something I just found in *Scientific American*. For people who believe our drug Czar, this has to be frightening." Mother handed me the magazine.

Marijuana is "a more dangerous drug than heroin or cocaine," I read. Authority for this statement is United States Commissioner of Narcotics H. J. Anslinger. Mr. Anslinger's statement was made as part of a report on narcotics appearing in the bulletin of the Federal Bureau of Investigation. *Science Service* quotes Mr. Anslinger:

> I am surprised to learn that certain police officers have been inclined to minimize the effects of the use of marihuana... These officers should review some of the cases that are reported to the Bureau. They would, I am sure, be convinced that the drug is adhering to its Old World tradition of murder, assault, rape, physical demoralization, and mental breakdown. A study of the effects of marihuana shows clearly that it is a dangerous drug, and Bureau records prove that its use is associated with insanity and crime. The user loses the power to resist emotions, and may commit violence which knows no bounds, when disorders of the intellect have reached a point of incoherence. During this dangerous phenomenon, evil instincts are brought to the surface and cause fury to rage within the user.[9]

Mother, now just smiling and shaking her beautiful head of auburn hair, saw that I had finished reading the article. She said, "What study?

What records? Anslinger's falsehoods were presented to the FBI as fact, and given as sworn testimony before Congress. They were also presented as fact to parent-teacher groups, law enforcement agencies, and the press. Son, always be cautious about what you read. Newspapers and magazines print what government heads present to them. Do your own investigations. You have a good mind; think for yourself."

Our beautiful mother is ill

A month passed. Mother hadn't told us, but she was quite ill, hemorrhaging badly. She was petite, and yet so brave, not wanting us children to worry. A lady of the Christian Science faith lived next door and convinced her that with enough faith she would be just fine. We children were frightened. I washed her sheets hoping they would never be bloody again.

Doctors finally convinced Mother that if she didn't have a hysterectomy she would bleed to death. Because she was a veteran, she was able to go to the VA hospital in San Francisco; but it was difficult to find a home for youngsters 10, 12, and 13. We kids were taken to the Edgewood Orphanage in San Francisco, where we lived for six months. Watching some of the other children there we felt fortunate that we had parents. The orphanage was clean and we were taught to work. We peeled potatoes, helped the cook, darned socks, did laundry, and made our beds.

When our "sentence" was up, we were released to Mother, who was weak yet continued to work.

Stinson Beach – and a tidal wave!

We moved several more times. At Stinson Beach, mother rented a two-story knotty pine house right on the ocean, for $25 a month. It was for sale for $2,500. (I saw it recently; it was selling for $500,000.) I was now almost 12. Dad gave me a collie I named Lady, the love of my young life. She and I would hike along the ocean examining everything that washed in. We did find some beautiful driftwood, and she swam with me in the cold ocean water.

I attended a one-room school, much like the one in the TV series *Little House on the Prairie*. Our teacher was Mrs. Saddler, in her early thirties, an amazing lady who taught all six grades. She loved to talk about Alaska, and I promised myself that one day I would go there. I was in the fifth grade.

We had lived at Stinson Beach for six months when one night there was a strange silence. Generally, the sound of the ocean waves would lull us to sleep; but not this night. About dawn we heard sirens and over a loudspeaker we heard a man's voice: "Tidal wave! Evacuate all lowlands NOW!"

As we kids frantically pulled on clothes, Mother looked out the window and saw a wave at least 50 feet high bearing down on us. She yelled out, "Duck, everybody, we're going to get hit!" Then the wave crashed over the house. The entire building tilted away from the ocean as windows shattered and ocean water poured in. The house was now skewed at a 30-degree angle. "Are you all OK?" Mom screamed. Our little mother was so brave. She got the girls together and said, "Now, let's just be calm. We'll get out of here." Just then a rowboat, the size that would be a lifeboat on a ship, appeared, and I had the momentary mad fantasy that we were on the Titanic. The men sat next to each other, each using one large oar. One of the men yelled to us, "Get in! Another wave is on its way!" We got to the road and stayed with friends for a week. When the roads were cleared for traffic, Dad showed up to help us out. He was living in a two-bedroom apartment over the garage and gas station he now owned, and asked if we children would like to live with him for a time. Mother was exhausted and didn't object. Sister Carol and I accepted Dad's offer. Sis Margo stayed with friends.

By 1940 I had attended more than two dozen schools in my 12 years, and had learned little scholastically. As much as I would miss being with Mother, moving in with Dad meant stability. It was painful when Dad told me I couldn't have my precious dog, Lady. He was concerned that she would be hit by one of the many cars coming and going through the garage. We had had four dogs prior to Lady, and three of them had been killed by cars. The one exception was Buster, who was part Chow. At least his tongue was purple. I don't remember what happened to Buster. Buster was gay. Buster was cool. There was an ugly guy who lived across the street. One day I saw Buster humping the guy's leg. Buster had his eyes closed. I think Buster and the dog down the street just took off. Dad returned Lady to her former owners. I decided then that I would never have dogs when I had children; the loss was too painful.

The government continued to report that marijuana was being sold or given to youngsters in grade school. As usual, the official pronouncements failed to match my own experience. No one ever approached any of the kids at any of the schools I attended, selling or giving away marijuana, not once. Most kids didn't know what marijuana was.

Dad had established the Fairfax Garage back in the twenties, sold it, and bought the Ross Garage, about five miles away, in 1940. I met his new wife, Mary, who was about an inch taller than my mother and had a full figure. She worked in the garage. She not only kept the books but pumped gas, washed windshields, and checked oil. In those days regular usually sold for 17 cents a gallon, and dropped to as little as 11 cents during price wars.

During that summer vacation Dad offered me a job working in the garage for 15 cents an hour. I learned how to pump gas, wash cars, lubricate them, change oil, replace brake linings, and go on service calls with Dad, who had the local AAA franchise.

I also had a seven-mile newspaper route for *The San Rafael Independent*, Marin County's major daily. It was great business training, as I had to buy the papers, keep books, and collect from my customers each month. Many doctors, lawyers, prominent business owners, and CEOs of big businesses were on my route. I was fascinated by their beautiful homes and swimming pools, and decided that one day I would have the same.

At age 12 I joined the Boy Scouts. We spent two weeks at a Scout camp in the High Sierras. During a three-day hike we camped by a lake. The scoutmaster told us not to go swimming, but it was hot and humid and I couldn't resist going in for a short dip. The water was so clear I could see large boulders 50 feet below. When I raised my head I saw a snake coming straight for me. I flailed my arms frantically, but it was like a nightmare. I wasn't getting anywhere – let alone *away*.

The scoutmaster hauled me out. My adventure pleased him not at all. "David, that was a water moccasin," he said. "They are deadly." I decided that I would become a very good swimmer – somewhere else!

First "radio show"

When I was in the sixth grade, each classroom had a loudspeaker over which bulletins and announcements were broadcast each morning. I asked the principal's permission to do a daily 15-minute radio show to be broadcast to my class, and she okayed it. The following week the show began. There was recorded fanfare music, three minutes of current news, and five minutes of a soap opera with music and sound-effect records I'd bought. "*The Railroad Kid*" was a serial I wrote and (of course) starred in. There were other student actors, too. I did a mock commercial for "Ever-stick fingernail polish." After a couple of weeks, the principal, Mrs. Jenkins, asked if I would mind if the show were broadcast to the entire school at the beginning of the next school year. *Mind?* That was my first rush.

Kissed by an angel

My sisters had switched places. Sister Carol had moved in with Mother, and Sis Margo had taken her place with Dad, Mary, and me. Carol and Mother were now living in Beverly Hills, and Carol had met actress Jane Withers, who had played the "bad girl" opposite Shirley Temple and had already appeared in dozens of movies. Mother invited me down for the summer and Carol asked if I would like to meet "Janie." What 13-year-old boy wouldn't?

In her home, the young star had her own beauty parlor and soda fountain, and she made us sodas. She was beautiful, with exquisite large brown eyes. She was just 16. Jane's family loved Sis Carol, who had grown into a lovely lady, also 16.

I asked Jane if I might have a photo of her. She wrote, "To Davy, one swell fella. Love, Jane." She then kissed the photo, leaving her lipstick print on it. When she noted my hungry smile she leaned over and kissed me right on the mouth. My first kiss, from any woman other than my mother. And from a *movie star!*

We were invited to spend the summer at Jane's summer home at Lake Arrowhead, in the San Bernardino mountains. Their chauffeur, a wonderful black gentleman dressed in suit and tie, picked us up from Mother's apartment the next morning in Jane's new Ford station wagon. Jane's home was magnificent, knotty pine and right on Lake Arrowhead, with its own boat dock. It was a wonderful summer.

A whole generation will remember her as Josephine the Plumber in commercials for Comet Cleanser, but I'll always remember her as a lovely young woman at the wheel of a gleaming Chris-Craft with "Janie" painted on the transom.

World War II begins

In December 1941 I was still 13. Sis Margo and I were both reading in bed on the morning of the 7th. I had just finished an article in *Popular Mechanics* about Henry Ford experimenting with an auto that "grew from the soil." The car panels were said to be stronger than steel. One of the ingredients of these miracle panels was compressed hemp.

I had moved on to another magazine article about how alcohol prohibition had generated a mammoth drinking epidemic among children, as prohibition made it common to obtain liquor in unregulated back rooms. Alcohol prohibition had been passed with a campaign of "Save the Children from Alcohol"; it had been repealed with a campaign of "Save the Children from Prohibition"! I was laughing about that when abruptly Dad called us into his and Mary's bedroom.

Their little white plastic radio with its glowing red dial was on and Dad and Mary looked very upset. "What's happening?" both Sis and I asked. "President Roosevelt is saying that the Japanese have attacked Pearl Harbor. This is a sad and tragic day, kids. We were told World War I, the Great War, would be our last. Wars are started by politicians, but fought mainly by foot soldiers." We were stunned.

Gasoline was immediately rationed to three gallons a week unless you were involved in the war effort. Out of a fear of air raids, car headlights were "blacked out;" showing only small slits of light for night driving. And the speed limit was reduced to 35 miles an hour to conserve fuel. Young men were enlisting; many more would be drafted. I wished I were old enough to be a Navy pilot. Two of the young men who worked for Dad went into the service.

Dad had just bought a new 1940 green Ford four-door. At dinner one evening he said, "Inflation is terrible. This car cost $800! It will be our family car, but we're also starting a taxi service. Lots of people who can't get gas will need that service , and we'll provide it."

"Super idea, Pop," said I.

My school broadcasting show now included news beyond the campus, reporting on local boys who joined the service and on how the war was progressing. Early in the war a peace parade was held in San Francisco and I took a bus into the city for the event. A man was selling sailor hats in red, white, and blue, with "V for Victory" on the side. I had 25 dollars with me. The price was 35 cents per hat. Visions started circling in my eyes, and the word "wholesale" whispered in my ear.

I offered the man $25 for 100 of them. He accepted. The next day at school I wore one and lots of kids were impressed. That day during the broadcast, I made a slight change in my sponsorship. Ever-stick fingernail polish was out. Over the PA system I announced, "Prior to school today many of you commented on my patriotic hat. I have a limited supply; but as many students as possible should wear them and demonstrate our support for our boys going overseas. They're only 50 cents each. I look forward to seeing you at lunch break. Have a great day, and remember: V for Victory!"

My box of hats and I were waiting for the lunch bell to ring. When it did, out poured the kids, and the hats sold out within a half-hour. When we returned to class my teacher handed me a note to go immediately to the principal's office. Wow, I thought, it's too bad all the hats are sold, perhaps she wants one.

"David, I missed your show and commercial this morning because I was at a conference. I see that you have been a busy newscaster. Please be advised that today ends your popular series. We do not use our school's public address system to sell merchandise. I've had seven students come to my office saying they were hungry. I could see where their lunch money had gone – each of them was wearing one of your hats. You're dismissed. Return to your class."

"I'm sorry, Mrs. Jenkins. I didn't realize how much the students wanted to support our boys, many of whom will never return from war." Neither my contrition nor my patriotism moved her an inch.

Saturday morning Dad asked me to go with him on a service call to San Geronimo, some 15 miles from the garage. Someone had a dead battery – not much excitement there. Dad got only three dollars for each service call, and seven dollars when the tow truck went out. When we reached the stranded motorist, I attached the jumper cables to his battery and the car started right up. I had him sign the standard AAA receipt.

As I started to get back in the truck Dad said, "Go around to the driver's side, Son. Drive us home." My *heart* got a jump-start. He'd never let me drive before. I put it in gear and we were on our way. I was thinking, this is the most fun I've ever had!

Mary was waiting for us as I drove in. She gave me a hug and said, "Congratulations, driver." For the first time, rather than calling her Mary, I said, "Thanks, Mom!" Tears ran down her cheeks and I gave her a hug. I had never called her "Mother," but I felt she had definitely earned being called "Mom." Dad took me to the state Department of Motor Vehicles office to apply for a learner's permit. He signed an application revised to reflect wartime conditions. It stated that, owing to a hardship (in this case the difficulty of finding help when so many workers were now in uniform), I would be allowed a full adult driver's license when I was 14.

I had just got my license when a man came into the garage driving a yellow midget racer. He asked if I knew anyone who would like to buy it for $175.

In my mind I answered him, "Yeah, me!" Aloud I asked him to wait, and then I found Dad under a car and told him all about it. He came out and opened the hood, ran up the engine, winked at me to signal his approval, and said he had to go back to work. I settled into the negotiation.

"The upholstery is cracked and the tires should be replaced," I said. "I'd like to buy it but all I have is $130." He accepted it. I was so excited I couldn't stay still. I waxed the little racer, painted the long tailpipe that ran along the outside from the engine to the rear end a nice bright silver, had new upholstery installed for its single seat, and put some decals that read "Supercharged" on both sides of the hood.

Most of the kids took dancing lessons. I didn't, and my lack of skill embarrassed me at every dance. The prestige that little racer gave me more than compensated. When the kids saw it they all wanted a ride, which I was happy to give them (especially the girls). When I drove alone down the highway, heads would turn, horns would honk, and people would wave.

Dad now had me driving the 1940 Ford taxi. I loved it, and my salary had been raised to 25 cents an hour. Many of the older ladies would ask for me to drive them. I received many 50-cent tips.

Hemp for Victory!

In l942, much of the war news was painful to read. Amid the large black headlines of our ships being hit by Japanese torpedoes were stories that struck me oddly.

The government had switched gears and now was telling us that our military desperately needed hemp. Children in 4-H Clubs were asked to grow at least a half-acre of hemp, preferably two acres each. It was now *mandatory* for farmers to attend showings of the film the U.S. Department of Agriculture made in 1942, *Hemp for Victory.* Hemp-harvesting machinery suddenly became available at little or no cost to the farmers, and some 300,000 acres of hemp were to be harvested by 1943. Here are excerpts from the sound track of *Hemp for Victory:*

> In l942, patriotic farmers, at the government's request, planted 36,000 acres of seed hemp. The goal for l943 is 50,000 acres of seed hemp. Now with the Philippine and East Indian sources of hemp in the hands of the Japanese, American hemp must meet the needs of our Army and Navy as well as our industry.
>
> [Here we see workers] spinning American hemp into rope yarn or twine in the old Kentucky River mill at Frankfort, Kentucky. All such plants will be turning out products spun from American-grown hemp: Rope for marine rigging and towing; for hay forks, derricks, and heavy-duty tackle; light-duty fire hose; thread for shoes for millions of American soldiers; and parachute webbing for our paratroopers.
>
> As for the Navy, every battleship requires 34,000 feet of rope – American hemp will go on duty again: hemp for mooring ships, hemp for tow lines, hemp for tackle and gear; hemp for countless Naval uses both on ship and shore, just as in the days when Old Ironsides sailed the seas victorious with her hempen shrouds and hempen sails.
>
> *Hemp for victory!*

The need for hemp was so great that farmers and their sons who grew it were *exempt from serving time in the military.* If they grew hemp today, where do you suppose they would serve time? (As soon as the war was over, of course, we were again told that hemp was a dangerous narcotic in the same category as "deadly" marijuana.)

During the summer after I graduated from Ross Grade School, life moved rapidly. Dad sold the Ross Garage and we moved to San Rafael, where Dad bought an auto parts store.

I outgrew my beloved racer. My legs got so long I could barely shift gears. My options were limited: have my legs shortened or sell the racer. The decision wasn't easy, but in the end I sold it, for $225.

Mother again invited me to spend summer vacation with her and Sis Carol in Beverly Hills. I accepted and got a job detailing out cars at a large car lot. I asked the owner of the lot if I could get a commission if I sold a car while he was out to lunch.

"Sure kid, $25. What do I have to lose?" He soon learned.

I had some fine opportunities to demonstrate our goods. A couple of ladies came in and saw just the car they wanted. Off we went on a test drive, all the way to Hollywood. They said they would seriously think about buying the car, and let me know "tomorrow." Tomorrow came but the ladies never did. Several other ladies appeared and with generally the same outcome. It didn't take long to realize that I was being used as a free taxi. I decided it was time to stop being taken for a patsy.

Pushed around by the wrong guy

There was only one late-model car on the lot, a yellow '41 Cadillac convertible. The auto manufacturers had switched over to war production, and 1941 was the last year they'd built any civilian cars. I wanted to drive that Caddy. My boss was out to lunch when this guy came in wearing Levi's and an old denim shirt and a stubble of beard. He walked right over to the Cad, and said, "Let's give her a drive, shall we?"

I said, "Sure," and slid behind the wheel. The battery was dead. So I said to this bum, "How about a push?"

He asked, "Don't you have a service truck?"

I told him, "Just please put your back up against the rear bumper and push. "

He really put his back to it. We had gone a half-block when I put the car in first gear and let the clutch out. He almost fell down, but the car wouldn't start. I said, "Push faster and I'll drop it into second gear."

All he could say while gasping for air was "Yup." He did as he was directed, but the damn thing still wouldn't start.

He pushed me all the way around the block and back into the car's parking stall. He was dripping perspiration. It was tough for him to speak but he was able to get out, "I might be back when she's running."

He was walking off the lot when the owner came running toward me.

"Mr. Rankin," I called out. "You're going to love this. That bum was going to let me give him a free ride, but I let him give me one." Mr. Rankin raised his arm – to shake my hand, I thought, until I noted that his hand was curled into a fist!

"I saw what happened, you little shit. D'y'know who that *bum* was? That was Gary Cooper! You're fired!"

My next challenge was working at a radio repair shop. After cleaning the shop for a couple of days I asked the owner if I could learn more about repairing, and also drive the panel truck to pick up and deliver radios. A few days later he asked me to join him on a service call. I was sure I was already climbing the ladder of success.

We pulled up in front of a Beverly Hills mansion with iron gates. The lady of the house took us into the living room, which overlooked an Olympic-size swimming pool. "We're having a dinner party this evening, and the radio console isn't working. Can you fix it here?"

The boss peered around the back of the set after checking the off-on switch. He tapped some exposed tubes. "It will have to go into the shop, but we'll have it back for you in time for your party. I'm sorry to say that it will cost $50, plus parts."

I looked behind the set too, trying to appear professional. "The plug is out of the wall," I said. "Let's plug it in!"

Rather red in the face, he did and, miraculously, it worked. He was so disconcerted that he forgot to charge for a service call. On the way back to the shop, he didn't speak. When we arrived, he just said, "Get out. I never want to see you again!"

Hollywood in those days was exhilarating. You could attend the *Lux Radio Theater* for free. It was a real theater where weekly shows, most often dramas but sometimes comedies, originated. If you arrived early enough you could sit within 15 feet of the stage. When the *Lux Radio Theater* ended, on the same stage it was time for the deep-voiced announcer to intone, "*Your Hit Parade*, sponsored by *Lucky Strike* cigarettes!" Their new star was a skinny young man with a bow tie and a protruding Adam's apple, a singer named Frank Sinatra. Between his numbers, while the band played the Top Ten Songs Of The Week, you could wave to Frank, and he would wave back if he was in the mood.

For three weeks I waited in line to see the ever-popular Jack Benny radio show. Three times I got close to the front, and three times the usher lowered his hand and said, "Sorry, no more seats available. Try again next week."

The following week I borrowed a trombone case from a friend and just walked through the performers' entrance along with the real musicians. I ended up on the stage, sitting next to the much-loved tenor, Dennis Day. Each week he sang a solo, and played the innocent boy next door in the comedy sketches.

When the band began playing, he asked what I was doing there, and why I wasn't up playing with the band. I told him the union had called me at the last moment, and that I just realized I'd left the key to my trombone case at home. He was very sympathetic.

Twenty years later, I interviewed Dennis Day for CBS television in Hawaii. When I reminded him of that incident he laughed and laughed. (I also interviewed Jack Benny about the same time. I asked him if he ever got nervous before a broadcast. His answer: "I throw up before every show.")

San Rafael High School; almost expelled

Even after the adventures I'd had in Southern California, it was exciting to return home and begin high school. My first day at school I was flattered when a very nice senior befriended me. He obviously wanted to help a lowly freshman get off to a good start by letting me in on a school secret.

There were two "Mr. Wellses" at San Rafael High, our principal, Mr. Wells, and a math teacher whose name was spelled Welz. "Mr. Welz is short and pudgy. So freshmen won't confuse the two names, Mr. Welz likes to be called 'Porky.' You'll meet the other Mr. Wells, our principal, in the near future."

I went out of my way to find Mr. Welz's room. I waited until I saw him leave for the lunch break, and sure enough he was squat and piggy-faced. As we passed each other in the hall I called out to him cheerfully, "Good morning, Porky, my name is Dave Ford." He must have been in a hurry because he glanced at me but didn't stop. After lunch I passed him again and said, "I hope you're having a good day, Porky."

That afternoon the senior's prediction that I would soon meet the principal came true. I was summoned to meet Mr. Wells. He was a tall man of about 50, with black hair graying at the temples. He had an easy smile, and I felt comfortable with him.

"Sit down, David. May I ask you a question?"

"Of course, Mr. Wells."

"David, why have you been calling Mr. Welz 'Porky'?"

"I didn't mean any disrespect, sir. I understood that's a nickname he prefers. And he does look a bit like a pig."

It was at that moment that Porky appeared, red-faced and fuming, from behind the oak door of the principal's office. "I want this kid expelled now!" Porky squealed.

Mr. Wells interceded. "David, you were suckered in by a senior, no doubt. Mr. Welz has only one name, as far as you're concerned, and it's Mr. Welz. Do you have it clear now?"

I was terribly embarrassed, and I apologized to Mr. Welz. I was not expelled. That time.

My favorite subjects that year were speech and dramatics. In drama class I met an upperclassman named Glenn Vernon Hughes, to me then and always Vern. He starred in a number of the school plays and his performances were outstanding. He was also Commissioner of Assemblies, whose responsibility was to produce school shows. I was in a couple of school plays that year, and I also took wood shop, electrical shop, and auto shop. These enabled me to maintain my hobby of buying, renovating, and selling used cars.

My goal was to be in radio, even if only as a hobby at first. I made an appointment to visit San Rafael's radio station, KTIM, and prepared a proposal for a radio show aimed at teens. I met the station owner, Hugh Turner, and presented my idea. *Junior Jamboree* would be a one-hour live show in the studio each Saturday morning. There would be quiz contests between rival high schools, live music by teen-age performers, and interviews – including more than one on what drugs teens were using.

"Fine idea, David. You find a sponsor and I'll hire you for a 13-week contract." His polite smile told me that he didn't think he'd ever see me again.

I approached a number of potential sponsors. The last one was *Hoy's Radio and Record Shops* in San Rafael and San Anselmo. I was ecstatic when Mr. Hoy said, "Let's give it a try!"

The show was a huge success. The live audience response was impressive. KTIM had an amazingly talented pianist, Jack Risso, who was one of our featured attractions. Halfway through one show, while Jack was playing a concerto he fell off the piano stool and began thrashing about on the floor with foam oozing out of his mouth. The kids applauded at such a funny prank. The only problem was that it was no joke: Jack was an epileptic. I signaled the studio engineer to spin a record while I attended to Jack.

Back from a fishing trip in my first car, a midget racer, wearing my V for Victory sailor cap in 1942. That year I began driving a taxi for my dad. Wartime rules allowed me to get a driver's license at 14.

At 16 I created, produced, and emceed a top-rated teen radio show, Junior Jamboree, *broadcast from KTIM in San Rafael.*

He was replaced by an equally talented pianist, Fae McNally, a 15-year-old student – who smoked pot. Fae could improvise great jazz. He would roll an orange across the keyboard and play Kitten on the Keys while high on grass. He could also roll a joint with one hand. He would smoke a joint and go to the movies just to watch the cartoon. He'd get a good laugh, then leave.

His home life was not good. His dad, a heavy drinker, caught Fae smoking grass. He told him if he ever caught him again with that "violence-causing drug" he would turn him over to the police. Fae eventually switched to alcohol.

I heard that that the famed crooner Bing Crosby was at the Fairmont Hotel in San Francisco, so I tried to arrange an interview. He wasn't available the first time I phoned, so I left a message.

An hour later I got a call. "Hi, ol' buddy, how ya doin'?" It was the unmistakable voice of Bing Crosby. I tried not to be too excited by the friendly "ol' buddy" – I knew it was a signature phrase for him.

"Hi to you, Bing! I was wondering: if I brought a crew over to your hotel, could I do an interview with you?"

"Of course you can, ol' buddy. How about six tomorrow evening?"

"That would be perfect, Bing, thanks."

Then Bing said, "See ya tomorra, John."

"Bing, the first name is Dave."

"Isn't this John Ford?"

"No, Bing. This is Dave Ford. I do a radio show for kids in Northern California."

Click!

Apparently Bing wasn't as interested in an interview when he found out I wasn't an Oscar-winning movie director.

Alcohol versus pot

On the radio show I interviewed hundreds of teens on the drugs they "saw" being used. In those days it was generally pot or alcohol. One feature common to many of the interviews was the kids' impression that alcohol frequently caused violence, including date rape, while the most earth-shattering effect of pot was "the munchies." Drinkers sometimes attacked girls. Smokers attacked French-fries.

I also interviewed celebrities, including vocalist Frankie Laine and actors Humphrey Bogart and Lauren Bacall. One result was that I was invited to parties where marijuana was smoked openly. At first I was dazed. Then I asked the marijuana smokers, "Aren't you afraid of becoming violent?"

"Dave, pot makes you feel relaxed, not violent. Marijuana is nature's tranquilizer. It's medicine – and it's far safer than other drugs." It was then that I decided to do some serious research into why government and big business continue to demonize marijuana and hemp.

Making love for the first time

I had just turned 16 and was almost constantly preoccupied by admiration for those beautiful, spirited young ladies in school. I took the girls for picnics, to movies, or out to lunch, and was occasionally rewarded with a kiss; but a couple of them said, "If you touch me down there, you'll have to marry me."

A lovely Italian student, my age, lived just a block from my home; and we began walking home together. One afternoon she asked me if I would like to join her doing some homework. "Sure," I said.

Janice asked me to wait until she checked to see if, by any chance, her father was home. "No one's home," she reported. "We can study in my grandfather's old room in the basement – he's not here anymore."

The little room held an Army cot, a dresser, a small desk and chair. On the dirt floor of the basement I noticed a large wine vat, about six feet high and about 12 feet around. We sat on the bed and opened our books. In about one minute, we were necking. She pulled down the shade and we undressed each other, kissing and exploring each other's bodies. I was glad that I had a condom in my wallet that had been there for three years, waiting for such an opportunity.

Soon we were making real love. Wow, I thought, *this* is the most fun I've ever had. In about 15 minutes I experienced a full-blown explosion, but I didn't stop: I wanted her to feel the same ecstasy. (Boy, did this beat solitaire!) Then she screamed, "Oh Davie, Davie!"

Seconds later there was a pounding sound. It must be my heart, I thought. God, no, it was the door! "Janice, is there a boy in there with you? Why is this door locked, and why did you scream?"

"Daddy, I didn't know the door was locked. I'm doing my home work and I saw a mouse." Good girl, I thought.

"Open this door now or I'll smash it open!"

I've never seen anyone get dressed as fast as Janice. I was frozen in terror; all I had on was the condom.

"Go. Go! He'll kill you!" whispered Janice.

"Where can I go?" I whispered back.

"I don't know! There's only one door down here. Just go!"

I grabbed my clothes and stumbled against something cold and smooth – the wine vat, with a ladder on the side of it. With my clothes under my arm I climbed up the ladder and down the other side – into four feet of wine.

I heard a slap, and something like "Don't you ever lock that door again!" and then a lot of Italian. Next I saw a flashlight on walls. I was so frightened I hoped I wasn't about to have an accident in his vat of homemade Italian wine, what the locals called "dago red." More yelling. Then the door slammed shut and I heard a key turn in the lock.

It was quiet upstairs. Janice must have convinced him she'd been alone in the basement. I felt relief that she wasn't being hurt. And that I was alive. I was thirsty, so, like a horse drinking water, I lowered my head and sucked up some wine.

After a long period of silence, I climbed up and out of the vat and peered around. What happened to the condom, I asked myself. What if it ended up in her father's dinner glass of wine! I thought giddily. I was drunk.

It was getting dark, but I could see a screened air vent about a foot and a half square, low on one wall. My escape route beckoned. I pulled the screening off, paused for a brief prayer – please God, don't let me get stuck in this vent – and, naked, pulled myself through it. I huddled in the shrubs, put on my dripping clothes, and staggered off toward home.

Mom caught me trying to slip into my bedroom. She looked at my wine-soaked clothing in utter disbelief and asked, "What happened to you?"

"I fell into a friend's wine vat while we were fooling around. I'm sleepy. May I pass on dinner?"

"All right, son. I'll leave a plate for you in the refrigerator."

I stumbled into the shower, washed clumsily, and left my clothes on the floor of the shower. I passed on dinner, all right. I also passed *out*. I awoke at midnight with a throbbing hangover.

The next day in Study Hall, Janice and I sat next to each other, rolled our eyes, and smiled sheepishly. I discovered that lovemaking was a lot sweeter than ice-cream, and I decided I wanted to savor as many flavors as possible.

Groucho Marx swears by (at) me!

San Francisco radio personality Marjorie Trumbull heard about the success of *Junior Jamboree* and kindly invited me to co-host a broadcast of her classy show at the Mark Hopkins Hotel on ritzy Nob Hill. The show was called *Top of the Mark*, after the restaurant on the hotel's top floor, famous for superb food and a spectacular view of the city and its sparkling blue bay. Its gimmick was a four-star luncheon served to the host and guest. In exchange for the lunch and the use of a studio with one of the world's grandest views, Marjorie would compliment the hotel, the food, and the view.

That week's guest was the zany Groucho Marx, known for his snappy comebacks. Heavy traffic and rain made me run late that day. I reached the hotel only five minutes before air time. It was still raining and there wasn't a parking spot in sight. I parked in a loading zone a block away, ran to the hotel, and rushed up to the studio. The engineer's arm was already raised and his finger poised to cue the announcer to introduce the show when I flopped into my chair.

Groucho looked at me and deadpanned, "Late again, huh?"

We all survived lunch, and the interview was going quite well. Dessert was apple pie à la mode and, to help Marjorie plug the hotel and its food, I asked Groucho, "Isn't this pie delicious?"

With a perfectly straight face, Groucho said in his classic Brooklyn accent, "It's the worst apple pie I've ever sunk my teeth into."

Marjorie winced. I said, "Thank you for your recommendation, Groucho."

Groucho replied, "Think nothing of it."

I said, "I didn't."

Groucho added, "It sounds like you're stealing my material."

After the show ended, Groucho accepted my offer of a ride to his hotel. When we got outside, it was still raining. Belying his name, he took the lousy weather in good spirit. You might even say he took it in stride: he pulled his topcoat over his head and did his signature funny walk for me – stooping down and taking giant strides.

"Where's the car?" he asked, at just about the same instant that those words were racing through my own head. I was afraid to tell him I didn't have a clue. It *had* been there before the show. Rain had now soaked Groucho's topcoat. All I could hope for was that I made a minor mistake. "It's on the next corner." Groucho wasn't walking funny at all now, and water was dripping from his cigar. The next corner appeared, but my car didn't.

I spotted a police officer and asked if he had seen a blue 1936 Ford. "I just came on duty. Saw one parked in the yellow, and had it towed."

I was mortified. "Ah, Groucho, did you hear what the officer told me?"

"I'm not totally deaf, you stupid little bastard."

"I'm not little. I'm six foot one!" I said.

At that point, repartee deserted Groucho, and he deserted me. The last I ever saw of him, he was running through the rain and melting into the crowds.

Motorcycles, alcohol, and marijuana

At 16 I purchased an Indian motorcycle, a beautiful machine, like new. Within a week I had joined a motorcycle club in San Rafael. Most of the guys in the club were older, ranging from their twenties to their forties.

The second week the gang gathered for a weekend in Santa Rosa. We met at a cafe in San Rafael, where I saw several young ladies chatting with the guys. I asked Tom, one of riders, if the ladies were riders.

"Naw, they like to ride with us. Go ahead, pick one up if you like. We ain't jealous. Get the redhead if ya can."

"Thanks," I said. The redhead was about 18, wearing Levi's, an old leather jacket, and a scarf. I wandered over.

"Good lookin' leathers ya got, guy," she said.

"I hope to break them in on this trip," I replied. I had to admit to myself that the heavy tan and brown leather jacket and large black leather gloves I was wearing were cool.

I introduced myself, and she responded with, "I'm Bunny. Can I ride with ya?"

"Sure," I said.

It was thrilling to hear and feel the rumble of 16 high-powered bikes cranking up. We headed up Highway 101 toward Santa Rosa, 40 miles north. It was eight at night and dark, and before I realized it the bikes were moving at 70 miles an hour, faster then I'd ever gone. We were 10 miles out when Jerry, about 40 years old and leading the pack, stood up on the seat of his bike. He was doing 80 or 90, and without a hand holding on to anything. I shuddered, remembering the several beers he'd had before we started our ride. Bunny was holding on tight. "Move it, Dave," she said. "Jerry will join up with those two riders up ahead. When he pulls between them, we'll pass 'em all up!"

By this time I had fallen so far behind, I could barely make out the distant taillights. When I twisted the throttle and closed the distance, I realized that two of the taillights weren't on other bikes, but on a big-rig crawling up a grade at 40 miles an hour! Jerry came to the same realization far too late. In a flash he dropped into the saddle, grabbed the handlebars, and threw his motorcycle onto its side, wheels toward the truck. He was now lying on the bike as it disappeared under the truck, metal shrieking, sparks flying. The rest of us were barely able to stop our own bikes in time. My heart was pounding. Surely Jerry was dead.

The truck pulled off the road as we got off our bikes and ran toward the downed rider, horrified at what we'd see. The truck driver's face was ashen. Jerry was still lying on his bike as several of the guys pulled it from under the truck. As we formed a circle around him he stood up, dusted himself off, and laughed! "How'd ya like that lesson, ladies and gentlemen?" I turned aside and puked. I think the motorcycle's crash bars saved his life. At the bar-restaurant in Santa Rosa most of the guys drank about a half dozen beers. I had one, and danced with Bunny. After dinner we headed for their favorite motel.

The night wasn't chilly, and the motel had a large patio. The gang soon gravitated into two separate groups. In one, guys were drinking boilermakers (shots of whisky, chased with beer). They swapped insults and soon began fist-fighting. Knives came out of boot tops. They were cutting each other up and acting like they were having fun! In the other group, the grass smokers remained mellow, and just sat around in a circle talking and laughing.

I was exhausted. "Bunny, what do you say we retire?"

"I'm ready, Eddie! Or was it Dave? Only kidding!"

I soon learned how she'd earned her nickname.

Motorcycle rider loses his leg

The next morning we went to the motorcycle races. I was sitting with Bunny in the front row, as close as we could get to the race track. It was exciting – then suddenly *too* exciting, when one of the lead riders slammed into the wall right in front of us and his right leg went flying in the air. Red lights went on and the race stopped. To my astonishment the now one-legged rider crawled over to where his other leg landed – and strapped it back on! Bunny laughed when she saw my bloodless face. "Oh, that's Reggie. He lost his leg in a race 10 years ago. This makes the third time he's lost the same leg!"

Sunday night we headed home. Blackness closed around us when we left the lights of Santa Rosa and Petaluma behind. Suddenly, my headlight went out! I couldn't stop. We were going so fast that I was certain we'd crash if I tried to pull onto the shoulder. I rode on, eyes glued to the winding dotted line dimly visible in the starlight, until we reached a stretch of highway were there were lights enough to stop safely. I reconnected a wire that had shaken loose and we rode home, too slow for Bunny, plenty fast enough for me.

Police officer knows marijuana is medicine

A few weeks later I joined another of the club's rides to Santa Rosa. On the way, a fellow in his late thirties, Tommy, was side-swiped by a car passing him. The car didn't even stop. Tommy's bike careened off the road, flipped on gravel, and landed on his left leg. His leg was crushed; blood poured from the wound, and Tommy was screaming in pain. Fortunately, a California Highway Patrol officer appeared on his motorcycle and radioed for an ambulance. While the officer was on the radio one of the bikers fired up a joint and put it to Tommy's lips. Tommy took several deep drags; within minutes he started relaxing. The officer only said, "That'll ease his pain." It did. Shortly thereafter the ambulance arrived and took Tommy to the hospital, where his leg was amputated above the knee. I quit the bike club that week.

I was now more intrigued by cannabis, even though I hadn't yet smoked any. I was pleased when I read about the La Guardia Report, which once again contradicted the falsehoods of the government's continuing drumbeat of hysterical marijuana propaganda.

La Guardia Marijuana Report, 1944

New York Mayor Fiorello La Guardia authorized the New York Academy of Medicine to establish a committee to evaluate the dangers of marijuana. In 1944, after four years of investigation, the committee of eight physicians, a psychiatrist, and four New York City health officials concluded that, at worst, marijuana was a relatively harmless intoxicant and the *smoking of it did not lead to an increase in violent crimes, use of other drugs, or other antisocial acts*[10] (italics mine). But my elation soon turned to frustration. The U.S. Government's response soon became obvious: Don't confuse us with the facts; our minds are made up.

Me, in a whorehouse?

That summer I took the course in Senior Red Cross Life Saving. After I passed, I began long-distance swimming in the San Rafael Canal. One day I recognized another swimmer as the father of one of my school buddies. He was Swedish, tanned, with silver-gray hair and a handlebar mustache. I guessed him to be in his mid-forties. I watched him swim for at least a half mile on his back, using both arms the way one would row a boat, rather than the alternating overarm backstroke I'd learned.

I introduced myself and asked him about that backstroke. In a heavy Swedish accent Mr. Furrin said, "You can swim miles that way and not get nearly as tired as doing crawl. Come try, boy." I did, liked it, and soon added a frog kick with my legs. We swam together for an hour.

While resting in the balmy sunlight he glanced at his watch and said he had to leave. I asked where he was headed.

"I tell you, but you no tell my son Hooki, OK?"

"I promise."

"My wife die long ago. I go to wonderful whorehouse in Petaluma. Lots of fun. It's been there since World War I."

"Oh yeah," I smirked. "Same women?"

"No, no", he answered seriously. "Pretty young girls. Many go college. Cost only $3.00, or $5.00 for half and half.'

I didn't want to sound ignorant, but I guessed it wasn't something to put in your coffee, and I had to know. "What's half and half?"

He looked at me with pity in his twinkling blue eyes. "Half suck. Half fuck."

"Oh, I've only had the last part," I said. "Could I go with you sometime?"

"You no tell my boy, and I take you. I go tonight at seven. I come by your house. Honk one time. You no out front, I go."

I told my folks I was going to a rehearsal. When I heard that single honk I was out the door and into his car like a shot. He hit the gas and we were on our way – oh my God, to a whorehouse. The trip took about forty minutes.

"Vallejo good whore town, too. Navy town. Go down Georgia Street. Almost every old hotel is whorehouse. Same prices as Greenhouse in Petaluma." We crossed railroad tracks next to a river. The house was dark and I was sure the place was closed. He knew what I was thinking. "No worry. She's open for business!"

Mr. Furrin knocked on the door of the green Quonset hut. Thirty seconds later a peephole opened. "It's me, Hookin. I have good young friend with me. He OK."

I could feel her eyes on me. Then she opened the door and I could smell cologne. It was exciting. The "madam" I guessed to be in her mid-thirties, an attractive brunette with wavy hair. She shook my hand. "Honey, is this your first time with a lady you pay for?"

"Yes," I answered nervously.

She smiled and pressed my hand. "Just relax. You'll be just fine. It won't hurt at all!" Then she disappeared through a door on the far wall.

She reappeared with seven young surprises in tow, all wearing Frederick's of Hollywood's very sexy outfits: black high-heeled shoes with clear plastic heels, negligees you could almost see through, and nothing underneath that my avid eyes could detect. Each lady was dressed differently, and they looked as beautiful, fresh, and clean as any in *Playboy* magazine. Several of them I guessed to be in their early twenties. Mr. Furrin got up, smiled, and took Darlene's hand.

Each of the remaining six came over to me and introduced herself. "I'm Lorraine. You'll like me. I love young boys!" "I'm Joy. I just love to make love. You'll come back for me." "I'm Baby, but not in bed. Come with me, honey."

I stammered, "My name is David." I shook hands with each of them. Then I took Lorraine's hand.

She led me down a dimly lit hallway to a small bedroom with a double bed. A wall mirror, dresser, and wall-to-wall carpeting completed the furnishings. Lorraine had a lovely smile and figure. She appeared to be about 20. "Is this your first time, honey? Your voice sounds familiar but I don't think I've ever seen you here."

She tilted her head and gave me an appraising look. "I have a suspicion that your real name *is* David. Most guys use different names, like we do. I'm just thinking out loud; but some of us girls listen to *Junior Jamboree* and you sound just like that guy."

"Yes, it is my first time, and I am nervous," I stammered – not sure I wanted to tell her that I was indeed the guy who did *Junior Jamboree*.

"You won't be nervous, honey Just wait and see how wonderful I'm going to make you feel. You're a cutie!" I was feeling more relaxed already.

Lorraine took a porcelain washbasin from her dresser, filled it with warm water, and placed it on the carpet. A bar of Ivory soap was floating in it. She removed her baby doll nightie, then squatted and washed between her lovely thighs. It was exciting to watch her, and she was aware of the effect. She washed with a smile, saying, "I want to be all clean for you, David. Now you take off your clothes, honey. You can hang them right on the back of the door."

When she finished washing she poured out the water and refilled the basin. She asked me to hold it for her. She gently and sensuously washed me with the soapy water. As she did it she was purring, "What a nice big boy you are, honey, I can hardly wait!" I noted that she examined me carefully, and I was grateful she wanted to be certain that I was free of disease. (In those days we didn't have to worry about AIDS, nor did we have to wear condoms.) She carefully and gently dried me. I noticed a red rose tattoo low on her abdomen and asked about it.

"David, I'm a little embarrassed to tell you. That rose was done when I was young and foolish."

"How old were you?" I stammered.

"Fourteen, David." Tattooed in script under the rose were the words, '*Pay as you enter.*'

I handed her the five-dollar bill. "Thank you, big fella. Would you like two dollars change?"

"No, thank you."

"Ahh," she purred, "you want half and half don't you, David?!"

I nodded and she guided me over to the bed. "Lie down, honey. Don't keep me waiting. I need you badly!" She lay between my thighs. Her cologne was intoxicating. She took me into her sweet warm mouth and began something new and glorious.

Soon she rolled onto her back and asked, "Do you mind if I use just a little KY jelly, cause you're such a beautiful big boy?" I figured she probably said all these things to each guy. But it worked for me.

I thought, *this* is the most fun I've ever had. I hadn't realized how awesome lovemaking could be. I had one hand under her head and was looking into her eyes. I started to kiss her, but she turned her head to one side.

"It isn't you, David. We girls only kiss the ones we're in love with."

"Thank you for telling me," I said, a bit embarrassed.

Within a few minutes I had a climax like never before. Just in time too, because there was a knock at the door. Grateful that this time it wasn't an angry father, I got the message and said, "Thank you, Lorraine. That was super."

"Thank you, David."

I got up and began to dress. "Not so fast, David." Lorraine got that little white basin and gently washed and dried me. I glanced at her bedside clock. It had been exactly 13 minutes since I entered this little piece of heaven, her room. She was not only smart, knowing just what to say to have the most happen in the shortest time; she didn't talk about anything other than making love. Wise lady. In future encounters I learned that these ladies are natural psychologists. They know what to say, not only to make a man feel comfortable and good about himself, but also to bring him to climax as soon as possible without making him feel rushed. Lorraine kissed me on the cheek and invited me back to see her again.

On the next *Junior Jamboree* show, I dedicated the song "Sweet Lorraine" to "my friend in Petaluma, who lives in a pretty green house." In future weeks songs went out to the other ladies of the Greenhouse: to "Darlene, the beautiful lady with that long cigarette holder" I dedicated "Smoke Gets in Your Eyes"; to Baby, Jimmie Lanceford's "OK for Baby." Knowing that only a select few listeners knew I was dedicating songs to lovely whores was a rush. Now, I didn't care if the ladies knew who I was. In fact it made it more electrifying. I looked forward to every visit to the "green house."

That late fall of my 16th year, Dad took us all to spend a week up in the Sierras. He had rented a cabin in the pines that smelled almost as good as cologne. There were picnic tables, barbecues, ping-pong tables, and a river we were told still had gold in it. It was beautiful. The thought of a week of it made me feel like yawning until my jaws cracked.

A train's whistle could be heard from our cabin. I was told it went to Reno, about 75 miles east of our camping grounds. The next day I hiked to the railroad tracks. A slow-moving freight train was crawling up the hill. Memories of my intraschool broadcasts flashed before me: my serial adventure "The Railroad Kid," the story of a teen-ager who ran away from home and rode the rails, and of the life he encountered. When the engine disappeared around a curve, I scanned the last seven freight cars, and spotted an open door. I began running alongside. When I pulled even with that door, I hauled myself up and climbed in. I was alone.

About two hours later the train again came to a crawl as it neared

Reno, and I jumped off. In five minutes I was in town. Walking into a gambling casino was a thrill, until I saw a sign: NO ONE UNDER 21.

Before the casino staff could eject me, I quickly thrust three quarters into a slot machine. I won nothing. I had one quarter left and was prepared to lose that, so I plugged it in, pulled the handle and stared in delight as three dollars in quarters clattered into the cup. Wow! An old guy was waiting to play my machine, so I said, "Go ahead, sir, I don't want to lose my winnings." He put in a coin and four bells turned up; he had won $75. "Congratulations," I said to him; ("Son of a bitch," I muttered to myself). I hitch-hiked back to the camp.

The next spring I made an appointment to present a creative idea to the manager of Albert's Department Store in San Rafael. I suggested that for a week prior to Easter they have a six-foot Easter bunny running around the store and hopping from counter to counter.

"And who might you suggest for this role, David?"

"Well, sir, I was thinking I would make a great rabbit, and I could rent a rabbit outfit in San Francisco. I'd pay for the outfit if you would pay me four dollars an hour."

It was a deal. I had great fun and the kids loved it. The local newspaper did a story and printed a photo of me. I was told that was the most the store had ever paid anyone.

The next Christmas I rented a Santa Claus outfit and advertised myself in the paper as a freelance Santa, for $10 per home visit. The first call I received was from the same store that had hired me as an Easter bunny. In addition to gigs elsewhere, I worked at Albert's during the afternoons and early evenings while kids were still awake. The store was packed after my photo appeared in the paper. I had fun with the children, but the most exciting diversion was when high-school girls came and sat on my lap and wiggled around as they had their photos taken.

One evening, my last call was at a Rotary club in Mill Valley at 9 p.m. I had brought my buddy Vern Hughes along, and he and I handed out gifts to the children and generally had a wonderful time. When it was over, several of the men took me to the Two AM Club next door, and invited my friend Vern come along. They told the bartender, "Anything Santa wants is on us." I was sure they knew I was underage. Before that night I'd had only a few beers.

I thought, "Shucks, if they think I'm old enough, I might as well have a free drink." The only drink I could think of was a Tom Collins.

After the fifth one I lost count of how many I downed. I had enough sense left to ask Vern to drive us home. It was a grim ride. I recall hanging my horribly aching head out the passenger-side window. Suddenly nausea overwhelmed me, and I was puking through my fake beard. That was a noteworthy lesson. I'm thankful that grass, wonderful no-hangover pot, came to be a big part of my life rather than liquor.

My first joint

The first time I used cannabis was early in 1945. I was 17, and was with my friend Fae McNally, now 16. You'll recall he was the featured pianist on my radio show. One night while going over the following week's radio show with Fae, he suggested I enter the Lions Clubs International's public-speaking contest for California and Nevada. "There's only 12,000 in the contest so you have a chance," he chuckled.

"Thanks for your confidence, Fae," I said, "but I just don't have the time to research and practice for such an event."

Fae pointed out that many performers, especially jazz musicians, use marijuana. It gives the feeling that time slows down by at least 50 percent. "With marijuana, we find we have plenty of time to add extra notes to the music, and that's what jazz is all about. Grass heightens creativity, too. Might help you with that speech."

Fae lit up a joint, took a drag, and handed it to me. The setting was comfortable and my trust in a good friend made me confident. My years of curiosity prompted me to accept the joint, and I emulated his inhaling technique. Wisely, he had explained the usual sensations, and presently I experienced a pleasant relaxed state where free-flowing ideas began and a feeling that time slowed down. Fae stated the required speech title and handed me paper and pen. Within an hour I had written a speech, with an attitude that I was humoring my friend.

Ironically, the required title was, "Can youth, by local leadership, strengthen the responsibility of government?" I traveled around the state competing with numerous other student speakers, and I won first prize, a scholarship I could use at the college of my choice. I was invited to give the talk at the Lions International convention soon to be held at the Civic Auditorium in San Francisco.

Face to face with 14,000 Lions; pot helps

Daniel had nothing on me. There were *14,000* Lions out there. Doing radio, where many thousands *may* be listening, is far easier than speaking live to thousands you can *see* are listening. Radio allows you to convince

*At 17 I became a real, live rabbit! I sold the managers of San Rafael's largest
department store on the idea of making me their Easter Bunny for $4.00 an hour. (I
should have sold this idea to Hugh Hefner a few years later, for even more.)*

PART TIME SANTA CLAUS.—Hiring himself out as a Santa Claus to families in Marin who desire the services of a St. Nick for the benefit of their youngsters, is David Ford. 221 Union street, San Rafael, a Marin Junior College freshman. He makes arrangements with parents, fills a sack with appropriate gifts and is Johnny-on-the-spot when the kiddies appear. Ford is using his earnings to pay part of his education costs.

Acme wire service

...So naturally I played Santa Claus too, Christmas 1947... which led to my decision never to drink hard liquor!

yourself that perhaps no one is out there. Eight months had passed since I had written the speech after smoking my first joint; I was expected to give that speech live before a large – live! – audience in a matter of minutes, and 432 butterflies were square-dancing in my belly.

Backstage at the Civic Auditorium I was fumbling around in my pockets looking for a mint when my fingers discovered a roach (comparable to a cigarette butt) in my jacket pocket from the time that I had written the speech. I made a beeline for the exit. Just outside I lit up and took two puffs, and within a couple of minutes the butterflies flew away. I took a deep breath and went back inside, to center stage and the microphone.

Thousands of those people were talking among themselves. I stood there in serene silence. Gradually the conversations ceased until at last you could hear a pin drop. That night's delivery was my best ever, and the applause from 14,000 curious and attentive Lions and their wives was far more intoxicating than any drug.

They presented me with a three-foot gold trophy, inscribed with my name, along with those of the winners from years past. My high school held a special assembly and I was given a gold watch, inscribed. I thanked everyone involved in the contest, along with the teachers and students. (I smiled to myself, thinking: I should have also thanked the pot.)

It's 4:20, Louie!

High Times is the country's most straightforward drug magazine, reporting on both the positive and negative effects of drugs. Editor-in-Chief Steven Hager and one of his senior editors, Steve Bloom, tell the story of two San Rafael High School students in the early 70s, who may well have created the now internationally known code phrase "4:20."

Steve Waldo claimed that he and his friends coined the term while at San Rafael High. School let out at 3:10 and, because many of them had after-school activities, they usually arranged to meet 70 minutes later. Their standard rendezvous was the statue of Louis Pasteur near the entrance of the school parking lot – right where my buddy Fae and I used to take a toke or two of pot after school, 25 years earlier! They signaled a desire to meet by saluting each other in the halls and saying, "4:20, Louie." *High Times* put it fittingly: "420 has become another reason to extol the virtues of marijuana and challenge the folly of prohibition." 4 Truth 4 Liberty 4 Justice, 4:20.

On a Saturday in April my friend Hookin, whom we called Hokie, (the son of the gentleman who introduced me to the joy of sex at the Greenhouse in Petaluma), joined me on a drive to Stinson Beach, where my mother and sisters and I had lived through a tidal wave when I was 12. Though it was a cold overcast day, Hokie decided he'd go swimming. I was alarmed, because I knew these waters to be treacherous. "Hokie, please don't do it. The water is cold and you'll freeze your butt off. There are also riptides out there today."

He breezily ignored me, removed all his clothes but his undershorts and high-stepped out to meet the large waves, diving through one. He swam about 200 yards out while I watched nervously. Suddenly, he disappeared, then he resurfaced, screaming for help. I could barely hear him as he moved farther out to sea. Even though I'd earned a senior Red Cross lifeguard certificate, I didn't want to go after him without a surfboard or flotation device; but nothing offered itself. I found myself tearing off my clothes as I dashed for the water. It was rough and the waves were immense. I swam over them rather than dive through, as I didn't ever want to take my eyes off Hokie: If he went under I could lose him.

When I was 10 feet from him, I dived under the water, grabbed his ankles and turned his body so that his back was toward me. Allowing a drowning person to face you can be a disaster, especially one 6 feet tall and weighing 175. I began the struggle of swimming toward the distant shore with Hokie in tow. Waves were crashing over us; the current was strong; Hokie was fighting me, and I was becoming exhausted.

"Hokie, listen to me," I urged. "I can stand up. So can *you.*" Actually, I was treading water but the deception mellowed him out. *Anything* to prevent his panicking and killing us both. I kept up the calm talk until he relaxed, and he became far easier to tow. Soon we *could* stand up, and now I just held his hand. "Stand up, Hokie."

"Shit, I can stand!" A few minutes of wading, feeling the undertow straining to haul us back into deep water, brought us to the beach at last, thanks to an incoming wave.

"Hell", said Hokie, "I could have made it just fine on my own!"

I'd've encouraged him to go try it again if I hadn't been exhausted.

Its siren rapidly growing louder, a red jeep with surfboard and all the necessary lifeguard equipment came bounding over the dunes. The siren dwindled to a slow growl as its driver stepped down. "I'm Sheriff Bill Woodington. I saw that rescue with my binoculars from up on the hill. Got here as soon as I could. Do you have a Red Cross senior life-

San Francisco Examiner
CCCC✥   MONDAY, JULY 28, 1947   **13**

ORATOR—Winner of the annual Student Speaker Contest of the Lions Clubs of California and Nevada yesterday was David Ford, 18, of San Rafael, shown holding his trophy and receiving a kiss from his sister, Carol. With him are his parents, Mr. and Mrs. Ernest Ford. In addition to the cup, young Ford won a **$500** scholarship to the university of his choice.

—Photo by San Francisco Examiner.

San Francisco Examiner, July 28, 1947

On a dare, I entered the Lions International Public Speaking Contest, and won first place. Sis Carol congratulated me with a kiss while Mother and Dad looked on.

WINS LIONS' STUDENT ORATORY

Dave Ford of San Rafael, winner of the | 000 contestants, is congratulated at Califor-
scholarship in the Lions' student oratory | nia Hall yesterday by his sisters, Margot
st which started out with a total of 12,- | (left) and Carol.

San Francisco Examiner July 28, 1947
A double delight — kisses from two exquisite young ladies, sisters Margo and Carol.

saving certificate, young man?"

"Yes, sir," I panted.

"Would you like a job as a lifeguard here this summer?"

"Me?" said blue-skinned Hokie.

"No, not you, son."

"I sure would, Sheriff", I said.

"Where do you go to school?" the sheriff asked.

"San Rafael High, sir."

"That's fine; I'll also have a lifeguard from Tamalpais High School." We shook hands on it.

Hired as lifeguard – alcohol, pot, and girls

As soon as high school let out for the summer I pre-taped radio shows and headed for my job at Stinson Beach. My lifeguard partner from our rival high school, Tamalpais, had just arrived; Val was a nice person, tall and slim but in excellent shape. We were provided with a small cabin and a red jeep that was well-equipped, much like those on the TV series *Baywatch*. We were on the job every morning, cruising the beach by 8:30 a.m. Stinson Beach can be tranquil, with friendly seagulls gliding over gentle waves; but generally the water was far from placid. Each day we had to help several people out of trouble. It took a couple weeks to get used to the grasping tangles of seaweed that would clutch our legs as we rushed to a swimmer's aid: There are sharks at Stinson, and more than once the touch of seaweed convinced us we were about to lose a leg.

When visitors came to our cabin I never mentioned pot; I'd drink a Coke or some other soft drink. There were times when a couple of young ladies remained with us in our cabin for the night; and each time it happened, I was surprised to find that at least one of the girls would produce a joint. If they offered me a hit, I would join them with the tacit understanding that word would never leave our cabin, or I could lose my job. It was surprising to have discovered, in those early years, that girls used pot as much as guys did. Frequently it was to scare away those mean butterflies of menstrual cramps; but often it was just to have a fun time with no hangover.

Incidentally, *pot was as strong in the 1940s as it is today.* One or two puffs of medical-quality cannabis, at a higher cost, was all that it took then, and all that it takes today. (If it's being used medically, more might be required depending on the illness.) Alcohol encourages the lowering of inhibitions far more than grass does. You've heard the cliché, "Candy is dandy, but liquor is quicker." Grass isn't "quicker": It produces relaxed camaraderie and closeness, and an inclination to explore those feelings, if both partners desire each other, but grass is not an aphrodisiac. When the government says that smoking a joint leads to unsafe sex and pregnancy, that is another despicable lie – and, like other propaganda about cannabis, was borrowed from the lore of alcohol use!

Lifeguards soon learn that many swimmers get into trouble in the water after consuming alcohol. The warming effect of alcohol encourages some people to remain in cold water longer than their bodies can tolerate. After drinking alcohol too many swimmers become overconfident, and won't heed lifeguard warnings. Some inebriated beach-goers who dive into shallow water break their necks, becoming permanently paralyzed. We never witnessed such tragic consequences among those who smoked pot before swimming. Beach rules banned all drugs, including grass and alcohol; with several thousand people there at one time, however, it was impossible to prevent all use.

I am not condoning use of any drug, including grass, while engaged in any sport, or when working, driving, flying, using mechanical equipment – when pursuing *any* activity that demands sound psychomotor skills. I am simply comparing the effects of the two drugs.

One day the ocean was especially ferocious. People were trying to beat a sweltering day, and our boss, Sheriff Woodington, estimated the crowd at 7,000. We ran the jeep up and down the beach constantly, its siren wailing, warning people to stay out of the water. That day we pulled eight people from the ocean.

At mid-morning I spotted a man, barely distinguishable, motionless on top of a gigantic wave that was cresting and about to smash into the sand with its thousands of gallons of deadly weight. I leaped from the jeep, plowed through the mean surf, and threw myself into that twenty-foot wave. I caught the man and dragged him back to calmer waters just seconds before the breaker crashed onto the shore. Val helped me carry him from the water's edge. I guessed him to be in his mid-forties, about six feet, and weighing about 180 pounds. He was cold.

I immediately began artificial respiration, working feverishly as a crowd surrounded us. I asked Val to call an ambulance. The man's body was turning blue, and I wouldn't stop to let Val or anyone else touch him.

When you're working to save a life, you frequently become tender and protective toward him, as if he were a member of your family; that's how it was for me that day. An hour passed while I continued resuscitation efforts. Then I saw a fire-truck, an ambulance, and a police car approach. A man in a dark suit pushed his way through the assemblage of onlookers. He opened a penknife and knelt beside us.

"Get away from here!" I yelled at him; "Someone get this nut out of here!"

"I'm the coroner, son. Move aside," he said.

I continued performing compressions; I couldn't believe what I was seeing. The coroner stuck his penknife into a vein in the man's arm. "You can quit now, son. This man was dead when you brought him in."

Tears filled my eyes as I abandoned my futile efforts. The next day the *San Rafael Independent* ran a front-page photo of me trying to resuscitate that poor man, and relating the story.

Even today, my heart sinks each time I read of a drowning. Every time I was able to save someone from drowning – and every time I couldn't – brought home to me the plain truth, that there is no excuse for drowning if people learn to swim, and don't panic.

My summer of lifeguarding taught me some valuable lessons, and with the summer ending and school about to begin, I bid a reluctant farewell to Val, Sheriff Woodington, and some of the lovely young ladies I met while at Stinson Beach.

I left behind the young ladies of that summer, but autumn brought new chances to renew my discovery that for sheer adventure and fun nothing could beat sex. One Saturday night I invited a classmate named Roann to go out to dinner and a drive-in movie. At soon as the screen showed "The End," our adventure began. We drove to McNear's beach, about five miles from San Rafael, snuggling and teasing along the way. Roann was darling – ivory-haired, blue-eyed, five foot three, around 115 pounds. I parked on a side road and we continued kissing and fondling while I folded the front seat back into a bed. (That car hadn't left the factory with fully reclining seats. I learned a lot of useful skills in auto shop.) Within minutes we were far more comfortable. And naked. And making joyful love. We were both about to climax when there was a pounding on the driver's side of the car.

"Roann, hold me up," I whispered. She put both hands in the center of my back and pushed me upright. I opened the driver's side window about four inches. A flashlight shone in my eyes. It was a cop.

"Yes, sir, officer. Is there a problem?" I asked, trying not to sound naked.

"Let's see your driver's license, please."

Still holding me up with one hand, Roann fumbled through my pants and handed me my wallet. I clumsily found my driver's license in the dark and handed it to the policeman.

"Would you care to step out of the car, Mr. Ford?"

"Um, Officer, I'd rather not; I have a cold. My friend and I were just visiting here off the main road."

"It's past midnight," the officer said. "You kids should be home. Take the lady home, Dave. You're not setting a good example for the teenagers who listen to your show."

"Yes, sir. You're right, officer."

Red to the ears, we struggled into what clothing we could find quickly and I started the car. Roann was understandably terrified; her father was a judge. "Dave, I really prefer not to end up in court. I'm going back to Johnny; his car doesn't turn into a bed."

Across the street from our home lived an Italian family with a daughter about 24 years old. She was gorgeous, about 5' 9" with chestnut hair and long tanned legs. She was bright, already an executive with the telephone company. We exchanged smiles when we passed on the street, and I fantasized.

My illusions shriveled when she married a World War II veteran. Then three days later he vanished. She was heartbroken. The following day, I found her crying in their backyard. I gave her a hug and told her how sorry I was.

"Hell," she sobbed, "I'm going to call in sick. Would you like to stay for a glass of wine?"

"I would, Dorothy."

After we drank a glass, I decided I had nothing to lose by being friendly. "Dorothy, I just tuned up this convertible and was going to test-drive it. Would you care to join me?"

She smiled. "This will be a chance to wear that beautiful mink coat my parents gave me for my wedding present. I'd love to go with you." I opened the car door for her, lowered the top, and headed toward Mt. Tamalpais. After a half hour of conversation she relaxed. She told me how much she loved sex, and that her husband was hardly interested. I felt sorry for both of them.

We parked on a turnout overlooking the ocean. Harry James with his magic trumpet was playing "Bye Bye Blues," which couldn't have been more perfect. I put my arm around her and was delighted with her response. Within minutes we were undressing each other. I was so ready that I had difficulty pulling off my trousers. I suggested that she sit on her fur coat, thinking that that would feel extra sexy for her. She nodded, handed me a tube of KY jelly, and inserted her diaphragm. I'd heard about this process but had never seen it performed before. Nor had I ever seen such a beautiful woman's naked body, with her long brown hair silhouetted by the full moon.

She nestled sensually into the mink coat. And screamed.

Attempting to contain her fury, she slowly sizzled, "Where-did-you-put-the-tube-of-KY?" Uh oh. It was no longer in my hand. Oh God! She slowly sat up and felt under her lovely bottom. Her hand came out covered with some of the KY. The rest was now smeared all over her fur coat. "Please take me home – *right now*."

Now my pants slipped right on. We dressed in silence. As I started the car to head for home, Glenn Miller's band was playing "In The Mood." "Yeah, perfect," I thought, and turned the radio off.

Dorothy forgave me after a few days, fortunately, but I wasn't having good luck with the local ladies. Equally fortunately, I knew where to go when Lady Luck takes a holiday.

The next night I returned to the Greenhouse in Petaluma. This time I went alone. I had been continuing to give the ladies there "plugs" on my radio show, and the madam was so appreciative that she presented me with two lovable ladies for the price of one!

A week later I mounted my motorcycle – not what you may be thinking. It was for a ride to Vallejo. I wanted to see whether Mr. Furrin was right about the whorehouses there too. I reached Vallejo in forty minutes, around 10 p.m., and began walking down alleys off Georgia Street. It didn't take long to spot the men coming out of the rear entrance of a two-story wood-frame hotel. I walked past several sailors who were leaving. I held my breath and knocked on the door. It slowly opened a scant two inches.

"What you want, boy?" came a feminine growl.

"I want a girl. I'm no problem, and I haven't been drinking."

I heard the chain being removed and a tall, attractive black woman invited me in. She wore a white smock, and appeared to be a maid.

"You Navy, boy?" she asked in a mellow, friendly voice.

"I'm in high school."

She looked at me with suspicion. "You got three dollars, boy?"

"I've got five," I said with a smile. She laughed deeply.

"My oh my, you young kids do learn fast. Come in to the waiting room."

There was a fellow in a wheelchair who looked like a teenager. His legs had been amputated at his knees. A war casualty, no doubt. Two blind men, each with white cane, perhaps in their sixties. They were whispering excitedly to each other. Another man looked as though he must weigh 300 pounds. For the first time I realized what a service these ladies were performing for men who might otherwise never experience lovemaking. (And no doubt reducing date rape by sex-hungry young men.)

In a few minutes, the maid returned with eight young ladies. She led two of them over to the blind men. They took the men's hands, and it was obvious that they all knew each other. The men smiled, got up, and were led away. One by one, the maid led the girls to the waiting men. Finally only one girl was left. In her late twenties I guessed, auburn hair pulled back into a pony tail that trailed to her waist, large emerald eyes, and freckles. She wore an ivory satin robe, three-quarter length.

The maid said, "I'll bring in more young ones for you in a few minutes," and the lady with the charming freckles looked down at the floor.

"No, please don't," I urged. "I want this lady with the beautiful scarlet hair."

Those brilliant green eyes looked deep into mine. She took my hand. "I'm Gail. I'm kinda old, almost 28, but I'm still fun." She smiled and led me to her room.

Her bedroom was much like the one I had seen at the Greenhouse. "What name would you like me to call you?" she asked.

"My real name. David, or Dave." I felt a warm connection with Gail.

She asked my age.

"I'm 17." I told her I lived in San Rafael. She said she came from Kalamazoo.

Gail went through the same ritual with the bowl of warm water I'd encountered at the Greenhouse. When she removed her robe I was treated to a lovely sight: Her long legs were beautiful, and every other inch of her was ravishing. I asked her if most of the ladies enjoyed this work.

She answered, "About a third of them are lesbians, or bi, and do it strictly for money. They're good actresses, frequently faking orgasms to excite the man so he'll climax as soon as possible. Some of us are just addicted to sex. After my monthly three days off, I can hardly wait to get back to work."

Gail began undressing me. When she finished she was on her knees in front of me with the pan of warm water. As she washed me she started breathing hard, and I knew this was going to be special. She smiled up at me and said, "I'm going to rape that beautiful big cock."

What excited me about Gail was that she was really into the enjoyment of sex. She guided me over to her bed. "Just lay on your back and relax, baby." Gail could have written the stage directions for the movie *Deep Throat*. (Now I realize why Woodward and Bernstein's mysterious informant in the Watergate scandal was called "Deep Throat": He was nowhere to be seen!)

As Gail was going down on me superbly, she was rubbing herself against my leg. After a minute or so she had an orgasm such as I have rarely witnessed since, thrashing and moaning. There was a tap on the door; a lady's voice softly asked, "Are you all right, Gail?"

"Oh, yes," moaned Gail.

We could hear the maid's chuckle. "Gail, you are a wonder!"

When I was atop Gail, she wrapped her long soft legs around my back. Our rhythm was perfect, and without losing a stroke she rolled us over so that she was on top. She would move in circles, and then would hump wildly. She would have me almost out of her for a few seconds, and then all the way in, then out again. When I squirted, Gail had such a tremendous orgasm that she had tears in her eyes. I feared she was about to cry, but instead she released a beautiful laugh. What fun! What an education! What a lady! What an orgasm!

When I was dressed and about to leave, I pulled out another five-dollar bill and asked if it might be possible to do it again. She smiled, and knocked on the door. It opened slightly. She whispered something to the maid, handed the bill through, closed the door, and laughed. "OK, baby, you're on!" Soon I *was* on – and off again!

When I was finally washed and dressed, I asked Gail what her favorite songs were. She answered, "Cole Porter's 'Night and Day' and George Gershwin's 'I Got Rhythm,' played and sung by Louis Armstrong." Then she stared at me, and laughed. "I *thought* I recognized your voice. You're Dave Ford! You should be ashamed of yourself. You've been dedicating music to our friends – and our *competition* – up at the Greenhouse in Petaluma, you naughty boy! Lots of us girls listen to *Junior Jamboree* on Saturdays."

In love with a prostitute

The evenings that Gail was off work, during her period, I invited her out to dinner, and a couple of times to movies. One day we went riding on the motorcycle, a surprise picnic in the bike's saddlebag. We rode out into the countryside where wild buttercups covered the grass, and picnicked under an idyllic oak tree.

We had held hands but never kissed – I'd never *tried* to kiss her. She frequently insisted that I not pay for my numerous visits to her business establishment, but I refused to be a "free rider."

In the next six weeks, I visited only Gail – several times a week. She became one of my revered friends, and a mentor on how to please a lady. One night after making love with Gail she asked me if I would like to come back when she got off work at 2 a.m., and spend the rest of the night. I phoned my folks and said I was going to spend the night at a friend's house. Slightly duplicitous maybe, but still truthful! Dad laughed and said, "Have fun, son. But be careful."

I realized then how unfair it was that ladies didn't have the sexual freedom that men enjoy. To kill the time, I went to a late-night movie, *Forever Amber.* Pretty risqué for those days. When I returned at two, Maria, the maid, was even friendlier than usual when she let me in. She said that Gail was with her last client and would be with me shortly. When I started to sit down in the usual waiting room, she shook her head and led me to a room I'd never seen, a large, comfortable living room Some of the ladies had already showered or bathed, and they were chatting and having drinks. Clearly, I was in a place few customers ever saw. I felt special and proud. Gail had no doubt told them I was a special friend.

Within five minutes, out came Gail in a pair of black satin harem pants with side slits. A black crop top emphasized her full breasts, and black shiny pumps with five-inch heels completed the outfit. I stood up when she entered the room, happier than I'd been in weeks. I wanted to think she had dressed up just for me, but surely not, I told myself.

"Sorry to make you wait – just got out of the bathtub. Do you like this new outfit, Dave? I got it thinking of you."

All I could stammer out was, "You bet, Gail." She sat next to me on the divan, and for the first time she kissed me on the mouth. I was certain that I was in love with Gail.

She opened a small silver box and showed me some sweet-smelling buds. We had chatted briefly about grass, and I'd told her I'd used it, but we hadn't explored the topic any further. Now she rolled a joint and said, "After work it's relaxing to smoke a little pot. And it's super medicine, too. Many of us girls use it for menstrual cramps, headaches, and chronic pain. A couple of times I took a few hits before inviting a gentleman into my room, and those orgasms with grass were the wildest ever. But Maria heard my screams of joy and she realized I must have smoked pot. She doesn't mind what we do after the clients go home, but she won't allow smoking on the job, so I had to quit while at work." Her eyes twinkled. "Too bad."

"Another rule: no one can sleep in our rooms with us," said Gail. "I hope I didn't lead you on. I invited you to spend the night because I didn't want you driving home after smoking grass. You can sleep here on the divan, and leave in the morning. OK, baby?"

"Makes sense," I said.

Gail lit up, took a hit, and passed the joint to me. It was fine weed. Within a few minutes I felt a warm glow and an irrepressible urge to smile. I told Gail about my pal in Petaluma with the tattoo. I didn't mention Lorraine's name, in case Gail knew her. Gail laughed and said, "We have a young lady here who is very popular with the guys, but she doesn't have much in the way of breasts. To be frank, she's flat-chested. She has a tattoo on her belly too. Hers says, *"In case of rape, this end up!"*

I cracked up. It goes to show that a woman's sexuality is not only in her breasts, it is between her thighs, and underwear manufacturers don't take measurements down there. If any of you ladies have small breasts, please keep that in mind. Madison Avenue makes far too much of big breasts. If you have them, that's great. If you don't, that's great too.

Gail's sense of humor took over. I asked her how precocious she was as a child. She laughed and said, "When I was 10, one day I ran into the house to ask Mom if I was old enough to have a baby. She said, 'Of course not, darling.' I asked, 'Are you sure, Mommy?' and she said, 'Definitely.' So I went outside and said, 'OK, fellows, same game!' It didn't take me long to realize that sex is one of the most beautiful, wholesome things that money can buy!"

Maria came into the room with a tray of sandwiches, cookies, milk, and iced tea. The food tasted especially delicious; grass is renowned for enhancing taste and appetite. Maria looked me right in the eye and said, "You are the only boy who has ever been invited back here. This you do not tell your friends, and never mention the smoke."

"You have my word, Maria."

I told the girls about an incident the previous week in The Pig and Whistle, a very nice restaurant in San Francisco. I had been giving the waitress my order, when suddenly she stopped, ripped the check off its pad, flipped it over, and began writing furiously. She handed it to me, looked me straight in the eye, then ran off. It read, "I could not help but notice that your fly is wide open, and that you are very much exposed. I'll go into the kitchen and drop a tray of dishes so as to distract the customers' attention. This will give you an opportunity to zip up your fly. P.S. I love you!" Gail and all the ladies howled.

Rose said, "I never heard that one before. My guys will love it!" We told more stories and smoked more pot.

I told them about a friend of mine named Fun. I had been pondering a question and asked her: "Fun, what is your definition of being in love?" Fun tilted her pretty head in thought and then, smiling, answered, "Being in heat!" The ladies nodded their heads and we all laughed in agreement.

I asked Rose if she'd mind if I asked a few questions about their work.

"Not at all. Shoot. No pun intended!" she laughed.

"Are the girls safe here?" I asked.

"Yes. Only about half of the girls have pimps, and those leeches are never allowed in here. This environment is far safer than working the streets. I had to do that for a while, and I hope I never have to do it again. Too many of those girls are picked up by men in their cars, used sexually, and then robbed and beaten up, or even murdered. Lots of them are young girls who have run away from home. Many of them are from good Christian families; I was one of those. When they can't find jobs and run out of money, a pimp will latch onto them and 'turn them out' – get them started working the streets."

I asked Rose if she could compare pot with alcohol. "We won't allow a man to be with a girl if he's been drinking. Two reasons: First, they generally can't get it up. And second, they frequently get mean and even violent. With grass, which we can smell on their breath, they're mellow. And wow, *they* get it up."

"How about payoffs?" I asked.

"From here to Sunday," she griped. "Not only to the cops who demand free pussy, but also to the politicians. Once, I'm positive I recognized a judge here. Maybe that's why they keep it illegal," Rose laughed cynically.

At some point, I fell asleep and awoke refreshed at 10 in the morning. There was Maria in a starched white smock, very quietly tidying up the room. She handed me a towel and whispered, "Some of the girls will sleep till noon. You can take a shower, and then come into the kitchen. Ham and eggs will be waiting for you." She led me to the shower, pointing to the kitchen on the way. It was only later that I learned from Gail that Maria wasn't a maid – that she owned the business.

Interviewing Humphrey Bogart and Lauren Bacall

I was feature editor of our school paper, *The Red 'n' White*. As a budding journalist, I was asked to write a gossip column as well. It was aptly named *Dave's Dustpan*.

In November of 1946 Humphrey Bogart and Lauren Bacall were making the movie *Dark Passage* at the notorious state prison at San Quentin, just a few miles from San Rafael. I set up an interview with them, and Liston Sabraw, the editor of our school paper, joined me.

The film crew was shooting a scene in a small clearing along the Paradise Cove road, which faces San Quentin and San Francisco Bay. On the ground lay Bogart and another man, seemingly injured, and in great pain. Suddenly a car door slammed and Lauren Bacall pushed through the brush to rescue the two men. The director Delmer Daves yelled, "Cut! That's a take," and all the actors relaxed.

Liston and I got up and chatted briefly with both stars. They were polite and presented the same naturalness of manner and expression we were so familiar with on screen. I noted that everyone there called her by the name she was born with, Betty. She was only 22 when that movie was made, and had a great, feline face, a sultry voice, and a sweet slim body in addition to great acting talent. *Dark Passage* was their fourth film together, and it wasn't difficult to see why Bogart married her.

Me, in San Quentin?

I wanted a more in-depth interview with Bogart, so a day or two later I went to the prison and asked if Mr. Bogart was still there filming, and if so, where I might find him. I got permission to enter the prison, was directed to Bogart's location, and rode my motorcycle to where a black limousine was parked. There was Bogart in the back seat, with a gun in his lap, a prop for his next scene. What I remember now, more than the interview, was a grim omen of Bogart's future. The windows were closed, except for the one next to him, which was open only two inches. Cigarette smoke was seeping from the window and the ashtray was full of cigarette butts.

Humphrey Bogart died about 10 years later, at 57, of cancer of the esophagus. Tragically, he was but one of dozens of entertainers, along with millions of others, killed by nicotine: Yul Brynner, Nat King Cole, Harry James, Lucille Ball, John Wayne, Zeppo Marx (Groucho's brother), Bette Davis, Sammy Davis Jr., Steve McQueen, James Franciscus, Edward R. Murrow, and David Janssen, star of the television series *The Fugitive*, who died at 48 of a heart attack. It was reported he smoked three packs of cigarettes a day. There is no report anywhere of anyone dying from grass alone.

The next Sunday, Gail wasn't working; it was her time of the month. We took off on my motorcycle and found a lovely spot in a meadow overlooking the harbor, where we shared a joint that I just happened to have with me.

I also had a gift for her. Between my hobby of reconditioning and reselling cars and my radio show, I was doing very well financially and I wanted to give Gail something special, something that would let her know how special *she* was.

"Close your eyes, Gail," I said.

Gail smiled and complied I slipped a jade bracelet onto her wrist.

"Open your eyes, Gail."

Her big green eyes, usually mischievous, filled with tears that spilled down her lovable freckled cheeks. "You're the first man to give me a gift. It's beautiful! Thank you."

Whenever she turned serious, she would call me "Davie."

"Davie, would you consider spending some time with me in Florida? I'll be leaving shortly, and I'll be there for the winter." I was surprised and flattered. "I'd love it. I don't know what obligations I'll have here, but I can tape a couple of shows, and I promise I'll fly down for at least a couple of weeks during Christmas vacation."

I held her in my arms, stroked her face with one hand, and ran my fingers through her beautiful scarlet hair with the other. And we kissed. With grass, the sensation of touching a person you truly care about is magical. Your mind and body are focused on that moment.

"When I'm in Florida, I don't live in the whorehouse; I have a nice apartment. It will be really fun to come home to you, Davie. And I can cook, too!" She was lying on her stomach now, so I massaged her neck, shoulders, and back. After a nap, we rode around for an hour, than went to a Chinese restaurant and had a seven-course dinner.

I asked Gail if she'd had any serious romance in her life. She laughed and said, "There was Johnny, about two years ago. He wasn't too bright, but he wanted to marry me. I asked him, 'Johnny, don't you realize that I'm a nymphomaniac?' And Johnny said, 'I don't care if you steal, as long as you're faithful to me!'"

"Davie," she promised, "I'll write to you every week when I get to Florida."

But she didn't.

Expelled from high school

In 1946, with encouragement from my "brother" Vern, I ran for Commissioner of Assemblies and won the post. With the aid of a couple of hits of quality grass, I could come up with ideas and write a script in less than a quarter of the usual time. The largest and most elaborate production on the schedule was the Christmas show, *Santa's Toy Shop*. The school's theater was as well equipped as most theaters featuring professional stage shows, and I was eager to see what feats of wonder I could produce.

The show was set in Santa's workshop. After all the work of making toys for all the youngsters, Santa was tired and drifted off into a long winter's nap. A toy soldier in an old-fashioned uniform began to march mechanically. Music began, "March of the Wooden Soldiers," and he gradually became more limber and danced to it. When the music finished, he woke up all the other dolls. A jack-in-the-box sprang out of his box and played "Swinging On A Star" on an accordion. A boy doll, wrapped in red cellophane tied up with a large green bow and sitting at a grand piano (my friend Fae McNally) woke up and played "Silent Night." An 18th-century doll with a white powdered wig and ornate costume sang "White Christmas." Some dolls danced, others performed acrobatics, still others sang "Santa Claus is Coming to Town" and "O Holy Night".

For the finale, all the dolls were to sing "I'm Dreaming of a White Christmas." As snow fell outside the shop window, stage lights would dim to blue. The curtain would close as the dolls returned to slumber.

Two days before the show, word spread throughout school that whoever dropped the snow would be expelled. I went to the school's stage manager, Mr. Day, who was also the art teacher, and asked him about the rumor.

"Well, ah, it would be a dangerous thing for someone to be up there above the stage. The faculty met and decided that it won't happen."

At first, I felt sick with disappointment. Then I had a sudden thought and said, "I can have the wood shop make a box on hinges. It could be secured safely, and with the pull of a rope, the snow could still be released. Would that be OK?"

"Well, it answers the safety question, David, but I'll have to check with the rest of the faculty."

The next day the same rumor persisted. I went back to Mr. Day. "I hear that now even the box isn't acceptable. Why didn't someone tell me?"

Mr. Day smirked and said, "You've gotten a little too big for your britches, Mr. Ford. We felt it's time to let the students know that the faculty is running this school, not you students!"

I was heartsick and said, "We're supposed to have a student government. The students deserve to be *heard* on this issue, at least."

"Forget it, Ford." he said. "What this school needs is a good expulsion. That would shape it up."

Not if I could help it! was my first thought, but I was so determined to give my show the finale I'd planned I was willing to run that risk.

Because any Commissioner of Assemblies might work long hours preparing a show, I had been given a key to the school. At midnight I let myself in and cut up paper 'til I'd filled four big boxes. I then carried two of them, one box at a time, up a two-story vertical metal ladder, and placed them at the center of the catwalk directly above the stage. I placed the other two boxes of shredded paper at the foot of the ladder, as decoys.

Ominously, the day of the show was Friday, December 13th. The entire school was buzzing. The word was everywhere: If anyone drops snow in the Christmas show he'll be expelled. The students were all certain now that the snowfall couldn't happen. Yet in these rebellious teenage hearts, the hope was still alive.

It was time. We had 100% attendance; not a single student wanted to miss any part of this show. The house lights dimmed as the curtain slowly opened. After writing the show and directing all the rehearsals, I wanted it to be perfect. I was backstage managing the details. Five male teachers were backstage with me making certain no student even *thought* of carrying a box of "snow" up that ladder.

The show was going beautifully. The word had gotten around that the snow was supposed to start falling as the dolls launched into the second verse of "I'm Dreaming of a White Christmas," but no one knew what I had done the previous night, and tension was growing. I could hear my heart pounding in my ears as the second verse began. I casually walked over to the teachers and asked how they liked the show.

With a snicker, Mr. Welz said, "We think it's just super."

With that, I cried in a loud stage whisper, "LOOK!" and pointed toward the orchestra pit. As they turned toward the pit, I pulled Mr. Day away from the ladder and began climbing like a wild monkey. Mr. Simontacchi, the math teacher, grabbed my foot but I was able to free it from my shoe and scrambled on up the ladder to the catwalk. I crawled rapidly on my hands and knees to the center of the catwalk and dumped the first box of paper. Even from above it was spectacular.

The applause was thunderous. As I dumped the second box of snow, the kids were screaming with joy. I descended the ladder, knowing that the welcome awaiting me at the bottom wouldn't be as warm. Mr. Day knocked me to the floor, Mr. Welz bent my arm behind my back, and Mr. Day grabbed one of my legs. The teachers began to realize how ridiculous they looked restraining me, and their grip became uncertain. The curtain was closing so I shouted to my lighting technician, "Millard, open the curtain!" He reversed direction and as the curtain opened, I broke free and ran to center stage.

I grabbed one of the live microphones. "Kids! How did you like the show?" They'd answered my question before I asked it. Many were now standing on their theater seats, screaming with delight. The snow was still twirling and blowing over the audience.

One of the male teachers yelled, "Dismissed! Dismissed! Clear the theater!" Knowing that five angry teachers were waiting in the wings to renew their attack, I was desperate to stall for time, but what could I say now? Then it came to me:

"Kids, do you think I should run for student body president?"

Yells of "Go Dave go!"

There was still no escape, of course. When I left the stage two teachers frog-marched me to the principal's office with both arms twisted up behind my back.

The principal, Mr. Wells, asked calmly, "Who informed David that no snow was to be dropped?"

Mr. Day, ruffled but trying to retain control, said, "I did."

"When?" asked Mr. Wells.

"Several days ago."

"I see," said Mr. Wells.

He turned to me. "David", said Mr. Wells, "I have no alternative but to expel you from San Rafael High School. You are not to return to this school – until after Christmas vacation."

I couldn't believe my ears: I had an ally! Those teachers stormed out of the principal's office and slammed the door behind them. Mr. Wells said, "Merry Christmas, David. Nice show!" I was so happy I had tears running down my cheeks. In those more formal days, the most I could do was shake Mr. Wells's hand – but I wanted to hug him.

The show was repeated and broadcast for the *Junior Jamboree* radio show on the stage of the El Camino Theater in San Rafael, complete with snow. Every seat was sold out. Students brought their parents and friends from other schools.

A broken heart

Gail had departed for Florida the month before. Each day I checked my mailbox. No mail from Gail. I couldn't understand it; she was always so sincere with me, and I loved her for that. I decided to see if I could get her address and phone number from Maria.

When Maria appeared at the back door and recognized me she opened it wide, and gave me a bear hug. I felt better already.

"Come into my apartment, David, and sit down," Maria said gravely. "It's painful to tell you this. I didn't know how to reach you, or I would have phoned or written. Gail couldn't get a job in Florida at the 'house.' They said she was too old."

"Is she here?" I asked, excited.

Maria shook her head. "She was probably ashamed to get in touch with you. I know she cared a great deal about you."

"Where is she?" I demanded, suddenly frightened. "What do you mean, she cared? What happened to her?"

"She apparently decided to work the streets with a pimp." I felt sick to my stomach.

"He took all of her money except cab fare, and money for food and rent. Gail apparently held out on him once." Maria began to sob. She held my hand tightly. "Oh, David! To teach the other girls a lesson, he put her eyes out with a metal coat hanger and cut off her breasts. Her screams didn't bring help. When they found her, she had bled to death. I just heard about it last week. I'm sorry, David."

I was shaking. I could barely see through my tears to drive home.

It's *illegality* that makes business dangerous for prostitutes – and their clients. Lacking a legal right to police protection, those who meet in back alleys to exchange money for sex risk being ripped off, exposed to AIDS, abused, or even killed, just like those who meet in the same back alleys to exchange money for drugs.

Returning to San Rafael High School was difficult. For several days I seriously considered not returning to school, but I decided that Gail would want me to continue my education. She had always encouraged me to be the best person I could be, as my mother and father had.

Marijuana – and the student body president?

I t was winter 1947. Dozens of kids urged me to run for student body president. Mr. Day, still feeling his humiliation after the Christmas show, was determined I would not win. He made it clear to me he would use his power as stage manager to keep me off the platform during the candidates' speeches.

For several days I tried to think up some creative, legal way to win the election. I could think of nothing – until I fired up a joint. My desire was to give students more power so that they would be interested in running for office and improving the country as adults. Maybe ours would be the generation to finally put people ahead of politics.

Within a few minutes ideas began flashing. Wow! Yes! After years of turning out trucks, tanks, and other war machinery, the automobile companies were just then retooling to manufacture new civilian cars for the first time in years. The Ford Motor Company, understandably eager for people to choose Fords when they satisfied their long-frustrated desire for new cars, came up with a clever advertising image: a lady fortune-teller, looking into a crystal ball, with the caption "There's a Ford in your future."

"What luck! Ford Motor Company has geared up to make me student body president!" I thought: "I'll get a team of kids to go to all the Ford dealerships around, and grab up all the brochures that show the fortune-teller. We'll cut out the lady, the crystal ball, and the caption, and paste them on the inside of students' lockers – most kids leave them unlocked. Put 'em in the teachers' lounge! Scotch-tape 'em to car bumpers! Tape them to the glove compartments of students' – and teachers' – cars! Yes – especially Mr. Day's!"

And that's exactly what we did. If the kids at San Rafael High didn't know they had a President Ford in their future, it was not for lack of any effort by us!

I was a rebel with a cause. My campaign was not just about dazzling stunts, or even about winning what, in many schools, was nothing more than a popularity contest. My platform promised that, if I was elected, we'd rewrite our school constitution. Some teachers felt I was seditious. To round out the picture, I would be running against the classic "clean-cut all-American boy." Liston Sabraw was bright, handsome, a magnet for feminine adoration, the editor of the school paper, and – yes, our star quarterback.

My buddy Vern Hughes had already graduated, but he made a sign that went across the entire width of the hallway that led to classes. It featured a big red apple, with a little worm wearing a freshman's beanie sticking his head out, saying, "I'm for Dave Ford too!"

Mr. Day and his henchmen spread the word: "If Ford puts one foot on the stage to give a campaign speech, he's expelled permanently." The day before the scheduled campaign speeches, an envelope was delivered to me in my first class after lunch. In it a note read, with ominous simplicity, "David, report to my office immediately after school. Edwin A. Wells, Principal." All afternoon I dreaded the approach of the closing bell. I worried that perhaps I had gone a bit too far in my campaign. I'd heard that one of my campaign helpers had glued one of the "There's a Ford in your future" on a box of condoms that was discovered in the glove compartment of one of the attractive female teachers. Could that be what I was summoned for? Or could it have been for the ads that were taped inside Mr. Day's desk drawer and on the steering wheel of his car?

The bell finally rang, and I trudged apprehensively to Mr. Well's office. "Sit down, David." He laid a clean sheet of paper on his blotter, uncapped his fountain pen, and drew a rectangle with a small square at each end. "David, this rectangle is the stage. The small squares that I have drawn are where the American flags are located. The little squares are *not* part of the stage. Am I making myself clear, David?" His twinkling eyes said it all. For some reason I could not guess, he wouldn't say so out loud, but he was clearly telling me that I could walk up the stairs to the stage, stand on one of the little areas about four feet square, and give my speech – legally! I laughed, and once again had to stop myself from hugging him. He shook my hand and wished me "Good luck." I thanked him and left.

The next day when the bell rang for Assembly, every seat in the auditorium filled. I got there early to grab a seat in the front row. The house lights dimmed. Mr. Day began introducing the speakers for the various student body offices. Finally it was time for those running for president. Liston Sabraw presented his speech, and I had to admit it was good, and the audience around me applauded enthusiastically. I was next.

My heart was pounding. Before I could get out of my chair, Mr. Day quickly walked from center stage down to my front-row seat. He whispered in my ear, "Looks like this just isn't one of your lucky days, Ford. No Ford in our future. How sad."

I got up, walked right past him and up the four stairs, and stood in the small square – conveniently next to the American flag! Without a microphone I knew I'd have to project strongly, so I lifted my chin and began by saying, "Good afternoon. It's nice to be here today!" Applause and laughter followed for about thirty seconds.

Mr. Day, whose face was now red with anger, looked at me, looked at the flag, and realized he'd lost again. He came over and tapped me hard on the shoulder. "Clever, Ford. You're not going to be a martyr. Go to center stage. Use our microphone, and give your losing speech."

I won the election by a landslide. Soon we had formed a conference with representatives from 16 high schools in the North Bay Area. We established a student court to handle inter-school fights at football games (generally started by kids who sneaked alcohol into their soft drinks). We also wrote a new school constitution giving the students more power in their own government.

That was my last year of high school, and some of the most fun I ever had. I was honored to present the graduation address, Friday, June 13, 1947. (I was a bit concerned when my parents, for a graduation gift, presented me with two suitcases!) Just before summer vacation, I was selected to be lifeguard at the Odd Fellows resort on the Russian River. Soon I was on my way.

My accommodation was a tent with a cot and a dresser. The job wasn't nearly as frenetic as being a lifeguard at the ocean, but there's subtle danger lurking in any river. Undercurrents can churn under a calm surface; tree branches moving under water can terrify a swimmer if he gets entangled. I was on the lifeguard tower, or in a white rowboat with a red cross on it. As at Stinson Beach, a frequent problem for me was people going into the water after overindulging in alcohol. I pulled several of them out of the river dazed and throwing up water.

Saving lives is all in a day's work

An incident of that kind occurred late one afternoon of my first week on the job. I heard a man's scream coming from under the diving raft. By the time I got there, there was no one to be seen. I dived under the raft, and by incredible luck connected with an arm. I pulled the man to shore and gave him artificial respiration. It was obvious to me that if I'd taken as much as a minute to find him, he'd have been a dead man. When he was finally revived and the water pumped out of him, he admitted he had drunk too much. When he came up under the raft, he panicked, forgot where he was, and slipped under the water.

During the fourth week working on the river I had to pull an 18-year-old out of the river. Her name was Rosemarie. She had been playing hide-and-seek with friends, going under water to "hide." I'd seen this game get dangerous before, so I gave her 15 seconds to reappear and then I went for her. River water isn't always clear. I made four dives before I grabbed a leg. It was not moving, and she was upside down.

I pulled her ashore, and began artificial respiration. When she revived, she looked into my eyes and said, "You saved my life. I panicked and didn't know which way was up." Her mother was hovering nearby, clutching a crucifix that was on a chain around her neck.

It's surprisingly easy to get vertigo when under water, and simply not know which way is up, particularly when the water is murky. It's also surprisingly easy to handle vertigo. The important thing is to remain calm. If you have a good breath of air in your lungs, just relax your body and let that air buoy you up to the surface. Let a little air escape, and follow the bubbles; they'll be rising to the surface. If you're out of air, try to remain calm and look where the water is lightest.

The next day, Rosemarie climbed the ladder to the lifeguard platform where I was sitting. She asked me, on behalf of her parents, if I would join them for dinner that evening, and then the two of us would to go to a dance. "I'd be pleased to," I said. Rosemarie was about five foot three and armed with a delicious figure. She had black wavy hair to her shoulders, glistening gray eyes, and a devilish smile.

Her parents were grateful and gracious to me. The dinner was superb. Before dinner, her father said grace while we all held hands. There were religious pictures on all the walls – not exactly what I was used to.

After I thanked her folks for dinner, Rosemarie and I headed to an outdoor dance in Rio Nido, a nearby town. The dance floor was filled with teens who were passing around bottles of booze in paper bags. As soon as we had the backs of our hands stamped with ink so we could come and go as we pleased, Rosemarie looked around inside. She said, "I don't drink. Do you mind if we just sit in your station wagon for a few minutes?"

"Not at all.' I said.

I was confused, until Rosemarie reached into her breast pocket and removed a joint! "Do you smoke grass, Dave? If you do, I promise that whatever we do together will be strictly between us." We shook hands to seal the deal, and lit up. I took a hit as she exhaled her smoke into my ear. Interesting lady. We returned to the dance where Rosemarie got a sample of my dancing. She was a good sport and we were having fun. I noticed that she received many admiring stares from envious guys. On the slow songs, our bodies melted together.

When we left the dance it was after midnight. We parked overlooking the water and necked passionately for a while until my hand began to move over her body. Then her hand stopped mine. Rosemarie was frank, and made it clear to me that she was a devout Catholic and intended to get married in a white wedding gown. "You know what I mean, don't you, Dave?"

"Yep," I responded.

"I will be a virgin when I get married," she said. I can't say I was happy about her covenant, but I respected it. We returned to the resort. She kissed me goodnight with a well-educated tongue.

My days off were Mondays, and the next three were spent with Rosemarie. We shared a strong sexual attraction, and on picnics we did everything imaginable except go all the way. She had beautiful hands an octopus could have taken lessons from. Rosemarie and I both knew this was just a summer fling and enjoyed it for that. She was headed for Stanford University in the fall and was planning on obtaining a Ph.D. in psychology.

Then one night, a couple of weeks before their departure, when we were lying by a secluded area of the river and necking passionately, Rosemarie put something into my hand. The little sweetie, I thought, a present – probably a religious statue. Then I realized that it was a tube of Vaseline! She kissed me in the ear as she placed my hand under her panties and on her lovely bottom. I was blown out, but didn't feel the need to ask why she handed me that little gift.

She and her family departed two weeks before the end of summer.

Before summertime and my job ended, I pulled a few more youngsters and adults from the hungry river. I also enjoyed a few dates with young ladies who didn't take religion quite so seriously.

Getting even with William Randolph Hearst

In the fall of 1947, at 19, I enrolled in the College of Marin. On February 8, 1948, the front page of *The San Francisco Call-Bulletin* announced an oratory contest, sponsored by 12 of the 29 newspapers in the Hearst chain. The Rupert Murdock of his day, William Randolph Hearst also owned dozens of radio stations, magazines, and movie studios, as well as thousands of acres of timberland. The contest was "to select the cream of the nation's college and high school orators." There would be a cash prize for the best original oration about Benjamin Franklin, delivered without notes. The next day a full-page spread bore a banner headline that screamed out "BENJAMIN FRANKLIN ORATORICAL CONTEST," and a quote from California Governor Earl Warren (later Chief Justice of the U.S. Supreme Court): "The Hearst newspapers are to be commended for sponsoring such a wholesome, patriotic project, and I extend my best wishes to all of this year's contestants."

I became one of those contestants – not because I had any great admiration for William Randolph Hearst. To me he was neither "wholesome" nor "patriotic." To understand why I did enter the contest, you need to know a little of the history of that time. Even before I began research for my speech, I knew Hearst had been a prime mover in the prohibition of cannabis and hemp. It may have been a little off the subject of the speech, but I wound up doing more research on Hearst than on Benjamin Franklin. What I learned only made me more determined to win. It became obvious that his prohibition efforts were for his own enrichment rather than any "noble-but-misguided" purpose. For years his newspapers had demonized marijuana for no purpose but to sell papers. Hearst was the pioneer of yellow journalism.

In my research at the library, I learned that when alcohol prohibition ended in 1933 Congress cut the budget of the Federal Bureau of Narcotics and Dangerous Drugs severely. Narcotics officers were out looking for jobs in the very depths of the Depression. The nation's first drug czar, the Bureau's power-driven chief, Harry J. Anslinger, didn't want to join them – indeed, resented the drastic reduction of his force of narcotics officers. Anslinger realized he desperately needed a new evil to pursue if he was to save his Bureau from being further diminished.

His quest for a new evil took Anslinger to newspaper mogul William

I was a senior lifeguard on the Russian River when I was 18, after spending the previous summer as an ocean lifeguard at Stinson Beach.

One of my special friends at Russian River.

Photo: American President Lines

As a teenager, I visited the magnificent President Cleveland, and said to myself,
"Someday I'd like to own that ship." I may have been blowing smoke then — but years
later I almost bought it!

Randolph Hearst, with whom he had an acquaintance. Indulge me in a little creative reconstruction for dramatic effect:

Anslinger: [As they shake hands and sit down] ...I'm so desperate, Mr. Hearst, I've been thinking of making catnip illegal for cats."

Hearst: [Pouring his guest a whiskey and offering him a cigar.] Nah nah, Harry, cannabis is the thing to go after. With your gift for deception you're the kind of guy who might just pull it off. Invent horror stories that make cannabis sound deadly. We can start a war on this drug. You furnish the horror stories, I'll furnish the war! And keep saying things like, "It's for the safety of our kids." Using kids to panic parents works beautifully. And "We don't want to send the wrong message." Never mind that nobody's sending any messages at all for the moment. I'll print the stories, and sell tons more newspapers, and you'll have that new evil you need to pursue.

Anslinger: Good try, Mr. Hearst, but cannabis *is* medicine. It's been used and trusted around the world for thousands of years. We can't change those facts.

Hearst: You think so? Harry, the facts are what my newspapers, magazines, and radio stations say they are. Try this on for size: "In Mexico, cannabis is sometimes called marijuana. Loosely translated, it's 'the weed that intoxicates.'" That reference to intoxication will take it out of the realm of medicine, and using the Mexican name will tap into the fears of the bigots. In my tabloids, uh . . . newspapers, I'll refer to those tranquilizing cigarettes as "reefers."

Anslinger: That's great – but it's still medicine.

Hearst: Of course it is, but our scare stories will make people so terrified of marijuana they won't even think of it as medicine.

Anslinger: It'll make criminals of people who use marijuana for medicine, or to get a free buzz! Alcohol companies don't want the competition marijuana provides. I'll wager they will kick in millions to support our crusade to "save the kids."

Hearst: Not bad, Harry, but don't stop there, man. Tobacco

companies know that cann – uh, marijuana – isn't addictive, and that no one has ever died from it. They'll surely contribute money to our campaign. The heads of the tobacco cartels are Pinocchios just like us. I wouldn't be surprised if someday they swore before God and the Congress of the United States that nicotine isn't addictive! And don't forget the pharmaceutical companies. They'll help big time. Cann – uh, marijuana – cuts into their profits now. They can't patent an herb. They want to force people into paying for expensive *synthetic* drugs that can be patented, and make them billions of dollars.

Anslinger: What do you think of this idea? I go before Congress and swear that marijuana is a stepping-stone to heroin addiction. It's not, of course, but you're right: people believe what you print in your newspapers, especially when you quote a high government official directly. Why, between us we can get them to believe that marijuana causes violence, and turns people into criminals or lunatics, or both! Mr. Hearst, with your newspapers and my imagination, we can create a war on marijuana. And think of the jobs we can say it will create. We'll need builders to put up prisons, guards to run 'em, cops and judges to fill 'em, probation and parole officers – that is, if we ever let those vicious marijuana criminals get out of prison! [Laughs nastily.] And of course we'll need more prosecutors, clerks, bailiffs, janitors, secretaries, politicians – not to mention advertising companies to create propaganda that marijuana is the most violence-causing drug in the history of mankind! [Both men laugh.] We'll sell the government on using the National Guard to do home searches that our military cannot legally do.

Hearst: Terrific idea! And I see a solution to a little problem I have. We'll blur the distinction between marijuana and industrial hemp, make people frightened of both, and get both of them banned. Hemp isn't intoxicating, but it's stiff competition for my thousands of acres of timberland. One acre of hemp can take the place of four acres of trees, so you should get lots of support from the big timber companies. In fact, if we roll hemp into the campaign, we can line up lots of powerful allies. Cotton growers hate the weed because it doesn't require near the finicky treatment cotton needs. The oil companies can't like the competition industrial hemp gives to petrochemicals and to gasoline. The synthetic fibers like Rayon coming out of DuPont will find it easier to penetrate the market if they don't have to compete with hemp fiber. That company alone should be eager to contribute to a good cause. Continuous scare stories about marijuana might be the magic key to get hemp prohibited around the world. Harry, go to the League of Nations! Scare the hell out of 'em. Convince them that marijuana is at least as dangerous as heroin, and treat it as such!

Anslinger: [Getting up to leave] Well, you've been in the movie business, Mr. Hearst, so you know nothing's scarier than a really creepy film. I can get a movie produced that will be so frightening parents will think they need us to save the youth of America from a deadly drug. We can call it *Reefer Madness*!

Hearst: [Shaking Anslinger's hand at his office door] I love it, Harry. Actually, marijuana is so mellow compared to alcohol that if you kept it legal, kids probably wouldn't use it. You know how it is with "forbidden fruit"!

I'm sure both men were rocking with laughter as Hearst closed his door. (Today, about 75,000 Americans are incarcerated for being in possession of cannabis.)

How the first drug czar created the war on marijuana.

Anslinger kept his bargain with Hearst. He realized he needed to generate venomous propaganda. He convinced sincere organizations that marijuana was so dangerous that making up horror stories was justified to save the kids from a "horrible marijuana death, or insanity."

In 1936, to drum up public support for the prohibition of marijuana (which was in fact banned in 1937), the propaganda film *Reefer Madness* was produced. It opened with this warning:

Marijuana is a violent narcotic. Its first effect is sudden violent, uncontrollable laughter. Then come dangerous hallucinations, followed by emotional disturbances, the total inability to direct thoughts, the loss of all power to resist physical emotions, leading finally to acts of shocking violence – ending often in incurable insanity. [11]

And that was only the introduction!

These lines echo the phrasing of Anslinger himself, who said, "Marijuana is a highly dangerous drug, inciting its users to commit crimes of violence and often leading to insanity."[12] His misrepresentations may be the reason that the Federal Bureau of Narcotics' name was eventually changed to the Drug Enforcement Administration (DEA).

Anslinger collaborated with fiction writer Courtney Cooper to produce a story that appeared in American Magazine in July 1937, which said in part, "An entire family was murdered by a youthful marihuana addict in Florida. When officers arrived at the home they found the youth staggering about in a human slaughterhouse."[13] Numerous other lurid stories began appearing in magazines and newspapers, most of them ending with such statements as: "I was fearless after smoking marijuana cigarettes. I would not have done this without marijuana."[14]

Such stories were fabricated by Anslinger and reported as news in Hearst's papers and magazines. In Anslinger's book, *The Murderers*, he says: "I wrote articles for magazines, and our agents gave hundreds of lectures to parents, educators, social and civic leaders. In network broadcasts I reported on the growing list of crimes, including murder and rape. Much of the irrational juvenile violence and killing that has written a new chapter of shame and tragedy is traceable directly to (marijuana) intoxication."[15]

Only the most ardently irrational drug-warrior (crazed perhaps by excessive exposure to drug propaganda) could take *Reefer Madness* seriously today. Its most faithful viewers these days are pot smokers, who get a huge kick out of seeing themselves caricaturized as demented addicts, their eyes rolling maniacally. (The movie is especially entertaining if watched after a hit or two.)

The style has changed over the years, but the substance has not. Today's drug czars and other DEA propagandists honor the Founder's memory by following in his footsteps, keeping alive the agency he saved from oblivion in the '30's by the means he pioneered: an unremitting stream of distortions and outright falsehoods about cannabis. Those who know the truth behind those pronouncements feel impelled to wonder sometimes if Anslinger is still alive. (Researchers interested in balanced information may double-check anything the DEA reports with publications from a variety of dependable organizations on the Internet.)

Anslinger groups pot with heroin – as it is today

One thread of Anslinger's propaganda was the claim that marijuana was a "stepping stone" to heroin. In their unquestioningly fearful response to that lie, Congress and the state legislatures have created harsher penalties for marijuana offenses – up to and including life imprisonment – charging that these measures are needed to reduce the number of heroin addicts!

The ironies abound: The government arrests millions in its pursuit of a "drug-free America" – and can't keep heroin out of its own prisons. Many addicts did not encounter heroin until they were sent to prison for marijuana-related "offenses." Irony crosses the line to outright farce when at one moment Anslinger claims marijuana is "worse than heroin" and at another damns it as a stepping stone to heroin... We need to worry about a stepping stone to something that's not as bad as the stone itself? How about honesty?

The Federal Bureau of Narcotics propaganda against marijuana – what it called its "educational campaign describing the drug, and its identification and evil effects" – included posters in railroad and bus stations, and anywhere large groups congregated, that featured phrasing that was simply hysterical:

BEWARE!
YOUNG AND OLD – PEOPLE IN ALL WALKS OF LIFE!
THIS
[photo of joint]
MAY BE HANDED TO YOU BY THE FRIENDLY
STRANGER.
IT CONTAINS THE KILLER DRUG "MARIJUANA"
A POWERFUL NARCOTIC IN WHICH LURKS
MURDER! INSANITY! DEATH!

Why I wanted to win the Hearst oratory contest

After all I'd read about Hearst's collusion with Anslinger in the wholesale slander of a drug I knew well from happy experience, I felt it would be a thrill to win a Hearst-sponsored contest by writing my speech while high on that "deadly" drug, marijuana. It was time to tackle the speech. I spent a couple of hours at the library, this time reading up on Benjamin Franklin. Once back at my own desk, though, I lit up a joint, took a good hit, and wrote the entire speech in 45 minutes.

It was exciting and a privilege to meet the finest student speakers. We were all nervous about speaking before large audiences. We shook hands, many times thinking we were meeting the winner of the highly publicized contest. Suspense built with each presentation. I always tried to interject a bit of humor into my talks; I credit pot for encouraging a smile while writing a talk! The first I heard I'd won was when I opened the newspaper.

On April 30, 1948, a half page of the *San Francisco Call-Bulletin* was devoted to the outcome of the contest:

MARIN YOUTH IS ORATORY WINNER
Benjamin Franklin Champ Chosen

Original thought, a fine platform presence and a spirited delivery made David Ford of the College of Marin the Northern California Benjamin Franklin oratory champion today. Ford, one-time state champion in the forensics contest of Lions International, earned his title in close competition last night in the University of San Francisco auditorium...

The prizes, $500, a gold watch, a portable typewriter, and a trophy, were only frosting on the cake. To have *beat Hearst* in a private but very satisfying way, whipping him with the help of the very herb he demonized – I felt it only equitable to light up a joint and dedicate it to the lies Hearst and the government told about one of the world's safest medicines and highs.

I had noted during my time at the College of Marin that quite a few students smoked grass instead of drinking alcohol. Yet to this day, due primarily to the false scare stories about pot, too many kids still choose alcohol, and many of them die because of alcohol's dangerous consequences.

Even though they acknowledge the dangers, many of these young people use and abuse alcohol only because marijuana is illegal – and because consequences born of hysteria have been injected into the law. They know that a beer bust will get them a wrist slap, while getting caught smoking a joint is likely to end their college careers by cutting off access to financial aid. A person can murder, maim, and molest

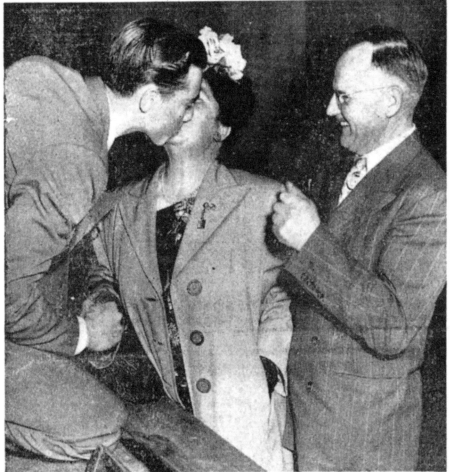

BLUE STREAK EDITION · **TELEPHONE YU 6-5151**

THE CALL BULLETIN

(AN INDEPENDENT NEWSPAPER)

CALL AND POST, VOL. 161, NO. 65
THE CALL-BULLETIN, VOL. 183, NO. 65

FRIDAY, APRIL 30, 1948   **5c DAILY**

Champ College Orator

David Ford, college division winner for northern California in last night's Franklin Oratory Contest finals here, receives congratulatory kiss from his delighted mother, Mary. Standing by is the champ's smiling father, Ernest. The San Rafael youth is College of Marin student. (Story and more photos, first page, Second Section.)
— Call-Bulletin Photograph.

San Francisco Call Bulletin April 30, 1948, front page

While at the College of Marin, I won the Hearst National Public Speaking Contest, to get even with William Randolph Hearst for lying about cannabis. Mom earned this kiss: she always encouraged me to speak out.

children, and be a violent alcoholic, and that person can still get federal financial aid for college; but get caught smoking a joint and you pay your own way through college. Under federal law you can also end up in prison. This result is especially unjust for those who don't have parents who can afford to pay for their kids' education, including, disproportionately, members of minorities – many of them already victims of a drug war that, if not racist in its intent, is certainly racist in its effects.

Top salesman, with the help of cannabis

When the speech contest was over, and my two years at the College of Marin ended, I felt it was time to seek my fortune. In those days, Los Angeles looked like a land of boundless opportunity, so I packed my two suitcases, and headed south in my 1939 Nash convertible. It was an all-day drive.

The next day I rented a furnished room in Pasadena for $5 a week. I checked the paper for jobs and one caught my attention: Grolier, publishers of *Encyclopedia Americana* and the *Book of Knowledge*, promised me I could "Make $200 a week!"

Grolier had its main offices on the 16th floor of its own large building. I'd heard this was a top-quality operation with a conservative dress code, so I dressed carefully for the interview in slacks, white shirt, sports jacket, and tie. I liked *The Book of Knowledge,* and wanted to sell it. The sales manager for the 11 western states was Mr. Snellgrove, a short intense man in his 50s, with gray hair, gray suit, and a thin white mustache. "David, we'll try you out for two weeks." I paid him a $15 deposit for samples, shook hands, and left. I then bought a brown leather briefcase and had my name stamped in gold on its side.

I went back to Pasadena, found a little restaurant where I ate dinner, and then retired to my room to figure out a selling formula. An ashtray on a side table gave me an idea. I lit up a joint, and some incense to mask the aroma of the grass. (Joints are "fire-safe." The tobacco in most cigarettes is adulterated to keep it smoldering, and a few moments' inattention can – and far too often does – lead to a deadly fire. A joint, on the other hand, will extinguish itself within seconds if no one's "toking" on it.)

In 10 minutes I had a method I was certain would work.

First I got a "criss-cross directory", one that listed phone numbers by address rather than subscriber. I selected a promising area and stayed on the phone as long as it took to make six phone appointments at homes in a neighborhood. I soon found that, on average, two of the prospects made it a point not to be home, two "qualified out" (decided they were not interested), and two turned into sales.

When I returned to the Grolier offices a week later, I had down payments or payments in full for 10 sets of *The Book of Knowledge*. Mr. Snellgrove was so amazed that he asked the secretary to call all the sales managers into his conference room. When they were all assembled, he said, "David, you are *amazing*. Most of our trainees either call with questions every day or two or simply disappear. When we didn't hear from you, we thought you must have found another job. Even our experienced salesmen bring in an average of one or two sales a week. You've got over $1,000 in commissions coming to you. How do you do it?"

I smiled and said, "Professional secret," and left.

I continued averaging 10 to 12 sales a week, which gave me quite a comfortable income. I would often leave my room Friday night and drive to Santa Monica Beach. It was so free and safe in those days. I'd buy food, make a campfire on the beach, cook my dinner, and spend a night or two camping right under the stars. There were bathrooms and showers nearby for campers' use.

One Monday I went to the offices as usual to drop off new contracts and pick up my commission check. I was immediately called into Mr. Snellgrove's luxurious private office. "David," he said, "come in and sit down. You've become the top salesman in the Western division in a remarkably short time. We'd like to make you a sales trainer here at the main office. You would train current sales people as well as new recruits, for one hour each Friday. You'd receive $50 each week for the hour session." He leaned back in his leather swivel chair. "You've got real potential, David; one day this office could be yours. You'd make $50,000 to $75,000 a year. What do you say?" I told him I'd be honored to be their trainer. I began the following Friday.

With the state of my fortune, I felt I had earned a new car. I shopped around and ended up at the Kelley Kar company. These are the Kelleys that put out the Kelley Blue Book that reports the prices used cars are selling for. I chose a current-year Oldsmobile 88, a blue convertible with red leather seats and just 4,000 miles on it.

I informed the salesman, a Mr. Hersinberger, I'd already arranged financing through my bank at a much better rate than he was offering, and that the bank would pay them off in full. "That's just fine with us," smiled Mr. Hersinberger, so I signed the contract and took delivery of the car.

Then I got a call from my bank: Kelley had refused to accept a payoff. I immediately drove back to Kelley's. Mr. Hersinberger was out for the moment, so I asked the salesman who "had the floor" what the problem was, given that Mr. Hersinberger had agreed to a full payoff.

He replied, "We sell our cars at such low prices that we have to make a little back on the interest. You will be required to follow the rules of the contract you signed, Mr. Ford."

I was furious and told the salesman I insisted on seeing Mr. Kelley.

"No one sees Mr. Kelley, son; that's why he has people working for him. But just to please you, I'll call him." He got on his phone. I could see the half-open door to Mr. Kelley's office, but couldn't hear what he was saying.

"Mr. Kelley doesn't care to speak with you, son. He just said that you must live up to your contract, like any good customer."

I stalked into Mr. Kelley's office, ignoring his secretary's shriek, "You can't go in there!"

Mr. Kelley looked up at my entrance and said, "Don't push your luck, sonny. The contract speaks for itself."

I pulled my driver's license from my wallet and slapped it down on his desk. "My uncle is Edsel Ford, of the Ford Motor Company. How'd you like a million-dollar lawsuit thrown at you for misrepresentation? I assure you it will make the newspapers." I snatched my driver's license right out from under his riveted gaze, and turned to stride out of his office.

"Just a minute, Mr. Ford!" (All of a sudden I was no longer "sonny"!) "Miss Thompson, get Mr. Hersinberger in my office."

The salesman appeared. "Mr. Hersinberger, call Mr. Ford's bank and tell them we will be happy to accept a payoff on the 1949 Olds convertible." I could hardly keep from laughing as I left the lot. I had no idea who Edsel Ford was, except that *he* was an authentic Ford.

A new love; grass also aided her creativity

I was hunting for a method to teach the Grolier salesmen to memorize several pages of a presentation quickly, in minutes rather than hours.

During high school and college I had studied hypnosis and used it on myself to absorb information rapidly. I now wanted to check on the latest techniques, so I went to the Hollywood library, where an attractive young lady helped me find the books I needed to brush up on hypnosis.

I researched my subject until closing time, then asked the librarian if she would care to join me for dinner. I was pleasantly surprised when she accepted. Her name was Ethel Balch. She was separated from her husband Roger, and had her own apartment. Over the next month, we went out to dinner several times and became intimate friends. Before the month was out, she accepted my invitation to move in with me.

It was time to find a nice apartment to replace the room in Pasadena. After a short search we struck gold, a complex called the Greenbrier. It consisted of around 200 units, many of which came with dishes, bedding, and maid service. Most of the tenants were in the movie business – directors, actors, musicians, writers, choreographers. Many of them did their practicing around the swimming pool, the focal point for gatherings.

Ethel was a marvelous artist. I nicknamed her "Cat," from Ernest Hemingway's great World War I novel, *A Farewell To Arms*. My Cat painted in oils and her work was outstanding. She frequently smoked grass while painting and once I asked her why.

"It helps me keep focused on my work. I'm 'into it,' and my mind doesn't wander. It opens my mind to new techniques, too, like using the pallet knife." Like so many people who use grass, Cat didn't drink much booze. At most, a couple of times a week we'd enjoy a glass of Cabernet Sauvignon or Chardonnay with our dinner. She said, "Making love with grass is sorcery. Your body feels as though it's purring, and when you truly care for the other person you're so into him with empathy and a feeling of love, that outside thoughts don't distract. That beautiful happy feeling lasts one to two hours. And those seemingly longer orgasms are totally wild."

She added, "I found while painting you can let yourself go into a light trance. You are always in control, however; the plant allows you to be totally into what you are currently doing. You can even tune out music or any other external noises should you prefer to do that. I love it!"

Everyday life at the complex was a constant show, watching the actors, dancers, writers, and musicians rehearse. Most of them smoked grass openly. Even the building manager and the "straight" tenants began to smoke grass and reduce their alcohol intake. Many in show business frowned on alcohol, especially those who had experienced its unfavorable consequences firsthand. The Greenbrier presented a true opportunity to enjoy life, liberty, and the pursuit of a mellow high. No snitches. No DEA. No police. (God, please tell the politicians that it's the War on Drugs that is causing the violence, and they should please mind their own business – and cut back on the booze.)

We were at the Greenbrier for over a year and I can't remember a single fight. Happiness and laugher prevailed. These people were not "pot heads," but rather hard-working, tax-paying professionals, who thrived on creativity and didn't like hangovers.

Several months after we moved in, at poolside I met Joe, a home-remodeling contractor, a 30-year-old with classic Irish features. He and I fell into a routine of playing ping-pong frequently, and over the next couple of months Ethel and I grew to like him and his 23-year-old lady Joann very much. Like Joe, Joann was Irish, with long black hair, green eyes, and natural pink cheeks. The four of us smoked grass together, played cards, swam, went to shows, and ate out.

Life was wonderful. I still kept a strict schedule of making at least 10 sales a week. Cat and I were getting along beautifully, settling happily into a dream come true. To have a best friend and lover in the same incredible woman; to go to parties, restaurants, and the theater on weekends – I was totally happy.

One night Cat didn't return home until 4 a.m. She tried to slip into bed without waking me, but I had been worried about her and was only dozing lightly. First I was relieved, but her slipping quietly into bed soon started me worrying in another way.

"Cat, talk to me. What's happening?"

"First, please remember that I love you, Dave," she pleaded. "I went to see Roger. He begged me to."

I bristled. "Did you make love?"

She began to cry.

"I asked you a question, Cat." I turned on the bedside lamp and looked her in the eyes.

As tears rolled down her cheeks, she answered, "Yes, we made love."

I got out of bed and began emptying her dresser. I found her suitcase and began stuffing her things into it. I wasn't quite 21, very immature, and very hurt. "Get dressed."

"Please, Dave. It will never happen again." She got dressed, still crying.

I was in pain too – a new kind of pain that I wasn't used to bearing. I thought, "I'm in love with her, and I'm throwing her away."

Without a word we got into my car. "Where does he live?" I asked.

"Please, Dave – don't do this!"

"Where does he live?" I asked again. She gave me the address. I drove there, handed her some money, took her suitcase to the front door, and left.

I returned to what had been our apartment, crawled into bed, and pulled the covers over my head, but I couldn't sleep. I thought about smoking a joint, but I associated grass with happiness, and I didn't want happiness. So I drank some wine and got sick.

I was ashamed of the way I had handled the trauma – discarding her like someone taking a cat for a ride, and dumping it – but my hurt pride was stronger than my good sense. When Joe got home I told him I'd go to work with him if he would consider moving. I associated the Greenbrier so closely with Cat that I had to get away.

"Yeah, sure, Dave. What caused you to change your mind?"

I told him what happened. "I'm damn sorry, Dave." He thought for a few moments, then said, "I've been thinking of opening an office in San Diego. Check and see if you can give up your apartment, and we'll leave before you change your mind, OK?"

I drove to Grolier's offices and told Mr. Snellgrove that I needed some time off, that it was a personal matter, and that I'd be in touch. He could see that I was very upset, and said, "Dave, please come back to us." I thanked him, shook his hand, dropped off my samples, and left. I spent the next three weeks out by the pool, feeling sorry for myself.

During the third week by the pool, I had overcome my gloom enough to teach a young lady named Terry how to do the double backstroke. Afterward she invited me to lunch.

When I reached her apartment, on the table were three sandwiches and a joint. Terry said, "Gwen and I share this apartment, do you mind if she joins us for lunch?"

"Not at all," I replied. I recognized Gwen from the pool. She was a professional dancer in her early twenties.

After lunch we sat around the table on kitchen stools and shared the joint. Gwen excused herself for a minute. She returned behind me, and placed her hands over my eyes. "What would you like for dessert, Dave?"

"Surely you don't have apple pie?" I asked naively.

I heard a rustling of fabric as she answered. "It's not news to us that you've been brooding over Ethel, your 'Cat.' We want you to be 'smiling Dave' again."

When Gwen removed her hands from my eyes, I swiveled around on the stool. Both she and Terry were naked and grinning. "Dave, are you ready for a very special dessert?" I could only smile and embrace them both.

That dessert was just what I needed, and it sure beat apple pie.

A loving gift from Mother

It was just a couple of days before my 21st birthday that I drove to the Beverly Hills area to see my mother and my sister Carol, with whom I kept in close touch. Mom presented me with a poem she had written for me. I needed and appreciated that poem more than gold and still read and revere it today. She was the dearest of mothers, and I'd like to share the poem with you.

To My Son
(With all of a mother's love)

What do I wish for thee, dear Son,
As I gaze tenderly into your eyes?
That, knowing your purpose right,
You may rely upon your strength,
And with Godlike discrimination,
Ever choose the wise!

To be noted for your agility of thought,
your gentleness of manner,
And your steadfastness of heart
(Qualities that can never be bought).
To strive for integrity and candor,
Undaunted by the ruthlessness of men,
And when disappointments overtake thee,
Smilingly to start again!

To be not misled
By the outward charm of a face,
A pure, clear heart hath magic that is dear,
And finer to embrace.

I wish for thee such happiness, my son,
    You, whose life has scarce begun;
To be part of the universe,
    Yet by none enslaved.
The noble acts your life portrays
    Shall be forever scored upon my heart
        As though engraved,

And I will stoop to gather
Pebbles clear and bright
To build a shrine
    Where I may worship silently by candlelight,
And recall the journey
    Begun so long ago with you,
When summer smiled, and I was young
    And eager too.
Ah, then I had much more
    Than just myself to give!

But now the Autumn hovers near
    And bids me guard each passing year,
Thus, as I look again into your face,
Hardships seem to vanish, leaving scarce
        a trace,
For I behold in your dear eyes,
    The soul of a boy
Now to manhood grown –
    Tender, loving and wise,
Yet the prayer and the wish
    Are ever the same –
God help my son to play the Game.
— *Adele Mason Ford*

Under the poem she wrote in longhand,

No goal for you, David, is too high!
Proudly,
Your mother.

That is only one of dozens of beautiful poems she wrote, many of which were published. I cherish this one most of all. I hope I haven't let her down.

Two days later Joe and I drove to San Diego in my car, leaving his behind for Joann. We located a three-bedroom, two-bath apartment on the ocean, and while Joe checked out the town I had a phone installed, with a 50-foot cord. I decided to try the same method for obtaining leads I'd used for Grolier. The phone reached right out to the sandy beach, which made a dandy office. In three weeks I did fairly well learning the business and obtaining leads.

I was still depressed about Cat, constantly wondering what she was doing. One evening when I was alone at the apartment Joe phoned and said Joann was going to spend the weekend and he was going to pick her up at the airport. About an hour later they arrived. I went out to the car and opened the door to welcome her. She held her arms out to me for a hug and as we embraced she whispered in my ear, "Hi, Dave. Be sweet."

For a moment I was at a loss, and then I noticed right behind her was Cat! Neither of us spoke. She came into my arms, and I just held her while we both shook.

Joe broke the silence. "A little surprise, Dave! I hope it was OK. What do you say we four go out to dinner like old times?"

Cat had tears running down her cheeks. "What would you like to do, Cat?" I murmured to her.

She said softly in my ear, "If its OK with you, I want to go to bed with you right now, baby."

"Thanks, Joe. But why don't you and Joann go ahead and have fun. We're going to hang out here."

I showed Cat around the apartment and then brought some snacks out from the refrigerator and set them on the coffee table. "Are you hungry, Cat?"

She smiled and responded, "Only for you." She opened her purse and produced three joints. She put one to my nose to let me savor the aroma. I lit it and took a hit, feeling its warmth in the back of my throat as I put the joint to her lips. After a couple more puffs, I took her hand and led her to the bedroom. In minutes we were in bed, kissing, holding, and loving each other from head to toe. She was as delicious as I remembered. I hadn't realized how much I had missed all of her.

I had been thinking our relationship was only physical. I realized

My wonderful mother was also my greatest teacher.
She taught me to find the answers for myself.

Photo: Powers Modeling Agency

Beautiful sister Carol was a Powers model, and my best friend. When I had tuberculosis
at age five, she was only eight – but often acted as my nurse.

now that it was more. Grass is not physically addictive, but I do believe that two humans who are mutually attracted can be physically addicted to each other; and for them, making love while high is indescribably beautiful. We made love many times that night. We didn't need to say a word, seeming to know what the other was communicating. It was totally awesome. We would make love, and she would fall asleep in my arms while I stroked her hair until I fell asleep. Less than an hour later we were making love again, insatiable.

We rarely saw Joe and Joann. They hung out in Joe's bedroom for the weekend while Cat and I hung out in mine, and the sweet aroma of high-quality grass permeated the apartment. We spent many weekends the same way, sending tickets for the ladies to fly down and join us. Together we frequented some of the area's finest restaurants and theaters.

As attracted as I was to Cat, however, I was more cautious now about trying to establish a permanent relationship with her. We talked about it and I think she understood that, to me, trust is one of the most important qualities of *any* relationship, whether the relationship is romantic, family, or business. I loved Cat, but I was afraid to trust her.

Oregon and Alaska, with loving adventures

We had been in San Diego for a year, and the business was not thriving. In fact, business was downright slow. This created a cash-flow problem that was exacerbated by Joe being a big spender who gave lavish tips. I was rapidly depleting my savings and thinking we needed a change.

My mother and Sis Carol had moved to Oregon, and Joe felt Oregon would be a better location for the business. At the end of a weekend with Cat, I told her where Joe and I were planning to move. She said she wanted to divorce her husband and marry me.

I was skittish, still afraid of being hurt again. I said, "Cat, I need to be alone for a time. Can you understand, baby?"

Her face fell, but she said, "I do, Dave. Be careful. And don't forget me."

I drove her to the airport, and wished her the best of luck with everything in her life.

Ten days later Joe and I were on our way to Portland. We headed for what we were told was the finest new high-rise apartment complex in the area, the King Tower. There was a valet to park the car and a doorman to open the lobby door for us, both wearing handsome uniforms. Part of the building was being operated as a hotel, but my unit had never been lived in. The apartment was fully furnished, except for towels, bedding, and utensils. I called for a maid and asked if she might find something for the night. I handed her a $20 bill.

She returned pushing a cart with everything I requested and more: two green woolen blankets, sheets, towels, dishes, and flatware, as well as pots and pans. "You'll have to keep these, sir. Once they've been used, I can't take them back," she said with a mischievous smile. I didn't want her to get into any trouble. I handed her another twenty. "*Thank* you, sir."

That night I invited Joe and Joann to my apartment for T-bone steaks with Caesar salad and all the trimmings. We smoked a joint first to enhance our enjoyment of the meal. When Joe excused himself to use the bathroom, Joann smiled and said, "I'm so happy Joe switched from drinking Scotch to smoking grass. You wouldn't believe it, but he used to get mean and even hit me. Now, he's a perfect gentlemen. Not to mention a better, longer-lasting lover. And those *long* orgasms are soooo wonderful!"

The next day I drove to Lake Oswego to visit my sister Carol and my mother. It was marvelous to see them again. They had a charming cottage, and Carol and I enjoyed swimming in the magnificent lake. Carol was a model for the Powers agency and she is still beautiful.

I felt like working hard again. Joe and I went out and made the sales. Some customers' homes just got new picture windows or a new porch. Other jobs were bigger, with new siding and roofing, and whatever other remodeling work they needed. We hired three carpenters and kept them all busy. Four months passed and the construction business was booming. I paid off the balance on my car and now had a couple of thousand dollars in my savings account.

One night on the way home I stopped in a bar, *The Zombie Zulu*, for a beer. I met a young nurse about my age named Hilda. She had a nice personality and a pretty face. I asked what her favorite meal was. "Probably lamb chops, green peas, and baked potato." I took the big gamble and invited her to dinner at my apartment the following night. She accepted. When she arrived, Tchaikovsky's "Sleeping Beauty" was playing on the phonograph. By lucky chance, it also happened to be one of Hilda's favorites. We chatted for a while, then I asked her as casually as possible what she thought of pot.

"Some of the nurses slip a joint to some of the cancer patients they can trust, who are nauseous from their medications and chemotherapy," she answered. "The prescribed medications just don't do the job for some people, or make them sick to their stomachs. And most of those medications are physically addictive. I think cannabis is the most underrated medicine in the world. I don't understand why it's illegal."

"I prefer not to drink liquor. I smoke grass instead," I said. "What do you think about that, Hilda?"

She smiled, and said, "You wouldn't have any handy would you?"

"If I did, would you care for a hit or two?"

"Sure would," smiled Hilda. "It's far better for you than alcohol." We took a few puffs, and danced and chatted until we were famished.

"Hope you have plenty of food, Dave, grass makes me so hungry." We both got the giggles. Grass frequently does that; everything seems funny.

We enjoyed the candlelight dinner. The shimmering city lights six stories below, and a half-dozen candles in the apartment, added to the feeling of enchantment. I hadn't planned on seduction that first night; more than anything I wanted Hilda's trust. It just happened. We were dancing after dinner, her breasts pressing against my chest. We began kissing, and almost before I realized it we were in bed. I slowly undressed her and saw that under her clothes was one of the most beautiful bodies I'd ever seen. Fortunately, she was as ready for love as I was.

We dated for about six months, going to movies, dances, and restaurants. She allowed me to give her a couple of new dresses that showed off her lovely figure. The only problem was she was a devout Catholic and began feeling guilty about making love. She wanted to get married. I still wasn't ready, and we slowly drifted apart.

My first airplane; almost landing on a cow!

At 22, my next love was a fantasy come true. As my savings account balance began to mount I found myself staring toward the sky, watching small airplanes cruising over Portland and dreaming about them.

One day I ventured into the office of a small airplane dealership, owned by a Mr. Johnson. "I'm thinking of buying a plane," I told him. "Do you have any clean, low-time aircraft for sale?"

He showed me several used little planes and in the process impressed me as an honest man. I didn't know planes, but I knew cars and what to look for, and I didn't feel comfortable with any I saw that day.

He could tell I wasn't satisfied with what I'd seen. "Next week I have a Cessna 140 coming in on a trade for a new plane. It has only 310 hours total time on it; it's like new. It'll be priced at $2,000 – is that in your price range?"

"Yeah, I'd like to see it," I replied.

Several days later I stopped at Mr. Johnson's hangar, and there I saw a petite aluminum-bodied plane, with green stripes and a single bench seat, just big enough for two. I walked around it and peered inside.

The upholstery was like new. There wasn't a scratch on the plane.

I asked, "Is this the Cessna that came in on a trade?"

A young mechanic in white coveralls replied, "Yeah. I'd like to own this one myself. The boss told us to go over it carefully. We just gave it a compression check; it checks out like a new plane. I think it's sold, though; the boss is saving it for some guy."

I walked into the office. "Mr. Johnson, is that Cessna out there the one you mentioned to me?"

"Yes, it is. I've been holding it for your inspection before I show it to anyone else."

"Thank you! When can we try it out?"

Soon the mechanics were pulling it out of the hangar and onto the grass runway. "Ready for that ride, Dave?"

I nodded and eagerly climbed into the co-pilot's seat. Mr. Johnson pulled on the starter knob and the engine roared to life. I immediately loved the throbbing sound of the plane's engine idling. Like a thoroughbred race horse that couldn't wait to get on the track. "Would you like to take off, Dave?"

I hadn't told Mr. Johnson, but I'd never been off the ground in *any* plane! "No, sir, you go ahead."

He taxied out to the runway, pointed it at the far end, checked the magnetos and controls, and gave it full throttle. We rapidly picked up speed on the runway, Mr. Johnson slowly pulled the control wheel toward him, and the earth began to sink below us. I was so happy I heard myself laughing. We climbed to 2,500 feet and began slow turns, climbs, and glides.

"Here, you take it, Dave." I put my hands on the control wheel, but had difficulty keeping the plane level. "It feels good," I said.

By the time we landed I knew I had to have that plane. After a little friendly haggling, we arrived at a cash price of $1,750. I drove to the bank and picked up a cashier's check, and that afternoon the deal was closed. Mr. Johnson set up an appointment for me with a flight instructor for the next afternoon.

I couldn't wait 'til then to make a short visit to my plane – *my* plane! I climbed into the pilot's seat and looked at the mystifying dials and gauges. After an hour or so trying to memorize their appearance and locations, I got out of the plane, patted its nose lovingly, and said, "Your name is Silver. I promise to take good care of you. Please do the same for me."

I was at the airport at three the following afternoon, dusting Silver off and again studying the instrument panel. At 3:55 a 16-wheel semi pulled into the parking area of the airport. The driver climbed down and walked directly toward me. He was a big burly guy with windblown face, six-two, 220, about 35. He looked me up and down, and briefly eyed the plane.

"The name's Jerry. Got four bucks cash on ya?" I nodded and shook his vise-like hand. "First thing I want you to do is memorize the following before we even get into the plane: 'There are old pilots and there are bold pilots; but there are no old bold pilots.' Got it?"

"Yes. I'll remember that."

I've never met anyone who had a gentler touch with the aircraft controls than this guy. He demanded perfection of his students, which I appreciated and strove to achieve. His high standards paid off: In almost 5,000 hours of flying no one has ever received a scratch from any plane I ever flew.

On an overcast windy Saturday in May of 1951, Jerry appeared at the field at 5 p.m. I had the plane pre-flighted and ready to go. I opened the co-pilot door for him. "Not today, young feller. Today is your day to solo, and my day just to sit and rest." He grinned. "But it's still gonna cost ya four bucks!"

I was elated and at the same time my legs felt a little wobbly. "I want ya to fly over the Columbia River Gorge, and then do a landing at Troutdale airstrip. Then fly back here." I looked at him for a sign of reassurance, but all I saw was a poker face.

Without Jerry's 220 pounds on the other side of the cockpit, takeoff felt like being shot out of a cannon. I was airborne in 100 feet. I automatically looked over to my instructor for approval. Trust me, when you realize you're flying a plane alone for the first time – now, there's a rush! I made a good landing at Troutdale and headed back. All was going according to the book until a sudden heavy rain began pelting the windshield. Two miles south of the field the daylight failed entirely. I adjusted the red instrument lights so I could see them in the dark. I'd never flown at night, or in weather, let alone both! I could barely see beyond the propeller.

Below I saw headlights blinking off and on. I knew that the landing strip had no lights; I hoped that the blinking lights were from Jerry's truck. That *had* to be Jerry at the end of the strip!

I turned on the plane's single landing light and descended into the blackness. I applied full carburetor heat and cut the throttle. When I was thirty feet above the ground I saw cows on the runway – and the critters wouldn't move! I remembered to close the carburetor heat before I gave it full throttle, and climbed to 600 feet to go around for another landing attempt. Down, down I went again. The same nightmare was before me. Cows! Full throttle again, and again into the blackness.

Sweat was running into my eyes. "God, if I get this plane down on the ground, I promise I'll never fly again. I'll even consider getting married. Just let me live to make love again, and smoke a joint." Sorry, God.

Again, over the field at thirty feet. Cows or no cows, I was going to connect with the earth this time – and this time the cows parted like the Red Sea. The plane bounced once, then I was fast approaching the headlights and they were no longer blinking. I stood on the brakes until the plane shuddered to a stop. Perspiration was running down my face, and I was close to passing out. I pulled myself out of the plane. Standing by his truck, which *was* parked at the end of the runway, was Jerry. I dropped to my knees and kissed the ground. As I slowly stood up, I noticed that Jerry's pants were very wet in the crotch. I felt it wiser not to comment on that discovery.

Only... "Was I OK, Jerry?"

"You were OK, kid."

There was really nothing more to say.

The following evening Joe, Joann, and I were out to dinner. We chatted about business, but my mind was in the sky. I was mulling over my promise to God. Never to fly again? Never to soar and glide and play hide-and-seek with the silvery clouds? Never again to slip the surly bonds of earth? From what seemed a great distance came Joe's voice:

"Did you hear me, Dave? I asked what you thought of our opening a branch office in Boise, Idaho."

"Does it rain less there?" I asked.

Joann laughed and answered, "Hardly any rain at all, Dave."

Joe said, "I was thinking that in about a month we'd catch a flight to Boise and check it out."

Suddenly my mouth was moving without any benefit of the thought process. "Hey, you guys! This was going to be a surprise, but... I own a plane! I'll be ready for my private pilot's license in about a month. You'll love the plane, except it carries only two people." After dinner we drove out to the airstrip and I proudly showed them Silver.

Four weeks later I passed the written exam given by the Federal Aviation Administration with a score of 96, and was ready for the final step: a "check ride" with an FAA examiner.

I took off from my "cow pasture" at 7:30 a.m. on a windy rainy day, and landed at Portland International Airport at 8 a.m. An FAA examiner who looked about 50 years old appeared, carrying two parachutes.

"You Ford?"

"Yes, sir."

"Strap this 'chute on."

"But, sir, I don't think we can fit in the plane with the parachutes on."

"Are you conducting this check ride, or am I?"

"Sorry, sir."

With the chute on, I could barely move. The examiner was impatient. "Crank this sucker up and let's go. I have another examination at 9:30." I radioed ground control for taxi instructions, switched to the tower frequency when instructed, waited for a couple of heavy aircraft to take off. Then we were cleared for takeoff. Given full throttle, my gallant little plane lurched ahead, trying gamely to prove itself, despite the added weight of the examiner and those damned 'chutes. We finally rotated and were airborne.

After we cleared the area, he told me to fly north-northeast. "Climb to 2,500 feet and level off." When we reached altitude he told me to do every imaginable maneuver, including stalls and 360-degree steep turns.

Suddenly the instructor pulled the throttle closed. "You now have a dead engine. Where are you going to land?" Jerry had taught me to be constantly on the lookout for a landing area in case of emergency. I checked smoke rising from a factory to gauge the wind direction and pointed to a field.

"OK, go ahead and show me you can land in that field."

Crabbing slightly to compensate for wind drift, I lined up for the field. "You want me to just do a low pass over the field, sir?"

"Didn't you hear me say land this sucker?"

"Yes, sir. We have enough altitude that I'm going to glide a 360-degree turn to check for rocks or whatever else might be on the field." Out of the corner of my eye, I saw him make a note on his tablet. I couldn't stop hoping he wouldn't insist that I actually put my immaculate little plane down in an unknown field. As we passed low over some high-tension wires I waited for the command to give full throttle. No word.

Finally, the instant the wheels made contact with the earth, "Full throttle *now!*" I'm sure he never saw a throttle pushed in that fast. Seconds later we were again airborne.

"Climb to 3,500 feet and level off." As we were passing through

3,400 feet and still climbing, he again pulled the throttle closed, and this time he reached over with his left foot and kicked hard right rudder. He held the controls back so I couldn't level off, and we stalled. Soon we were in a classic, full-on tailspin. The earth whirled around three times before he snapped, "Now correct!"

I immediately neutralized the controls, but we were now in a nose-down attitude. I pulled the control wheel slowly toward my stomach, but there wasn't enough room with the parachute on. "I can't pull it back far enough!" Two more rotations. We were now down to a dangerous 1,000 feet. "Back. Back. Back!" he bellowed. We both pushed back so hard on the double-wide seat that it broke away from its locked position. Had it not, you wouldn't be reading this book.

Back on the ground, and that cursed 'chute off my back, the examiner signed my temporary license. The permanent one would come through the mail from Washington, D.C.

As he walked toward a waiting plane, over his shoulder he said, "You gave me a good ride, Ford." As I taxied for takeoff I wondered how he survived to middle age. I chuckled as I thought – perhaps he's not a pilot!

The following week, Joe and I flew to Boise. Joe joked that he wanted me to buy a four-place airplane so Joann could fly with us. He said flying turned him on, and he wanted Joann in the back seat with him! We rented a car in Boise, looked the town over, and rented a small office. Joe wanted to start contracting to paint homes as well as remodel them. We stayed a couple of days and rented apartments. We also sold a couple of remodeling jobs and hired two local carpenters to do the work.

It wasn't long before the Boise office was losing money. Joe was a fun guy and an honest man to work with, but it was a constant strain that I was frugal and Joe enjoyed blowing money. We finally decided to go our separate ways. We ended our business relationship amicably. I paid off the lease on the apartment, and cleared out the Boise office. I decided to sublet the Portland office for six months and explore Alaska. On June 12, 1953, I caught a commercial flight to Anchorage.

Adventures in Alaska; meeting an inventive pot-smoking prostitute

After a long and wearing flight, the plane arrived at Anchorage International Airport at 1:30 a.m. The sky was as light as at 9 a.m. in Portland. (*When* the sun is out! Portland is beautiful, but it doesn't get a lot of sunshine!) I understood now why Alaska is called "the Land of the Midnight Sun." I caught a cab and asked to be left off at the nicest hotel in town. The driver took me to the Lane Hotel, an old wooden two-story structure.

"I'm Mr. Lane," said a guy about sixty wearing a worn flannel bathrobe and rubbing the sleep out of his squinting eyes. "What do you want at this time of night?"

"A room, please," I said in a weary voice.

"We don't have no rooms. If ya want to, wait until someone might be checking out." He disappeared.

At 6:30 a man checked out and complained about the dirty sheets and towel. "May I please have the room the gentleman just checked out of?"

"$20.00 cash in advance."

I paid. "Will you please call me when the room is made up?"

"The room is ready now. Here's the key. Toilet and shower at the end of the hall."

The room was about eight feet by six feet, with a metal army cot and an old woolen blanket. A thin, gray, wet, smelly towel was about to fall off a rusted hook. The sheets were nasty. I went back to the desk and rang the bell. Out came Mr. Lane.

"I must have gotten the key to the wrong room. 106 has not been made up."

"It's been made up. If that room isn't good enough for you, Mr. High Society, go somewhere else."

"Fine. Just give me my money back."

"We don't give refunds. See the sign?"

I gave up. I went back to the room and collapsed on the bed. At noon, a banging on my door told me my time was up. I walked out into the glaring sun. Other hotels were filled and had waiting lists. My strolling took me past a used-car lot, where a red '48 Ford panel truck caught my eye. The price, $2,495. I drove it for a couple of miles and decided it would do nicely. After some haggling I got the owner of the car lot to accept $2,000 cash.

I cruised around town and spotted a single-story wooden motel with a For Rent sign. The room the landlady showed me was about 10 by 10, with an old iron-frame bed and a dresser that the Salvation Army would reject. "How much?"

"$150 a week," said the lady, "cash in advance."

"I'll take it starting today."

I located a building materials supply company. They wholesaled and retailed lumber, insulation, and about everything else one needs for construction work. They gave me names of two carpenters they said I could trust. I phoned the carpenters and set a time to meet them at the Golden Nugget Bar.

Bruce was one hulk of a guy I guessed to be about thirty. He was a good six foot four, with hands about the size of badminton rackets. I guessed his weight at around 230. Tom was around forty, a slim, trim 190 pounds, and about six foot three. He was wearing his carpenter's apron, with hammer, chisels, and tape measure all neatly in place. I told them I'd want them to install insulation, as well as doing some remodeling of windows, porches, and other minor carpentry work.

"Easy stuff, Dave," said Tom. We dickered over wages, came to an agreement, and shook hands. "Everyone calls me Shorty, if that's OK with you."

"That's fine, Tom. From now on you're Shorty. I'll be calling you in a few days, guys." I gave them my motel address, and then spent the rest of the day hunting jobs for my new workforce.

By nightfall I'd sold two jobs for insulation. Both customers were Native Alaskans. After I showed them how the savings on firewood could pay for the cost of installing the insulation in just a few years, I asked them to phone friends who had insulated their homes, and to compare the prices they'd paid with my estimate. I waited while they phoned, and sure enough I soon had contracts signed. I phoned Shorty to see if they could begin work the next morning.

"You bet, Dave!" We were on our way.

Shorty was a veteran who had been injured in World War II. By the end of that first day on the job, I saw that he walked with one shoulder several inches lower than the other. "Oh, my aching back! Dave, could you please follow us back to my house? I'd like for you to meet my wife." When we arrived at his home and he had introduced me to his wife Betty, he said, "I've gotta tell ya, Dave, I have bad back spasms. What eases the pain more than anything is a few hits of grass." He opened a small metal container on his coffee table, removed a rolled joint, and lit up, drawing in a few satisfying inhalations. After a few minutes I heard an unwinding sigh of relief. His facial muscles relaxed visibly. When he walked me to the door, his shoulders were straight.

"The reason I wanted you to come by the house was not just to meet

Betty. I wanted to ask, would you have any objection if I took a few hits of pot while on the job, as long as nobody's home? Believe me, I can work just as fast and hard when I smoke as when I'm straight. I've never had any type of accident on the job while smoking. As an added bonus I listen to my portable radio. Music, either jazz or classical, is more meaningful and exciting. If I didn't have muscle spasms, I'd still use grass – for music appreciation!"

"Go ahead and light up while you're working, Shorty," I said, and told him a little about what pot had done for me.

The conversation soon turned to the politics of cannabis. "Dave, I suspect that pot and hemp will remain illegal until our coin-operated politicians stop accepting money from corporations that deal in alcohol, tobacco, pharmaceuticals, cotton, and timber – that don't want the competition of an herb that can't be patented and used to make money for stockholders." Shorty's insight was right on the money; I could only nod my head on that one.

Within two weeks we were receiving referrals from happy clients and enjoying the feeling of prosperity. After work the three of us smoked grass at my motel room or one of the local bars that welcomed pot smokers. Shorty always wore his carpenter's apron, hammer and all, whenever we went to a bar, even if he'd had time to go home first. I thought it was a bit odd, but sensed I shouldn't ask about it. Bruce appeared happy all the time. He reminded me of Lenny, the immense brawny man in John Steinbeck's classic, *Of Mice And Men.* Like Lenny, Bruce was a lovable big guy with the understanding of an eight-year-old. Everyone liked Bruce, and when he smoked grass his rich deep baritone laugh was so infectious that we couldn't help but laugh with him. He didn't sing well at all, but when he smoked pot he didn't care; he just had fun singing and laughing.

One evening the men and I were having a beer, jawing about the day's work in an offhand way, when Shorty said, "About a week after Betty and I were married she noticed a green spot on her inner thigh and she was terrified. She went to the doctor and he took a biopsy. He asked her to wait in the office for the results." By this point, Bruce and I were on the edges of our chairs. "Finally, the doctor came out and said, 'This is nothing serious at all, but I have to tell you that your husband's earring is not gold!'"

Bruce didn't get it. He said, "I wish I had a wife, so's I could tell stories about her!"

While Shorty and I were still laughing, a tall sensuous lady came over to our table and asked if she could speak with me confidentially. "I'll be back shortly, guys," I said. Shorty winked at me.

The lady invited me to join her at her table. She was alone. She appeared to be 25 or 26, with shimmering clean walnut hair that fell to her shoulders. Her baby blue eyes were a contrast to the fire-engine red of her lipstick. She looked and sounded much like Lauren Bacall. Her name was Diane.

She opened a gold cigarette case, withdrew a long cigarette, and lit up. As soon as I smelled the pungent aroma, I chuckled and said, "Can't you get busted for smoking grass here?"

She blew a smoke ring toward me. I took a deep sniff, and winked. "Alaska is more honest than most states. The bartenders know that violence isn't caused by grass smokers. On the contrary, the quietest people in our bars are the ones who smoke grass for relaxation, generally after work. They might have a beer, but they don't drink much. They're still welcome. Would you care for a drag?"

"Sure." I took a hit and closed my eyes in appreciation. The smoke was sweet and mild.

She smiled and said, "Yeah, we grow good smoke in Alaska." She uncrossed her legs and leaned forward. "But down to business. I've noticed your sharp panel truck around town. I have a business proposition for you. I work at night. I could use your truck in my business. I'll pay you $50 cash every morning when I return it. It will be filled with gas, and I promise it will be as clean as when I picked it up."

"How do you plan to use the truck?" I asked.

"I travel around to the fishing camps and where men are working on the pipeline. I'm a whore, but an honest one. Your truck would be my 'bedroom.' What do you say?" One corner of her mouth turned up. "If you'd prefer to take it out in trade, that can be arranged, too."

I looked into her innocent-looking big blue eyes and smiled. "You certainly are a creative lady," I said. "How about this: Let's try it for a week. You can pick up the truck at the Andrews Motel at 9:30 every evening – starting tonight if you want. I'll need it back at 7:30 in the morning. I want a copy of your driver's license and your current address. If there is ever a time that you don't live up to our arrangement and the truck isn't returned in the morning as agreed, I'll report it stolen. I'm sure you're wonderful in bed, but let's keep this a cash transaction. Would that be satisfactory to you?"

She laughed as she said, "It's a deal. After all, my lipstick matches your truck – and I'll do it justice. I'm sure you know how lipstick got started."

"No, I don't. How?" I asked.

"Back in the days of Cleopatra, Egyptian courtesans who gave oral sex wore lipstick to advertise that service. When that was what men – or women – were looking for, they only had to pick out a whore who wore lipstick. Simple, yes?" I wondered how many sweet little Sunday-school teachers knew that.

When she left, I headed back to brief the guys on the truck deal. The bartender motioned me over to him. "I see that you smoke a little pot," he said.

"That's right. Any problem?" I asked.

"Not at all. I just thought you might like to know: Before Shorty quit booze and switched mainly to grass, that SOB used to get into fights here. He's almost as strong as Bruce. And ya never wanta tangle with Bruce."

"Bruce seems like a pussycat," I said.

"He's no pussycat when he drinks whiskey, believe me," said the bartender. "He's mellow on pot. Whiskey makes him want to fight." He polished a glass and added, "Grass is competition to whiskey. I wouldn't doubt the liquor industry helps in the government's propaganda campaign against marijuana."

"But... isn't smoke competition for the whiskey *you* sell, too? Doesn't it cut into your take when guys like Bruce and Shorty switch from booze to grass?"

"Do you know how many shots I have to sell to pay for the results of one brawl?" He grinned. "What I lose on booze, I save on breakage. This place has been a lot more peaceful since the word got around that I welcome guys who have a toke and a beer instead of a shot and a beer."

I was awake at 6:00 the next morning and looked out the window. The truck wasn't back. I was a bit chagrined over the deal I'd made in such haste. I reminded myself that the promised time was 7:30 a.m.; there was still quite a bit of time. On the other hand, I reflected gloomily, my truck could be halfway to Seattle by now.

At 7:15 there was a knock on the door. I opened it to a beaming Diane, who shook hands with me. When I opened my hand there was a fifty-dollar bill in it.

"Its nice to see you, Diane. How was business?"

"Better than I expected," she said.

I asked her if grass played a part in her lovemaking.

"I don't use it with clients. With boyfriends I've had back home, darn right I use pot."

"Why?" I asked.

Diane now had the look of a teenager. Her gaze took on a dreamy look. "It's like your body is sweetly vibrating. And with the sensation of time slowing down, the lovemaking session seems to last a lot longer. Orgasms seem at least two or three times as long, and I have to say that they're also far more intense." I nodded. I knew.

She came back to earth, and with a pixie's smile added, "I like *things* in my mouth. But thanks to grass, not cigarettes anymore."

I chuckled. For a moment I considered the optional truck-rental payment she'd offered, but in the end decided I liked our friendly arrangement just the way it was.

Toward the end of the summer, she told me she wouldn't be needing the truck any more. When I asked why not, she replied, "Summer's almost over and I want to spend a few days with my parents in Denver before I go back to my regular job. Nine months of the year I teach school in Colorado. When I decided I'd come to Alaska and try being a whore for a summer, I told them I'd be tutoring youngsters here."

"So how has your 'tutoring' worked out?" I asked.

"I've had a great time. I get thanked for it. I get respect. I'm always thrilled that I get paid for it – more in one night then I make in a week of teaching. And contrary to what many women say, I enjoy a *big* man. I don't usually walk bowlegged!"

I roared. Diane knew how to make a man laugh, and I wasn't surprised her summer had been a success.

In the two months of working in Anchorage, business had been good. Now I bid on a large roofing job, for barracks at the Air Force base in Fairbanks, some 500 miles north, and won the bid.

A couple of days later I took Diane to the airport and saw her off. Then I picked up Bruce and Shorty, and we headed for Fairbanks. We were sad to leave Anchorage, even though we knew the two of them, at least, would return. Much of the highway was gravel, but the red panel truck ran gallantly and by 4 a.m. we had checked into a Fairbanks motel.

A swinging lady and a swinging party; "No drugs – only pot!"

Before she left Anchorage, Diane had phoned a friend of hers in Fairbanks who she said was single, attractive, extremely enthusiastic about sex, and not a prostitute. "I bet you're going to have fun with Joyce, Dave. She's looking forward to meeting you. She'll introduce you to something I suspect you're not familiar with, but I think you'll enjoy it." I phoned Joyce that first night we arrived in Fairbanks, and asked if she might be available for dinner. "Looking forward to meeting you, David. How about the *Last Chance Bar and Restaurant*, at 7 p.m.? I'll be wearing a blue hat."

Joyce wore a blue hat, all right – and a crucifix on a gold chain around her neck. My hopes for the evening sank. I wondered if Diane felt I'd enjoy attending church.

We had a glass of wine with dinner. "Diane told me you enjoy grass," said Joyce. "I do, too – and if you're interested in what I'm about to tell you, it will work in just perfectly."

"Please continue," I said.

"David, I'm a swinger. That means that I go to parties with a guy – but don't spend the whole evening with him. There are other couples there, most of them married. Frequently six or eight couples gather at one of their homes. Sometimes it's just a party with one or two other couples. No alcohol or drugs are allowed, but pot isn't really considered a drug, and it's welcome. We swap partners for sex."

My eyes widened.

"I see that I now have your undivided attention," Joyce smiled.

"Don't couples get jealous?" I asked.

"No, that's the beauty of it, David. Alcohol isn't allowed for two reasons: First, many men can't perform after a few drinks. Second, I've seen jealousy when one or both of the partners are intoxicated. Other drugs, such as coke or meth, are fine for the ladies, but for the men, they're generally a let-down, if you see what I mean. Whereas with pot, people relax, feel close, and are into what they are doing, without their minds wandering. Then, a five-second orgasm seems to last at least several times longer, and most women find that grass introduces them to multiple orgasms," Joyce said.

She continued, "You noticed that I said we get together for *sex*. 'Lovemaking' is a word we reserve for couples who are married, live together, or are seriously dating. The thing I like best about swinging is that couples do it together." She swirled the last of the wine in her glass. "Let's be realistic. Monogamy is one of the greatest myths ever created. Most couples who say they never wander at least do so in their fantasies. Swinging couples are totally honest. They generally have sex in the same room with their mates, then they go home together and are more turned on for each other. They don't sneak out for a fast fuck, or lie to their mates that they're away on a business trip when they're in a motel. I have more respect for swingers who love and play together than I do for couples who lie and cheat apart."

"Interesting," I said. "What do you do if, say, the guy finds a really intriguing lady at a party, or the lady finds a sexually attractive man, and they want to get together again?"

"Good question. There is established etiquette. If the man wants to see the lady again, he first gets the approval of his own mate. He then phones the man she is married to, or lives with, and asks about the possibility of getting together again. The same follows if the lady would like to have another encounter with a man. That rule is never to be broken. They never swap without permission all around. By the way," smiled Joyce, "there's a party tomorrow night at an Army officer's home. Would you care to be my date?"

I nodded.

"Then pick me up here at eight o'clock."

I had three rolled joints in the pocket of my midnight blue sport jacket, which topped gray slacks, black shoes, and white shirt and gray silk tie. Joyce was a knockout in a short, low-cut dress of black silk; stockings and high heels really showed off her stunning legs. The officer's home was tastefully furnished. Five couples were there, including Joyce and me. From the men's haircuts I guessed that they were all in the service too. I was pretty nervous; perhaps Joyce expected me to be, and that's why she made it a point that we arrive about an hour after the others. They were dancing, passing joints around, and pausing to sample foods that were on trays around the large living room.

When the music stopped, Joyce introduced me around as "Dave, the contractor." The couples were friendly, attractive, in their late twenties to early forties. It was refreshing to note that the guests had brought joints rather than bottles of liquor. I fired up one of mine and handed it to Joyce who took an adept puff and then passed it along. We all small-talked until the music started again and I asked Joyce for a dance. Fortunately for me, the music was slow so my limited dancing skills weren't overwhelmed. And the way Joyce danced with her thigh between my legs was positively uplifting. Soon, the pot took effect and I relaxed and fell into the rhythm of the dance. With the grass I danced OK.

Two hours passed and nothing unusual happened. Joints continued to go the rounds. I began to wonder if Joyce had been putting me on. Then it happened. I was dancing with Rhonda, a blue-eyed blond. She was warm and smelled delicious. Joyce was dancing next to us with a nice-looking guy, when suddenly, she dropped to her knees, unzipped his slacks, and began giving him head. That started a smorgasbord around the room. Within minutes clothes were flying off. Some of the couples were on sofas, caressing, kissing, making love – I mean, having sex! In a husky voice Rhonda whispered in my ear, "Hey, Dave the contractor, let's go find a bed." She led me into a bedroom with the blankets already neatly pulled down, leaving the pristine white sheets ready for action. We began taking off each other's clothes, both breathing hard. She whispered in my ear, "Baby, we must just leave the door open. My husband likes to watch. And it turns me on when he does. No need to rush. There are four bedrooms in the house."

Now naked, we spent twenty minutes devouring each other. Then she said, "Please, I can't wait any longer." That's all I needed to hear. I caressed and kissed her a bit more. "Stop teasing me," implored Ronda. Slowly I penetrated her. I remember wishing that I could dance the way we moved together. I leaned forward as I lifted her soft white butt, so that I was massaging her very core. I glanced into the mirror on the dresser – there was a naked guy standing not five feet away.

Rhonda felt my surprised start. "It's Richard – don't stop, he's loving it." I instinctively gave her a couple of slaps on her exquisite ass, and she began humping twice as fast. Within a few minutes we had one of those extraordinary mutual orgasms. I heard a loud animal sound and was shocked because it was coming from the depths of my being, and then I laughed because I was so happy. Rhonda understood and laughed too. I held her for a bit, savoring the peace and closeness. Then Richard tapped me on the shoulder. "That was great, guy. My turn, OK?" I understood. I picked up my clothes and left them alone.

I had a leisurely shower and dressed, but left off my jacket and tie. I ventured into the living room. Joyce had just finished intercourse with the guy she had been dancing with and they were getting up, chatting and gently caressing. Everyone else was apparently in other bedrooms. Joyce looked up at me with a great smile. "Can you go again, Dave the contractor?"

I smiled, took her by the hand and led her into the only empty bedroom. She was also an enlightened lover. After we came, I held her in my arms and she whispered in my ear, "Thank you, Dave the contractor."

While I was in Fairbanks, Joyce invited me to such parties two or three times a week. I really treasured the experience, and felt that it was a great adventure. I'd go into detail on more of the parties, but then this book would be too heavy! (Perhaps in the next book?) I was glad for having had it; but by the time I left Alaska for home, I felt I'd had enough of swinging. I was glad I wasn't in a steady relationship then. I'm sure I would be a bit jealous of my partner.

The barracks roofing work went smoothly. Within a week Shorty and Bruce were invited to join the enlisted men for drinks and poker at the base club. I was invited to the officers' club. I recognized a couple of the men from the parties. We just politely nodded, or exchanged a wink.

A couple of times a week I'd drop by to visit with the boys and their friends at the enlisted men's club. One Friday night I learned why Shorty always wore his leather carpenter's apron, complete with tools, even when he wasn't working.

Bruce and a stocky staff sergeant were sitting at a table, drinking and talking loudly. This was the first time I'd ever seen Bruce drunk, and it was a bit scary – he was a mean stranger. The soldier Bruce was arguing with was about six feet tall and a solid hundred and ninety pounds. Suddenly they were up and swinging at each other. The soldier hit Bruce on the side of the face. Bruce returned the blow so hard that the soldier spun all the way around. When the soldier's back was toward him, Bruce placed his beefy hands on each side of the soldier's throat and lifted him a foot off the floor.

The soldier's face was turning crimson. Frantically I yelled, "Bruce, let the guy go!"

With clenched teeth Bruce snarled, "He called me a dirty word. Said I do awful things to my mother. He'll never say that no more."

I spotted Shorty at a poker table at the far end of the room. "Shorty, quick!" I shouted. In an instant he was at my side. The soldier's face was now turning blue. "Bruce, it's me, Shorty – *your brother*! Let him go or I'm going to hit you with the hammer."

Bruce's eyes were bulging with hate. "He called me a motherfucker, Shorty. He's bad."

Shorty hissed in Bruce's ear: "Do you want to go back to San Quentin?"

"He's a bad man, Shorty, I gotta punish him."

Shorty pulled his hammer from the leather apron and hit Bruce a heavy blow on the side of his head with the handle. In less than two seconds it was over. Bruce and the soldier both dropped to the floor. There were four MPs on the scene, and they had their nightsticks out and at the ready.

"I don't know who started it, but I'll get him out of here right now," said Shorty.

"And don't ever bring him back," snapped one of the MPs as they half carried the soldier, who was gasping for breath.

Shorty looked at me with sadness. "I'm sorry. Bruce is my brother. Dad was a heavy drinker. When we were kids, and Dad was drunk, he'd beat on Bruce just because he was retarded. He's a pussycat when he doesn't drink, but once at a bar in Sacramento he almost killed a guy, and got two years in San Quentin."

"We have only a couple more days of work and we're out of here," I said. "In the meantime if Bruce needs to relax please give him a joint, and keep him away from any bar."

"You got my word, Dave."

After that incident, I was embarrassed to set foot in the officers' lounge; but at the end of our last day of work I did accept an invitation for an after-work drink from the contracting officer, Captain Mark Roberts. We sat at a corner table in the dimly-lit lounge. An attractive couple slowly danced by and I couldn't help admiring the lady. In fact I couldn't take my eyes off her. Captain Roberts observed my fixed stare and called the couple over to join us. "Dave, I'd like you to meet Captain Jim Barker and his lovely bride, Janice." I hoped my eyes didn't look as large as they felt! "Jim, Dave and his men have been doing some good roofing work on the barracks."

I forced my gaze from "Janice" to Jim. "Mark wasn't just being cute when he called Janice my bride," he said. "Five weeks ago we'd never even met. I just got incredibly lucky. Janice is a schoolteacher from Colorado. We met a month ago while I was in Denver on business. We hit it off right away, and here we are." I shook their hands and stammered out "J-Jim. J-*Janice.*" There was no question that this lovely bride was my recent panel-truck tenant, Diane!

Her smile and tight handshake said "I know you'll be discreet, Dave." I took a deep breath and said, "Congratulations, you two. You look great together. It's getting late, so if you'll please excuse me I'm going to retire." As I walked across the dance floor, "Janice" gave me a grateful wink.

Shorty played poker constantly when he was at the enlisted men's club. There were times that he won a thousand dollars only to lose it the next night. Our last night at the base, Shorty was invited back to the enlisted men's club. Shorty got Bruce interested in seeing a movie in town, so he'd be safely occupied. I was in the officers' club, chatting with a couple of them, when Shorty came running up to my table. "Could I please see you outside, Dave?"

I excused myself quickly. Shorty was so excited I was concerned that Bruce was in trouble again. He led me outside to the truck, then turned and said, "Dave, I just took my biggest pot ever, $4,400. It was quitting time, so I'm not obligated to play anymore."

"Congratulations!"

"Dave, would you take $4,000 cash for the truck?"

"You can probably find one less expensive, Shorty," I said.

"Maybe so, but yours is in top condition. I know the truck, and it's worth it to me. If I go back and play with those guys tomorrow I'll probably lose the money. Better I use it wisely now. You can use the truck till we're finished with the work here in Fairbanks. Whaddya say?"

I said, "Give me the $4,000 so you won't spend it, and I'll sign over the title to you right now and give you a receipt, paid in full." It seemed the right time to bring up a question I'd been wanting to ask. "Shorty, would you mind if I went back to Oregon, and we end our jobs in Alaska? I'd like to take a steamship down the Inside Passage to Seattle, and see more of your beautiful Alaska. I wouldn't mind leaving on the next ship."

"Do it, Dave. I'd really like to get back to my wife. And with a truck I can go for my contractor's license."

The next day I paid Shorty and Bruce up to date and wished them well. As they got into the truck, I could hear Bruce saying, "Someday I'm gonna get me a truck just like this one. All red, and with a mattress in it!"

That afternoon I purchased a one-way first-class ticket on the steamship that was leaving the next morning for Seattle, by way of Glacier Bay, Juneau, Ketchikan, and Vancouver Island. The ship was first class in every way.

The second night out, the water became rough. In the morning about 150 queasy, almost-seasick people, including me, were gingerly eating soft-boiled eggs, bacon, and prunes. The only breath of fresh air was a man, perhaps in his mid-sixties, with white shaggy hair. He smilingly balanced a full breakfast tray. How I envied him, wishing I had taken whatever seasick medication he had fortified himself with.

About halfway through our debatable breakfast, a boy of about 12 began walking down the marble stairway toward the dining area. He was tenaciously holding on to the highly polished brass rail to brace himself against the motion. Then he began swaying back and forth. And the sounds began: "Aaaa . . . uuhhh." All of us, I'm certain, were praying, "Please don't get sick, little guy." Suddenly, he threw up with such force that his vomit splattered all over the passengers sitting at the front table. Within 10 seconds all of us were sick. A lady with blue hair threw up into the grand piano. Then the pianist threw up all over her head. Only the white-haired gent was immune.

After a shower and change of clothes, I gingerly hobbled up to the promenade deck and slumped into a deck chair. There was only one person appreciating the breathtaking beauty of the glaciers and deep-blue ocean. It was the old gentlemen, the only one not ill in the dining room earlier. His deck chair was astern of mine. Out of his mouth protruded a long cigarette holder; but what really caught my attention was the pungent-sweet aroma that wafted from the hand-rolled cigarette it held.

As casually as possible I moved to within two seats of him and introduced myself. "Nice to meet *you*, son," said the old man. "The name's Ronson." He didn't hide the fact that he was smoking grass.

"Aren't you concerned that someone might report you to the captain?" I asked.

He smiled and looked at me with his twinkling red eyes. (Grass dilates blood vessels, allowing more blood to flow through them, resulting in 'redeye,' a common telltale.) "The only other person out here is you, son. Are you going to report me?"

I felt foolish. "Of course not." After a short pause, I asked, "Mr. Ronson, would you tell me how you kept from being seasick?"

"Actually, the medication was prescribed by a doctor," he said. "I'm a retired structural engineer. Years back I was diagnosed with muscular dystrophy and I was starting to worry that the muscle spasms in my legs would cause me to fall – and that would be no joke, because there were times I was out on a scaffold 10 or 12 stories above the street. That condition led to depression, which in turn encouraged early retirement. I finally had to use a cane, just to walk. I was told I would soon be in a wheelchair. Doctors prescribed medications that gave me vertigo, which assured a fall sooner rather than later. And their medicine didn't agree with my stomach.

"An old college buddy of mine from Stanford who's now in internal medicine suggested I smoke cannabis. Hell, I hadn't smoked grass since we were in school." Mr. Ronson took another drag. "He got me thinking, though. I remembered that grass relaxed me and provided a good night's sleep, with some damn sweet dreams," said Ronson as he continued his monologue.

"My doctor friend said that at the first twinge of muscle spasms, or of queasiness aboard ship, I should take a few puffs of pot. What it does to settle a stomach is a mystery, he said, but it almost always does the trick. Ol' Doc added, 'There's little question that it will take care of your depression and those muscle spasms. Hell, if it works, it's medicine!'

"My leg spasms and depression were gone the second day. Now I just smoke a couple of times a week. Do you smoke grass, son?"

"I do now and then," I offered. "I found that a glass or two of wine was relaxing, but frequently I ended up with a headache about midnight."

Mr. Ronson reached into his vest pocket and produced a nicely rolled joint. He smiled and handed it to me along with his lighter. I lit up and took a puff. After the second drag the stress and nausea began melting away.

"If they'd legalize the stuff, some of our stressed-out legislators might be able to relax – without the threat of a hangover," said Ronson, and added, "Forget the dog; *grass* is man's best friend."

Meeting my soul mate, Hazel

That picturesque adventure ended in Seattle. I caught a plane for Portland and took a cab to the King Tower, where my apartment awaited.

The next morning I found a letter from the manager of the apartment building informing me that I was two months delinquent in my rent. I had paid three months in advance before leaving for Alaska, so I immediately phoned the accounting office. A lady's voice answered, and I told her about the problem. Within a half hour she phoned back saying, "It's all straightened out, Mr. Ford. It was a mistake at the main office – please accept our apology. And where have you been for so long?"

I didn't know what she looked like. She might be married, or sixty years old, but I took a shot in the dark. "If you would allow me to take you to dinner this evening I'll be happy to tell you all about it," I said.

"Well, I just might take you up on that. I live at the Martha Washington. Would you care to pick me up at, say, 7 o'clock? And my name, which you obviously don't know, is Hazel Rose."

"What a pretty name, and you're right here in 'the City of Roses'! I'll pick you up at 7 p.m., Hazel Rose."

I arrived at the Martha Washington Inn for Young Women at 7:02, and rang the bell. A lady's voice boomed out through a loudspeaker. "Whom did you come to see, please?"

"Miss Hazel Rose," I answered.

A buzzer sounded. "Please come in to the waiting room." In a couple of minutes I felt soft womanly hands over my eyes. "Guess who?" came the familiar soft voice. "I hope it's Hazel," I laughed.

As her warm hands slipped away, I turned to see a stunning lady about my age, 23. She had the most beautiful shining black hair, thick, wavy, and falling to her shoulders, framing a radiant smile and deep brown eyes. She was smartly dressed in a white blouse, a gray sweater, a pleated gray skirt, stockings, and black high-heels. She had a gray coat under her arm. We shook hands and both smiled. "Did you think I'd be some old hag weighing 200 pounds?"

"As a matter of fact... nah, nah. Still, you are a lovely surprise." We had a fine dinner, and about two hours of conversation. Hazel had grown up on a farm in Lebanon, Oregon, one of nine children. After high school she opened a dress shop in Lebanon. It didn't do well so she decided to go to Oregon State College in Corvallis for two years, where she took accounting and shorthand. After dinner we drove to a scenic spot that overlooked Portland.

It was 11 p.m. when I returned her to the Martha Washington. "Thank you for a lovely evening," she said, and pressed the buzzer. "It was my pleasure," I assured her, and meant it. As she slipped through the door we squeezed each others' hands.

I didn't see Hazel for several days. Catching up with messages at the office was a bit overwhelming. But soon I began seeing her at every opportunity. I'd watch her work when she wasn't aware of me. I was proud of her that she managed to get a good job at the finest apartment complex in Portland. We went flying the first week; she loved it. We went to many restaurants, and began having dinners at my apartment. Something told me not to bring up the subject of grass.

I sold the 1949 Olds Rocket 88 convertible, and bought a new yellow 1952 Buick convertible with red leather seats. I knew it was foolhardy to lose almost 50% on a new car, which happens in a few years, but it was my first new car and my first time truly falling in love.

To break in the new car we drove to Lebanon. Hazel wanted me to meet her family. I liked them; but there were times when I didn't feel comfortable about "the old man," as Hazel and her siblings referred to her father. He was very autocratic: follow his directions, or get out. Fortunately for Hazel, she had managed to get out on her own. He told me how lumber companies gave him a hundred dollars cash each time they crossed his property to get to large timber, and that happened frequently. But it appeared that the family had no money. Practically everything they ate came from the farm. The house was old and rundown, their clothes worn. It was a bit of a puzzle.

Most of the time we flew to visit them. We'd buzz the farm to let them know we'd arrived, and soon one of the family would be at the Lebanon airport to meet us

A forced landing with precious Hazel

The following week Hazel joined me on a business flight to Boise. Before our return, I checked Portland weather, and the forecast was for "scattered clouds" at our ETA of 8 p.m. The darkness didn't concern me: By that time, I had over 300 hours of night flying. But it began raining hard as we neared the Willamette Valley. Daylight was rapidly failing, the ceiling was lowering swiftly, the wind was trying to overturn the plane, and we were unable to reach Portland by radio. I made the decision: We were going to make a forced landing. My first.

I recalled that on the way to Boise there had been an emergency landing strip near the Bridge of the Gods. I told Hazel that we might land momentarily.

"Whatever you decide, I know it will be OK."

I wished I had her serene confidence. It was totally black outside. With the plane's landing light on, about all I could see was the heavy rain. We felt our way to the ground. Fortunately, the runway was where I recalled it to be. We came to a grinding, shuddering stop just short of the end of the runway. My next fear was that the wind would flip the airplane over. I shouted to Hazel to jump out, grab the wing on her side, and hold on for dear life. It was an hour before we dared to let go of the wings long enough to get ropes and anchors out of the plane to tie it down securely. Finally some neighbors came to see what had happened. They kindly invited us to stay in their home for the night. I called Portland and closed our flight plan, and the next morning, I phoned in another, and we took off in clear blue skies.

One day I asked Hazel if she' d like to go skiing. Neither of us had ever tried it. I was curious, and Hazel said she was too, so one weekend we drove to Timberline Lodge at Mount Hood and rented ski equipment.

Hazel was wise and started with the beginners' slope. Being macho, I took the 5,000-foot chairlift to the top of the mountain. I pushed off. What fun! It was like flying. The only problem was that I didn't know how to stop! I got going so fast I was afraid to fall down. I figured out how to turn in time to miss some large trees. I took a couple of spills that should have broken both legs, but luck was with me and finally I arrived at the bottom, shaken but in one piece. Hazel was waiting for

At 22, I was really flying. Soon after I bought my first airplane I met Hazel, the love of my life, in Portland, Oregon.

Hazel and I, as much in love as we look, enjoying our first Christmas together, 1954.

me with a worried look on her pretty face. Some blowing snow had frosted her hair and made it look white. "You'll be even prettier someday when your hair is *all* white," I said. Her big dark brown eyes had tears in them as she gave me a hug. She was dear, and fragile.

We went into the lodge and drank hot buttered rum. We laughed at the same things. We loved the outdoors, swimming, camping, flying. We both wanted children one day. I felt closer to Hazel than any lady I had ever dated. I was convinced Hazel was my soul mate. There was no question in my mind that she loved me as I loved her.

I asked if she would care to spend the night at the lodge. She looked nervous, but said, "O.K. I trust you." I had known her now for almost three months, and something told me not to press her. After dinner we retired to a cozy room with a king-sized bed. We had done a lot of necking, but nothing more. Now, her body convulsed in spasms of distress.

"Daaave," (I loved the way she stretched out my name.) "I don't know if I can ever make love with you. I've got to tell you about it." She began to sob. I held her and stroked her lovely black hair.

"My... my... my... dad... *used* me. He raped me so many times." Her body was cold, shaking. "Please don't hate me, Daaave. I'm dirty."

"You're not dirty and I couldn't hate you. I love you!" Something I had never before said to anyone other than my parents. I felt I could cheerfully punch out "the old man."

That night she slept with her ski pants on. I made no attempt to make love to her. As she slept I stroked her hair and kissed her cheek. I was furious about what she had gone through; I wanted to save her, as if she were drowning. The next morning we had a fine breakfast and headed back to Portland.

The last thing I wanted to do was put any pressure on Hazel, but as the next three months went by a certain pressure on me built up. While we'd been dating I hadn't made love to anyone. I was getting to where I couldn't sleep more than three hours a night. My body missed the super relaxation that comes from making love.

My apartment, like the others at King Tower, had a miniature "dairy door" next to the entrance, for delivery of milk and small packages when the tenant was away. I rarely locked it from the inside. One night, in a deep sleep, I dreamed that someone was cramming his body through the dairy door and into my apartment. I awoke with a start – and realized there *was* someone in my apartment:

I saw a shadow moving. I wasn't certain whether I should leap at whoever it was, run yelling out of the apartment, or what. Instead, I froze in bed. It was exactly like a nightmare: you try to run, but can't move. The next instant someone was *on* the bed, and an instant later I felt a naked body next to mine. "Good evening," said Hazel's familiar voice.

"God, Hazel, please don't ever do that again!"

"Make love to me, Daaave, I really need it."

"In that case," I said, "it's OK if you break in any time!"

I was elated to discover that Hazel was a natural born hugger. This was such a change in her demeanor. We made wild love until daybreak, when I fell into a deep sleep. When I awoke Hazel was gone. It was 9 a.m. I should be at the office. But first I phoned the apartment's accounting office and was rewarded with the sweet sound of Hazel's bright answer. "Good morning. King Tower. Accounting office."

"Good morning, Hazel, this is Dave. Are you OK?"

"Of course I'm OK. Have a nice day, Mr. Ford!"

That night when we went out to dinner I mentioned what a marvelous and crazy time we had had last night. Hazel didn't respond at all; it was like it hadn't happened. I never mentioned it again.

It was now February of 1952. My mother and sister Carol were now living in Ashland, Oregon, not too far away. I invited them to dinner at the apartment, wanting them to meet Hazel, and hoping for their approval. They were polite. I was disappointed, but I hoped in time they would see in Hazel what I saw, and in time, come to love her, as I did.

The next evening I drove Hazel up to the beautiful rose garden park in the hills overlooking Portland. I presented her with an engagement ring and asked her to marry me. She cried with happiness and accepted. I was elated, but apprehensive. There were times that she had a faraway look, and times that she didn't want to be touched or held, and other times that she craved to be loved. I understood the horror inflicted by her father. I was positive that with my love and understanding, all would be well.

The following weekend we flew to San Rafael to meet my Dad and my step-mom Mary. They met us at the little airstrip only a few miles from their home. They were ecstatic, and loved Hazel at first sight. Hazel was so happy and proud, it was a thrill for me watching her show her ring to everyone we met. She wanted to be a June bride, so we set the date for June 29th. The wedding would be held at the First Christian Church in Lebanon. I asked Dad to be best man.

Me, married?

Dad, Mary, sister Margo, and her husband Vic were all there for the wedding. Sis Carol and mother had moved to Pasadena, near Los Angeles. Dad was a great best man. I was so nervous getting dressed in the men's dressing room of the church that I could understand how a groom might disappear without a best man with a more level head nearby. Margo, Vic, and I smoked a joint together to calm me down. Margo told me she used grass for PMS, migraine headaches, relaxation, and for enhancing lovemaking.

It was surprisingly spine-tingling to wait as Hazel's maid of honor helped her dress at the other end of the church. I'd asked Dad to please check and see whether Hazel was OK. He reported back that she was just fine, and wanted to know how I was doing. I asked Dad to tell her, "I'm still here!" When the music began my knees started dancing uncontrollably.

The church was filled mostly with Hazel's friends and relatives. When the organist began "Here Comes the Bride," and Hazel appeared in her white bridal gown, I was thunderstruck with pride and love. Hazel was indeed beautiful. Her inner beauty was visible as her radiant smile encompassed the congregation. In the past I'd chuckled with pity when one of my buddies got married. We guys had looked at a wedding as no more than the groom buying a license to make love whenever he wanted. This time it was different. This was the time I was leaving youth and its cynicism behind, and I was astonished and humbled that Hazel would be my wife and the mother of our children. And we would grow together. I was overwhelmed with love and tenderness and wanted to protect and shelter her. There was so much little scared child in her, and much that I didn't understand.

The ceremony was at 9 p.m. and the reception was in the church hall. When we finally left the reception it was almost midnight. We spent our first night at a lovely lodge in Walport, Oregon. For the first time I asked Hazel if she would care to try a little grass.

She said she didn't care for it. "It's OK if you want to smoke some, Daaave."

"It's OK, baby," I said. I never offered her any after that, and I didn't smoke again for almost two years. There was no withdrawal, any more than if friends of yours had moved away: You would miss them for a time, but you wouldn't go chasing after them.

The next day we left for our honeymoon at Laguna Beach, California, and Mexico. On the way we traveled through the redwoods, driving right through one of the magnificent giant trees, via an opening cut just wide enough for a car to fit through. Hazel wanted to see where I had been a lifeguard, so we stopped at the Russian River for a swim. Then on to San Rafael, where my parents threw a reception for their friends to greet us.

It was a fun-filled two-week honeymoon with plenty of swimming in the ocean, which Hazel loved almost as much as I. We dined at romantic restaurants, and went dancing several times. Hazel was the only lady that I now felt totally comfortable dancing with. Still, several nights a week Hazel would go to bed with Levi's on, and push me away. I got the message and would stay on my side of the bed. Other times she couldn't get enough loving. It was confusing, but I loved her and felt that in time she would be more comfortable.

We had decided to leave Oregon and move to Salt Lake City. It was exciting to be heading to a new nest, and we both felt uneasy around Hazel's father.

● ● ●

Even though I gave up smoking pot for a couple of years, I never gave up studying why the government felt it had to lie about this relatively harmless herb. I interviewed anyone who would answer questions about grass. "I'm researching marijuana, both medically and for relaxation, or what you might call recreational use. May I ask you a few questions?"

Some people would say things like, "It's a dangerous drug. I don't want to discuss it." Most people who were open to the subject, though, were angry at the government and had lost respect for law enforcement, which they felt was interfering with the private lives of people using a substance milder and far less harmful than alcohol.

Answers came from people in all walks of life – doctors, lawyers, entertainers, teachers, religious leaders, and even judges and police officers. So many condemned our country's ding-a-ling War on Drugs. Comments included:

From a judge: "The drug war is causing more misery than illegal drugs. If you add up expenditures by local, state, and federal government, including incarceration, this drug war is costing taxpayers many billion

Hazel in the cockpit of "Silver," proudly displaying her wedding ring.

dollars a year. Zero tolerance equals zero common sense. It only causes kids to hide a drug problem for fear their teacher or parents will overreact."

More than one frustrated teacher said, "Unless I restrict our 'education' to discussing only the *negative* effects of marijuana or hemp, I'll be terminated."

"There will always be some people who abuse both legal and illegal drugs," one young mother said. "No one goes to prison for alcoholism. No one goes to prison for cigarette addiction. Drug *abuse,* for legal or illegal drugs, is an illness and should be treated as a health problem"

A doctor said: "The billions wasted by the DEA prosecuting social and medical pot users, rather than big-time drug kingpins, should be spent on treatment for those with hard-drug problems. America's drug policies are perpetuating the reliance on law enforcement and interdiction with comparatively minor focus on education and treatment. The public wants treatment. Not incarceration. There's an immense difference between *use* and *abuse.* But the government calls *any* illegal drug use abuse. The hypocrites!"

What is harm reduction?

According to a policeman, "We will never stop drug use. We should be open to learn from other countries that *harm reduction* can minimize the bad effects of drug use by informing those who, in spite of warnings, use drugs anyway. An example: Kids at 'raves,' after-hours dance parties characterized by drug and alcohol use, are practicing harm reduction when they have Ecstasy pills analyzed by DanceSafe (www.dancesafe.org) to detect adulteration with other, potentially lethal drugs.

"Kids shouldn't use Ecstasy at all, but inevitably some will, and they can take a few precautions to minimize harmful effects: Get their drugs tested. Drink at least a pint of water and 'chill out,' rest for 10 minutes, every hour. Also, limit use to one pill per session to prevent death from overdosing. Most politicians don't have the courage to say that, even though they know it's true, and could save lives. Shouldn't all the options be examined?"

Apparently not. Recently a California Assemblywoman was pushing a rave-regulation bill that would — according to the bill's *supporters* — prevent organizations like DanceSafe from testing pills at permitted raves... in the name of "protecting the children" of course.

Far better to work in a nonjudgmental way to minimize harmful effects.

Methods range from *managed use* to *abstinence*, with *honest* drug education. One example is providing clean syringes for hardcore addicts, to reduce needle sharing and prevent the spread of AIDS.

Regarding AIDS, the United Nations reported that 68 *million* more AIDS deaths are feared by 2020. Ten billion dollars a year is needed for prevention.[16]

Wouldn't it make more harm-reducing sense to give up part of our $50 billion-a-year drug-war budget, including imprisonment, to save a possible 68 million lives, or would that be politically incorrect?

Ask Bill Maher. Sad that his outstanding show, *Politically Incorrect*, was canceled in 2002. Today, one must be careful expressing a personal opinion, no matter how honest. I predicted that Bill would return, and be even better known for his wit and honesty. His new show premiered February 21, 2003; a one-hour late-night news and comedy show on HBO.[17] Welcome back to TV, Bill Maher! We need heroes like Bill, and ABC's John Stossel, and government officials such as Orange County, California, Superior Court Judge James Gray and former New Mexico Governor Gary Johnson, to mention a few of the many courageous people who are not afraid to say the drug war is a hypocritical sham.

Every person agreed we don't want kids doing any drug. But they do – in part because drugs are illegal. Kids are rebels, like we were; they embrace a challenge! A father said, "Unlike legitimate businesses that sell alcohol, illegal drug dealers do not ID for age. They do push addictive drugs when given the chance, and they don't care if your kid is 12 years old." Have you ever heard of a liquor store owner jeopardizing his business by pushing beer outside a schoolyard?

Other comments: A surprising number of people confided that they "sold small amounts of pot to friends" because they knew the herb was top-quality, and that that should not be a criminal act. A police officer said, "Mandatory minimum sentences must stop. It should be up to the judge to decide whether punishment or treatment is required, and how much. If drugs were regulated, there wouldn't be a black-market profit for them, and we could be chasing real live criminals!" A mother said, "Without judges having discretion, people might as well be sentenced by computer."

The War on Drugs was designed to catch and imprison major drug kingpins, to stop corruption, encourage health, and reduce suffering and death from certain drugs. Is it accomplishing its mission? Hardly. When kids hear drug lies, they roll their eyes. Millions of Americans who once used pot, have, due to urine testing on the job, switched to speed, heroin, alcohol and other dangerous drugs that are out of the system by Monday morning.

Kids are going to experiment with drugs just as most of us did when we were young. I've had parents tell me, "We'd certainly prefer to have them experiment with pot rather than Ecstasy, alcohol, speed, or cigarettes." But then, I've also heard both moms and dads say, "So the kids use a little alcohol. At least they're not on drugs!" Somehow, these parents haven't gotten the message that alcohol causes more teen deaths than all other drugs combined.

Questioning people about grass was almost as satisfying as smoking a joint, I rationalized!

● ● ●

Hazel and I headed for Utah, with Hazel driving the Buick and me flying the plane. It was great fun. I'd buzz her now and then. Once I landed in a large meadow adjacent to a river, where we had arranged to meet if the site was OK for landing. It was, and it was isolated. I lifted her up out of the convertible, held her, and hugged her. I told her what a fine driver she was, and how lucky I was to have met her. We made love there next to the river, and then had a picnic before she got back behind the wheel and I took to the sky.

It was a thrill to watch her from the plane as she wove her way around the mountain passes with the top down and her long black hair flying in the wind. I wouldn't get too far ahead of her; I played hide-and-seek with the clouds, and then did slow flight just ahead of her at 500 feet in rural areas. I could see her wave and throw me kisses. Our rendezvous was at a little airstrip with a motel and restaurant about half way to Salt Lake. We had a fine meal and an exotic night. And in Salt Lake City we rented a new home.

On Wednesday, August 27th, 1952, I was driving home after work on an extremely windy afternoon. At a stop sign a youngster was selling papers. Holding up the *Salt Lake Telegram*, the city's daily newspaper, the boy was shouting, "Read all about it! Two planes smashed at Salt Lake Airport!" There on the front page was a photo of a plane, upside down, that had smashed to the ground the wing of another aircraft – my plane! With a sick stomach I sped to the airport. Someone had not tied down his plane properly; the wind had blown it up into the air and down onto the wing of mine. The wing was smashed, and there was fuselage damage as well. The other aircraft owner had no insurance and said he had no money. The repair estimate was $1,800, more than the plane cost. I had it rebuilt anyway.

I was missing my family and friends, and asked Hazel what she thought of our moving to Oakland, California. I pointed out that we'd be just a few flying hours from her relatives. "I'm ready. Let's do it, Daaave!"

Building muscles – and homes

We visited Hazel's family and my mother and sister Carol for a week, then headed for Oakland. We found a pleasant home to rent on 82nd Avenue.

On a warm summer Sunday afternoon, Hazel and I were enjoying a picnic and swimming at Alameda, a few miles from our home in Oakland. I mentioned to Hazel that a friend of mine, Cliff, wanted to open a health spa in San Rafael. His persuasive argument ran as follows: "We'll be the only health club in marvelous Marin County. We can call it the MarVel Athletic Club. I'll run it, and all you have to do, Dave, is invest the capital and promote the business! You'll love it. There's an airstrip just a few hundred yards from the vacant building. You could fly your plane over from Oakland and taxi in right in front of the spa. I can train the men. We'll just need a man to work with the ladies." Hazel was nodding her pretty head enthusiastically when we both were distracted by an amazing sight.

A youngster that couldn't have weighed more than 40 pounds was lying on his back in the sand with his knees pulled toward his little chest and his arms straight up. A man about 200 pounds was doing a handstand on the child's hands! We watched fascinated as the man then tossed the boy into the air and caught him. This tiny child was now doing a handstand on his father's hands, which were extended over his head. They performed every other acrobatic feat one could imagine. We ventured over and introduced ourselves.

The man was Bill Henry, and his five-year-old son was Billy. "Meet Mr. and Mrs. Ford, Billy."

Billy put his little hand out, looked us straight in the eyes, and gave us each a firm handshake, saying, "Nice to meet you, Mr. and Mrs. Ford!"

I told Bill about our plans for the athletic club and our need for a man to work with the women teaching weightlifting. I asked what his occupation was and how much he made.

"I work for the gas company and I make $375 a month."

"Would you be interested in working for the gym for, say, $500 a month?"

"Would I ever! That's exactly what I'd like to do!"

We went to their little home and met his pretty wife, Betsy. I phoned my partner Cliff to tell him the idea and check with him on the monthly salary. He thought it was great.

When I told Bill that I had Cliff's okay, he said, "I could give notice to the gas company and be with you in two weeks."

I invested the money, Cliff started buying equipment for the building that was to be the club, and I did the promotion. I set the grand opening for the Fourth of July. I lined up Mr. America, Roy Hilligan, to appear, and had us entered into an Independence Day parade. The morning of the Fourth, as I was gathering our group to head for the starting point of the parade, I found Roy in the dressing room getting into his little black bathing trunks. He greeted me cheerfully and handed me a bottle of baby oil.

He said, "You've been so nice to me, giving me $50 and all to come here today, I'm going let you grease me up!"

I said, "Ah... I'm honored, Roy, but I think Cliff has more experience in that area."

Cliff rolled his eyes at me, but was a good sport, letting Roy think it was truly a privilege.

For the parade we had our yellow convertible decorated with a large sign: MarVel Athletic Club. Hazel and Betsy sitting in the car added to the excitement, and the decoration, as both were beautiful. I had Billy walking in front of the car holding wooden replicas of large black weights that looked real. Painted in yellow was "500 lbs." All along the parade route Billy would drop to the street, get on his back and do a few presses with the weights that he appeared to be straining to lift. He and Bill would then perform some of their gymnastic stunts. They received thunderous applause. Our car, along with Bill and Billy, made the front page of the daily paper, the *San Rafael Independent Journal.*

I spent a day a week at the athletic club. Several months passed. When I learned that Bill and Billy used to live in Canada and ice-skated, I suggested that they try out for the Ice Capades. They were such a professional team I felt they were wasting their time at our gym. Bill said, "There's no way we could ever make it, we're not that good; but thanks for the thought."

Unwilling to give up, I phoned Los Angeles and spoke with the Ice Capades talent director. I asked when they were auditioning. "We're having auditions the middle of next month." I told him about the

Henrys. "Sure! Let's have a look at them," said the talent director.

I told Bill about my call to the talent director, and finally persuaded him that they should practice their skating and work out a routine. Bill said he was currently working on a prop that would enable them to do a finger-to-finger stand with little Billy straight over Bill's head. I suggested they both wear tuxedoes for the audition.

Five weeks later I rented a four-place Cessna. We took off in the plane on our way to Los Angeles and the Ice Capades. Hazel was sitting next to me and Billy and Bill were in the back seat. We were at 10,000 feet and about halfway to Los Angeles when Billy said, "I have to pee."

Slightly exasperated, I said, "Billy, I suggested you do that before we took off. Here's a Coke bottle."

Billy said, "I'm not going in any Coke bottle. I'm going on the ground!"

I could see that this was a conflict that I wasn't going to win: The thought of that lingering smell in the cockpit encouraged me to look for a handy landing spot. Far below was Pismo Beach. With the binoculars I was able to spot a hard-packed area of the beach where there weren't any people. As soon as I landed, bathers began running to the plane. We got Billy out and emptied and back into the plane before they reached us, and we took off waving and smiling at the bathers.

Bill and Billy were fabulous at the audition, and were hired on the spot, starting at $800 a week – a big jump from $500 a month! It wasn't long before they were making $1,500 a week. We lost a fine instructor, but I believed their talent should be used to their best advantage. They traveled all over the world, always sending us tickets for the finest seats. We did attend the show when they were in San Francisco, Oakland, or Los Angeles.

While at the Los Angeles performance, during intermission I went to the bar for a glass of beer. Sitting next to me was comedian Lou Costello, of the famous comedy team Abbott and Costello. (They made several movies in the 1940s that are still shown on TV. If you truly enjoy some good laughs, especially if you're a medical-marijuana patient; light up a joint and watch "Abbott and Costello Meet Frankenstein." Grass multiplies anything funny to make it hilarious. Of course, Cheech and Chong movies are also super hilarious on grass, as are the Three Stooges and cartoons!)

Lou had been drinking, and it was obvious that he was crying. I asked him if there was anything I could do. He just sobbed, "My son. My son." I put my arm around him and said, "I'm so sorry, Lou." I recalled that his young son, who, like Billy, was just five years old, had drowned in the family swimming pool just a few months earlier, and little Billy no doubt reminded him of his son. A few months later Lou died of a heart attack.

As the years passed Bill and I became great friends. "The Henrys" were now one of the featured acts of the Ice Capades. At 18 Billy elected to join the Air Force as a radar technician. Soon his crew was flying at low altitudes, frequently under 500 feet, learning to avoid radar detection. One tragic night their plane slammed into a mountain, and all aboard were killed. Bill was heartbroken. Three weeks later he was playing handball, trying to put the tragedy behind him. He fell dead of a heart attack at age 40. Perhaps his early death, and Lou Costello's, resulted from the devastating loss of a loved one.

Once again I was ready to move on. I had remodeled dozens of homes. Now the challenge I set myself was to make a good living building new ones. Searching for building sites, I found a number of irregularly shaped lots. I visited a man who worked for the city's building department and asked if he would be interested in drawing plans for irregular lots in his spare time, for $100 per plan.

He said, "I'll be darned glad to, son. Sure beats the five bucks an hour I'm being paid here. I could do one in a weekend." I showed him a pie-shaped lot and asked if he could design a house for it. He said, "I'll phone you this evening." About 8 that night he called. "I can do it. It will be only about 850 square feet, but it will have two bedrooms, one bath, and a garage attached."

I looked up the owners of the property and asked what they would take for the lot. "If you'll pay us $800 we'll take it." Having a man who worked for the building department do the plans assured me of county approval. That first house earned a profit of $2,500. Soon I was building three-bedroom houses, and eventually duplexes and triplexes. In those days the three-bedroom houses with hardwood floors were selling for $9,500. I could probably have sold them for more; but at such reasonable prices they generally sold and closed escrow within a month.

Growing more than tomatoes!

I started a small garden in the back yard and planted a few pot plants among the tomatoes. I enjoyed a good silent laugh hearing neighbors in three houses that surrounded our back yard say, "Isn't he a fine young man, tending his tomatoes!" I gave the grass to my friend Fae. I wasn't smoking it at that time, so growing it was like catching fish and throwing them back into the water.

Fae phoned me a few weeks later to thank me again for the pot. He said he divided most of it up among his friends. His words were slurred. "Dave, I'm trying to smoke only good ol' grass, but I'm an alcoholic now, and I can't seem to quit. After my dad whipped me and threatened to turn me over to the police for smoking pot, it just seemed easier to be a good American, forgo the grass, and drink the booze."

I never saw that great talented pianist and friend again. Fae died at age 42 from alcohol-related complications.

I couldn't keep the false horror stories about grass out of my mind. What troubled me almost as much as the death of my friend were some of the radio people I knew, who smoked grass and yet climbed on the propaganda bandwagon and did the government's dirty work. Anything that grabbed an audience was exaggerated and went out on the air or in the papers. I could see that it was only going to get worse, because the listeners and readers were taken in by those they trusted – newspaper reporters, columnists, and radio personalities, none of whom seemed to care about the facts when they were on the job. Grass-bashing garnered audiences, which translated to money. Once again, that old news credo proved true: "If it bleeds, it leads!"

Almost killed by my carpenter

I used the same framing crew on each construction job. Not only were they good workers, they were also nice guys. Jim was a little guy who had been a fighter pilot in World War II, and he constantly joked about giving me a flying lesson. By now I had over 2,500 hours flying time and had never scratched a plane. I didn't think there was much he could teach me, but I could see he was eager to climb back into the sky. One afternoon after work I invited him to give me that "flying lesson."

We took off from Oakland International Airport with Jim in the co-pilot's seat. We climbed to 3,000 feet and went to the practice area. Then I said, "Take it, Jim."

His hands leapt to the control yoke. "Yeah, this is more like it! I should have been flying all these years. This is a sweet little plane. Watch this, Dave!"

Before I realized what he was doing, Jim put the plane into a dive at full throttle, then pulled the controls full back. The plane climbed at a critical angle of attack, almost straight up.

"Here's how to do a loop, Dave." Then we were upside down and the plane had stalled out on top of the loop. It began falling – upside down. Jim's face was white with terror. His fighter-pilot instincts had abandoned him.

I yelled over the roar of the engine. "Nose *down*, Jim! Nose *down!*" The engine was screaming. "Give me the controls, Jim!" No response. He was frozen at the controls and I was unable to move them! The altimeter was unwinding faster than it could be read; in seconds we would smash into the ground at full speed. I reached for the fire extinguisher and hit Jim over the head.

His head fell forward. I pushed him back in the seat, then I cut the throttle, brought the nose down, and gently pulled back on the controls. By the time the plane was leveled out and under control, we were at a perilous 275 feet above the ground. We almost collided with an apartment building! I took the plane back to a thousand feet and radioed the control tower, declaring an emergency with an ill passenger, and requested an ambulance.

Jim was given eight stitches in his head. "Man, if you hadn't hit me we'd'a been dead meat, buddy. Please don't tell my wife."

"I won't. And I won't tell mine either!"

I had the plane checked out by Cessna mechanics. Almost all of the wing ribs were compressed. "You're damn lucky, Dave," one told me. "One more G and you wouldn't have *had* any wings." The estimate for repairs was $880 – too high. I did have it repaired, though, and then sold it. I vowed to myself that never again would I trust anyone else to fly my plane.

I found a four-place Cessna 170 at Los Angeles International with only 310 hours total time on it. I flew commercial to L.A., picked up that gorgeous plane and flew it back to Hayward, a small airport just down the Bay from Oakland. Hazel loved the large white plane with blue trim almost as much as I did. Now we could take friends along with us if we wanted to.

A few days later I awoke around 4 a.m., thinking about that lovely plane "Hazel honey, are you awake?"

"Yeah," answered a very groggy voice; "someone's voice just woke me up."

"How would you like to fly to Palm Springs for the weekend?"

"I can be ready in a half hour, Daaave!"

We showered, and I filed a flight plan and checked the weather. I phoned Desert Air Park in Palm Springs, made a reservation, and we were off, into a magnificent sunrise. Sometimes in the early morning the air is as smooth as a lady's thigh. The plane seems to love it, and it allows you to fly "hands off."

We landed three and a half hours later on the grassy runway lined with date trees. The temperature was 107. As we taxied to a tie-down area, I noticed that the plane next to ours had a picture of Charlie McCarthy on it. It belonged to the famous ventriloquist, Edgar Bergen, father of actress Candice Bergen. Frank Sinatra's plane was also on the flight line.

Hazel and I took many such trips, frequently taking off for a week or two at a time. We took friends to Las Vegas. We flew up to remote Lake Pillsbury in Northern California, where a World War II-vintage dirt landing strip was located right next to a great fishing and swimming lake. Hazel and I both enjoyed camping. We'd fly up to the lake, bringing food and sleeping bags, and sleep under the stars. We flew to numerous resorts for weekends or days at a time. Memories of camping at Yosemite National Park and other fun places are still with me, like enjoying the memories of photographs around my home, and wishing Hazel were here today. Tragically, that was not to be.

Death from grass?

Bert Waller was a friend of ours. At 24, he was making $20,000 a year at an advertising agency. In response to stress from advertising deadlines, Burt, like millions of other Americans, used alcohol to "mellow out" when he got home from work. He told me that, at times, after a few drinks, he took his frustration out on his wife, Jeannie, sometimes abusing her verbally, sometimes even smacking her.

During a "think tank" session he discovered that a few of the men smoked pot at home to enhance creativity. One of the men offered him a joint to take home. "I couldn't believe the relaxation I felt. The stress melted away and I came up with some fine creative work." Bert told me that he gave up alcohol for grass. I smoked with him at their apartment a few times. His wife, like Hazel, was afraid of pot, owing to the never-ending propaganda. Nevertheless, she approved of Bert's use because "he's a puppy when he smokes grass instead of drinking alcohol."

One day when Bert stopped by his dry cleaners to pick up a sports coat he'd left there a few days before, there was a delay. The manager apparently couldn't find the coat. Then two police cars screeched to a halt in front of the cleaning establishment, and before he realized what was happening, three policemen rushed into the shop with guns drawn. They grabbed him and handcuffed his hands behind his back. Bert was terrified. The manager cried, "That's him! Here's his sports coat with the marijuana cigarette still in the breast pocket!" Terrified, Bert ran. An officer hit him on the head with his nightstick; closing the wound required ten stitches.

The judge gave Bert nine months in the county jail for possession of marijuana and resisting arrest. It cost him $1,500 in attorney's fees, and he was fired from his job. He was raped while in jail. His wife left him – not because of the rape, but because she was humiliated that he had been arrested for marijuana. Bert found himself blackballed in the business because he had a police record. The experience made him afraid to smoke grass anymore and he went back to alcohol. Two months later he hanged himself.

● ● ●

It was now 1955. Hazel and I were 27, and we decided to move into one of the triplexes I had constructed. I enjoyed building, but found that once I succeeded in a business I wanted a new challenge. So I went looking.

I found S&B Motors in Hayward. They sold new cars and used ones that appeared new. S&B Motors had their own master mechanic and reconditioning shop; but few dealers in those days detailed their cars. The company was owned by the Bruner brothers. I applied, and got the job of selling on commission.

Roy Bruner was an outstanding salesman. He was a slim guy about 5' 7", 140 pounds. He smoked cigars and drank a fifth of Seagram's VO every day while on the job, although he never acted drunk. I asked him one day if he would ever consider smoking grass rather than drinking. He was offended and told me, "I don't do drugs!"

Hazel decided she wanted something to do while I was away at work, so she got a job with Welcome Wagon, giving small gifts from local stores to new residents, to encourage the newcomers to shop locally. I was proud of her, but I could feel tensions building up, for no reason I could see. She assured me that she was fine, but I was a little worried.

Hazel ill

I began to receive strange phone calls from Hazel at the auto agency. She would call me by different men's names. The first time I thought she was joking. After the second time, I drove home and asked her about it. She chuckled and said, "I was only kidding, Daaave. You know it's only you I love." I was convinced then, and now, that that was true; but there was something very fragile about her. She asked my opinion about everything, and she wanted me to pick out all her clothes. I still treasured it that she always called me "Daaave." Dragging out my name meant I was very special to her.

A week later she quit her job.

One night I was reading in the living room when I noticed that Hazel was standing in the doorway with her arms hanging limp at her sides. I happened to glance up as she fell flat on her face, without putting her arms out to break her fall. Terrified, I jumped up to help her. Her face was bruised and she appeared to be in a daze. "Baby, let me get you an ice pack for your face."

At first she just seemed dazed. Then she screamed, "My brain is coming out the top of my head!" I held her and tried to console her, but she kept screaming. I was nearly frantic as I called our family doctor. Bless the man, he came to us within minutes. After calming her down, he took me aside and said he believed she should have a psychiatric examination. He recommended Langley Porter, an outstanding mental hospital at the University of California's medical campus in San Francisco. They performed tests on Hazel and said they could find nothing wrong at that time, but told me to monitor her closely.

Then Hazel began coming down to the car lot. The closest I'd ever heard her come to swearing was "Judas Priest." Now she was using more descriptive language. She frequently stayed awake all night, ironing or sewing. And laughing.

"Baby, why are you laughing?"

"People are talking to me!"

We went back to Langley Porter. Again they examined her and again they told me they couldn't find anything wrong. I was really frightened by this time, and unable to get more than a few hours sleep a night. I began staying home days. She began screaming at night. Once the police came. They observed her for a few minutes, then looked at me and shook their heads in pity, and left. Again I took her to Langley Porter. This time she was out of control, laughing and screaming. The staff told me that I should leave her there for a full assessment. They phoned the next day, saying that Hazel was a very sick woman. They had a long waiting list for admissions, but they admitted her immediately.

I visited Hazel two or three times a week. Each visit was one of the saddest experiences of my life. Hazel was everything to me: I loved being with her, loved taking her places, loved her excitement. In some of my visits to Langley Porter, there were times when Hazel was totally rational, and would tell me she knew she was "crazy." When she *was* ill, she was certain she was fine. Going into the women's locked ward was surreal. Almost every time, some of the women and young girls were naked, masturbating and asking me to screw them.

One of the days that Hazel didn't recognize me she thought I was the actor William Holden. When I put my arm around her she threw a glass of grapefruit juice in my face. "Get away. You're not my husband!"

It was heartbreaking. I missed her; I loved her; I was frightened for her. When Hazel was in the mental hospital, I smoked grass several nights a week. It helped lighten my depression and helped me sleep. Marijuana became my medicine: Before I started using grass again, there were times that her illness made me so despondent that I couldn't find the energy to go to work.

I told her psychiatrist about her wearing Levi's to bed, sometimes for a week or more, then being ravenous for love for the following week. It was like riding one of those mechanical bucking broncos in a Western-type bar. I loved those latter times, yet it was distressing that they always ended abruptly, and the Levi's again appeared when we went to bed. When my honey was well, I'd never had a more exciting lover.

The doctors suspected that the incestuous relationship with her father may have caused her mental illness. They cautioned me that her condition could deteriorate as she became older. We had been married for just less than four years, and she'd been at Langley Porter for one of them. When she was finally released from the hospital in December of 1956 and returned home, she told me she believed that if we had a child she would be fine.

Moving to Hawaii – almost losing all our money!

One windy, frosty morning in February of 1957, a rusty four-door Chevrolet drove into the agency's lot. In the car were five happy young Hawaiians. They were all singing, and one was playing a ukulele. They began looking at cars, kicking tires, singing all the while. I introduced myself – more because I loved their infectious enthusiasm than because I saw a chance to make a sale. They told me how much they missed Hawaii, but that they had to fulfill a contract to sing at a night club in San Francisco. I asked how the weather was in Hawaii in February. "It's summer *all* the time!" one said.

I felt that a change of scenery was important for Hazel. Neighbors were all too well aware of her illness. One day I asked her what she thought of moving to Hawaii. "Let's go, Daaave. I'm ready!"

Hazel and I packed everything we owned into the 1956 yellow Cadillac convertible that I had purchased wholesale. It had only 3,800 miles on it.

Medical bills had reduced our savings more than I liked, but we had about $15,000 in the bank, and selling the plane gave us another $9,000. I was told that one should take cash to Hawaii, because it would take about two weeks for even a cashier's check to clear the bank. After I closed our accounts I drove away with just under $25,000 cash, in hundreds, five hundreds, and thousands. Just looking at all that cash made me apprehensive, and I decided I'd feel safer if I carried only $1,000 cash and brought a cashier's check for the balance. I headed back to our bank in Oakland. The convertible top was down on this sunny day. The parking space closest to our bank was two blocks away. While I waited in line at the bank, I instinctively gave a pat to the back pocket of my slacks, where I always carried my wallet. It was gone!

My legs began to buckle and I thought I was going to pass out. I stumbled out of line, then sprinted for the door, colliding with customers. It's a wonder the security guard didn't take a shot at me. I prayed as I ran: God, please let the wallet still be on the seat of the convertible! The light at the corner was red; I crossed against it and was almost hit by a taxi. As I neared the wide-open convertible, three teenage boys were looking it over. Gasping for air, I all but dove into the car. There against the back of the driver's seat was my wallet, with three hundred-dollar bills hanging out invitingly. I reached over the door and grabbed the wallet and loose bills. The boys looked disappointed that they hadn't seen the money first. This time I headed for the bank clutching the wallet in both hands.

A week later we boarded the *S.S. Leilani*. A hurricane met us two days out, and tormented us until we reached Hawaiian waters. Hazel and most of the rest of the passengers were seasick, but I remembered what the old gentleman on the ship from Alaska had taught me about grass eliminating seasickness. Whenever I started to feel nauseated I ducked into a bathroom and took a few hits of that sweet smoke, and my queasiness would evaporate in minutes.

I rented a car until our Cad was unloaded from the ship. After a couple of days in a hotel, Hazel and I found a charming Hawaiian-style furnished apartment in a two-story building that was almost new, with a swimming pool right outside our front door. Hazel was again as beautiful and as healthy as when we first met. She seemed like a new person already.

Meeting Henry J. Kaiser

Hazel and I lazed around for six months. During that time I met a business idol, Henry J. Kaiser, founder of more than 100 companies, including Kaiser Steel, Kaiser Cement, Kaiser Aluminum, Kaiser Gypsum, Kaiser Permanente Hospitals, and Kaiser Shipyards, where he built Liberty ships during World War II.

When we arrived in Hawaii in February of 1957 Mr. Kaiser was constructing the fifth floor of the Kaiser-Hawaiian Village hotel. He was building a floor a week, and when a floor was completed he would rent the rooms on it for $5 a night to any guest who could tolerate 24-hour-a-day construction. I hung around the construction site off and on, until one day I spotted him with some men who were white-chalking an outline on the dirt for the excavation of an Olympic-size swimming pool.

One of the engineers was saying, "Mr. Kaiser, it is now March 25. We thought you might like to dedicate the swimming pool, say June 30, sir?"

Mr. Kaiser had a surprisingly soft voice for such a powerful industrialist. "I think next Thursday evening at 7 would be a nice time. Please see that it's completed by then." Clearly he had learned that the faster a project was completed, the sooner it began to pay for itself.

When he had finished his business with the engineers, I introduced myself. Mr. Kaiser said, "It's nice to meet you, David, I hope we have the pleasure of meeting again." Not long afterward, we did.

He sold the hotel to the Hilton chain for a $12 million profit two years later.

Opening auto agency; locals try to put us out of business

I decided to open my own auto agency. I found a perfect square block of real estate standing vacant in downtown Honolulu. It had a small drab office structure and white painted metal light poles surrounding it. After a bit of research, I discovered that the Dillingham Corporation owned the lot, so I went to their offices and spoke with one of the executives about leasing it from them. "Sorry, Dave. That lot is prime property of 30.000 square feet, and we have plans to build the Ala Moana Shopping Center there. Until recently we leased it to a Cadillac dealer for $1,000 a month."

Knowing it can take a year or two to complete financing on a project like the one they planned, I asked, "Do you have your take-out financing yet?"

"No, but we'll have it before too long."

"I'll pay you $500 a month 'til you need to clear the site – I'll write a check right now for the first and last months," I said.

The executive laughed. "Good try, Dave, but why would we let you have it for $500 a month when we were getting $1,000?"

I replied, "Right now you're not receiving anything for it, right?"

He excused himself and left the room, returned within five minutes, and offered his hand. I wrote a check for $1,000. No contract was ever signed. I've never dealt with anyone with more integrity.

The next weeks were busy and exciting ones. In 1957 car dealers in Hawaii did not detail-out cars. They just painted prices on the windshields and put them on the lot. The engines were grimy and so were the cars, inside and out. The car lots usually had drab old shacks as offices; cars were parked haphazardly on the lot – no showmanship!

We painted the hollow-tile office white with coral trim and installed air conditioning. I repainted the light poles in spiraling blue and white stripes so they looked like candy canes. We put up bright lights and surrounded the lot with colored plastic flags. Professionals painted white lines on the pavement for 150 cars. I ordered two electric turntables from the mainland to feature "show cars." I had metal signs made that attached to the tops of the cars; one side read "Dave Ford Motors" and the other said, "ENTER AND BE SAVED!" in gold on white. On the roof of the office a sign said, "Dave Ford Motors, Home of Hawaii's Finest Cars." Music played over loudspeakers installed at the entrance facing bustling Kapiolani Boulevard. I proudly parked the yellow Cad right next to the entrance. I was having the time of my life – until I went to buy recent-model trade-ins from new-car dealers.

Creativity comes in small packages

The car dealers preferred not to have any competition from a young newcomer from the mainland with new ideas about marketing. Every one of them smiled and said, "Sorry, we don't have any cars for sale." I went to the banks and finance companies. Lending institutions would not advance me money, even though they would hold titles to the cars; they were in cahoots with the car dealers. What could a guy possibly do to outsmart them? I sat in my newly painted office and lit up a joint and...

A unique idea flashed. I would buy cars *retail!* These guys didn't know a sharp car from a rough one. I remembered that the Chevrolet dealer I'd approached had 10 1954 Chevrolets lined up in a row, each with the Blue Book price on the windshield. I knew that a sharp car will bring more than retail. I returned to the Chevy dealer. Two of the cars had low mileage and not a dent on them. One of them had smooth tires. I drove them and assured myself they were excellent condition. "I'll buy these two," I said, writing out a check for the full amount. "I'll have them picked up in two hours so you have time to confirm that my check is good."

Revisiting other dealers, I ended up buying 12 cars, with the same general result. The sales staff looked at me and laughed, clearly thinking, "This young idiot will be out of business in a month!" I had new tires installed on the cars that needed them. I hired two Coast Guard mechanics who had some spare time. They appreciated the opportunity to work on their days and evenings off at $1.60 an hour, and I had such confidence in their workmanship that I felt safe in offering a 30-day guarantee on every car.

I had the engines steam-cleaned and painted in the original factory colors, and the cars waxed and polished 'til they sparkled. They both looked and drove like new. I wanted the buyers to be proud of their cars.

Two of the cars now rotated on the electric turntables, a kind of exhibition not seen before in Hawaii.

Now I needed to get customers to the lot. I realized that newspaper stories attract more readers and interest than paid ads. Another joint came to my assistance. It made me recall a local women's organization called the Outdoor Circle, whose members included the wives of Hawaii's top business executives. They policed signs to see that they were in good taste, and the media were solidly behind them. (That support was at least partly self-interested: those ladies' husbands bought ads.)

I summoned a sign-maker and ordered a folding sign, six feet high, and put it up facing Kapiolani Boulevard. One side of the sign read "WANTED! Sharp CARS. CASH! HAWAII'S FINEST – DAVE FORD MOTORS." On the reverse side was the silhouette of a woman, obviously nude. Two days later the good ladies of the Outdoor Circle took the bait.

"Mr. Ford, *that* sign is to come down immediately. Humph!" I was polite, but made no promises, and they took their indignation to the media.

The next day a large photo of the silhouette of the nude lady appeared in Hawaii's major newspaper, *The Honolulu Advertiser.* Dozens of people came to see this "naughty" sign. Our first sale was to one of the onlookers, who paid $400 over Blue Book. My cars rolled out the door.

I then phoned the newspaper and told them we were about to dress the lady on the sign and asked if they would like to take a photo of the event. Out came a photographer, who snapped pictures as the artist made the "dramatic" (and entirely pre-arranged) changes. The next day another large photo in the paper showed the artist at work. The story read:

REAL COOL NUDE GETS PROTECTION FROM CHILL
Well, the eye-catching girl on the sign at Dave Ford Motors on Kapiolani Boulevard is still there, but she's better fortified now to protect her against the current wintry blasts.

Three weeks ago Dave Ford, manager and owner of the firm, decided business was a bit slack. He figured he needed a sign to lure customers, and what lures 'em better than a fetching-looking gal? So he painted a sign and embellished it with a nude girl. It was just a simple line drawing – a side view – and left everything to the imagination.

People stopped to look – almost everyone is an artist, in his own way, when it comes to a shapely form. Business picked up and Dave likes business.

On Tuesday, the Outdoor Circle drove past. Said Dave: "The lady introduced herself, pointed to the sign, and said she was a representative of the Outdoor Circle and that the sign had to go. She said that sort of art might be okay in San Francisco, but not in Hawaii. She was very firm, and I could see she meant business," said Dave, who, as we said, likes business.

Well, the sign was too expensive to tear down so Dave decided to give the young lady a new spring outfit. All it took was a paint brush. "Her former glorious self is now only a memory," sighed Dave when an Advertiser photographer came to call. The girl on the sign is wearing a hula skirt and a halter top. "Whoever is going to look at her now?" said Dave.

Well, *I* looked at her, every day, and thanked her for shivering, naked and unprotected, in the icy winds of a Hawaiian winter for a few days to get my business off to a flying start.

My dear Hazel was the healthiest she had been in a long time, partly because at this time she was visiting a psychologist twice a week. I gave her a two-year-old air-conditioned Oldsmobile that she loved to drive. She would sometimes meet me for lunch and we'd go to the Ala Moana Beach Park. We'd swim and visit for an hour or so, and enjoy some wonderful Hawaiian dishes for lunch, and then I'd return to work. I still did not smoke grass at home, but that was no hardship because, like the majority of pot smokers, I used only two to three joints a week. Grass smoking in Hawaii was casual and generally accepted; people either drank liquor or smoked grass. "No big t'ing, brah," as they'd say in Hawaii.

Business picked up and I hired three salesmen. People began coming in to sell their cars. I kept only the sharpest ones. Any trade-ins I took that I couldn't put in top condition I wholesaled to other car dealers.

I ordered professionally painted Masonite placards – *$25.00 Down!* – and placed them on the windshields of our cars. The other car dealers told me I was crazy, and cheerfully gave me such conventional advice as, "Hey brah, you go broke selling cars for $25 down."

I just laughed and said, "Maybe you right, brah."

But they weren't. Here's how the $25 down worked: We took the $25 subject to financing. We informed the client that the total monthly payment would be $100. If we could obtain financing, the $25 applied to the purchase price; if not, we returned the money in full. The gimmick was that we used two lenders, a bank and a finance company. We would take a credit application and call a finance company for a signature loan of $300, to be repaid at $25 a month. The $300 would go to the bank as the down payment on a conventional auto loan to be repaid at $75 a month. Total payment: $100 a month. If the customer's credit history was good, most banks were happy to accept $300 as a down payment on just about any car up to $2,500.

We began doing the first television advertising for cars in Hawaii. A mobile television crew would come to us and we'd do live commercials. In one, the sales crew carried a very light car over to the camera and one shouted, "Yo, Dave! Here one car folks will like. Good mileage this one!" In another, I popped out of the trunk of one of the cars. I'd invite the folks to come in for a demo ride, and enjoy free coffee and doughnuts.

Cannabis again became my medicine

I had the mechanics reconstruct a 1932 Ford coupe, a classic "Deuce," install a V8 engine with "full house," and turn it into a racing stock car. The door carried a big number 82 and *Dave Ford Motors*, and I raced it at the Honolulu Stadium each Saturday night during racing season. It was a thrill to be lined up at the starting line, revving up the engine, trying to keep from letting the clutch out until the light turned from red to green. Then, suddenly, we were peeling rubber and screaming down the track.

There were some fine local guys who really knew how to drive their stock cars. And it seemed as though they weren't too concerned whether they (or I) got killed. They knew how to cut off a new guy and drive him into the wall for some brutal smash-ups. Just being able to walk away from one of those crashes was a victory in itself! Ambulances were always standing by. It was during one of those early crashes that I injured my back. Several orthopedic surgeons told me I needed surgery to correct a damaged disc. Before surgery, I was prescribed heavy medication, Vicodin for pain and Valium for muscle relaxation. These drugs made me sick to my stomach much of the time, and I began to feel physically addicted.

The third surgeon I visited was amazing. "Mr. Ford, don't ever have surgery on your back unless there is nothing else that will eliminate the problem and the pain." He then demonstrated some exercises I was to do.

"I've followed your exploits in the papers," said the doctor, "including your auto racing. Can I tell you something in total confidence?"

"Yes, doctor," I said.

Then he blew me out with his knowledge, and courage. "Mr. Ford, if you know someone who has some top-quality marijuana, you should try it. It'll eliminate those muscle spasms, as well as reducing the pain."

"Thank you, doctor, you're amazing. I already smoke grass for relaxation, creativity, and sometimes for sleep. Now I'll use it as medicine." With the aid of the grass, and exercises, I keep my back pain and spasms under control to this day.

After learning to hold my own on the racetrack with the local drivers, I elected to play it safe and let one of our mechanics race the car.

No other dealers competed with our type of advertising, or with our attractive detailing of the cars. Before the end of our first year, dealers gave up attempting to drive me out of business. They began inviting me to buy their new-car trade-ins. The banks all but begged me to borrow money from them; one gave me an expensive gold pen set. I thanked them all, but told them we didn't need them anymore. By the end of that first year, we had netted $84,000, and had over 50 cars on the lot, all paid for. (I credit most of the creativity for our success to grass.)

Suddenly pot dried up on Oahu. Pot smokers switched to alcohol or other drugs. After a few months without grass, one day someone offered me a cigarette. I was not aware of their horrible addiction rate. I really didn't like nicotine, but began smoking it anyway.

A couple who had purchased a car from us invited Hazel and me to dinner several times on the luxurious fifty-foot yacht they lived on. Two staterooms had king-sized beds, there was a modern galley, a bar, and even a grand piano. One evening Donald and Janet phoned and invited us to join them and another couple to go water skiing the following morning. Hazel was thrilled. The plan was that Donald and I would take the yacht to Kehii Lagoon, about 10 miles west of the Honolulu Yacht Club. "This tub needs the cobwebs blown out, but even at full cruising speed it's a lot slower than John's speedboat. He can take the ladies joyriding while we transport this slow tub. Then we'll have a barbecue on board and all hit the skis," said Donald.

We cast off at 9 a.m. on a balmy Sunday. The twin diesels were purring as we moved out of the harbor. "Do we have plenty of fuel?" I asked.

"Sure do. Five hundred gallons of diesel and 10 gallons of extra gas stowed below for the speedboat."

Two uneventful hours later we anchored in the smooth waters of the lagoon. Donald cut the engines while I was on the top deck filling the barbecue with charcoal. Donald said, "Why don't we get the coals going? When the gang joins us, all we'll have to do is throw on the steaks and grab the salad from the reefer."

I squirted charcoal lighter over the coals and Donald tossed me a lighter. *An American In Paris*, one of my favorites, was playing on the hi-fi as I thumbed the lighter near the charcoal. There was a violent explosion, and I flew like a rocket. Before I knew it, I was under water, then another explosion brought me to the surface. I instinctively put my hand to my face. It felt numb. Where was Donald? my confused mind asked. Where are my shoes? And where is my nose? My face must be blown apart. Don't panic, I kept repeating to myself, thankful for my lifeguard experience.

I could barely see. Explosions continued. I yelled for Donald until I realized it would be impossible for anyone to hear my voice over the continuing explosions. Moments later a speedboat came by and a man helped me in. "Have you seen anyone else in the water?" I implored.

"Only you," yelled the man.

"How bad is my face?" I stammered.

"It wouldn't look bad if you'd wipe the seaweed off of it."

I wiped off the slick seaweed and again gingerly felt my face. "I'm OK," I said mostly to myself, "my nose is back."

Now that the explosions had stopped, I started yelling for Donald again.

"How did the explosion happen?" asked my rescuer.

"I don't know. Could you please circle the boat and see if we can find my friend?"

"Could that be him running along the shore?"

"Yes!" I said with great relief. "Could you please take me as close as you can to the shore?"

He eased in to about 20 feet from the rocky shoreline. I thanked him and slipped into the water. The concussion had blown my shoes off, and my feet began to bleed as I waded ashore and ran along the rocky beach yelling for my friend.

We moved to Hawaii in February 1957 and opened "Dave Ford Motors – Home of Hawaii's Finest Cars." Pot helped me create promotions like the $25 down payment. "Hey brah, you go broke selling cars for $25 down!" The first year we netted $84,000.

Photo: Honolulu Sodium

Racing our hopped-up '32 Ford publicized the auto agency – and injured my back. Cannabis saved me from surgery.

Real Cool Nude Gets
Protection From Chill

Well, the eye-catching girl on the sign at Dave Ford Motors on Kapiolani Blvd. is still there, but she's better fortified now to protect her against the current wintry blasts.

Three weeks ago Dave Ford, manager of the firm, decided business was a bit slack. He figured he needed a sign to lure customers, and what lures 'em better than a fetching-looking gal?

* * *

SO HE PAINTED a sign and embellished it with a nude girl.

It was just a simple line drawing—a side view — and left everything to the imagination.

People stopped to look. Almost everyone is an artist, in his own way, when it comes to a shapely form. Business picked up and Dave likes business.

ON TUESDAY, the Outdoor Circle drove past.

Said Dave, "The lady introduced herself, pointed to the sign and said she was a representative of the Outdoor Circle and that the sign HAD to go.

"She said that sort of art might be okay in San Francisco, but not in Hawaii.

"She was very firm. I could see she meant business," said Dave who likes business.

* * *

WELL, THE sign was too expensive to tear down so Dave decided to give the young lady a new spring outfit.

All it took was a paint brush.

"Her former glorious self is now only a memory," sighed Dave when an Advertiser photographer came to call.

The girl on the sign is wearing a hula skirt and bra.

"Who ever is going to look at her now?" said Dave.

Honolulu Advertiser

*Our nude lady got dressed when the good ladies of the Outdoor Circle applied pressure —
very public pressure, exactly as planned!*

When I reached Donald, he was sitting on a rock with his face in his hands, sobbing. "Thank God you're OK, Dave. But our boat! We must get to a phone and call the Coast Guard and see if they can locate the speedboat."

He exclaimed, "What an idiot I am! I forgot that gasoline fumes seek the lowest point and can fill up a boat. I should never have stored the gas below." He paused, and I could see a memory cross his face. "Geez! I was about to go below and get us a cold beer. Another couple of seconds and I would have been blown to bits."

We spotted John's speedboat and waved our hands. They came as close to shore as possible, dropped the anchor, and waded to shore. Hazel put her arms around me and said, "Thank God you and Donald are OK."

Insurance covered a portion of their loss. Within six months they bought another yacht of about the same size, and invited us to join them on the maiden voyage. We politely declined.

Death of a salesman

One of our best car salesmen was 50-year-old Addison Smith. "Ad" was a fine salesman who helped the business grow to seven sales people in just over a year. The only disappointing thing about Ad was his smoking. I smoked nicotine then too, but Ad *always* had a cigarette smoldering in an ashtray or dangling from his mouth.

His almost constant cough worried me. "How about quitting, Ad?" I'd ask.

"Come on, Coach," he'd tell me. "Give me a break! I can't quit; I've tried too many times. I'm down to two packs a day!"

"At least see a doctor, will ya?" I begged.

After several weeks of nagging, Ad finally did see a doctor. A few days later he took me aside. "Uh, Coach, I think I need a little time off." I told him we'd miss him at the lot, and urged him to get well soon.

A week later I learned that Ad was in Queen's Medical Center in Honolulu. I went to visit him. "How are you doing, pal?" I asked.

"Oh, I'm fine, Coach. Just a little case of lung cancer."

I was dazed.

Ad smiled and reached under his pillow and removed a pack of Lucky Strikes (a jarring brand name, just then). He flipped one between his lips and lit up.

"You've got to be kidding, Ad. What would your doctor say?"

Ad smiled pathetically, tilting his head, "What the doctor doesn't know won't hurt him!"

"Ad, that's not funny. You've got to quit now," I implored him.

Tears welled up in his sad blue eyes. "I can't, Coach."
Three weeks later Ad was dead.

• • •

Hazel and I enjoyed our one-bedroom apartment with the swimming pool right outside our front door. The coconut trees swayed with the balmy trade winds, and the two-story building's Hawaiian architecture was idyllic and relaxing. We both wanted children and we were now convinced it was time to begin. We were 29. Hazel now seemed less affected by her father's molestation. She still visited the psychologist twice a week, but she was stable. My love and admiration for her was complete. Our love for each other convinced me children could now be a blessing. By August of 1958 it was confirmed that Hazel was pregnant. We were both elated.

Hazel was doing beautifully with her pregnancy. She watched her diet, we swam almost every day, and she got plenty of sleep. We went to shows, picnics at various beaches, and sometimes to dances. We enjoyed dinners at friends' homes, and had them to dinner at our little apartment.

The car business was going well, too. We enjoyed an exceedingly content clientele, and we were now giving a conditional one-year guarantee on our cars. One of our customers recommended us to the wife of world-renowned criminal attorney George T. Davis, and she bought a car from us for their son. So did the wife of one of the executives of the Dole Pineapple Company.

One afternoon a local man, unmistakably a descendant of the original islanders, came to our agency, parked the Chevrolet that he had purchased from us, removed the keys, and handed them to me. With a face that might have been chipped out of granite, he said, "I don't like this car and I want my money back."

I told him that I'd be happy to talk to him about it, and invited him into the office. Hazel happened to be present. I pulled his file. He'd had the car for only two weeks. "Would you care to share the problem with us?" I asked.

"My wife doesn't like the color, and the brakes are bad. I should have known better than to deal with a *haole* (Caucasian) car dealer. I don't trust them."

Hazel's exquisite thick black hair almost stood up on the back of her neck. "Don't you talk about my husband that way! There is no more honest person in Hawaii than Dave. I can tell you that if there is

Hazel and I eager to celebrate New Year's Eve in Hawaii

something wrong with the brakes, Dave will have it fixed. Now, what's the real reason you've brought this pretty car back?"

Abashed by her outburst, the hard edges in his face softened. "The fact is after I bought the car a local buddy of mine said if I could get my money back he'd sell me one for $200 less."

I asked, "If your brakes are repaired, which we'll do, don't you feel that you'll be happy with this car?"

"Yeah. And I'm sorry. I was just feelin' bad that I didn't buy the car from my old buddy."

Our handsome son is born

March 6, 1959. The exciting day arrived and our son was born at Kapiolani Maternity hospital in Honolulu. Both Hazel and our little David Guy were in great spirits. Hazel had a relatively easy birth and our son was perfect in every way. That was my Father's Day!

When I took my two dearest ones back to our apartment we were met by applause from our friendly neighbors as well as a visit from our manager. After complimenting us on our son, she said, "As you both know, we don't allow children. In order to be fair to the other tenants, I have to give you the standard month's notice to find another apartment." Within a week I had located a cozy guest cottage on Kahala Avenue, just above Diamond Head. It had a swimming pool, which we were invited to use. Hazel and I would tow little David around the pool on a water mattress. He loved it.

We had found a house lot in the Waialae Golf-Course Subdivision, directly across from the Kahala Hilton Hotel. I sketched floor plans that Hazel liked, and we retained Hawaii's most prestigious building contractor, Pacific Builders, to construct the home for us and install a swimming pool. Eventually, it would also have maid's quarters and a Japanese-style guest cottage.

As Hazel recuperated from the birth, we opened a second car agency. We had been informed that the Ala Moana Shopping Center would be breaking ground within 60 days so we needed another location. And big changes were about to take place.

On August 21, 1959, Hawaii became the fiftieth state. Less than two months earlier, on June 30, a Qantas Boeing 707 had touched down at Honolulu International Airport, introducing jet travel to Hawaii and greatly expanding tourism. Before statehood, residents were much like a big family, but the atmosphere seemed to change overnight. In 1959,

243,000 people visited the Islands. Today, tourism is an $11 billion industry employing more than 180,000 people.

● ● ●

When David was three months old, we took him down to the ocean. Hazel and I had spent many hours swimming at the foot of Diamond Head, while above us sprawled the awesome mansion belonging to Doris Duke, heiress of the Duke tobacco fortune. The home is comparable to the palace William Randolph Hearst built at San Simeon, California. We fantasized about someday being invited to visit the Duke mansion. Ultimately I did make that visit... but not with dear Hazel.

Ms. Duke had hoped to moor her yacht in the cove where we now swam. The sleepless, capricious ocean, however, had other ideas, and wouldn't allow any boat to anchor there. For us, though, the water's restlessness was part of the attraction. The rough water surging in and out of the little cove was exhilarating to swim and play in. Some of the most fulfilling times of my life were spent there with Hazel and little David. We wanted to teach him to love the ocean, so in the swift-flowing shallows we would take turns raising him high over our heads, then plunging him into the rough ocean water. He rewarded us with the music of laughter that only a baby can give you.

Almost every week I would take his little foot and place it against one of mine. It was so tiny, and yet I could already see rapid growth. He rarely cried, and he would look right into our eyes with his big baby-blues and give us a toothless smile.

Breaking a world record – aided by pot

The media reported that Dr. A. Leonard Diamond, professor of psychology at the University of Hawaii's Psychological Research Center, was about to conduct a project on sensory deprivation. The project team was seeking a volunteer. Captivated, I visited him and asked how they planned to run the experiment.

He replied, "We feel that if a volunteer is submerged in murky water for at least 24 hours we can accomplish our goal. We'll learn a substantial amount regarding human isolation. We'll be studying both the physiological and psychological reactions."

"Dr. Diamond, if I could put the entire project together could I be that volunteer?"

"I can't see why not, so long as you can prepare yourself physically."

I asked that he write me a letter stating their objective, and acknowledging that they had selected me as the subject. When he handed me the letter we shook hands on the agreement.

All my life, I've enjoyed taking risks, pushing out the edge of the envelope, but only when I was convinced I had a good chance to accomplish the goal safely. This project was especially attractive to me because the information gathered might help others. As a father and husband, I was concerned about the risks of the dive, but I was convinced that with proper training the risk would be minimal.

Helped by industrialist Henry J. Kaiser

The day after my meeting with Dr. Diamond I made an appointment to meet with Henry J. Kaiser "regarding a scientific project to be conducted by the University of Hawaii." After recollecting our first encounter, he agreed to meet me at his new Kaiser Foundation Hospital in Honolulu.

I explained that my plan was to get the U.S. Navy to provide the necessary diving rig and teach me how to dive, and that we would need medical doctors to monitor me before, during, and after the submersion. Mr. Kaiser was intrigued. "If you're willing to take that kind of risk, David, the very least we can do is to provide all the necessary medical assistance you require. If you should need hospitalization at any time, rest assured that our facility will be totally available at no cost." That generous offer was a thrill, coming from probably the world's greatest industrialist and one of the finest men I ever had the pleasure to know.

Mr. Kaiser owned the NBC television and radio affiliates in Hawaii. I suggested that, if his engineers could install a microphone inside the helmet of my diving suit, I would broadcast every 20 minutes, 24 hours a day, and report my physical condition.

"That's a splendid idea. If you get the diving outfit, I will see that our engineers accomplish what you suggest." (During our conversation I learned that Mr. Kaiser was up every morning at 3 a.m. so that he could telephone his companies around the world.)

Next I made an appointment to visit the Navy commander at Pearl Harbor. I told him that this would be a fine opportunity to improve the antiquated design of the standard diving rig. "I'll give you a call and let you know if we want to be involved," he said.

It seemed that it would also be a good opportunity to attempt to break the underwater world record, which had been set accidentally by a Navy diver in 1944. After the Japanese attack on Pearl Harbor on December 7, 1941, the Navy began a salvage operation that was still under way in 1944. A deep sea diver had been using a torch to cut through the heavy plates of one of the ships in Pearl Harbor's West Loch, when the ship rolled, and buried him alive in the mud. His air lines were intact, but it took other divers days to dig him out. He was pinned down there for 74 hours and 55 minutes, a world record. We could only imagine the terror he endured before he was finally rescued.

The following day the Navy phoned to say that it wanted to be a part of this scientific research. The next challenge was to line up a large shirt manufacturer, Hale Niu, to donate 50 green shirts that would be imprinted with their trade name and *Underwater Medical Research Team*. The shirts would be worn by the volunteers who served food to the

Navy divers, members of the University of Hawaii's department of psychology, and others who would aid in the mammoth project. I enlisted the Hawaiian Land Company, a subsidiary of Dillingham Corporation, who promised to provide two cranes, (in case one failed when it was necessary to bring the diver – me! – to the surface) and operators at the submersion site around the clock. Finally, we needed a platform that could be submerged.

The owner of Pacific Builders, Jim Humpert, agreed to construct a platform with a large wooden chair that would be anchored to the floor so that the diver could sit in it. I suggested that they paint their name and logo on the platform, as the entire event would be covered by radio and television. "Agreed!"

In addition to his dozens of international corporations, Mr. Kaiser told me about his upcoming construction of an entire community. "It will be named Hawaii Kai, and will be located on 6,000 acres of Bishop Estate land. It will be a planned community for 60,000 people, featuring 12,000 homes, seven schools, and 2,000 one-acre parks. Included will be businesses, shopping centers, high-rise condominiums, and waterways to the ocean, as well as a golf course." It's worth noting that he was in his late 70s when he took on this last project, and completed it.

As much as I was tempted, I didn't have the temerity to ask Mr. Kaiser if he smoked grass. I daydreamed about asking him, and hearing him answer, "Of course. How else could one person come up with so many successful ideas and completed projects?" I could also imagine the DEA saying, "If he hadn't smoked marijuana, he might have *really* amounted to something!"

U.S. Navy trains me to be a diver

The diving rig weighed 210 pounds. On the inside of the helmet were two plungers that the diver operated with his chin. One valve brought air into the suit, one expelled it. If a diver is fatigued he may accidentally press the intake air valve, filling the suit with too much air. In that case the buoyancy of the suit and the weight of the brass helmet blows the diver upside down, and in a second or two water can fill the helmet, and drown him before he has a hope of getting right side up again. It was vital that the correct actions become automatic. I had some practicing to do!

To train for the experiment, I worked out at the YMCA each day for two hours, using the punching bag, swimming, and riding an exercycle.

From home I jogged three miles and then swam two miles in the ocean. As the big day drew near, Navy divers trained me for three weeks in the ocean near Pearl Harbor.

A site near Fisherman's Wharf in Honolulu was selected for the dive. Cranes, generators, and tables for sensitive instruments were assembled. The Kodak company provided motion-picture film to record the event. TV crews staked out sites for their cameras, and tents were set up for divers who would be tending me during the experiment. More tents were erected to create space for 80 volunteers who would support the technical crew; and of course one for the University of Hawaii's Department of Psychology. Engineers from Kaiser Broadcasting Company began working around the clock to wire the helmet for radio broadcasting, carefully sealing all the wiring.

Hazel enjoyed watching me work out. As the arrangements moved rapidly toward the day of the dive, I was asked to give a press conference. Newspapers, radio, and television did stories each day about the dive and increased public interest. Photographers began following me as I jogged, swam, and worked out at the Y. I was receiving weekly physicals at Kaiser Hospital from my appointed physician, Dr. Sing. He was scheduled to be at the dive site or on call during the entire submersion. The press was told that I wanted to remain under water for 80 hours.

I go for the record

Finally the day arrived, Thursday, October 23, 1959. At 8 a.m., Fisherman's Wharf looked as if preparations were being made to send a man to Mars. Several hundred curious onlookers watched from the sidelines. Generators and cranes filled much of the space on the wharf, and an ambulance stood nearby.

Numerous newspaper stories now quoted Dr. Diamond's statement that "The experiment will lead to important knowledge of human reactions to isolation." Professional deep-sea diver E. R. Cross, as well as members of the U.S. Navy, wanted to know specifically what breaks down first in a man – the mental or the physical function.

Operators stood by a vast array of medical equipment in a large tent that was my first stop when I arrived. The medical team shaved areas of my scalp, chest, and legs, and attached electrodes to capture brain waves with an electroencephalograph and to monitor heart function with an electrocardiograph. Dials and gauges for all the medical apparatus, including the intercom, were tested and re-tested.

TV cameras gaped at me and radio and TV personalities interviewed me while I was being prepped. In an unprecedented innovation, a urinator was connected to the diving suit. The national *MD Medical News Magazine* had flown a reporter and photographer from the mainland. As a technician began to insert a rectal thermometer about the size of a marking pen, the *MD* photographer edged forward to shoot a picture, but at that point, I put my foot down.

The Navy men helped me into the suit. Before they put the helmet on, I asked to kiss Hazel and my handsome seven-month-old son. I would have liked to hold them in my arms but I was too wired up. Finally two Navy men hoisted the helmet, placed it over my head, and bolted it into place. It was now 1:20 p.m.

"This is Dr. Diamond, David. Can you hear me?"

"Yes," I answered, "loud and clear."

"Dave, this is the engineer. Please do a radio check."

Everything seemed to check out OK. I felt like The Man in the Iron Mask, claustrophobic and apprehensive. The hissing of the air began. I asked them to open the faceplate and wipe my face; sweat had run into my eyes. Then I was asked to stand up and walk twenty feet to the platform. The suit itself now weighed 215 pounds. I weighed 185. It took all the strength I had to walk to and climb onto the platform, and slowly sit down in the oversized chair that would be my home for the next three days and nights. The crane with its 30-foot boom gently began lifting the platform and swinging around to lower me into the Pacific waters of the Kewalo Basin. I could see people waving and saluting. I couldn't hear anything but the hiss of air entering the helmet.

I gave an awkward salute to Hazel and our son, and threw them a kiss. There was now no way I could get out of this on my own. I had to trust the good people around me, and their equipment. My thoughts raced, and not in the happiest directions. If the generator failed and the emergency generator wasn't started immediately, I'd use up the air in the helmet in three minutes, and suffocate – not exactly a comforting thought at this stage of the operation. The platform sank beneath the surface and green-blue water slowly rose to envelop me, and closed over my head. Visibility was no more than two feet. The sounds of hissing air and escaping bubbles were all that I could hear until a ghostly voice broke through.

"This is Len Diamond, Dave. Are you OK? Are you getting enough air?"

"Yes," I answered. "I'm OK."

The University of Hawaii needed a volunteer for a study of sensory deprivation. After weeks of training by Navy divers, I was lowered into the Kewalo Basin to begin a planned 80 hours underwater. That brass helmet was heavy – and, Hawaii or not, that water soon got cold.

Perhaps the world's greatest industrialist, Henry J. Kaiser created Kaiser Steel, Kaiser Aluminum, Kaiser Broadcasting, Kaiser Permanente hospitals, and many other companies. He built hotels, ships, dams, and highways, and supported my record-breaking dive wholeheartedly. And he was my friend.

"Let us know when you reach the bottom, Dave. The platform is sinking rapidly now. Sorry there's such poor visibility in this area, but as you know, that's necessary to the experiment. You'll do just fine. We know that from all the tests you've taken. You're well prepared. But remember, if you're able to remain down there for 12 hours you will begin to suffer from sensory deprivation. You will begin to wonder where you are. You will become disoriented. And that's what we need to happen. Do you hear me, Dave?"

"Yes, I hear you." Moments later there was a shaking thud as the platform settled onto the muddy bottom and into three feet of silt. Clouds of mud reduced visibility to zero. I tested an old cliché: I truly couldn't see my hand in front of my face. I felt as though I were blindfolded and turning in circles. In about a half hour the slurry of mud settled back to the ocean floor, and visibility went all the way back up to two feet.

Dr. Diamond administered tests of mental agility, to provide a baseline for comparison with results of similar tests after the physical and mental deterioration to come.

The suit leaked from the beginning. Within three hours the water was up to my neck and my teeth were chattering. Broadcasting and answering questions from the psychologists, adjusting air with my chin, and constantly concentrating on not being blown upside down kept me busy but not warm. I was already becoming fatigued, largely by the shivering. Water should not have come into the suit for several more hours. The leaks were later attributed to the holes drilled through the breastplate of the suit for the wires connected to my body. After 12 hours I was feeling the claustrophobia divers commonly experience during long dives.

A quarter-inch copper tube had been cut through the helmet and led to where my mouth could accept liquid food. "It's time for your feeding, Dave." Down came two divers. They had improvised a rubber bag that was filled with Sustagen, a high-protein, high-calorie, low-residue liquid which also included vitamin supplements. Over the course of the dive they added to the Sustagen 1,300 milligrams of Noludar, a hypnotic. The drug's purpose was to make me more susceptible to sensory deprivation and hallucinations (it worked!) and at the same time to help me relax as much as possible under the circumstances. The liquid squirted into my mouth as a diver rolled up the bag like a tube of toothpaste.

Kaiser Broadcasting covered the dive as promised. Every 20 minutes whoever was on the air for them would cut in and ask me what I was experiencing.

"Can you see any fish down there, Dave?"

"Sure do," I answered, and described the types and sizes of fish that swam close enough for me to see them.

Local radio stars George Groves and Hal Lewis were on top of the project, and were excellent. It was clear in their interviews that they were truly concerned about my teeth chattering after just three hours under water, and about my general health. I could tell that to them I wasn't just broadcasting fodder, some guy pulling a stunt.

I want cannabis down my air line

Twice, two young ladies in scuba gear swam up to the face plate and kissed it. I smiled, and they performed a little water ballet within two feet of me. Several times the support crew put Hazel on the radio to talk to me, and that was a tremendous boost for my morale. Then came the voice of Dr. Diamond.

"Dave, you've been down there now for 36 hours. We've gotten some fine information. The longer you stay down, the more useful information we can obtain. What do you say? It's totally up to you."

The water temperature was 18 degrees lower than my body temperature and the cold was biting into my bones. I told them I'd stay down as long as I could stand it, but my body was feeling as if I'd been locked into a medieval torture chamber. Bones and joints that weren't becoming cramped and cold were entangled by wires and tubes, and were numb. I thought: if only someone could blow a few hits of grass down my air line, it would make the pain and discomfort go away.

Loneliness was overwhelming me. I couldn't sleep, or so I thought. Suddenly I was paralyzed by fear: I had blown upside down and I was drowning! I saw a fence covered with snow as the cold murky water closed around my face. God, I moaned, why did I allow myself to get into this intolerable environment, to die like this and leave Hazel and our little son? The bubbles were now coming out of my mouth as I gasped for a last breath of air.

"Dave, this is Dr. Spicer. Why did you scream? You've been asleep for almost two hours."

My body was shaking and convulsed with cold. "Am I asleep?" I asked.

"No, you're awake now. Apparently you've been hallucinating. You must eat. You refused your last feeding."

"I'm so cold, so cold," I heard myself saying, over and over.

"This time, Dave, we've made your drink taste like chocolate. You'll like it. The diver is on his way. It's imperative you drink. This will warm you up."

My body was trembling continuously now and I couldn't stop my teeth from chattering. The urinator did not work, and uric acid fumes were stinging my eyes. I had an inexplicable dread that I was doomed. I ached to go up to the surface; but even stronger was the urge to be a good sport and accept the agony in order to provide as much medical information as possible.

"The divers are there now, Dave. Put your mouth on the feeding tube. Is your mouth on the tube, Dave?"

"Yes. Yes!" I moaned in a haunted raspy voice coming from 185 of pounds of pain. Suddenly the liquid food was squirting all over my face and into my eyes. I was so exhausted I had forgotten to place my mouth over the feeding tube. I must wipe that syrupy liquid out of my eyes. Then my dazed brain realized that was impossible. My intellectual lassitude flashbacks became whimsical. I wanted those "mermaids" to come back to perform again. My right hand and foot were now totally numb.

Seconds from death

Minutes now seemed like hours. "You're doing just fine, Dave," said Dr. Diamond. "You're at 71 hours. Four more hours and you'll have broken the world's record. You have already contributed much to science. Do you still want to remain down for a total of 80 hours? If you do, we'll help you. If not, we're ready to bring you up now."

I was almost deaf and crazed from the hissing air but I murmured, "I'll stay down for the 80 hours." After three days and nights with only an hour or two of sleep, my thinking was far from lucid. Every muscle of my being that wasn't numb or shuddering from cold was in agony from spasms. The thought came to me again: if only some person would exhale some pot down my air hose. It would stop those muscle spasms. I started hallucinating again: I was in our little guest home on Kahala Avenue and Hazel and our son were desperately trying to remove the deep sea diver's helmet from my head.

Before I realized what was happening, I began gasping for breath. I was barely able to make my mouth move. "Please. . . air. . . I'm suffocating!" No answer, and fear turned to hopelessness. The platform was shaking. The heavy wooden chair I was sitting on began to slide off the platform into the ocean. I was barely able to place my numb arm around a cable. The chair vanished. It seemed as though I was moving. Two shadows appeared in wet suits and put their arms around me. Was I dead? That constant, thunderous hissing of the air – stopped. It was peaceful now, not a sound. But I was gasping for air; I was strangling, and the water was up to my chin. Suddenly, brightness shattered the gloom of the murky water. The platform broke the surface of the water, like a breaching whale thrusting its body to the heavens, gasping for air.

But for me there still was no air. Blackness began to envelop me. It seemed that many shadows were holding me upright. One held a large knife and he was raising it as he came toward me. I tried to back away but I couldn't move. The shadow raised the knife and plunged it into the diving suit. I thought he was stabbing me, and that I didn't feel the blade penetrating my body only because I was numb. Water gushed from the suit.

Then suddenly, I could breathe! I sucked in huge gulps of air. The blackness that had been encompassing me began to lighten. The dying cells of my body were coming back to life. I could hear wrenches rapidly turning the brass bolts of the helmet, as the face plate was opened.

As the helmet was lifted off, my chin fell forward onto the breast plate. Hands lifted my head up and a voice said, "Inhale deeply, Dave... that's it." It was Dr. Sing. I began to focus my eyes.

Several voices were speaking at once. "Are you OK now, Dave?" I didn't respond. "Were you aware that the generator quit? We couldn't get the emergency generator to start. We're so sorry." My exhausted brain tried to focus. Another voice: "It's 5:52 p.m., October 25. You just broke the world's record for staying underwater in a deep-sea diving rig. You were down 76 hours and 42 minutes. Congratulations!"

Ambulance doors opened, ready to take me to the hospital. I stared at people surrounding me, and tried to nod, but the flash bulbs were hurting my eyes and the Hawaiian sun was blinding me. I did notice that the shirts of those around me were sweat-soaked.

"Are you OK, Dave?" It was Dr. Sing again.

I answered feebly, "I'm very cold and numb." As they cut the diving suit off me I gazed at my wrinkled white hands. I was in some sharp pain. How I wished someone would put a joint into my mouth! I

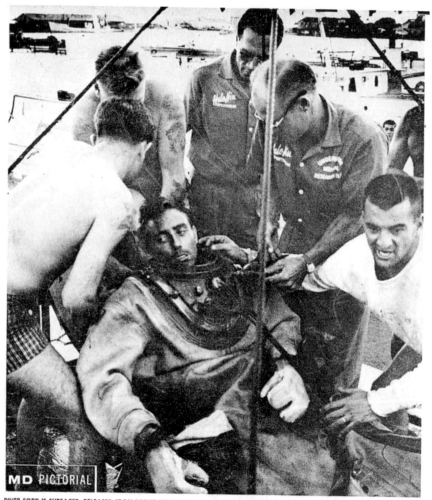

MD PICTORIAL

DIVER FORD IS SURFACED, RELEASED FROM DIVING SUIT AFTER SETTING AN UNDERWATER ENDURANCE RECORD OF 76 HOURS 32 MINUTES

ETIOLOGY OF AN ENDURANCE RECORD

COOPERATING in an unusual research project on human endurance were the University of Hawaii, the United States Navy, Kaiser Medical Center of Honolulu. The object: to put a diver underwater for an undetermined length of time and register effects of prolonged isolation and monotony by depriving him of varieties of sensory stimuli normal to his environment.

MD, AUGUST, 1960

Originally planned to establish an endurance record, the project presented vast possibilities for the study of perceptual distortion and induced schizophrenia. Under the supervision of the University of Hawaii's Psychological Research Department, Kaiser Hospital physicians conducted extensive physical examinations before and after the descent, local merchants

PHOTOGRAPHED BY ROBERT GOODMAN

and radio station contributed a heavy duty crane, diving gear, electronic and sound equipment, food. Navy divers attended the subject during submersion.

The purpose: to measure any corollary between physiologic and psychologic change in a nongravitational atmosphere, demonstrate that preparation for vertigo-like disorientation minimizes panic in the sufferer.

CONTINUED   37

MD Pictorial

The national publication MD Medical News Magazine covered the dive, along with the Hawaiian media. The generator failed, and the emergency generator wouldn't start. When I was hauled to the surface after 76 hours and 42 minutes, I had less than 30 seconds of air left in the helmet.

almost begged for it. An ambulance siren stopped all of the questions from reporters and doctors. The sound was like a trumpet hitting a new impossible note. Men in white now lifted me onto a stretcher.

Navy diver Rocky Cochran climbed into the ambulance with me. As the siren wailed on its way to Kaiser Hospital, he said: "We could have lost you, Dave. We couldn't get the emergency generator started, and the crane wouldn't start! We tried to pull you up by hand, which no doubt severed your intercom wires. We tried telling you not to worry, that we were bringing you up. It must have been terrifying for you, as you could have known only that you were suffocating. Over a minute went by before the crane's engine caught. We divers estimated you had less than 30 seconds of air before you would have passed out."

"How are Hazel and David?" I asked groggily.

"They're just fine. Hazel spent hours down here with your son. She is really proud of you."

At the hospital, I asked if I could have a hot bath. I couldn't stand up. I asked to see a mirror. The stubbly beard was no surprise, but I was shocked when I saw that my lips were blue and cracked. Four competent nurses lifted me into a bathtub, and gently began to wash me. "Please put more cold water in the tub; the water is too hot," I pleaded.

"The water *is* cold, Mr. Ford. We didn't dare put you in warm water." My body was still shuddering from the cold, yet the water felt scalding. Minutes later a gurney arrived and took me to a private room overlooking the ocean. I feebly thanked the nurses for putting hot pads in the bed. "There are none, Mr. Ford. It will take your body several hours to adjust."

A newspaper photographer climbed into the window and shot a couple of pictures, and then was gone. A few minutes later Hazel and our smiling little son appeared in the doorway. I wearily held them in my arms. The next thing I knew, 12 hours had passed and Hazel was back with copies of the *Honolulu Advertiser* and the *Honolulu Star-Bulletin* for the past three days. All had front-page stories of the dive. Two issues of The *Advertiser* gave it banner headlines and included front-page pictures and details of the dive. An *Advertiser* story published the second day began...

DOWN FOR OVER A DAY, DIVER AIMS TO STAY
Diver Dave Ford was still underwater at midnight last night, 35 hours after he slipped below the water of Kewalo Basin on a "mission for science."

...and continued over four columns.

On Monday, October 26th, the *Advertiser* came out with another banner headline: "DIVER DAVE FORD BREAKS ENDURANCE RECORD." There were two front-page pictures with captions below. Another headline read: "COMPRESSOR FAILURE ENDS DIVE." An excerpt:

> Diver Dave Ford emerged from Kewalo Basin at 5:52 p.m. yesterday to claim a new world underwater endurance record of 76 hours and 42 minutes.

It was a five-column story and some of the details told of the medical success of the dive. That was the most important thing to me. The front-page story, with photo, in the *Honolulu Star-Bulletin* stated in part:

> Mechanical trouble with the compressor that pumped air to diver Dave Ford led his handlers to call off the record attempt at 5:52 last night, a few hours short of his 80-hour goal. But a new record for a man in a diving suit of 76 hours, 42 minutes was set, and the scientific research objectives of the "isolation experiment" were completed, according to Dr. Leonard Diamond, University of Hawaii psychologist.
>
> At about 3:45 p.m., Dr. Diamond, who was in charge of the experiment, said: "As far as the University is officially concerned, we have completed our research. It's up to Dave if he wants to go on." Forty-five minutes previously, Ford had seemed determined to go on. His voice, tired and weak-sounding over the intercommunications system, he asked for the time, calculated a few minutes, then said to one of his people, "Let's make the 80-hour goal a reality. I can do it."

I remained in the hospital for three days. Pinched nerves left a thumb and one of my toes numb for several weeks afterward. Uric acid caused sores on my legs that lasted for a month. It was good to be back home with my family. For the first time in my life I had had enough of being in water. I recuperated for a week before returning to the auto agency. I was content to watch as Hazel took our son into the pool, and felt no urge at all to join them.

The August 1960 issue of *MD Medical News Magazine* featured a six-page photo spread that presented a medical perspective of the dive under the title: "Etiology of an Endurance Record." Following are a few quotes:

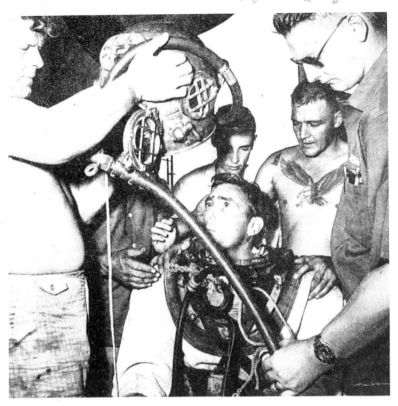

BEFORE AND AFTER his weekend immersion in the waters of Kewalo Basin for 76 hours and 42 minutes, Dave Ford is pictured above and below. Above, the helmet is about to be put in place. Below, immediately after being taken to the hospital after air compressor failure forced an end to his experimental siege, Ford begins his first real rest in a long time.

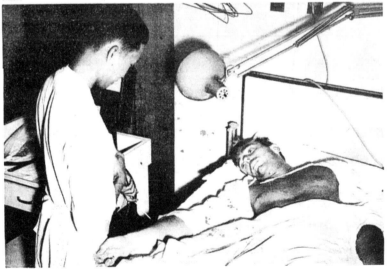

Honolulu Advertiser, October 26, 1959

After three days underwater, I spent three days in the hospital. Navy hard-hat diver Rocky Cochran told me I was lucky to be alive.

Cooperating in an unusual research project on human endurance were the University of Hawaii, the United States Navy, and Kaiser Medical Center of Honolulu. The object: to put a diver underwater for an undetermined length of time and register effects of prolonged isolation and monotony by depriving him of varieties of sensory stimuli normal to his environment. The project presented vast possibilities for the study of perceptual distortion and induced schizophrenia.

Under the supervision of the University of Hawaii's Psychological Research Department, Kaiser Hospital physicians conducted extensive physical examinations before and after the descent. Navy divers attended the subject during submersion. The purpose: to measure any corollary between physiologic change in a nongravitational atmosphere, and to demonstrate that preparation for vertigo-like disorientation minimizes panic in the sufferer.

Having prepared the subject for immersion by intensive investigation into ego motivation and personality structure, clarification of panic responses, anticipation of danger and disorientation, the Hawaiian research team was ready to survey their acquired data: vertigo due to gravitational suspension was produced; visual and auditory distortion occurred with accompanying hallucination."

I was grateful for reports like these. They gave me an external view of an experience that had been intensely internal and personal – but I always felt they shortchanged the contribution of the Navy divers. Through those long three days 12 Navy divers were on site 24 hours a day, to see whether I was in trouble, and rescue me in the event of any emergency. They were not in wet suits. On their dives to check on me they wore only bathing suits and scuba gear. Several of them were badly stung by jellyfish. I will never forget their courage and help.

During those years, television's *Sea Hunt* series, starring Lloyd Bridges, was one of the most popular TV shows ever. Bridges was in Hawaii at the time of the dive, and while I was still in the hospital he extended me a dinner invitation. He treated me to dinner at *The House Of The Golden Dragon,* a restaurant in the Hilton Hawaiian Village Hotel, and we enjoyed chatting about diving and his film career as we smiled for photographers.

I recuperated rapidly, and within a month I was back to normal physically – and I eventually returned to playing in the swimming pool with Hazel and David.

Pot helps me make an adventurous career change

Business had never been better at our auto agency. Hundreds of people came in to visit and ask about the dive project, and we made many new friends and customers over the months following the dive. Our new home was completed in time for Christmas, 1959, so we celebrated by bringing my parents over from the mainland. They had never met their grandson, whom they had adored via pictures and our praiseful reports. They were especially gratified that shortly after they arrived, David took his first steps. He was just over nine months old, and we thought he was the most brilliant child in the world. We began teaching him to swim when he was a year old.

Shortly after the dive we had another visitor. Jim Humpert, Pacific Builders president, came to our auto company one day. "Dave, I want you to come work for me. I've scrutinized your operation and have been amazed at your promotional skills. I recently learned that you are now the third largest car dealer in Hawaii, and no doubt rated first-class in creative advertising. Have you had any experience in the construction business?"

I briefed him on what I had done in that field. I understood that he had 300 men on his payroll, and did little sub-contracting. "What did you have in mind, Jim?"

"I want you to be my sales manager. I doubt I can pay what you're currently making. However, like me, you'd drive a new white Cadillac convertible every year. You'd get credit cards for entertaining and for gas. Also, any big deals you put together, I'd cut you in as a partner."

"Let's go to lunch and chat about it," I suggested.

We lunched at Canlis. "Dave, I've run Pacific Builders for five years. I'm convinced we construct the finest homes in Hawaii. Yet I'm losing around a hundred thousand a year. I need someone who obviously knows business and promotion to turn Pacific Builders around. What do you say?"

I had been feeling the time was ripe for a new challenge, so I said I'd take a look, and we agreed in principle on a salary. "I'll get out of the car business within six months," I said, "since it would take me that long to move our inventory."

I paid for the lunch. Jim grinned. "Do you know that you're the first person who ever picked up a tab when they were with me? Everyone thinks because I have money, why should they pick it up?"

"I invited you to lunch," I reminded him. I told Jim I wanted to do an evaluation of his company before committing myself.

Meditating with cannabis

After a short private session with pot, it took less than two hours rather than days to come up with suggestions for Pacific Builders, and then to make the career change.

My report recommended: "Continue building fine homes. Also get into commercial construction, including high-rise condominiums. Much of the commercial work could be sub-contracted. Don't pay your Realtor a salary, but rather have him on straight commission. On the tailgate of each of your trucks, rather than showing the name of the manufacturer, such as Ford or Chevrolet, cover it with metal painted the same color as the trucks, then paint *Pacific Builders* across the tailgate."

I had checked on some of the people who'd had Pacific Builders do preliminary plans for them. Many of them had shopped them to other builders. "Your company frequently is ending up with not even a thank you for a set of free drawings!" I recommended, "Do not gamble the company's money to draw free preliminary plans. Hire an artist who can paint a rendering in water colors showing what the finished home would look like." I said that the company should require a $500 deposit from the client for residential preliminary drawings, and a $1,000 deposit for commercial work. If the client elected to build with Pacific Builders, the deposit would apply to the contract. If he chose to go elsewhere, he would first have to pay a reasonable cost for those preliminary plans, not to exceed the amount of the deposit. If he wanted the rendering, he'd pay $300 for houses, $500 for apartment buildings.

Jim Humpert was enthusiastic. "Can we shake on it right now, that you'll start in six months?" We shook, and he proudly showed me my large new office. It was impressive, with two telephones, an intercom, a speakerphone, and access to Jim's secretary for dictation. I hired two outside salesmen to work on straight commission, and an artist for $900 a month.

The company painted all its trucks yellow, with *Pacific Builders* in red. I had received outstanding results with television spots for Dave Ford Motors, so I suggested we have our own television show. Jim and I would do the commercials. We worked out a deal with the CBS affiliate, KGMB-TV, to produce *Pacific Builders First Run Theater*. I got the sub-contractors to contribute money toward the production of the show, and we ended up making $200 a week over costs. Far more importantly, the show produced thousands of dollars in new business.

Most people saw Jim's habitual stern look and heard his deep baritone voice and thought of him as unapproachable. I thought about his very serious public demeanor and decided to use humor in the commercials to balance it. After all, people watch television to be entertained – and it had been my experience that you could keep viewers from wandering off to the kitchen if the entertainment didn't stop when the commercials started. I convinced Jim that our commercials would have more spontaneity and more impact if we didn't script them and rehearse them. When I said, "Trust me," he agreed.

The day arrived when we were in the studio for taping the first commercials. A camera showed an incipient bald spot on the back of Jim's head of mostly black hair. When he saw the bald spot in the monitor, Jim yelled, "Cut! Cut! Cancel the contract! We're not going on television! I look like the rear end of a baboon. I didn't know I had that bald spot. Forget the show!"

I quietly asked the crew, "Just please hold everything for five minutes." I ran to a shoe-repair shop across the street and bought a can of black shoe polish, ran back, and smeared some of it on the back of Jim's head, totally covering the bald spot. "What the hell are you doing to my head, keed?" I asked the cameraman to shoot from the same angle again.

"Now, don't you look handsome, Jim?" I asked.

Jim, glared at the monitor, lowered his head to see the crown, began nodding, and then grinned. "OK, we're back in business."

Photo: Hilton Hawaiian Village

Lloyd Bridges, star of many major motion pictures and perhaps best known for his hit TV series Sea Hunt, wanted to hear all about my world-record dive, and invited me to dinner at the Hilton Hawaiian Village.

Photo: Pacific Builders publicity dept.

After the dive I was retained by Hawaii's finest builder of homes, Pacific Builders, with 300 employees, and became Vice President.

I set the tone for our commercials in the very first one. Here was this 200-pound six-foot tycoon whom everyone in the office called Mr. Humpert, and here this new guy begins calling him "Jim." When the cameras rolled I asked him, "Jim, why are you always so serious?"

"Life is serious," said Jim.

To which I replied, "Really?"

I reached behind me, picked up a custard pie, and slapped Jim across the face with it.

Pick your own cliché: His expression was priceless. The silence was deafening. After what seemed like an age he burst into laughter at his own seriousness.

That night the show aired and the next day at least a dozen new prospects wanted to meet him. Luckily, I had figured him correctly. Underneath that relentlessly businesslike exterior he had a real sense of humor. Fortunately for me!

Pot creativity – uncovering a "corpse"

Once or twice a week after sleeping a few hours, I would go into my den at home, smoke a little grass, and write five or six commercials in an hour or two. They normally would have taken a couple of days. Those written while I was high on grass were totally professional. In several I used a little audio-visual magic to increase impact. I'd clip one frame from the night's movie and insert it into a rear-screen projector, which made anyone in the studio look as if he were in the film. Then for proper atmosphere I'd tape 60 seconds of the film's music, with no dialogue. Here are two examples:

The classic horror film *The House Of Wax* starred Vincent Price as a gifted creator of wax figures. One night he was caught in a fire, and the resulting disfigurement deranged him. When he opened a new wax museum in another city, instead of sculpting figures as before, he began to steal bodies from funeral homes and dip them in wax. I used a frame of the film at the point that he climbed into a funeral home to steal a body, and recorded a minute of the movie's spooky music. I then dressed in the same type of black cape and hat that Vincent Price wore to hide his disfigurement. When the commercial began, the audience did not realize that the film had actually stopped. I made it look enough like I was creeping through the window of the funeral home that the audience thought it was still seeing Vincent Price. I lifted a sheet from one of the bodies, and Jim Humpert sat up and did a 30-second spiel for Pacific

Builders. Almost before anyone realized what had happened, we were back into the actual movie.

During the war movie, *Target Zero*, with actor Chuck Connors, there was a tremendous explosion on the battlefield. I cut the film at that scene. Again, it was as though we were now in the movie. I was dressed in a World War II army uniform, complete with backpack and dummy hand grenades on my belt. The movie's music and battle sounds continued. From out of the sky fell a plastic lady's leg that I'd borrowed from a department-store mannequin. (She didn't mind.) I caught the leg, faced the camera, and told viewers that there are no accidents, and no one ever blows up, when one builds with Pacific Builders. And before the audience could catch its breath, we were back into the movie.

Most of my commercials were far out, but they created intense interest and high ratings. Some of the show's other sponsors waited a year to have commercials on the show.

Lloyd Bridges was one of my first interviews. Most folks remember him from the television series, *Sea Hunt*, but he also appeared in dozens of motion pictures; among them *East of Eden, Sahara, Around the World Under The Sea, High Noon, Bear Island, Master Race,* and *Airplane*. Actors invariably appear average-size or larger on screen, so it's always a surprise to meet them in person. As I recall, Joan Crawford stood five feet tall, while Lloyd Bridges stood six feet four. His work in *Sea Hunt* gave him a keen interest in diving, and that was what prompted him to invite me to dinner after my dive. I not only admired him as an actor but also enjoyed interviewing him, as he had interviewed me during that dinner.

Why I refused to interview Elvis

Living in Hawaii for 30 years offered me many opportunities to use a bit of creativity. I never offered money for an interview, nor was it ever requested. By phone, I would ask to speak to the stars themselves and, surprisingly, I got through to them 95 percent of the time, and they almost always accepted my request for an interview.

In July of 1961, Elvis Presley was in town putting the finishing touches on his movie, *Paradise Hawaiian Style*. I wanted to interview him, so I dialed the number of Waikiki's first plush high-rise hotel. A few seconds later, blasting my ear was a loud familiar voice: "Aloha! Kaiser Hawaiian Village Hotel. Kimu speaking. For who you like talk?"

Hawaii was more authentic in those days than it is today, not yet spoiled by high-rise buildings and millions of tourists. Perfect mainland-

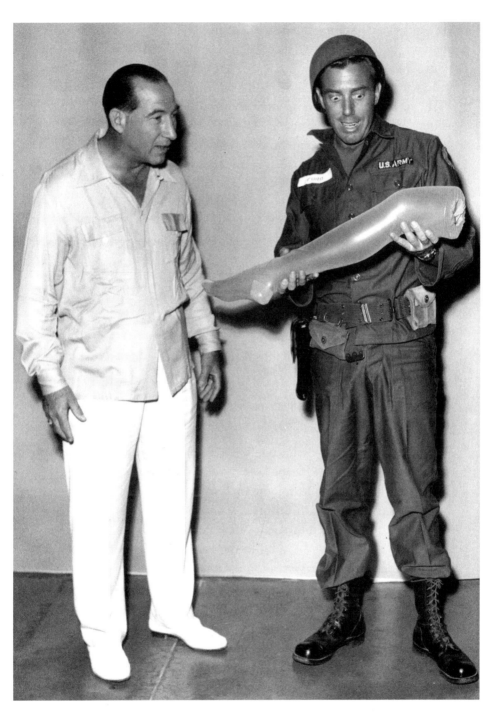

I talked Pacific Builders president Jim Humpert (left) into backing a new show on KGMB TV, the CBS affiliate in Hawaii, that featured top Hollywood films. At first, it was a little harder to drag him into the zany commercials I wrote, but they kept the viewers from heading off to the kitchen during station breaks — and he loved all the new customers they brought us!

style English was not a job requirement in those early days of Hawaii's statehood, and I enjoyed slipping into the friendly patois of islanders like my friend Kimu.

"Eh, Kimu! This Dave Ford. I like you ring Elvis Presley, yeah?"

"Yeh, sure Dave. Eh, brah, surf's up. You surf yet today?"

"Naw. Wish I could, Kimu."

"OK, brah, maybe see ya on beach later today, eh? I now ring Presley."

A few seconds later a man's voice sounded. "Elvis Presley's suite. What can I do for you?"

"Good afternoon. This is Dave Ford with CBS television in Honolulu. Who am I speaking to, please?"

"This is Colonel Parker. I presume you want an interview with Elvis, is that right?" said the Colonel.

"Exactly right, Colonel." I said.

"How long would you like?" asked the colonel.

"How about 20 minutes, Colonel?"

"You're sure 20 minutes would be enough?"

"That would be a perfect length of time, Colonel. *Mahalo.*"

"How about 6 p.m.?"

"Perfect, Colonel, and thank you."

"Oh, there's just one thing, Mr. Ford."

"What's that, Colonel?"

"Bring a cashier's check with you for $20,000."

"You're putting me on, I hope."

"Do I sound like I'm putting you on?" said the Colonel.

My face was flushed with outrage. I was positive Elvis would have been happy to do a free interview. "Colonel, Elvis loves the people of Hawaii. He contributed $25,000 to the Pearl Harbor Memorial. I'm sure he would do the interview if you just ask him, sir."

He was not happy. "Elvis wants to do what I want him to do!"

"I'll pass on interviewing Elvis then," I said; "How about interviewing you, Colonel? How much do you charge?"

"I don't give interviews." said the colonel.

I said, "Please give Elvis Aloha from his thousands of Hawaiian friends."

"Yeah, sure," said the colonel.

I liked Elvis, partly because he loved Hawaii. I also felt he was manipulated by Parker, who owned up to 50% of him. His "quickie" movies made plenty of money – for the colonel. Elvis wanted to become a top-notch actor, and felt he could have achieved that goal with proper drama coaching, which he never got. I believe the colonel thought he would lose control if Elvis became a major motion-picture star. What Elvis wanted was unimportant. Such frustration may have contributed to Elvis becoming a drug addict. In mid-2002, Elvis' best friend, Joe Esposito, said on the Larry King show that it was too bad that Elvis didn't just stick to pot. If he had, I have no doubt Elvis would be alive today.

Some of the famous people I did manage to interview during my years with KGMB-TV included Bing Crosby and his brother Bob, Reverend Billy Graham, Wayne Newton, Charlton Heston, Don Ho, Lloyd Bridges, Milton Berle, Richard Boone, Jonathan Winters, Margaret Whiting, Cab Calloway, Robert Cummings, Sophie Tucker, Dennis Day, Harry James, Richard Widmark, Kay Starr, Mr. and Mrs. Arthur Murray, Edgar Bergen, Eva Gabor, Dame Margot Fonteyn, Mahalia Jackson, Tiny Tim, Vic Damone, Duke Kahanamoku, Liberace, Hilo Hattie, James Shigeta, Jimmie Dodd (the first Disney Mouseketeer), and two of Hawaii's governors, its first, William F. Quinn, and John Burns.

Interviewing Cab Calloway – a genuine "reefer man"

Cab Calloway was one entertainer I'd long hoped to interview, and it finally happened. He was the star at New York's Cotton Club, and a bandleader through the '30's and '40's. Cab worked with Ethel Waters, Louis Armstrong, Dizzy Gillespie, and Duke Ellington, among other greats. An outstanding jazz singer and dancer, his hits included *Minnie the Moocher, Blues in the Night, That Old Black Magic* – and *Reefer Man.* In my interview, I asked Cab if he would care to mention an adventure about grass. (I'd already set myself a goal of encouraging as many people as possible to come out of the closet regarding the use of grass.) Cab just smiled and winked. Understandable.

Many more people use pot than surveys reveal

The government has people so frightened by the possible consequences that many are afraid to admit their use of marijuana. I've asked many hundreds of people about this. Answers are generally: "If you were asked to participate in a confidential survey, and were asked if you use, or ever used, marijuana, would you admit it?" About 99 percent have said something like, "Are you serious? I don't trust the government, or any such surveys. I'd say no, of course!" I wager that the incidence of marijuana use is at least triple what the government reports. After lectures, while I autograph books, I've had doctors, scientists, teachers, college students, pharmacists, professors, waiters and waitresses, and several police officers, among others, tell me confidentially they've used pot for years. Many say they take it to help them manage stress, alcoholism, depression, sleep disorders, nausea, PMS, phantom limb pain, or chronic pain. Others, to enhance lovemaking. Still others, just for fun, for a lot of laughing. One teacher said, "The only thing pot ever killed – is a gallon of ice cream in one sitting!"

Interviewing Bing Crosby; I ask if he uses grass

I heard that Bing Crosby would be spending a few nights on Oahu at the Kahala Hilton Hotel. I left a message saying that he owed me a call.

About an hour later, while I was editing film, our operator rang my office and said, "Bing Crosby is on the line, and asks to speak with you."

I said, "Thank you. I've been expecting his call." Who could resist the chance to say that!

On came that unmistakably mellow voice. "Mr. Ford, I'm returning your call out of courtesy. However, please be aware that I rarely give interviews anymore. I imagine that is what you were calling about. Right?"

"Bing, please don't hang up on me," I said. "You did that to me 18 years ago when you were in San Francisco. You thought I was the great director and your personal friend, John Ford. When you found out I was just a high school kid, you hung up on me."

"Did I really?" he asked. "Refresh my memory, ol' buddy."

I rapidly went over my earlier call to him, telling him that I had had a popular teen radio show, *Junior Jamboree*, and that I had wanted an interview with him.

"I'll tell you what I'll do," Bing said. "We're leaving tomorrow morning for Los Angeles. If you have your crew ready at the airport's VIP lounge at 6:30, I'll give you that interview that I owe you. OK?".

"You bet, Bing. Please remember the name is *Dave* Ford, not John Ford!"

He laughed and said, "See ya in the mornin', Dave Ford."

During the 1960s, video was used only in the studio; on location we shot film. At 6 a.m., the cameraman, lighting director, still photographer, and sound man were set up in the VIP lounge of United Airlines.

At 6:30, no Bing. The flight was due to take off at 7:30. The camera crew began to dismantle their equipment. "Give him five more minutes," I implored. At that moment a black limousine pulled up to the main terminal, and I ran to it. Getting out of the limo was Bing, his wife, Katherine Grayson, and their two children, Harry Jr. and Mary Frances. I took hold of Bing's arm. "You must be Dave. I'm sorry, but it doesn't look as though we'll have time for that interview."

"Bing, my job may depend on it."

"OK, but it has to be a fast one."

"It's a deal," I said. I guided Bing to the camera. "Roll it," I said. Bing sat down and the interview began.

We were four minutes into the interview when the children barged in. Four-year-old Mary Frances calmly walked right up to us, wearing a plumeria lei. I sat her on my lap. She said, "Would you like some Black Jack chewing gum?"

I said, "Sure," and took a piece.

Bing said, "You like Dave, huh? Would you like him to go back to Hollywood with us?"

"Yes!" said Mary Frances.

When the interview was concluded, Bing said, "Now, that was fun! Is there a chance that I can buy a copy of that interview?"

"No, Bing. But I'll *give* you a copy of the film."

A few weeks later I received a personal letter with "Bing Crosby-Hollywood" printed in blue. It was dated, Oct. 8, 1962, and it read:

> Dear Dave:
>
> I've just gotten back from Europe and found the can of film awaiting me. I haven't had an opportunity yet to run it, but first time I get in the office where we have a little projection room, I'll put it on the screen. I'm very interested in seeing how it turned out. It must have been good for a few laughs, anyhow. Thank you so much for remembering your promise and sending it on to me. I appreciate it a great deal. Warmest personal regards to you and the staff.
>
> As ever, Bing.

I got a copy of everyone's favorite Bing Crosby movie, *The Bells of Saint Mary's*, and broadcast it on December 13, followed by the interview. Newspapers, TV stations, radio, and our own news department generated some positive publicity, and some related the details of how I talked Bing into that interview.

Bing Crosby was certainly one of the most relaxed stars I ever interviewed. I didn't put him on the spot when the camera was rolling, but afterward I couldn't resist asking one burning question as I escorted him to the newsstand to buy some pipe tobacco.

"Bing, I couldn't help but wonder, with your super relaxation, if at home you might put a little grass in your famous pipe?"

He looked me right in the eyes and rewarded me with a generous grin and a wink.

In a later interview Barbara Walters asked Bing what he would do if he ever caught his daughter smoking marijuana. To the best of my recollection, his exact words were: "It should be legalized!" I chuckled, hoping that I may have encouraged him to *almost* come out of the closet.

Since my interview with Bing, I've had various musicians tell me that in fact he smoked a lot of pot, and that it did keep him mellow. Bing once had a serious alcohol problem and grass was certainly the right remedy for him. I knew too that Bing idolized the great trumpeter and vocalist Louis Armstrong, who was an avid pot smoker. Gary Giddins confirmed in his book, *Bing Crosby: A Pocketful Of Dreams,* "Armstrong also introduced him to marijuana."

There goes the false propaganda that pot gives users a dropout mentality! I wish I could take the credit for introducing our courageous country-western singer and actor, Willie Nelson, to cannabis. Willie has truly opened the door. He is another relaxed entertainer who relies on pot's stress-relieving quality. He gives cannabis full credit for ending his alcohol problems. You may have heard Willie say: "Stress is the greatest killer on this planet, and the greatest medicine for stress is still cannabis."

The brilliant actor Woody Harrelson also deserves immense credit for his honesty and courage in discussing his use of grass and educating the public about the thousands of uses of nonintoxicating hemp. And how about one of the country's top criminal attorneys, Tony Serra? Serra openly admits his use of pot, with a lawyerly qualification: "not during court."

Co-hosting the Jerry Lewis telethon; many wheelchair patients use cannabis

For two years I co-hosted the Jerry Lewis Muscular Dystrophy telethon for the State of Hawaii. As I interviewed patients backstage, it became clear to me that a majority of people in wheelchairs suffer from muscle spasms. Due to their medications most wheelchair patients also have

Pacific Builders First Run Theater featured celebrity interviews as well as great movies. One of my favorites was with Milton Berle, who was always "on." I spoke with "Uncle Miltie" again 25 years later – about marijuana.

Jimmie Dodd was the first of Walt Disney's Mouseketeers.

For two years, I had the privilege of co-hosting the Jerry Lewis Muscular Dystrophy telethon for the state of Hawaii. Sadly, Mickey Rosha, the dear young man in the wheelchair, died shortly after appearing on the show.

little appetite, and many become seriously gaunt. Many of them confirmed that they used marijuana to ease those spasms and to create appetite, and lamented that pot is not covered by health insurance. Would patients risk prison for using this Schedule I drug, and pay the high cost of medical-quality cannabis, if it didn't work? No way.

Milton Berle interview

Comedian Milton Berle was a truly funny man. For many years he starred in the *Texaco Star Theater.* Some of "Uncle Miltie's" movies included *Broadway Danny Rose, Cracking Up, Lepke, The Muppet Movie,* and *Who's Minding the Mint?* He was also featured in *It's a Mad Mad Mad Mad World.* When I was in Los Angeles a couple of years ago I met with a friend in show business, Toni Webb. She invited me to the Friars' Club, where many people in the entertainment business have lunch because it's one place they won't be bothered by autograph hounds.

Milton Berle was there and he invited us to join him at his table. During our meal, he asked me what I was doing at that time. I just happened to have in my pocket a jacket to my book, *Marijuana: Not Guilty As Charged,* so I brought it out. Note how sharp this guy was at 90:

He said, "Dave, that stuff is good for glaucoma, right?"

I said, "Yes, it is, Miltie."

So he took the book jacket out of my hands and rubbed it across his eyes! (The FBI had Uncle Miltie under surveillance for marijuana use for a while but was unable to prove it.)

Most of the dozens of interviews I recorded were pretty straightforward. The one with Tiny Tim began as anything but. One day in 1968, I tip-toed down the corridor of the Hilton Hawaiian Village Hotel to interview the gentleman who has received reviews that ranged from "He's really a genius that knows how to capitalize on what today's audience expects" to "He's an unpredictable kook" to "He's completely mad." I soon learned he could be considered a little of each.

My knock on the door brought Tim's manager, Mark Hammerman, who invited me in. Tim looked me over with a smile, walked out onto the lanai of his 26th-floor suite, peered over the railing, then swung his leg over it and said, "It sure is a long way down! Hey, Mr. Ford, watch me do a handstand on this railing."

Hammerman, with the cool nonchalance of a head zookeeper walking into a cage of lions, said, "Please don't do that, Tim."

DAVE FORD INTERVIEWS TINY TIM

A FEW FORGETTABLE MOMENTS WITH SHOW BIZ'S BEAUTIFUL PEOPLE

I went tip-toeing down the corridor of the Hilton Hawaiian Village Hotel on my way to interview Tiny Tim. From the numerous stories I've heard regarding him, I must admit I was looking over my shoulder to see if anyone was watching as I gingerly knocked on the door of his hotel suite. Still ringing in my ears were such statements as, "He's completely mad," "He's really a genius that knows how to capitalize on what today's audience expects," "He's an unpredictable kook."

In today's rapidly spinning world, I soon learned he could be considered a little of each.

My knock on the door brought Tim's manager Mark Hammerman, who cordially invited me in. Tim looked me over with a friendly smile, walked out onto the lanai of his twenty-sixth floor suite, swung his

leg over the railing and said, "It sure is a long way down."

Mr. Hammerman with the cool nonchalance of a head zoo keeper walking into a cage of lions slowly walked over to his charge and said, "Please don't do that Tim." While grabbing for my camera I couldn't help but to notice that Mr. Hammerman had a hand on his heart. As I cocked my camera ready to catch the possible action shot of the year, I looked to see if Mr. Hammerman had his other hand on his wallet. After getting Tim to sit down on a chair, we began our chat.

FORD: Are you enjoying your first trip to Hawaii Tim?

TIM: I love Hawaii. Everyone has been so friendly to me, and of course they grow a lot of pineapples here. That's a real thrill because I love pineapples. I think they are one of the greatest fruits, and one of the most forgotton fruits, and taken for granted fruits.

TV Time

I had a contract with TV Time (comparable to the national TV Guide) that allowed them to print as many of my celebrity interviews as they wished. They did at least a dozen. This is a portion of the Tiny Tim interview... which began with a scary moment on a 26th-floor balcony!

FORD: Speaking of fruits, I understand you brush your teeth about six times a day, and among other things you use payaya powder. Would you elaborate?

TIM: I'd say an exact count would be, let's see — one, two, three, four, about five times, yea. Papays powder isn't readily available, you have to get it at a health store. When I can't get a hold of it, I use three dentifrices at one time, in fact, four. I use salt to get out the dirt. Number two, I use Crest toothpaste which is the greatest around. After that I use Pepsodent, and on top of that I use Ultra-Bright. I top it off with Ultra-Bright, to keep 'em white! I use Crest in my mouth to strengthen the teeth against cavities. Crest is the greatest.

FORD: You're giving an excellent commercial for Crest.

TIM: It's only true. Many tooth pastes are like golf clubs. I think a lot of manufacturers realize that. You can use three or four at a time for different effects, but nothing beats Crest. It doesn't whiten the teeth, but it strengthens them. I leave some in my mouth when I go out to strengthen my teeth.

FORD: I see. (Actually I saw it was time to get to another subject) Tim, who is your favorite male vocalist?

TIM: Dean Martin, Frank Sinatra, Jimmy Morrison.

FORD: How about female vocalists?

TIM: Doris Day, and also Mary Hopkins.

FORD: Who is your favorite actress?

TIM: Catherine DeNue.

FORD: And actor?

TIM: Gene Barry. If I were to go back to the past, I'd say Byron G. Harlon, Henry Burr, Charles Harrison, and Rudy Vallee.

FORD: When did you let your hair grow?

TIM: Six years before the Beatles. I did it because it went along with the high voice that the good Lord gave me.

FORD: As time goes on do you think men will use cosmetics?

TIM: I believe in using perfumes and creams. Men should be sure if they use cosmetics they are not obvious.

FORD: Successful actors frequently have the desire to become vocalists and vice-versa. Do you have such desires?

TIM: Yes. I'd like to play in horror movies. I'd like to be a creature that comes down from Mars. A girl would bring me around to the neighbors, and they would say, "Oh, my goodness!"

FORD: If you could live anywhere in the world, where would you choose?

TIM: New York.

FORD: How did the name Tiny Tim evolve from Herbert Khaury?

TIM: One of my many managers came up with it.

FORD: Any marriage plans, Tim?

TIM: I could never get married. I like to be alone. But young women just to look at thrill me, and stimulate me, in the pure sense of the word. One should never do that which is not permissable before marriage.

FORD: What is your favorite food?

TIM: I get a kick out of anything I can get a hold of, especially pies and salads.

FORD: What do you like best about show business?

TIM: The fantasy and glamour.

FORD: What do you like least about show business?

TIM: Bringing (he spelled out the word) S-E-X into movies.

FORD: During World War Two you patriotically tried to join the service about eight times, is that correct?

TIM: (Wild laughter for about fifteen seconds) I always loved the services. I did volunteer about that many times.

FORD: Why were you turned down?

TIM: Some said they were crowded! Some said, "The record shows that it's better that you stay out." (At this point Mr. Hammerman interjected, "Didn't you have Bronchitis when you were a kid?") I didn't have it when I went down there. I went into the psyciatrist, I had passed my examination.

FORD: With the psychiatrist?

TIM: No, but everything else. Then I went and told them I wanted to join up so I could go to the moon.

FORD: Were you wearing your hair long at the time?

TIM: Oh, no, no, no!

FORD: Didn't you have some problem matching up shaded rectangles, triangles, etc.?

Continued on Page 70
TV TIME / 13

When we finally got Tim off the near-death railing and settled into a chair, he seemed content to focus on the interview, much to my relief. Tiny Tim was intriguing.

Foreboding of tragedy to come

We were nearing the end of 1960. Our son David was doing great, and Hazel and I both idolized him. Hazel, however, was again experiencing disturbed episodes. "When I'm OK, Daaave, I'm great. But the times I'm ill, I'm afraid I'll hurt myself or David." I tried to reassure her how much he and I loved her, and that she would be fine again, as long as she continued to see the psychologist.

By the end of my first year with Pacific Builders, its financial condition had turned around. The red ink turned black and I was promoted to Vice President. Shortly thereafter, I located two square blocks of land owned by the Bishop Estate and was able to secure a 55-year lease to construct an apartment complex of 175 units. Jim would own two thirds and I would own one third, with an investment of $35,000 on my part. I arranged financing with a first mortgage for 12 years, after which time Jim and I would own the complex outright. By that time Jim would receive approximately $40,000 a month, and I $15,000. Construction was completed within a year, and I named the complex Pacific Gardens, linking it to Pacific Builders. We took photos as construction proceeded and used them in our television commercials.

Jim Humpert had been married five times and was once again single. And lady-crazy. I introduced him to several women who had visited our offices. They were impressed by seeing us on television and no doubt had also heard that Jim was rich. He went to bed with the first lady that night, and next day bought her a new car. To the next lady he presented a four-carat diamond ring. Soon he was flying these ladies to neighboring islands in his custom-built twin-engine Beechcraft.

"You can't do that, Jim," I pleaded.

"Come on, keed. We're taking in $50,000 a month."

I said calmly, "As you well know, that money is progress payments from the banks; it's not profit. Jim, you don't have to squirt every lady you meet."

"I know that, keed, but I'm having a ball. (Maybe we'd have been better off if he'd had just *one*.) We're growing. Don't worry, with your help we're making plenty – I can afford to spoil a few broads."

Six months later Jim asked me to sign a second mortgage on Pacific

Gardens. "Keed, our accountant tells me we're getting a little short. I need to borrow $20,000. I'll pay it back within six months. I *promise*. Just put your John Henry right here." He handed me a pen, and I signed, reluctantly. I feared that this was the beginning of the end of all our success. I had worked hundreds of hours of my own time putting the deal together. I frequently took Hazel and David with me to the project and we watched the construction with excitement, while Jim was gone for days at a time with his ladies.

Terror from home

What worried me far more than the possibility of losing Pacific Gardens was Hazel phoning me at the office with horrifying calls. "Darling, you know how much I love you and David... and it's raining outside..."

"Yes, I know, baby. I'll be home in a couple of hours."

"Daaave, you know David will one day have to go to war. It's best that I kill him now...."

"I'll be right home, baby. Wait for me!" I'd leap in my car and speed the eight miles home. Sometimes when I arrived she acted as though she didn't know who I was, and would call me by some other name.

On one of these occasions I found her rocking David in her arms. "I just took a whole bottle of aspirin, Daaave. I decided that, instead of killing David, I'd kill myself." I grabbed David and Hazel, and sped to Kaiser Hospital, where they pumped out her stomach. She had indeed taken the bottle of aspirin, and this kind of thing happened more than once. It got to where our switchboard operator would say, "Mr. Ford, I understand that you're in conference closing a deal; but I know you'll want to take this call."

Once when Hazel phoned, she said, "Darling, Daaave, it's time for David to go to heaven. We're going for a ride. Goodbye," and hung up. I told clients there was an emergency, and I was out of there. I sped home at 90 miles an hour. Hazel's car was gone.

Where would she have taken him? I knew that she enjoyed taking him to play peewee golf in Waikiki... but she wouldn't take him there if she were going to kill him. Where else? Then I had it. She loved to drive to Sandy Beach, which was past Koko Head, 15 miles from where we lived. I jumped back in the car and raced along Kalanianaole Highway, desperate to reach her in time. I had just passed Hawaii Kai, and there she was, driving about 15 miles an hour. I drove alongside her, and honked. "Pull over, honey!" I yelled.

She turned into a parking area next to the bay. Her eyes were glassy and vacant. "I'm taking David somewhere special. We're going to visit God."

I slipped into her car. I put David on my lap and gave them both a big hug. Slowly, I took the keys out of the ignition of her car. "Let's go for a ride in the convertible. You both like that, right?" Hazel looked confused but followed me into the convertible. I locked her car and left it there.

When we arrived home I fixed them something to eat, and once more called her psychologist, Dr. Spicer, with whom I'd been consulting more frequently of late. I told him about Hazel's behavior earlier that day. He was aware that the situation was becoming serious. I asked him what I should do. "As I've suggested to you before, the solution is to have her reside at Kaneohe."

"I don't want to do that, put her in another mental hospital," I said. When she was rational she knew she was ill, but felt that she could handle it.

One evening when I came home I heard Hazel laughing. It was a laugh that I'd heard before, and it sent shivers down my spine. She was in the den and the door was locked, so I called, "Hi, honey. It's me. I'm home from work, I'll have dinner ready shortly." (I generally did the cooking)

"We don't need dinner. Little David just needs lots of ice cream. Momma has lots of ice cream in here for our little boy. Don't worry about us, we're just fine."

"Hi, David. How ya doing, son?" I asked.

"OK, daddy," came the little two-year-old voice. I phoned Dr. Spicer. "Leave them alone tonight unless she sounds depressed. Come and see me in the morning." I didn't sleep all night. In the morning, when the laughing stopped I poked a wire through the hole in the center of the door handle. I quietly opened the door to find Hazel on the couch and David on the floor, both sound asleep. I picked up David and took him into our bedroom and let him sleep for a few more hours, then got him up, bathed him, and fixed him breakfast.

I left Hazel sleeping. In case she awoke I left a note saying that I was taking David for a ride, then I took him with me as I went to talk with Dr. Spicer in his office in Waikiki. At times, I felt David knew something was not right with his mother; yet no matter how strange she acted, his love was unconditional, as was hers. I'd never seen any child more loving or good-natured. Dr. Spicer had some toys in his front office and pointed David to the box of brightly colored objects. He was superb at entertaining himself, and the doctor and I talked for an hour.

"Are you making progress with her, Doctor?" I asked in despair.

"Counseling her is like trying to get hold of a handful of spaghetti. It's imperative that you keep a close eye on her. I've already contacted the hospital in Kaneohe and told them that she may have to be admitted in the near future. The paperwork is complete; so if you should need it, it's just a phone call away."

When we got home, Hazel was still asleep. In the sad days that followed, her condition deteriorated steadily. She slept in jeans when she slept at all, which was only an hour or so at a time. She laughed during the night. Frequently she was up all night long, wandering around the house.

One night when I put my arm around her, she pulled away sharply and said, "Don't you ever touch me again, old man!" Even more than her physical revulsion, "old man" went through me like a knife – it was the way Hazel and her sisters and brothers referred to their father.

One morning she began screaming and smashing dishes. "I want something to kill myself with!" I tried to hold her and tell her I loved her, and that everything would be all right, but she kicked and scratched me. She was so powerful I couldn't restrain her. Desperate, I called Dr. Spicer. He told me to phone Kaneohe immediately and ask for them to come and get her.

That was the most painful phone call I ever made. I was crushed. Hazel trusted me. I felt like a traitor. This was my little family. I never loved anyone the way I loved Hazel. My head was spinning. What if she decided to kill herself again, and take David with her? I was sick to my stomach. I had to protect our son. She adored him. I knew in her heart she would agree with me.

Within an hour they arrived. She was screaming and breaking dishes. They put her into a straitjacket. I was crying. They took her to the hospital, while I followed in the car. The doctor said, "It's in her best interest that you don't see her for a week. At the moment she's let go completely, and is in a padded cell so she won't hurt herself." I returned home almost blinded by tears.

I hired a nanny to care for David while I was at work. I visited Hazel twice a week, when the hospital staff let me. There were times when she was rational, and they allowed her to come home for a few days at a time. She was again diagnosed as a chronic schizophrenic and manic-depressive, a condition known today as bi-polar disorder. She herself frequently knew when her condition was worsening, and that she should return to the Kaneohe facility. A few weeks later, when she was home for a weekend, we learned that, despite precautions, she was pregnant. News that a year before would have overjoyed me left me only deeply concerned, as Hazel was on Thorazine, and receiving shock therapy.

When she was at Kaneohe, I missed Hazel and my heart went out to her. When she wasn't home, I smoked grass more frequently to reduce the stress and depression. Then the opportunity presented itself to fly again, and I welcomed any escape from my gloom.

The CBS affiliate in Honolulu broadcast to the whole state, and the Pacific Builders TV commercials had led to jobs building homes and apartment buildings on several of the islands. Many of these projects included swimming pools. Our pool contractor had bought a four-place Cessna 175 in order to save airfares for his workmen; but he was having a problem passing his flight exam. He heard that I was a pilot and asked if I would fly three of his men to Hilo on the Big Island. I told him I'd be happy to.

He needed six men delivered to Hilo, and he said, "I have another pilot lined up with a rented plane. He'll carry the other three men." The other pilot's nickname was "Crashy." He'd earned it by crashing a number of planes when he was a pilot in World War II. More recently and more locally, a newspaper story had reported that he'd gotten drunk one night and "borrowed" a B-25 that was on display at Honolulu International. He took it for a joy ride and almost hit the Aloha Tower at the harbor in downtown Honolulu, a landmark designed to welcome visitors to Hawaii.

We were all scheduled to meet at Honolulu International for a 3 p.m. takeoff. I filed our flight plan, checked the weather, and fueled the Cessna. Our six passengers were still standing by at 3:30 – no Crashy. Finally, he showed up. I was now concerned. I told him I didn't want to land in Hilo after dark. Weather there was notoriously unpredictable, and often included sudden heavy rain. In addition, this would be my first flight over 200 miles of ocean. Crashy was not to be rushed, and wasn't finally ready to take off until 4:30. We agreed to communicate via radio during the flight, and to stay in visual contact.

We were cruising at 5,500 feet when we reached the Big Island. At Upulu Point, 70 miles west of Hilo, it began raining. And getting dark. And we were still 40 minutes from touchdown.

We passed Akaka Falls, only eight minutes from landing; it was now dark and raining hard. For added thrills, there was thunder and lightning. I radioed Crashy and said that if I couldn't see the field within three minutes I was going to abort our landing in Hilo, and head for my alternate field, which was Kamuela, fifty miles northwest.

"Dave, just follow me!" Crashy insisted.

We were now in heavy turbulence, and hail was hammering the windshield. My three passengers were understandably nervous. "Are we OK? Do you have parachutes?" they asked.

"Everything is fine, but we're going to land at a field where the weather is better," I said. Crashy disappeared into the blackness of rain, hail, thunder and lightning. I radioed both Crashy and the tower reporting our destination change, got approval to increase altitude, then climbed to 9,500 feet. We broke out of the storm and into a lovely night lit by the moon and stars, and landed without a bump 45 minutes later.

The contractor took a commercial flight to Hilo, where he rented a car and picked us up, congratulating me on the decision to abort the Hilo landing. The field in Hilo was down to a half mile visibility and in heavy rain when Crashy landed. One of his passengers puked all over the rental plane. I hadn't realized how much I had missed flying – especially in good weather!

● ● ●

In the early to mid-1960s, a horrifying incident led the state government to encourage fishermen to kill as many sharks as possible. Along with adults and other children, a 12-year-old boy had been diving off a raft at a beach park in Lanikai, near Kailua, on the Island of Oahu. The raft was less than a hundred yards from shore. He dove into the water and was only 30 feet from the raft when a shark attacked him and tore his right leg off. He screamed for help, but people were too terrified to go in after him. He died from loss of blood.

On the following Saturday Jim invited me to join him and Walter Dillingham, his cost estimator and foreman, on a shark hunt. Jim flew his twin-engine 10-seat Beechcraft, with me as co-pilot, to Upulu Point on the Big Island of Hawaii. Jim had arranged for some hands at a local ranch to kill an old horse and leave it in the sun for several days. The airstrip at Upulu Point was only yards from an area of the ocean that drops off into 100 feet of water. Ten work hands dragged the foul-smelling carcass into the water while the ranchers were drinking beer and whiskey. I couldn't help but feel that if they'd been smoking grass instead, they wouldn't have been so enthusiastic about killing. (Ask police officers if they've ever answered a call regarding domestic or family violence, when the only drug used was pot. Then ask them about domestic violence cases in which alcohol is involved.)

It couldn't have been more than a few minutes before the fins of giant sharks began circling the bloated carcass. In seconds, they began ferociously tearing apart the dead beast. A tiger shark at least 18 feet long swiftly and deftly went straight for the head of the already mutilated animal. Blood stained the water for yards around the feeding frenzy, but we could clearly see the tiger shark tear the head of the horse off in a single terrifying, sawing bite with its razor-like teeth.

We were on a rock ledge within 25 feet of the carnage. The cattlemen were in an excited "high," and began shooting the sharks with rifles. They sincerely felt, due to the media propaganda regarding "deadly shark attacks," that they were saving lives by killing these animals, who in fact rarely attack humans. I was reminded of how some police, because of government propaganda, are hyped up to catch those "depraved" people who use or grow marijuana.

When one of the sharks was in its death throes, the ranch hands impaled it with spears connected to ropes, and eight men dragged it backward toward shallow water. When a shark is dragged backward its stomach comes out its mouth. We were just feet from the thrashing animal, which was gushing blood.

This experience was not for the faint of heart. My stomach convulsed. I was in a precarious position standing on a large slippery rock, and as the shark was pulled to its inevitable doom within a few feet of me, I began slipping into the ocean. An alert young Hawaiian cowboy seized my arm and stopped my slide. In the scramble my dark glasses flew into the deep water. "Hey, brah, those expensive specs?"

"Not really," I said. The words no sooner left my mouth than the young fellow dived into the bloody water! Sharks were creating whirlpools with their circling attacks at what was left of the horse carcass. A minute passed. Suddenly, up popped the cowboy – with my glasses in his hand! I reached out and pulled him up onto the rock.

"Are your specs OK?" he laughed as he handed me the dripping glasses.

"They're just fine. But you shouldn't have gone into the water. I was certain you were already dinner for at least one shark."

"Hey, brah, sharks don't eat Hawaiians!"

Damn. He really believed it.

Jim was having a great time watching the action. I went for a walk and finally sat in the plane and reflected on life.

When David was two I had brought my mother to visit us for a month.

She adored him, but she was tired, and like many true poets and philosophers she sought the truth – and, hopefully, a rainbow. Yet she was disappointed in a life that didn't seem to have a happy ending. I was reminded of that poem she had written for me those many years ago, on my 21st birthday. Some of the words came to me. "...*But now the Autumn hovers near/And bids me guard each passing year...*" I was thankful she was not with me on this day. I feel she would have said something like, "We should learn to understand these graceful creatures."

Interviewing Wayne Newton

Most people go to Las Vegas to gamble, and I'm no exception. In my case I was betting my travel expenses that I could obtain interviews with Wayne Newton, the versatile solo stage performer; and Harry James, one of the world's greatest trumpet players. I felt as though I'd picked up a royal flush at one table and blackjack at the next when I arranged an interview with each of those unique talents in less than an hour after arriving.

Wayne was just 25 when I interviewed him, yet was making $15,000 a week performing at the Flamingo. That figure didn't include his shows on the road, or his acting fees. I caught two of his stage shows, and it was obvious to me that he loves performing for a live audience. That they love him was evident from the standing ovations. Wayne is not only a showman who can belt out a song, he's also an actor, a comic, a dancer, and, to top it off, he plays seven different musical instruments.

Our interview took place in the Flamingo Hotel. One of the many questions that I asked him: "Wayne, wasn't it about 1963 that you were pinch-hitting a show for a friend, and Jackie Gleason stood up in the audience at the end of the show and screamed, "For God's sake don't go on anyone else's show until you've been on mine!"

He answered, "Right, Dave, and that was really our first big break, as far as national television goes. We had never done a big show like that, and we hadn't had any hit records up to that time."

When the interview was over, Wayne slipped out of a side door to avoid some 50 autograph seekers. He looked back over his shoulder with a "little boy" expression, smiled, and said, "If there's anything I can ever do for you, Dave, just let me know!" Not many months after, I took him up on that kind offer.

Photo: KGMB publicity dept.

Cab Calloway, star at New York's Cotton Club and a top bandleader through the 30s and 40s. A great jazz singer and dancer, he made the song "Reefer Man" famous. I asked Cab if he would care to mention an adventure connected with pot.

Photo: Flamingo Hotel

Wayne Newton is amazing. At the end of our interview in Las Vegas, he said, "If there's ever anything that I can do for you, Dave, just let me know." Years later I did — and he did!

One of the world's greatest trumpeters, Harry James

Harry James, who was also avoiding a crowd of fans, appeared in the same side door that Wayne was exiting. They bumped into each other and laughed. James came over to our camera, shook my hand, and said, "Ready to go, Dave."

I was privileged to chat for 15 minutes with my trumpet idol. He was 20 when he joined Benny Goodman, the "King of Swing." Tall, thin, athletic, and a charmer, James was the perfect bandleader and went on to become one of the swing era's biggest stars. There's an outstanding movie featuring James' trumpet playing, called *Young Man with a Horn*, which starred Kirk Douglas, Doris Day, and Lauren Bacall. It's a wonderful story about a little boy who became a great trumpet player. Douglas played the lead, but all the trumpet-playing was done by Harry James himself. Frank Sinatra said in 1983, during his eulogy at James's funeral, "He was one of the finest musicians I have ever known." My sentiments too.

The Reverend Billy Graham

I interviewed evangelist Billy Graham twice. The first time was at the Royal Hawaiian Hotel in Waikiki in 1962 and the second was at the studios of KGMB-TV, the CBS television affiliate in Honolulu, in 1965. He was a delightfully humble man. As soon as we shook hands at our first meeting, I said, "For many years I've wanted to meet you, Reverend Graham."

"Please, Dave, just call me Billy."

You can't help but respect his philosophy and dedication to his work. Billy has personally known 10 Presidents: Eisenhower, Kennedy, Johnson, Nixon, Ford, Carter, Reagan, Clinton, and both Bushes. He has met the Queen of England, as well as hundreds of other world leaders. He has spoken to more people in more nations than any other person in history. He has preached to more than 230 million people live, and millions more via television. He has written 17 books, each of which became a best seller. (My sister Carol has read most of them.) He has appeared on Gallup's Ten Most Admired Men in the World 37 times since 1955. Yet his humility is equal to that of Christ, in whom his belief never wavers. He now suffers from Parkinson's disease and prostate cancer. He never complains. He looks forward to meeting God.

I found Liberace to be surprisingly humble, and gracious.

I interviewed Reverend Billy Graham twice. For someone who's known every President since Eisenhower, he's a very modest gentleman: when I said, "It's a pleasure to meet you, Reverend Graham" he replied, "Please, just call me Billy."

• • •

With Hazel in the hospital, I worked seven days a week trying to keep up with our 300 employees and to keep my mind occupied with something other than worrying. I frequently took David along on trips to inspect homes and apartments under construction.

Materials were disappearing from our warehouse. It appeared that some of the employees were helping themselves to lumber and other articles. Many of problems were due to Jim being gone for days at a time. "Jim," I said, "everything that you hired me to accomplish for your company is going down the drain if you don't monitor costs. I can't run this company by myself. It's getting to where you only show up to do the TV commercials and then you take off, sometimes for a week."

For the first time in our long association, he was angry at me. "It's my company. If it goes belly up, that's my business. I'll do my best to stop the stealing of materials, but don't tell me how to spend *my* money!"

I weighed the idea of arguing with him that my money and retirement were also involved. I felt Jim was insufficiently aware that he was professionally out of control. In addition to my concern about the business, I was terribly distraught over Hazel.

Smoking grass at night was an immense help to relieve the tremendous apprehensions about Hazel and the business, and it also helped me to sleep. Without it, I felt I was close to breaking down. The grass also aided me in writing the humorous commercials. Without it, I could not find humor in anything then. For the first time in my life, I was physically and emotionally drained.

Our beautiful daughter is born

When Hazel reached the sixth month of her pregnancy, the hospital released her more often for visits home. We had kept in touch with Hazel's sister, Mary Ann, and now she offered to come to Hawaii to help with David and the forthcoming baby. I immediately sent her airline tickets. It was good to have her with us, and she was a comfort to Hazel.

One evening, in the ninth month, we had just retired when Hazel cried, "My gosh! I think I'm going to have it right now!" I called the doctor and told him we were on our way to the hospital. Hazel got into a muumuu while I grabbed a shirt, slipped into my Birkenstocks – and almost forgot to put on a pair of pants! I grabbed the bag I had already packed for Hazel, with a nightgown, toothbrush, and other necessities. As we left the bedroom and entered the hallway Hazel screamed, "The baby's coming!" and immediately lay down on the floor.

I yelled, "Mary Ann, boil water and bring some string and scissors!" I didn't have a clue what the boiling water was for.

Within three minutes out slid a beautiful baby girl with a full head of black hair and skin the color and texture of the palest pink rose petal. She wasn't even the angry pink that most newborns are. Nervously, and yet excited, I tied off both ends of the cord and then cut it, hoping I had done it properly. When I finished, my hands were still shaking so hard, I couldn't dial the phone to call the ambulance company! I dialed 0, and asked the operator to send an ambulance.

The next day the paper featured a picture of a smiling Hazel in a hospital bed, surrounded by flowers, and with me looking admiringly at her. The story read:

DO-IT-YOURSELF BABY DOING FINE

The baby wasn't due until this weekend, but it came early and David Ford, the father, found himself delivering it in the hallway of his home at 4683 Waiiki Place.

Ford, Vice President for Pacific Builders, delivered a 7-pound, 8-ounce girl to his wife Hazel yesterday. The baby came 15 minutes before the ambulance. The Fords were in the hallway because they had been getting ready to drive to the hospital when Mrs. Ford exclaimed, "My gosh! I think I'm going to have it right now."

Ford had some help from his sister-in-law, Mary Ann Grenz, of Lebanon, Ore., who was visiting to take care of the Fords' other child, 2-year-old David Guy, while Mrs. Ford was in the hospital. Both mother and daughter were reported in fine shape later yesterday at Kapiolani Maternity Hospital. "At the hospital they were a little surprised that this was my first delivery," the father said. "I'm still a little tired."

We named our daughter Sandra Ann Ford. However, our love for the ocean led us to call her Sandy. It was the perfect name, as Sandy loves the ocean also, and is a fine swimmer.

After Sandy's birth in 1963, Hazel spent weeks at a time in the psychiatric hospital. One day she said, "It's important we talk. The psychiatrist said that it would be better for the children if they had a mother image that didn't have frequent psychological problems." She went on, "They told me that a man shouldn't have to raise a child by

Thursday, May 11, 1961 HONOLULU ADVERTISER

Jerry Y. Chong

Ford and Mrs. — after unscheduled event.

Do-It-Yourself
Baby Doing Fine

The baby wasn't due until this weekend, but it came early and David Ford, the father, found himself delivering it in the hallway of his home at 4683 Waiiki Place.

Ford, sales manager for Pacific Builders Inc., summoned the memory of a high school biology course taken 15 years ago and delivered a 7-pound, 8-ounce girl to his wife, Hazel, yesterday.

* * *

THE BABY came 15 minutes before the ambulance. The Fords were in the hallway because they had been getting ready to drive to the hospital when Mrs. Ford exclaimed, "My gosh! I think I'm going to have it right now."

Ford had some help from his sister-in-law, Mary Ann Grenz, of Lebanon, Ore., who was visiting to take care of the Fords' other child, 2-year-old David Guy, while Mrs. Ford was in the hospital.

* * *

BOTH MOTHER and daughter were reported in fine shape later yesterday at Kapiolani Maternity Hospital. "At the hospital they were a little surprised that this was my first delivery," the father said.

"I'm still a little tired."

Honolulu Advertiser, May 11, 1961

Two years after our handsome son David Guy was born, I had the thrill of delivering our beautiful daughter Sandy – who wasn't willing to wait for a ride to the hospital.

himself, without a mother-wife role model. I've thought it over carefully, and I feel that he's right. It's possible that when I'm having one of my episodes I could injure myself or the children."

Hazel wanted me to find a person who would play with the children, perhaps sew clothes for them, and take time to read stories to them. She said, "If you do find that type of lady, I want to meet her, to interview her. I would like you to get me an apartment in Waikiki so I can see the children frequently."

I was stunned, but the psychiatrist at the hospital agreed with her. "Your wife's mental illness is not hereditary. However, by being with someone who displays inappropriate actions or talk, children can pick up some of the peculiar behavior. It's imperative that you also understand that it's possible that she can harm herself or your children. You must think about making a radical change."

"I don't want that," I said; "one day Hazel will be well. I love this lady and I want to be there for her."

The doctor rejected my delusion: "The prognosis for her future is dismal."

I was exhausted, and concerned about the children being with her. I still loved her very much, and I'm sure she loved me. But now we had two children to care for; and this was one of the times that the children's welfare had to come before our desires.

Hazel spent so much time in the hospital during the following two years that Sandy barely knew her, and David understandably missed her. He was an exemplary brother. Frequently, he would sit and watch the baby when she was in her playpen; Sandy was a pleasure for all of us.

Marie, our nanny, resigned. When Hazel was home from the hospital, they were in near-constant conflict. So I did some research and hired a well-recommended lady named Larlane "Jo" Hinkle. Jo had a baby daughter, about Sandy's age, who would be a perfect playmate for Sandy. I had my worries, but at least one of my fears proved to be unfounded: Hazel didn't seem to feel any sense of competition with another mother and her child.

Jo was also a professional hula dancer and taught little Sandy the hula. Sandy became one of the most talented and beautiful hula dancers that I have ever seen. Her beautiful hands resemble her mother's.

Meeting President Kennedy – a morose year

In June of 1963 President John F. Kennedy visited Hawaii to address the Conference of Mayors. My press card and my affiliation with CBS television were the entrée that gave me the good fortune of meeting him. Seated less than ten feet from him during his talk, I was awestruck; several times he looked right into my eyes. I was delighted, and now totally convinced that I had made the best choice possible voting for this young energetic President. He was friendly, approachable, humorous, and teeming with youthful enthusiasm. His handshake was firm. His sparkling blue eyes seemed to touch one's soul. It was easy to see why so many people loved this president, especially the ladies. I had even more aloha for him when I heard that, to ease his back pain and other ailments, he smoked pot. With happy-grass, I can understand why he enjoyed sex so much!

That summer my mother was living in Southern California, and she was not well. Carol insisted that Mother go into the hospital. Our mother's GP suspected that she might have cancer and he wanted to run some tests. Mother was reluctant. Years earlier she had experienced roughshod surgery, a hysterectomy at the Veterans Hospital. The incision looked like something an almost blind sail-maker had done while drunk. Her once pretty stomach had been mutilated – and had become infected. Mother had good reason to be terrified, not only of the unknown source of her pain, but also of surgeons. The doctors finally convinced her to allow exploratory surgery. She died in the recovery room. No cancer was found. I was grief-stricken, my anguish all the greater because I had not been there to see her one more time.

Photo: David R. Ford

Meeting President John F. Kennedy at the Conference of Mayors in June 1963, in Honolulu, was a huge thrill. My press card and my affiliation with CBS television provided the entrée.

Photo: KGMB-TV publicity dept.

James Shigeta was born in Hawaii, and incredibly gracious. He starred in the movies Flower Drum Song and The World of Suzie Wong, and in the TV shows Simon & Simon and Murder She Wrote, among many others.

Mother had been a nurse in World War I, and was buried with full military honors at Arlington National Cemetery in Washington, D.C. A truly loving mother and talented poet was now history. I still feel her loss. And her love.

Shortly after mother's death, dear sister Carol at age 38 finally allowed herself to be married to a long-time sweetheart, Harold Lavelle, a road-building and demolition contractor. A multifaceted, talented man, he worked hard, yet was wise to enjoy life with his 63-foot sailboat, the *Navita*. Harold always had new top-quality cars and frequented the finest first-class restaurants. Both he and Sis Carol loved children, and ended up with three lovely girls.

● ● ●

The TV shows and commercials continued to generate new business. One afternoon a lady in her 60s came to Pacific Builders and insisted on seeing me. Her hair was bright red and her clothing was 1920s vintage. "Mr. Ford, I am Mrs. Hubert Tanner. I've been watching you on television for the past year. You're the man I want to put in charge of the design of my new apartment building, and to oversee the construction of it. I'm living in one of my other apartment buildings in Waikiki. I'd like you to come for a goose dinner this evening and examine the design I have in mind."

We took my car because she'd taken a cab to our offices. When we arrived I was astonished at the size of her penthouse, more than 3,000 square feet, with a view of Waikiki Beach and Diamond Head. Business letters were strewn over a good portion of the living-room floor, dozens of them containing undeposited checks made out to her.

"Will Mr. Tanner be joining us for dinner?" I asked, noting three places set at the table.

"Oh, Hubert died 20 years ago. But don't worry for a second that I don't have the money for our project. Hubert invented the marshmallow. Anyone who manufactures marshmallows must pay me royalties."

Any image I'd had of a proud and gently steaming goose on a silver platter faded when I saw her pull two packaged dinners out of the freezer. While she unwrapped them and set the microwave with obviously practiced fingers, I began picking up checks and piling them on her desk. Some amounts were in the thousands of dollars. Mrs. Tanner kept winking at me. We small-talked until the microwave's bell informed us that my goose was cooked. Actually, less than half cooked, as I found when we sat down.

*1963: Five-year-old son David loved the diver's helmet the Navy presented to me...
which made an excellent mailbox.*

Three-year-old Sandy with her pal and mine, my sister Margo.

I was still curious about the third dinner setting. "Will there be another guest?"

"You might say that. Here, Poofie! Here, Poofie!" Out of nowhere shot a shrill, yapping poodle that reminded me of an insane Siamese cat. Mrs. Tanner placed a china dish of cooked chicken livers on one of the plates. In two mighty leaps for dogkind, Poofie sprang onto the table and began slurping down her chicken livers within two feet of my dinner. Mrs. Tanner scooted her chair suggestively close to mine.

Often my hostess lifted a silver flask to her heavily rouged lips and took a long suck out of the glistening container. "I enjoy a little brandy with my meals. And sometimes in between." Another wink. Offering me the flask, she asked, "Would you like some, David?"

"No, thank you." I suppressed a gag reflex when Poofie began helping me eat my half-frozen goose – and again when Mrs. Tanner's hand slid up my thigh. "David, you remind me of my first husband, Roger."

For dessert, the three of us ate a half-frozen brandy cake.

The next morning I told Jim that I'd appreciate it if he took over Mrs. Tanner's project. "You might fall in love with her, and you wouldn't feel the need to present her with a four-carat diamond ring. *She'd* probably give *you* one."

"Not a chance. The receptionist told me the lady has eyes for you. You do whatever it takes to close that deal. Call her right now. You're the best, keed."

When I phoned Mrs. Tanner she invited me to spend a weekend at her oceanfront home in Lanikai, a beautiful area adjacent to Kailua, on the north side of Oahu. "I want to go over the plans and costs. I'm ready to start construction," she said. I told her that I had promised my son I'd play with him that weekend. (Hazel was back in the hospital.) "That's fine. Bring him along. You and he can use the guest cottage."

David and I arrived at Mrs. Tanner's Lanikai home at 2 p.m. on Saturday. It was an imposing home on a private beach. I'd priced properties like hers before, and was sure that the half acre of land alone was worth at least a half million dollars.

She answered the door herself. "Son, I'd like you to met Mrs. Tanner." With poise far beyond his four years, David looked her right in the eyes and shook her hand. I was proud of him.

"Nice to meet you, son. You're very polite. You and daddy play for a time, I'm going to take a rest."

David and I had played in the ocean, close to the house, for about a half hour when I noticed Mrs. Tanner sitting close by, watching and drinking from her flask of brandy. "All right, gentlemen," she called, "supper will be ready in half an hour." We went into the guest cottage, which was surprisingly neat, and showered and dressed for dinner.

When Poofie sprang up on the table to join us for dinner, David looked at me, tilted his head, and raised an eyebrow in amazement. He was unfailingly polite and made no comment to Mrs. Tanner. She kept filling my wine glass with an inexpensive Zinfandel, and after another half-thawed grocery-store dinner, out came dishes of ice cream for four. At last, something that was *supposed* to be frozen. David enjoyed ice cream and wasted no time eating his. In his haste he ended up with a bit of it on his chin. Before he could wipe it off, Poofie sidled up to him and licked it off. At first he looked at me as if he was going to be ill, but instead he laughed.

As Mrs. Tanner and I went over the plans David quietly watched television, and around 8:30 I took my little son across to the guest cottage. As I tucked him in I told him I'd join him as soon as I finished doing some business with Mrs. Tanner. When I returned to the house, our hostess was wearing a see-through negligee.

After success in many professions, I fail in the oldest one

"I bought this just for your eyes, Roger – I mean David! You know, I've had every hair on my body removed. Would you like to see now, or wait until we go to bed?"

"Mrs. Tanner, I think we should finish going over the plans. I promised my son I would join him shortly and sleep with him in the guest cottage."

"David, I noticed that you admired this property. I rarely use it. I also own five condominium apartments in the Ilakai (an expensive high-rise oceanfront condo in Waikiki). Each has two bedrooms, and all are on the ocean side of the building. If you'll agree to be my lover, I'll give you this home, and three of the Ilakai apartments. And if you're really good in bed, I just may give you all five!"

I said, "Mrs. Tanner, I think you're a fine lady, and I'm very flattered, but I'm married, and it's also our company policy that employees never become emotionally involved with clients, no matter how much they may like them." To maintain an appropriately earnest expression, I ruthlessly suppressed the many images that sprang to mind of clients Jim had taken to bed.

Her expression froze over. She said only, "I think it's time you join your son." I did, and David and I were soon enjoying the sleep of the innocent.

In the morning we went to the main house. The doors were locked and it was obvious Mrs. Tanner had departed, probably the night before. David and I went out to breakfast, and then I took him home, where he, Sandy, and I played in the pool. I'd recently added a curved coral-colored slide, and we all enjoyed slithering down its water-sprayed plastic surface into the pool. Little Sandy did it head first with glee, and she was only two years old. Both children were already competent swimmers.

Monday morning I entered Jim's office with some trepidation. The look on his face informed me that he'd already heard the news. "Mrs. Tanner phoned this morning. She's on her way down here now to formally cancel the contract."

At that moment a special friend of mine, a pretty ash-blond German lady named Lisa stormed into my office. Jim made a quick getaway, and I didn't blame him: Lisa was furious.

"I heard that you spent the night with an old red-headed woman!"

"Lisa," I said, "David was with me and we slept in her guest..." At that moment Mrs. Tanner stamped into my office without waiting for the receptionist to announce her arrival. Lisa's eyes blazed. She took one look at Mrs. Tanner's hair and grabbed it. It came off! It was a wig, and under it she was almost bald! As the ladies started to go at each other I stepped between them, grabbed Mrs. Tanner's wig, and put it back on her head – backward. I turned it around and tried to apologize to each of them at the same time.

Some bombs can't be defused, of course.

"Roger, I never want to see you again!" Mrs. Tanner stormed out of the office and Lisa wasn't far behind. I called Jim on the intercom. "Jim, I'm sorry if you heard a racket from my office. I was unable to convince Mrs. Tanner to remain with us. I'll come into your office and explain."

● ● ●

In mid-1964, Pacific Builders continued to enjoy an outstanding reputation for quality construction – and our president continued to play the high roller. When an attractive woman came into our offices for an estimate on a home or an apartment building, what do you suppose happened to the bottom line? You're right. If she went to bed with Jim, he refused to believe our cost estimator, and convinced himself that his own personal cost estimate was more accurate. Contracts for homes and even high-rise apartment buildings were signed. Construction went into full swing. I estimated that costs of his sexual misadventures and losses on construction he approved when he was "thinking with his other head" amounted to close to a million. He was spending money on his amours that the sub-contractors had paid us for commercials. Lumber companies, the electrical contractor, and the concrete company became understandably impatient about money that was past due.

Jim called me into his office in June of 1964. "Sign here, keed."

"Sign what?" I asked.

"This fourth mortgage on Pacific Gardens."

I was angry. "Jim, I refuse to sign any more of our retirement away. You hired me to turn your company around. Once I accomplished that, you went back to your old ways. You're proof that a stiff prick has no conscience. You can't seem to understand that you are going to bankrupt Pacific Gardens Apartments – *and* Pacific Builders."

"Think it over, keed. I'm sure you'll make the right decision."

"I don't plan on signing another mortgage." I shook my head and walked out of his office.

Soon after this latest dust-up with Jim, a friend of mine who was aware of Hazel's illness, and of the doctor's suggestion that I find someone to be a mother to my children, told me of a lady he felt I should meet, a professional vocalist named Theo Lane. He said she was an outstanding talent, but would much rather have children than a career. So one evening in May I stopped at the Romany Room, a well-respected night club on Kalakaua Avenue in Waikiki. As I came into the room Theo was on stage singing "People," which had recently been a chart-topper for Barbra Streisand. I was impressed by Theo's talent and stage presence. Her voice was a combination of Streisand and Eydie Gormé, with a little Lena Horne. When she finished her set, I mentioned our mutual friend and invited her to join me at my table. We chatted at length about her career. She said, "I've never wanted anything more in my life than to have children. That would be more fulfilling to me than show business, but it hasn't happened. My ex-husband and I didn't have any luck."

Hazel wasn't getting any better. I missed her terribly, but I began thinking of what the psychiatrists had told me about having a maternal role model in the home. I visited Theo at the night club a couple of times a week to get to know her. After several weeks I took her out to dinner. She then had me to dinner at her house.

I invited Theo to join the children and me for swimming in the pool at home. "I've never had more fun," she said afterward. The children liked her. I had told Theo about Hazel, that I would always love her, and that if we divorced, I would still be her best friend, and help her to shop, and to pick out clothes. Theo said simply, "That's as it should be."

I decided it was time for Hazel and Theo to meet, and that a dinner out would be the least stressful setting. At that dinner they appeared to understand and respect each other. After Theo left for home, I asked Hazel for her thoughts. "I think she truly cares for you, and for the children. If you feel she would make a good stepmom – and after meeting her I feel she could be – then do it. I don't know if I'll ever be able to be a full-time mother. I have spoken again with the doctors, and they feel this is the right thing to do."

Today, surveys show that cohabitation is the choice for 50 percent of all couples,[18] but in those days living with a lady "without benefit of clergy" wasn't "proper." More important, it just didn't feel right to me. I still loved Hazel, but I was drained and acutely concerned about the children. I agonized over what the doctors had told me, about children who grow up with a parent who's mentally ill experiencing behavioral problems later in life. I thought it over for several weeks. I conferred with Hazel several times, when she was lucid, asking if she truly agreed with the doctors about our divorcing, and she consistently said, "Yes, I do."

I found a nice apartment in Waikiki for her. She decided to share it with another woman patient whom she knew and liked, who had also recently been released from the hospital.

With gratitude, turmoil, and a feeling of something missing in my heart, I married Theo on November 6, 1964. I wondered if it was fair to Theo when I still loved Hazel. I had a sincere fondness for Theo, admiration for her talent, and for her honestly caring for the children. But would that be enough?

When Hazel visited the children in our home she seemed happy. I spent time with her helping her to readjust, buying her new clothes, and helping her to select groceries to stock her new kitchen. She was dating a Hawaiian gentlemen who had been a friend of hers over the past year or so since their meeting at the hospital. He was stable emotionally; he'd been in the hospital to free himself from a drug addiction. I was glad she had a friend. I hoped she might have a meaningful relationship, even though that hope triggered more than a twinge of jealousy. I realized that I had to let her go emotionally.

The most terrible tragedy of my life

On November 23, 1964, Jim Humpert again called me into his office and asked me to sign the fourth mortgage on Pacific Gardens Apartments. I said, "I still have to think it over, Jim."

I retreated to my office and closed the door. I was still feeling confused by the conflicting emotions about the divorce, and my heart was also heavy over what by that time I considered four years of wasted energy with Pacific Builders. The fun we'd had making the commercials, the excitement of helping an enterprise grow, all of it was gone. I thought I might as well sign the fourth mortgage. What difference would it make? I could see clearly now that both Pacific Builders and Pacific Gardens were going down the drain. Even my anger against Jim had dissipated. I felt sorry for him, as I would for any prisoner of his own obsessions.

Janet, our receptionist, rang me. "Mr. Ford, there's a strange-sounding caller on the phone for you. It doesn't sound like Mrs. Ford. Would you like me to have her call back?" Janet was very perceptive; I'm sure she had an idea of what Hazel and I had been going through.

"Thank you, Janet. I'll take the call."

"Mr. Ford?"

"Who is this, please?"

"I'm Hazel's roommate. I'm locked out of the apartment. I've tried to get in, pounding on the door and ringing the doorbell, but the door is locked from the inside. What should I do?"

"Go get the manager and have him open the door," I said. "I'll be there in 10 minutes."

When I arrived, two police cars and an ambulance had converged in front of the complex. I ran up to one of the officers and asked if Hazel was all right. He laid his hand on my shoulder. "I'm sorry to say that Mrs. Ford has apparently shot herself in the head, and is dead."

I bolted toward the door. Another officer grabbed me. "I'm sorry, Mr. Ford. You can't go in at the moment. The medics are cleaning up the area. We would like you to wait for about 10 minutes, and then go in and make an identification."

My head was swimming. I was about to pass out. An alert medic sat me down and pushed my head down between by knees. I had no idea where Hazel might have obtained a gun.

About 15 minutes later, a medic and a police officer helped me up, holding my arms. A voice like a distant echo asked, "Would you care to come with us now, Mr. Ford?" I followed the voice into the living room. There on the floor was Hazel, looking peaceful, her eyes closed. I knelt down and stroked her sleek black hair. The voice asked, "Would you please tell us who this is, Mr. Ford?"

I heard my hoarse voice say, "That's my wife."

"Thank you. We won't trouble you anymore. You'll be contacted by the coroner's office for details."

I was sick at heart and sick to my stomach. I wanted to go home and tell Theo and the children, but I couldn't. I was confused, crazed. Sandy was only three and barely knew who her mother was, but David was now five, and he knew her very well; he would miss her. Would she have done this if I hadn't divorced her? I had lost my soul mate; and regret and guilt have never left me since.

I found myself back at the office, needing a friend. The only one I could think of was Jim. Even though we had been angry at each other, I also cared for him as a person. I pitied him for his reckless decisions, but I knew he loved the company he'd created. I desperately needed a compassionate friend. I drove to Pacific Builders, walked into his office, and told him what had happened.

His response made me come closer to punching a man out than I'd ever been. "This should be the happiest day of your life," he said. "She's tried it enough times. Now she's free, and you're free. What more could you ask for, keed? Now, sign this fourth mortgage, and let's get back to work. What you need is more work."

"I quit," I said abruptly. I was so terribly disappointed in this person I'd felt was my friend that I could feel the tears running down my cheeks. I scribbled my name on the mortgage papers still on his desk. "You can pick up your car in a week," I said. I threw my credit cards on his desk and walked out.

The next days were agony. I went home and told Theo what had happened, and that I needed to be alone. I locked myself in the bedroom and cried all night. I don't know if there's anything more devastating than the guilt you feel when someone you love suicides. You cannot but feel there was something you could have done to prevent it. So often, the sad fact is that there is nothing you can do. For some people life is so painful that all they want is out.

A neighbor who was a doctor at Kaiser Hospital tried to give me a shot of morphine to ease the anguish. I rejected his kindness. Had I wanted to reduce the agony of Hazel's death I could have lit up a joint. I didn't. I wanted to suffer. I wanted to feel the pain she must have felt. I was so overwhelmed with grief for a lady whom I truly loved that I was selfish in my bereavement. I should have been with my son. He had to know something terrible had happened. During my more rational moments I wanted to hold David and tell him how much I loved him, and his mother. I couldn't pull myself together.

Two days after Hazel's death I took David for a ride to a new subdivision in Portlock, adjacent to Hawaii Kai, near the estate of Henry J. Kaiser. I parked on a hillside. "I'm so sorry that daddy has been crying rather than talking to you before now. I needed some time first to be alone. You know that mommy has been in the hospital for a long time, that there were times that she wasn't her usual happy self."

"But why were you crying, daddy?"

"I was sad," I said, swallowing and choking back tears. "Mommy was sick, and she went to heaven. She won't be with us any more, but she will always be looking down upon you, and love you and Sandy."

"Did Mommy die?"

"Yes, Mommy is in heaven." I held him in my arms and kissed him. Did he understand how permanent death is? I didn't know. We went for a ride to Sandy Beach, where Hazel and I had often taken David and his sister. David gazed out at the ocean, and looked confused. I held his little hand. A few days later I had David talk with Dr. Spicer. Afterward, the doctor told me that David was taking the news as well as could be expected.

When the mortician came for Hazel's clothes, I gave him a bright muumuu, as she'd always loved these colorful and comfortable Hawaiian dresses. Hazel loved her wedding ring and never took it off, even after our divorce. I made it clear she was to be buried with it on. I phoned her family again in Oregon. They wanted her to be buried in the family plot. I told them I would take care of it. When she was ready, I went to see her at the mortuary. She looked peaceful. Her thick black hair was still beautiful. I combed it back with my fingers, and kissed her forehead. I agonized over whether I should have brought David with me. I wanted to give him a chance to say goodbye, but the memory of my mother taking me to that funeral home when I was four kept coming to mind. I didn't want David to live with anything like that, so I didn't bring him. Should I have? I still don't know.

Photo: KGMB publicity dept.

After Hazel's tragic death and my sad and bitter departure from Pacific Builders, I threw myself into television full time. Like First Run Theater, my own show, Hollywood's Greatest Movies, included interviews. Even my grief couldn't withstand the wacky humor of Jonathan Winters. Only that table kept me from falling off my seat.

With Hazel's blessing, talented vocalist Theo Lane stepped in to be Mom for David and Sandy. Theo appeared on many TV shows, and was a featured vocalist in Japan. Here she's singing with Joe Castro's International Jazz Band: Joe on the piano, John Pool on drums, and Buddy Banks on bass.

Many of my TV commercials were family affairs. Theo wrote jingles for sponsors, and she and the children acted in some of them. More than one featured pies made with shaving cream. Mom Theo helped Sandy and David prepare to get even with Daddy – and David insisted on finding out how it feels!

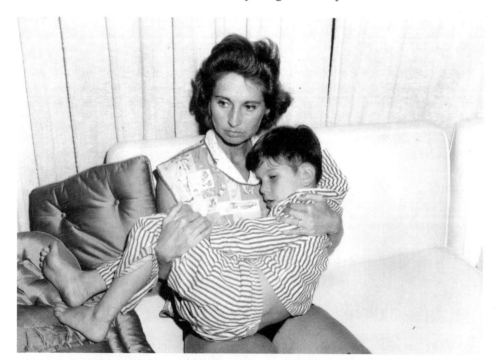

Theo, sleepy herself, gathering strength to carry a tuckered-out six-year-old actor to bed.

I told Theo that I was going to accompany Hazel on the plane to Lebanon, and attend the funeral. I had felt that Theo truly cared for Hazel, and empathized with the loss Hazel had to have felt. Now, the look on her face was cold. "The children have already lost one mother. If you want them to lose another one, you just leave with Hazel. When you get back, I won't be here."

For the first time I felt that I didn't know Theo at all. She knew I loved Hazel; but she seemed detached, almost emotionless. A shiver ran down my spine. My eyes teared with fury and disappointment. I had underestimated her insecurity, and expected too much from her. The children had bonded with her and I didn't want to have them hurt any more, so I didn't accompany Hazel's body to Oregon, or attend the funeral. I've always regretted it. From that moment on, our marriage was doomed. I felt that I couldn't take the chance at that time to have Theo leave the youngsters, but I had made it clear to them, and in private to Theo, that no one else would be their mother. Only "Mom."

Since the tragedy of Hazel's death, I have never allowed the children to have, or play with, a toy gun. David was probably the only little boy in Hawaii who received a soldier's outfit without a rifle.

Suicide is the eighth leading cause of death in the U.S., killing 30,000 people each year. More than 650,000 people make the attempt.[19] With 200 million guns in our country such tragedies will continue.

Meanwhile, I tried to understand Theo. She was insecure, both with her amazing voice and as a person. Her stepfather had physically abused her, once breaking her jaw when she was a child. She did her best with my children; she sang to them, read to them, made clothes and Halloween costumes for them. I believe she still loves them today. Yet her lack of confidence made it impossible for her to accept my leaving her, even temporarily, to bury Hazel.

David had shared a special bonding love with his mother, and I'm happy that he had that. She had driven him around the island many times, taken him out to lunch, and played peewee golf with him. He has always been so bright, I feel that he may have known at times that she was not well, but loved her more because of it. (I'm sure he had unusually good instincts. That time he and I visited Mrs. Tanner I felt he was aware she was "not quite right" – even though he was too polite to say a thing.)

I had him visit Dr. Spicer until the doctor felt he had adjusted to the horrible loss of his mother. In one of the visits, Dr. Spicer had David take an IQ test, and then called me in to show it to me, and to give me a copy. David's IQ was 135. I wasn't surprised. I'd never seen a child who could play so well by himself with mechanical toys. The preceding Christmas, when David was just four, Santa brought him, among other toys, a bicycle that had to be assembled. The next morning Dad tried putting the bike together. David watched with an amused expression for quite a while. Then he took the tools from my hands, and within a half-hour had the bike ready to roll.

I stayed home with the youngsters for a week, except to go out and buy a car for us, a two-year-old four-door Cadillac. Jim no doubt got the word and had my company car picked up the next day. The TV show was canceled.

A new career in television

Word spread that I was no longer with Pacific Builders, and might be available. In the four years *Pacific Builders First Run Theater* was on the air, many companies in Honolulu had asked that I personally do their television commercials. When I felt well enough to work I made an appointment to see Cecil Heftel, owner of KGMB TV and radio, the CBS television and radio affiliate for the Hawaiian Islands. I felt that a new challenge would help to mend the pain of Hazel's death. He was most cordial, and I began working with his TV station within the month.

I trademarked the name of my new show, *Hollywood's Greatest Movies*, and set out to obtain celebrity interviews. Most of the movies I selected were three- and four-star rated. That translated to a first-run movie each Saturday night during prime time. I had each show re-telecast the following Sunday morning, when those who didn't care for religious programs had little to watch. Soon, the show was receiving the highest ratings for that time slot. I declined to run any movie that had a suicide in it. For three years I was unable to watch any such movie, and I didn't want to be responsible for anyone else seeing them, either. I also rejected motion pictures that contained handguns used for killing.

The children were my greatest therapy in trying to put the tragedy behind us. I used them in as many television commercials as possible. I hoped that the recognition they'd receive from their peers at school would help increase their confidence, and diminish the pain of losing their mother.

Less than a year after my departure Pacific Gardens Apartments was in bankruptcy. Soon thereafter Jim and Pacific Builders went out of business. Hawaii lost a fine construction company and he ended up with nothing. Jim died in London of cancer in 1982 when he was 72. He phoned me just before his death to say goodbye. I was truly sorry for him.

Sandy – a comedian-to-be?

Little Sandy provided us with many memorable occasions for laughter. At her fourth birthday party, our neighbor Ruby brought her dog along. Sandy asked, "How old does your dog have to be to have a baby?"

Ruby said, "Three years old."

"I'm four," said Sandy. "I can have one right now!"

Sandy didn't stop there. She said, "Daddy, I was going to give you some of my birthday candy, but I didn't want you to get rotten teeth!"

The next morning around seven, I was awakened by my daughter shouting from the pool area. I opened the curtain, and there she was, standing on the diving board, stark naked, her golden little arms reaching toward the heavens. "God, I know you're up there. Come on out and talk to me!"

A few days later she said, "Daddy, I love you, and I never want you to die."

I was deeply touched. "Sandy, why were you thinking about death?"

Her answer: "Because you own the house, Daddy!"

That same year the kids' cat Georgie Girl had a kitten. Sandy wanted to know if she could take it to school for Show and Tell. She said, "It's pretty, daddy. I love it. While I'm at school could I sell it?"

While Sandy was still four, a good friend of mine, John Carroll, came over for a swim and brought his six-year-old son, Kirk. Soon, Sandy and Kirk disappeared. My parental antennae started twitching, so I started looking. I found the den door locked and promptly opened it using a wire. There were my four-year-old daughter and six-year-old Kirk, kissing. Kirk indignantly stated, "Close that door. This isn't a game for grownups!" Sandy had found her comic equal.

One day, Sandy asked, "Daddy, is farting inherited?"

● ● ●

Theo had sung with Joe Castor's International Jazz trio before our marriage and the two of them remained friends. We'd heard rumors that one feature of Doris Duke's fabulous mansion was a secluded lanaia king-sized bed suspended by heavy black chains; and that the heiress insisted on hearing live piano music when she made love. Joe mentioned that he and Doris had been married at one time.

We asked him if there was any possibility we could see the inside of the mansion.

"How about joining me for dinner there? Doris is in Spain at the moment, but we could go there for an evening. How about it?"

Of course, we accepted. The mansion is located on the side of Diamond Head. When we arrived the following Friday evening, we wondered if Joe hadn't been "putting us on." I pressed the intercom button.

A voice answered. "Mr. and Mrs. Ford?"

"Yes," I answered.

Seconds later the majestic iron gates opened. Joe was already there, and kindly showed us around. There was the private lanai with the ocean view – and the advertised king-sized bed suspended by black chains! Finally, we were ushered into another spacious lanai enclosed by glass walls, floor to ceiling, with glorious ocean views in three directions. A maid came in and offered us any choice of beverage. "Isn't it a little warm here this evening?" she asked in a friendly voice.

I looked at Theo. "It's fine," Theo smiled. Still, in a moment we heard a sound like a hydraulic lift and watched as the glass walls slowly descended into the ground. In moments we were sitting by the ocean on this beautiful lanai with no enclosure.

Joe ushered us into the dining room, which was like something you would find in a real castle. In fact, it reminded us of William Randolph Hearst's castle, Casa Encantada in San Simeon, California. A waiter appeared – and handed us menus! The service was better than at any restaurant, and the food finer.

Interviewing "the living dead" at the Hiroshima Atomic Bomb Hospital

Theo missed her professional singing career. When she was offered engagements in some of the finest clubs in Honolulu, we hired a nanny, Mary, to care for the children and to help around the house. Shortly after our first wedding anniversary, Theo received a contract for an engagement in Tokyo at $500 a week. I was happy for her, but she was a little nervous. I felt that being with Theo in Japan was important, that it would give her more confidence; so I offered to travel with her, she accepted, and I made arrangements.

The 20th anniversary of the detonation of the atomic bombs over

Hiroshima and Nagasaki would come around a few weeks after our arrival in Japan. Before we left I made plans to visit the Atomic Bomb Hospital in Hiroshima and interview some of the patients who had been in that hospital for all those years.

After making certain that the children were OK, we departed from Honolulu for Tokyo. At the Okura Hotel in Tokyo, one of the places where Theo was to perform, we were taken to a luxurious room. Her main engagement took place at a night club in the center of the Ginza in downtown Tokyo, The New Latin Quarter. It was exciting to hear her introduced in Japanese. She stood on a pedestal below stage level. When the 21-piece orchestra began playing, the pedestal slowly lifted 10 feet, and Theo rose into view, microphone in hand, singing to an appreciative audience. Some of the numbers included "I Left My Heart in San Francisco," "Falling in Love with Love," "Misty," "When the Sun Comes out," "Day in Day Out," and "Let Me Entertain You," as well as some songs she sang in Japanese.

We soon fell into a pattern. Theo worked until 2 a.m. By the time she unwound, bathed, and went to bed it was about 3:30 in the morning. I woke early and left the room around 8 a.m., while she slept on. I headed out with so many cameras that I must have looked like an American tourist.

"Don't let it happen again!"

On August 6, 1965, 20 years to the day after the U.S. Air Force bombed Hiroshima, I left Tokyo behind to travel to that city. I first visited the Peace Memorial Park, located within the square mile that the explosion of one atomic bomb literally vaporized. Join me in a visit to the Atomic Bomb Hospital:

The hospital was home for dozens of "living dead" who had been there for 20 years, ever since the bomb killed 200,000 of their neighbors. Through an interpreter I was able to talk with many of these patients. Most of them were so hideously disfigured they were outcasts in their own communities. Word spread among the patients that for the first time an American civilian was visiting them. From these lonely and forgotten ones, tears ran and arms of *welcome* were outstretched to *me*, an *American*. I had prepared myself for a hostile response. Instead, I was encouraged to ask questions.

I began the visit in the women's ward. The first lady I interviewed had no hair. She had no nose. Her eyes were bandaged. She, like the others, was terminally ill with radiation poisoning. In addition to open wounds and sores that never healed, many of these people suffered from cancers that were caused by the nuclear weapon. Many had leukemia or multiple myeloma. Others had malignant tumors characterized by an infiltration of bone and marrow, accompanied by anemia and kidney lesions, illnesses which were usually fatal by themselves. I sat on her bed and held her hand. I asked if she would care to talk about the day the bomb was dropped. She answered, "Yes."

"I was 13 when the Americans dropped the bomb. I was in our schoolyard chatting with schoolmates, waiting for the bell to ring for school to begin. I saw a blue-red flash. It was like another sun. Minutes later, thousands of people were screaming in agony. Many were naked from the concussion, their bodies black. Blood was coming from all their body openings. From many the flesh had been stripped, and hung so that one could see the bones. For some, it was like someone cut you with a razor at least a quarter-inch deep from shoulder to shoulder, then pulled the meat all the way down to your hips and then burned you with a blow torch. I didn't know then how badly I was injured. A school friend raised her hand for me to help her. I reached for her hand. Her skin came off like a glove, to the elbow. I vomited. Thousands of people were screaming and crawling to the river, desperate for water. As they drank, they died in horrible pain, filling the river like pieces of driftwood."

I listened to several such stories in the women's ward.

When it was too much of a challenge to keep back the tears, I asked to go to the men's ward. One of the men was without legs. He had open sores on his face and body. With tears in his eyes he said:

"Don't let it happen again. I saw mothers dead, black on the ground, skin stripped from their bodies. Some had sheltered their babies with their bodies to protect them from the blast. One baby was still alive, and was trying to nurse from its mother, but her breasts were destroyed. Some people died standing upright. Their eyes liquefied from looking at the blast. It was horrible." He began sobbing and squeezed my hand.

One patient said that "all communications were out. Total hysteria, screams of agony, and panic prevailed. Tokyo couldn't be contacted, or there surely would have been an immediate unconditional surrender. Hospitals were destroyed. The only medication for most of the victims was mercurochrome. Three days later, around 11 a.m., a second atomic bomb was dropped on Nagasaki, with similar results."

I said, "We dropped millions of pamphlets warning civilians to evacuate the cities."

He looked into my eyes. "No paper was ever dropped. No warning was ever given."

I held the hand of a dying patient. All I could say was, "I'm so sorry. We just wanted to end the war."

He said, "Our hatred is against the bomb, not the Americans. You are brave to look at us. Please spread the word that it must never happen again. There is no more agonizing way to die."

For the first time in my life I felt that euthanasia was a good thing, would have been a blessing to many of those tortured souls, whose suffering had not ceased for 20 years.

Today, a single nuke is 4,000 times more destructive than those first atomic bombs. In 1972 President Nixon raised the idea of using a nuclear bomb against North Vietnam. When asked about the inevitable deaths of civilians, he said, "I don't give a damn."[20] Perhaps you recall that during the 1991 Gulf War people wrote letters to the editors of newspapers, and called radio and television talk shows, suggesting that we nuke Iraq. Sadly, the same response was heard after the tragedy of September 11, 2001, when terrorists crashed planes into New York's World Trade Center and the Pentagon in Washington. If our people had any idea of the medical dimensions of what nuclear weapons render, I'm certain they would never suggest such a horrible death for anyone. We must prevent such weapons of war being used. It could happen to us.

The Japan Times did a story on our visit, "TV Host From Honolulu Gathers Material Here." The story followed for several columns. Japan is a beautiful country with friendly, caring people. Theo also received good press; she did well in Japan, and remained for several more weeks. For me, though, it was time to return. I was eager to be home again, and to see and play with the children.

● ● ●

On Monday, July 19, 1965, *The Pacific Business News* surprised us with a full-page story and photo:

TELEVISION'S LAUGH-PROVOKING DAVE FORD
INAUGURATES HIS OWN ADVERTISING FIRM
Dave Ford is once again up to his spellbinding tricks – tricks that catch and hold a television audience, tricks that make money for his clients. He has started an advertising business – the Dave Ford Agency – that has many top accounts. (Among them promotion and radio and television advertising for Times Super Markets, Ltd.)

But it was the Agency's first project, *Hollywood's Greatest Movies*, that put Ford solidly back in that familiar rectangle, the television screen. It all came about quite naturally. For four years, Honolulu's television fans kept up a regular acquaintance with Dave Ford because they watched a show called *Pacific Builders First Run Theater* on KGMB-TV. Come time for a commercial and onto the screen would pop the mischievous face of Dave Ford, alongside that of Jim Humpert, and after staging some unpredictable waggery, the two would start discussing the merits of Pacific Builders, the sponsor. Humpert was president of Pacific Builders and Ford was vice-president.

Before long, KGMB-TV (the CBS affiliate) was able to proclaim in a big newspaper advertisement that the latest TV ratings showed Dave Ford's show had captured 79 percent of the total viewing audience during that time slot.

The quality of the movies helps snare that hefty slice of audience, and so do Ford's interviews with celebrities when the film is finished. But undeniably, it's Ford's own puckish humor that keeps 'em hooked week after week. Quipped *Finance Factors'* Bob Maxwell in one of his Tiptopics columns in *Pacific Business News:* "Best Year Yet to Go Ford!" And as an official of Sealy Mattress Co. (one of Ford's sponsors) put it, many people watch "not always because of the motion picture presented, but rather to see what Dave Ford is up to this week."

Ford can be up to practically anything that's likely to intrigue the viewer's sense of humor and thereby set him laughing. For example, take a commercial Ford did for Andrade's men's wear. "At the end of that commercial," says Ford, "I mentioned that I was all set to go golfing – with golf shoes from Andrade's, my Ben Hogan slacks, and a little equipment of my own. At which point, I slapped on my crash helmet and goggles and headed out across the golf course in a wheelchair!"

Keeping away from violence, other than an occasional war story, and concentrating on family entertainment was an important consideration in the films I selected. I refused to do any commercials for cigarettes or alcohol. (If cannabis had been legal, however....)

Gossip columnists, such as Eddie Sherman, Wayne Harada, and Tom Horton, wrote about almost every trip we took, and all of the humorous commercials, and the interviews. The Sunday supplement of the *Star-Bulletin & Advertiser* did front-page pictures and stories in the *TV Week* section, such as, "A Ford with Lots of Drive," or, "Pies the Appetizer to Open TV's Dave Ford Show." They would go into detail on my background: "Scholarship Led to TV Career." Another half-page story had the headline "TV Emcee with a Sense Of Humor." Imagine the stories they might have produced had they known that I'd created most of my commercials and promotions after smoking a joint!

For once, Charlton Heston isn't Number One!

It was fun to be a celebrity, if only in Hawaii. Sometimes we went to the International Market Place in Waikiki to have dinner at Duke Kahanamoku's, with hundreds of other guests. A spotlight swung away from the stage and shone on our table. Hawaii's best-known entertainer, Don Ho, who was doing his show there at that time, would say something like: "Ladies and gentlemen, I'd like you to meet Hawaii's number one television personality, Mr. Dave Ford. Dave, would you kindly stand up and give our friends a wave of Aloha." There was a twinge of embarrassment as I stood up and waved. For me, my current fame was simply the result of years of just having fun with people. This recognition became common at Hawaii's night clubs and restaurants, and they frequently wouldn't allow us to pay the check. Consequently, we didn't go out as much as we otherwise would have.

The primo fun incident came when our film crew had the delight of filming an interview with Charlton Heston on the beach at Waikiki. He was on location, starring in *Diamond Head*. He's a bright guy who read a book a day while waiting for his scenes to be shot. When our interview was over, he and I strolled down Kalakaua Ave. to have lunch at the Royal Hawaiian. Along the way, two teen-age ladies stopped us and asked for an autograph. Heston was most polite. He pulled out a pen and asked if they had something to write on.

Flustered, the girls stammered, "Oh, no. We want Dave Ford's autograph!"

Heston laughed, handed me the pen and said, "How does it feel to be a big frog in a little pond?"

I said, "It feels great, especially right this second!"

I was saddened to hear in late 2002 that this powerful actor has been diagnosed with Alzheimer's.

He was certainly right about Hawaii being a small pond – but if ever I got puffed up and started taking the big-frog stuff seriously, there was always someone around to deflate me. Three brief examples:

Numerous resorts on neighbor islands invited us to be their guests. One day while traveling from Honolulu to the Big Island, a lady on the plane, who must have seen a commercial I'd done for Sears Roebuck, said, "I know you! Don't you sell underwear at Sears?"

It was a thrill when the Nielsen ratings showed that Hollywood's Greatest Movies captured 79 percent of the total viewing audience in Hawaii. Credit should go to the cannabis that inspired all those comical commercials.

I said, "You have an amazing memory. Thank you."

Another time I was walking down Kalakaua Avenue in Waikiki. An attractive lady stopped me and said, "Dave Ford. You're a Capricorn, aren't you!"

I said, "That's right. How did you know?"

She said, "Because my dog is a Capricorn!" (The mental picture of me licking her face sprang to mind.)

The capper, though, had to have been the man who came up to me one day while I was shopping for clothes and said, "Dave, I just want to tell you how much better you look – on television."

Hawaii's top radio personality smokes pot – on the air

One of the bonuses of being around creative show people is that many of them smoke grass at times to relax. Some use it for creativity, and it can also act as a mental stimulant.

I frequently arrived at KGMB early in the morning to edit films, line up costumes, or search the news wire for celebrities arriving in town. KGMB's TV and radio stations shared a single facility, and often I'd stop and watch Hawaii's best-known, most creative disk jockey and radio host do his show. Hal Lewis had given himself the attention-getting moniker J. Akuhead Pupule – "Crazy Fish Head" in Hawaiian. During the 1960s Hal was earning over $200,000 a year. He routinely did his entire radio show standing up. He was clever and bright, a caustic commentator who took shots at the mayor, the governor, and the police chief. In fact, at anyone and everyone who garnered attention. His popular show ran from 5 a.m. until 10 a.m., so he caught the morning commuters. After reading the morning papers he would comment on the news, and you hoped you weren't in it! "Aku" had the largest radio audience in Hawaii.

One morning I paused to admire him doing the news and making clever remarks – and my jaw dropped. Staring at him, I thought: surely that can't be a joint in his hand? It was! I pointed at it through the studio glass and gave him a big grin. He saw me, smiled, and held the joint out to me as if saying, "Have a toke if you want one." I slipped in and took a hit, while marveling at his unbroken focus on the broadcast.

I couldn't imagine myself doing the type of quick thinking that he did the whole time he was on the air. We're all different. (I know people who drink a cup of coffee to ensure a good night's sleep.) I've noticed, though, that lots of people think more clearly after a hit or two of grass.

"Aku" was commenting on the news, pulling records, doing commercials, and taking phone calls, all while smoking a joint! Proof that it works for some people. I'm free to mention Hal's name and his use of grass only because, sadly, he has died.

Interviewing Don Ho

Don Ho was a pleasure to interview. He's Hawaii's most notable and perhaps longest-shining star. He personifies Hawaii with his golden skin, black glistening hair, white straight teeth, and genial personality; he exudes the Aloha spirit, making everyone feel relaxed.

Don has the richly mixed ancestry of many islanders, mostly Hawaiian and Chinese, with a smattering of Dutch, Portuguese, and German. He was in the Air Force from 1954 through 1959, where he attended jet fighter school and later commanded a C-47. He began his early singing career at Honey's Lounge in Kaneohe, and he still gives the little lounge full credit for launching his perennially successful career. In turn, Don has always helped Hawaii's new talent; some years later Sandy danced professionally with his show for a time.

The revered Duke Kahanamoku

If you've visited Hawaii, no doubt you know of Duke Kahanamoku. He was Hawaii's hero and was acclaimed the world over as "The Father of Surfing." He introduced surfing to the world, starting with Australia in 1912, when he was just 22 years old.

Duke had set a world record in the 50-meter crawl and won gold medals in the Olympic Games in 1912 and 1920. In 1925 he received a medal for saving the lives of eight people whose launch had capsized at Newport Beach, California. The Duke was an icon of Hawaii: He was tall, handsome, and pure Hawaiian bronze. When I met him, his hair had turned to silver; but his body was still strong, and he was a fine swimmer at 75.

On one visit to the Kona Village on the Big Island, I met Duke Kahanamoku while bodysurfing there. I'd long admired him and was delighted to have the pleasure of visiting with him. He invited me and my family to join him for lunch. His lovely wife, Nadine, took a photo of the Duke and me at the Kona Village. It hangs on the wall in my home in Sonoma, California.

The Duke suffered a stroke in 1967, and had brain surgery performed at Kaiser Hospital. It was my privilege to do the last interview with him late that year. I did the program in the style of the popular old TV show

This is Your Life, asking family and friends for their memories of him. I asked Nadine if there was something she could tell us about Duke that wasn't already known. She smiled impishly and said, "When we were invited to the Governor's Mansion in Honolulu for long dinner parties, after dinner Duke would quietly crawl under that large table and go to sleep." I thought that was delightful, and so typical of true Hawaiians, who are not impressed with big government or politicians. Duke died on January 22, 1968.

On September 9, 2002 I was excited to return from the post office with the first of the new 37-cent stamps commemorating our Duke. A tribute to a great Hawaiian athlete, and friend to all.

Wayne Newton was our special star

In 1967 I was asked to produce and emcee a fund-raiser for the Disabled American Veterans. There was a live audience of 10,000 people in the Waikiki Shell on Sunday, July 30, to watch a show that featured most of Hawaii's finest talent.

Even professional entertainers become nervous before performing. One of the group vomited. Someone passed joints around, and a few of the more nervous took a couple of puffs. I empathized with them – so much so that I took a couple of hits myself. Pot often works better than Valium or the alcohol that some entertainers use to relax. The strained expressions dissolved. Then those mellow people went out on stage confident and professional – and performed their numbers beautifully.

The show was going admirably when someone backstage said, "Dave, I just heard that Wayne Newton arrived in town a short time ago for the concert he'll be doing Friday evening."

"Super!" I exulted. "Please find out where he is. Tell him what we're doing, and that he told me when I interviewed him in Las Vegas that if he could ever do me a favor, he'd be glad to. Tell him that just appearing on the stage for a moment would be that favor!"

Within a half hour there was Wayne backstage, shaking my hand. With him was his brother Jerry and comic Jackie Kahane. Wayne said, "We've been up all night, Dave. But just tell me what I can do to help."

I grinned. "Wayne, if you'd just go out there and say 'Hi' to the folks, and thank them for contributing to the DAV, that would be terrific. Of course, if you felt like belting out a song, I wouldn't stop you!"

Wayne went out, with an enthusiasm you'd expect to see in a newcomer getting his first big break instead of a seasoned professional. He had

Duke Kahanamoku, pure Hawaiian bronze! Hawaii's hero, he was acclaimed the world over as "The Father of Surfing." It was my privilege to know him, swim with him, and interview him. In 2002 I was excited to see the new 37-cent stamp with our Duke on it (inset).

In 1968, David was nine, Sandy was seven, and I was 40. Both children were already excellent swimmers, and Duke's ardent admirers.

never practiced with our big band, yet this super showman, Mr. Las Vegas, belted out three snappy numbers, "Won't You Come Home, Bill Bailey," "Bye Bye Blackbird," and "Red Roses for a Blue Lady." The next day the *Honolulu Advertiser* featured a six-column story with the headline "VARIETY NICELY SPICED IN DAV BENEFIT REVUE." The story mentioned that the show "was easily the year's best entertainment package" for the crowd of 10,000. And it went into detail on all of the numbers performed. It gave everyone involved a nice personal credit, and mentioned the surprise appearance of Wayne Newton. The story ended with:

> The revue was five months in planning. With so many stars in town, it's nice to see such cooperation and showmanship. Everyone worked hard to present a totally professional show, and how could it have been otherwise? Everyone was a pro.

Wayne Newton again demonstrated what a kind-hearted and generous guy he is.

Those of you who visited Waikiki before 1970 may recall the Queen Surf. Here was a piece of true Hawaiian paradise and charm: wide open, with a grass-thatched roof and five or six thousand square feet of dance floor, stage, and bar. The Queen Surf presented some of the finest Hawaiian shows in the islands. Being next to the warm waters of the Pacific, with palm trees swaying in the gentle trade winds, added to the enchantment. Hawaiian songs and music drifted out onto the beach, along with the aroma of sweet marijuana. You couldn't help but be entranced by the kaleidoscope of glittering gold and crimson sky, as the sun nestled slowly into the western horizon.

One super entertainer and personal friend I met at the Queen Surf was Sterling Mossman. I wanted to interview him. Not only was he the talented man who produced the show *Barefoot in Paradise* at the World's Fair in 1964, but he also was the director of the Barefoot Bar at the Queen Surf. I had the privilege of knowing this man of Hawaii, who was a great performer, vocalist, dancer, and guitarist. He was also a police officer. He rose from the ranks of Patrolman to Lieutenant of Detectives with the Honolulu Police Department. He never even suggested the possibility of busting anyone for smoking pot. He told me, "Alcohol causes hell. Marijuana causes peace."

Cannabis helps Hawaii's great talent Kui Lee find peace

Featured on the Ed Sullivan television show, Kui Lee was a songwriter whose ancestry was Hawaiian with a flavor of Chinese and Scot. Kui was a Hawaiian James Dean, but a rebel *with* a cause – he sought to break through superficiality and phoniness – a style that came through with feeling. *"Ain't no big thing,"* developed from pidgin English, was a phrase meaning that nothing is serious enough to worry about, and that became Kui's trademark. One of his most popular songs, "I'll Remember You," was made famous by the melodic voice of Andy Williams, sung frequently by Elvis Presley, and recorded by 30 other major vocalists. That song, and 80 others, including "The Days Of My Youth," "Rain, Rain, Go Away," and "My Hawaii," were written by that young Hawaiian, who deserves to be remembered.

Kui was one of the brightest stars of the Queen Surf. There were times Kui and I visited between his shows. And there were times when we smoked grass next to the ocean that we both loved. Kui had smoked grass for relaxation and to increase his creativity while writing new songs and acts. Now he smoked grass to relieve the pain from the cancer that had spread from his lymph glands to his lungs. He also smoked grass as a relaxant and stress reliever. He smoked grass to help forget the fear of dying. He smoked grass to help him smile again. And he smoked grass to help him sleep. The cannabis worked for all of those things. When he knew he was dying, Kui wrote, *"When the Time Comes."* He rarely slept or rested.

Years earlier, while Kui was seeking Hawaiian talent for his show, a young lady came to audition. She had taught hula in New York, and was an expert on the ukulele. This lovely lady was olive-complexioned, with large brown eyes and long black hair. She was regal. She was Nani. And Nani could sing and dance like no one Kui had ever met. Her confidence gave Kui confidence. He knew she was a lady. And if he did something wrong on stage, with Nani there with him no one would laugh at him. Nani and Kui fell in love. I later learned that Nani was at the hospital in Mexico with Kui when he died, at age 34. He asked her to cook a Hawaiian dish that he especially liked, and she left to do it. When she returned, his bed was empty and she was told he was dead. She had to be sedated.

Divorce

The marriage with Theo ended after three and a half years. She did her best to be a good mom; but it had to be a difficult position for her from the beginning, knowing that I still loved Hazel. After the divorce, Theo got a booking to return to Japan, and soon departed for Tokyo. The children wondered why they didn't hear from her. With the divorce I suspect she desired a total break. I knew it was difficult for her, but again the children had lost a mom. I forged a number of letters from her and read them to the children.

I had four or five different commercials pre-taped for each sponsor, along with a taped introduction for a specific movie, and a taped interview. I managed to reduce my in-studio time from six or eight hours a day to three or four hours a week. Now I had time to relax during the day while the children were at school, and lots of time to spend with them when they came home.

Sex can be a joint venture

Walking down Kalakaua Avenue in Waikiki one day, I was surprised by how many many young women I was passing. I asked a young newsboy, "Hey, brah, what's with all the *wahines* (ladies)?"

A big Hawaiian smile, and then "Dave Ford, you not know? Teachers' convention, brah. Wish I was older!"

I gave him a salute of "Mahalo," and began walking slower.

Within a few minutes a young lady tapped me on the shoulder. "Excuse me, sir, but could you please tell me what time it is?"

I looked at my watch. "In 17 seconds, it will be exactly 11:42 and one half."

Big smiles from two attractive ladies, in their early twenties I guessed. The first one's friend asked, "Could you kindly tell us where there's a good but reasonable place to eat lunch?"

"Do you like pizza?" I asked.

"We love it."

"And do you like a beer with your pizza?"

They both answered, "Yes!"

"I'll tell you what. There's a little grocery store a few doors down. I'm headed there, and then farther down the block to a super pizza parlor. I'm going down to the ocean to sit in the sand and have lunch. If you would care to be my guests we could do that together. What do you say?"

"We say, thank you!" said one of the young ladies.

Shortly after, I was sitting in the sand in front of the Moana Hotel with Barbara and Sally. Both were first-grade teachers, "and," Sally added, "we're roommates."

I just admired them for a moment. Sally was a tall, willowy brunette with big brown eyes and a pigtail, and Barbara was a little blue-eyed blond, with full breasts that pointed enchantingly right at me. I asked myself "What have I got to lose?" – and asked them, "Is there anything, any fantasy, that you ladies would like to experience while you're in Hawaii?"

They looked at each other, and giggled. Barbara answered, "We've fantasized for a long time about making love with one guy at the same time."

I was stunned, for about three seconds. "Is it possible that I might qualify?" I asked.

Barbara said, "Why do you think I tapped you on the shoulder? To ask the time?" We all laughed. She continued, "This is the kind of fantasy we would never dare to live out at home. We have a pretty nice hotel room, and we've been here five days, but darn it, we're leaving tomorrow. Dave, would you care to come up there with us?"

"I'll consider it," I said, laughing. As I got up and slapped the sand off my slacks, I remarked to myself how very young and pretty these young ladies were.

A half-hour later we were in their hotel room. I said, "Would you mind if I light up a joint?"

"Not at all", said Sally, "so long as you share it!" I never cease to be blown away by how many "straight" people smoke grass. If the government knew the actual numbers, they might consider abandoning their lies about a plant that's far less chancy than corporate pharmaceutical drugs.

It wasn't long before the joint was a proud little roach. Sally said, "I used to enjoy only hard rock. After my first experience smoking a joint, I don't know why, but I wanted to listen to classical music. I enjoy both now, but classical leaves me far more relaxed, thanks to pot."

"That's not unusual." I said. "Would you ladies mind if I took a quick shower? I think I'm a bit sandy."

Barbara laughed and said, "Why don't we see if the three of us can fit into the tub-shower?" It was a close fit, but none of us complained. We spent what seemed like hours sensually soaping each other up and rinsing each other off. The girls' tans were accentuated by their white breasts and their lovely white bottoms. By the time we dried each other off and slid into bed, we were ready to play. Each of us felt the mellowness and relaxation of the pot. We kissed, hugged, and stroked each other. The grass let us feel as though we had known each other for days rather than hours. Yet it wasn't the rushing to jump-on-their-bones feeling that alcohol so often produces, but rather a closeness, a camaraderie. The touching and holding became almost as satisfying as the intercourse. Barbara reached over to their nightstand and picked up a bottle of baby oil. We began oiling and massaging each other, until we were twisted into one big delicious pretzel.

We played for hours, and each of us had several super-long orgasms. I've never known a marijuana smoker, lady or man, who didn't recognize that the sense that time has slowed down causes the orgasm to be a blockbuster. I've also found that women who love sex are more adventurous and creative than most men. Men are simple creatures who enjoy sex mainly for fun – it feels good. Women feel that sex strengthens the emotional involvement. I suspect that they now also think, "Me wants lots of extra giant orgasms!" (Can't go wrong with a good vibrator, guys.)

● ● ●

The word was out that I was now single, and I began to receive invitations to gatherings. I still felt the never-to-be-forgotten pain of the loss of Hazel; to this day I still feel her love, and my love for her. But making love was natural to me, and was medicine for a broken heart. When making love, especially after smoking grass, I *feel* love, even though it may be temporary, for the lady (or ladies) that I'm with. For a little while I forget the pain and loneliness of Hazel's loss. It's as if I've taken a short vacation from remembering she is gone.

One day I returned a call from a lady who had left a message. I'd never met her, so I agreed to a rendezvous at a bar she named. She was pretty, in her early 30s, and the wife of an executive of Dole Pineapple. She had long brown hair that fell below her shoulders, green eyes and a neat figure. "I'm Juliet. Let me be frank, Dave. I've watched you for years on TV and I've always wanted to meet you. My husband, if you can call him that, is gone most of the time on business trips to Japan, Hong Kong, and the mainland. He never invites me along. He says it's company policy."

I told her that I didn't date ladies who were with other men.

"We're not really married. If I'm lucky, he makes love to me once in three or four months. He says he has too much business on his mind. I think he has another lady. Please? I'm horny! I have a hotel room rented. If you're by any chance available, I'd certainly love it if you would care to be my friend."

If what she's saying is true, I rationalized, it's not like I'm infringing on another man's wife. "I'd be honored to be your friend, Juliet." So we were soon in her hotel room and bed. She was a wild lady, and terrific fun. After several hours we showered and I took her back to the Tahitian Lanai, on a lagoon, with its thatched Hawaiian roof and decor, including original black velvet Leeteg paintings. It's where we'd met. As we parted, she asked for a "date" three days later.

"Noon, Thursday," I said, "at the Barefoot Bar. It's right on the ocean, with great food. You know the spot?"

Juliet winked, and nodded her pretty head.

Black and white and red all over

Noon, Thursday. I was there. And so was Juliet – and so was her maid, wearing a black dress and a white apron, right out of an old movie. Juliet introduced me to Lulubelle, who was about 20 and seriously attractive, with luminous eyes and dark chocolate skin. I started to extend my hand. "Don't shake her hand, she's a maid," Juliet snapped. "I'll be taking her back home before we leave, David. I brought her along only because she talked me into bringing her into town to buy a dress. Ignore her. Now, order us a drink, dear."

Lulubelle looked downcast.

"Lulubelle, can I have the pleasure of offering you a drink?" I asked.

"No, thank you", she said politely. When our martinis were served, Juliet said, "You don't even have a boyfriend, Lulubelle. What's the matter with you? All you do is stay in your room when you're not cleaning or cooking. Can't you get a man?"

"I'm kind of shy, ma'am. There aren't many black gentlemen in Honolulu. Your home is beautiful, but it's 15 miles from town and there's no transportation."

"Lulubelle, I don't know why I keep you. You're not very bright, are you? In fact, I'd say you're pretty stupid." She tossed back the last of her martini.

My whole body felt as though it was turning red with embarrassment for Lulubelle, and outrage at Juliet. I dropped five dollars on the bar for the drinks. I hadn't touched mine. As I stood I said very formally, "Please let me take you wherever you're going, Lulubelle."

"*We're* going, David," Juliet said. "Leave that black piece of shit."

"You're wrong," I said. "Lulubelle and I are leaving."

I looked Lulubelle straight in the eye, and lifted her elbow gently. She nodded mutely, and stood. We walked out.

"Come back here!" shrieked Juliet, as the door swung shut.

I led Lulubelle to the car and opened the door. Tears were streaming down her face. "I tried so hard. When she drinks she's always like that to me. I'd already decided if she abused me again, I'd quit." A little smile came through the tears. "I guess I just did. So happens I phoned some people this morning who offered me a job. They know Ms Juliet and her husband. They said I could move into their home tonight, and they would go get my clothes tomorrow." She added, "Ms Juliet even rubbed it in to me how much fun she had with you, Mr. Ford."

"Please, Lulubelle, the name is Dave, or David. Sadly, alcohol affects too many people that way. Incidentally, to celebrate your new job, would you by any chance care to make love with me?"

"I surely would, Mr. Dave."

"It's just plain Dave, OK?"

A Japanese friend of mine owned a motel catering mostly to Japanese clients. I phoned to reserve a room, and my friend said, "Number seven will be waiting for you, Dave. The key will be in the lock. I wish you a happy afternoon."

Lulubelle loved it. It was a cozy room with a king-sized bed and a slow-moving ceiling fan. She said, "I don't like liquor. When I was home in Alabama, we used to smoke grass. My daddy used to have bad things happen when he drank liquor. He'd go out in the streets at night and get into fights. But he started smoking happy grass, and now he doesn't drink liquor anymore and doesn't fight. He said, 'Baby, when I'm drunk I want to fight. When I smoke happy grass I just want your mommy and me to hug.' You don't smoke it, do you, Mr. ... uh, Dave?"

I couldn't help laughing. "Lulubelle, I just happen to have a couple of joints in my car. I'll be right back." I ran out, opened the trunk, lifted up the upholstery padding, and – voila! – there was the thin silver case, holding two nicely rolled joints and a lighter. When I returned, I heard the shower running. In a few minutes out came Lulubelle wearing a Japanese kimono and a pair of Japanese slippers. I lit a joint and handed it to her. She took a couple of puffs. "I'm going take a shower," I said. "See ya in a couple of minutes, Lulubelle. If you'd be more comfortable, please slip into bed." After the shower I put on the other kimono and slippers.

Lulubelle was in bed so I dropped the robe and slippers and slipped in beside her. I held her and looked into her enchanting big brown eyes. The grass was working: We both wanted to hold each other and kiss.

She was truly beautiful in every way, her spirit, her smile, and her loving energy. We made love, I don't remember how long, but I noted that the sun was sinking in the west. We were in tune with each other, and what a difference that makes. Her skin was smooth as satin. It wasn't just the pot. I felt very close to her. It was difficult to tell her that I had to leave. I told her I was divorced, and that I tried to be home every night to be with my children. We showered together, and dried each other.

We drove to her new job. I waited outside to be certain everything was OK. She came out in about five minutes and came around to the driver's side of the car to shake my hand. This lady had class. Out of the corner of my eye I saw a lady looking through the window. "I told Mrs. Stevenson that you were a friend of mine, and were kind enough to drive me here. Everything is fine. I have a nice room, and Mrs. Stevenson, I can feel it, will be comfortable to work for." Her beautiful eyes began to cloud up.

I said, "Lulubelle, I noticed that there is a bus stop on the corner. I'd love to see you again. Would you like that?"

"Yes, oh yes, David!" She smiled. "First, I almost cried because I thought I would never see you in person again."

"Do you know when your day off is?" I asked.

"Tuesdays."

"OK, how about you taking the bus to the Aloha Tower. I'll meet you there Tuesday at 11:30 a.m. Would that be OK?"

"Yes, David."

"I'll see you Tuesday. Aloha." I waved a goodbye, and headed home.

Lulubelle and I met each Tuesday for three months. I usually ordered a Japanese lunch for us. We had fun using chopsticks. While we ate, we'd talk about her job. We'd smoke a joint before we ate, so the food would taste that much more delicious, and increase our appetite – our appetite: of course the grass enhanced our lovemaking, too.

By the end of the third month, I felt that the relationship had to end. We were in bed, and had just made love when she said, "David, I've told my mother all about you. She makes the most delicious fried chicken with dumplings and grits that you will ever taste. I told her I'd be bringing you home to meet the family soon. And when we're married, she'll love making all the food for the reception."

I was dumbfounded. It had never been my intention to lead her on.

I held Lulubelle and stroked her young face, as I told her, "I have a special love for you, Lulubelle, and I always will. I just can't face the pain of marriage again. I should say, the pain of divorce. I didn't in any way mean to hurt you." She looked very disappointed. "I'm very sorry, Lulubelle."

"It's been too long since I saw my momma and daddy," she said. "I think its time I go back home." While she was in the shower I checked my wallet. I had three hundred-dollar bills. I drove her to within three blocks of where she works, as I usually did. I held her in my arms. "Lulubelle, I know you would never make love for money, and I've never offered you any. I only want to help you just a little with your transportation home. I want you to take this." I put the folded money in her shirt pocket. I was pleased that she accepted it. She just slowly nodded her head, almost in a daze. I said, "If you ever need me, please phone me, or write to me."

She looked into my eyes. "I love you David." I watched until I could no longer see her. She was darling. I never again heard from her. I hope she found a husband as good to her as she deserved.

● ● ●

Television had been good to me financially. In addition to the income from my show, I was writing a column in the weekly *TV Time*, which was comparable to the mainland's *TV Guide*. Still, I felt it was time for a change. When the time came to renew my contract, I decided not to, in spite of my admiration for Cec Heftel, owner of the CBS affiliate in Hawaii.

He later served as Hawaii's U.S. Congressman and in 1984 ran for Governor of Hawaii. I think he would have been outstanding. He lost only because his opponent made false accusations. We corresponded while he was in Congress, and in a letter in 1981 he told me that he felt that legalization of marijuana would be worth discussing as an option, going so far as to say "...it would perhaps be more satisfactory than the present situation."

Becoming an importer – and finding warm adventures

I had always wanted to travel around the world, and be able to write it off on taxes, so I decided to become an importer. It didn't take long to answer my next question: What should I import? Hawaii is known for its beautiful Monkey Pod wood, whose grain contains unique patterns. It's used for salad bowls, plates, and serving trays. By this time, however, Hawaii had few such trees remaining. I decided to travel to Thailand, Taiwan, and the Philippines, where Monkey Pod trees were still abundant. I was soon to find that the Far East is fascinating.

By the time the plane landed in Bangkok, my body felt as though it needed replacing. I checked into the hotel and asked to be directed to the massage salon. A young lady in a white smock showed me to the shower. When I emerged, she asked, "Please to disrobe. Get on table." As I did, I thought gratefully: How nice it will feel to get those knots out of my aching back, and spasms out of my legs!

I was on the massage table for only a minute when I saw that the masseuse had removed her smock. She was naked. I said, "You pretty lady. But all I want is massagie, please." She said, "I no know how massagie. I only know how fuckie!"

Wearily, I rolled off the table, gave her a tip and a little hug, and said, "You nice girl. Me like 'fuckie' you, but me tired now."

In my room, I ran a hot bath. I was just beginning to relax in the tub when a violent earthquake shook the building. Moments later I heard someone moving around in the other room. I thought: How nice! One of the hotel staff had come up to reassure me. I felt comforted as the guy looked around the room for me. I was about to say, "I'm here in the bathtub," when I noticed he was going through my pants pockets, transferring my wallet into his hand! I leaped out of the tub, and dived for him. The unexpected sight of a large wet naked Caucasian leaping at him and ripping the wallet from his hand, caused him to soil his pants before he ran from the room. (The sound and odor could not be mistaken.) I connected the chain on the door, dried off, collapsed on the bed, and fell into a deep sleep.

I didn't find what I was looking for in Thailand. In Taiwan, however, I found exceptional wood carvings and exquisite dishware. I purchased some items and had them shipped home. One of the storekeepers spoke excellent English. He said, "In Peitou there are imposing houses of prostitution that no adventurer should miss. It will be an experience you will long remember." He wrote the address on a card and handed it to me.

Flagging down one of the little pedicabs, I handed him the shopkeeper's card, pointed to the address, and sat down in the rear seat. The driver headed rapidly out of town. In 10 minutes we were in the countryside. Suddenly, he veered out across a dirt field and stopped the cab. He flashed his headlights three times. A car moved slowly toward him, and it too flashed its lights three times. I didn't care to wait for more flashes. I removed a large pen from my vest pocket and stuck the end of it into the back of my driver's neck. "Back to town," I yelled, and pushed the pen deeper into his neck. Fortunately, he fell for my improvised "gun." He flashed his lights once, turned the cab around, and pedaled hard for town. At the first stoplight I leaped out of his cab and ran into a store as he sped away.

Making love using Thai cannabis

I had better luck on my second try. Peitou was a delightful place, sited on a bubbling river with waterfalls. Across the river from the town proper were about a dozen little hotels. The driver pulled up in front of an attractive one, and a young Chinese boy opened the car door with a smile.

I registered and paid the $12 U.S. in advance. The desk clerk told me that that amount included a young lady for the night, but he made it clear that she would leave my room at 8 a.m. He presented me with a pair of slippers, which I immediately put on – the local custom – and then he showed me to a room. Soon, a "mama-san," an older Chinese lady, appeared with a bottle of warm rice wine and two glasses, along with what appeared to be two joints on the tray. "You like smoke good mary-wanna?"

"You bet", I said, handing her two U.S. dollars.

"You like young lady?"

"Yes, please, mama-san."

She smiled and departed. A few minutes later she reappeared with three young ladies. They were all lovely, clothed in traditional Chinese robes. The shopkeeper had told me that the girls were not older than 19.

I selected a young lady with shimmering black hair down to her slim waist. She waved goodnight to her friends, who silently departed.

She was the very image of the beautiful Asian courtesan of legend. She didn't need to speak English. Her body language spoke for her. She led me to the bathroom, motioned for me to remove my clothes and sit on a stool. I fired up a Thai joint and offered it to her. She smiled and shook her head. I took two hits. The warm floor was tiled green with a drain in the center. Next to us was a steaming tub of water. She sensually dipped a bucket of warm water from the tub and poured it slowly over my body. She took a large soft sponge and washed me all over, and worked shampoo into my hair. After thoroughly soaping me up, she rinsed me off slowly with warm water from a hose. The grass heightened the pleasure and relaxation.

When I climbed into the large bathtub, it was only to soak; I was already perfectly clean. She washed herself in front of me, then joined me in the tub where she began massaging my head, neck, arms, and back. The water was hot and relaxing, and it continued to pour into the tub and overflow into the drain in the center of the green-tiled floor, so the tub remained full to the brim with water at the same hot temperature.

After about 15 minutes she gestured for us to get out of the tub. She dried me with a large white towel, took my hand and led me to bed where she drank some rice wine and I took a couple more puffs of the smoke. We made love during much of the night. She was marvelous, and able to convey the feeling that she truly cared for me, stroking my hair and face. A rare and exquisite show of tenderness. Around 7 a.m. she awoke and began to massage me gently. We reenacted the bath sequence of the night before. About 7:45 she looked at the little clock on the dresser wistfully. I gave her a tip, a kiss on the cheek, and a salute of "Thanks!" and a thumbs-up.

She laughed, and beckoned me toward the bed with her forefinger. She now held her forefinger straight up, as if to say, "Just one more time?" I was surprised, but not certain if that was what she meant. There was only one way to find out, so I gave her a hug and she hurriedly began removing my clothes! That was one of the warmest and sweetest good-byes I've ever encountered.

The Philippines

Next, it was off to the Philippines, with their attractive green rolling hills, and the smiling friendly faces of the residents who like Americans. There are thousands of Jeeps that were left there after World War II, now chromed to the hubcaps. The poverty there is tragic: Youngsters as young as five years old sleep in doorways, and, sadly, many of them survive by selling predominantly American cigarettes. I learned that they sell them primarily to pay for their own nicotine addictions. While our Uncle Sam prohibits non-lethal marijuana in our country, he allows the export of the world's most death-dealing drug, nicotine.

After checking out a half dozen or so companies manufacturing products from Monkey Pod wood, I selected one. The owner was knowledgeable, and keenly interested in immediate new business. The family-owned operation manufactured salad bowls, serving trays, and other carved items.

I had also noticed Capiz shell ornaments for Christmas trees, and place mats decorated with the same beautiful shell. "Can Capiz shell be inlaid onto the Monkey Pod wood?" I asked.

"Yes, sir. It could be."

I drew a number of items on a large piece of paper: a butterfly tray, a fish tray, a long serving tray, a large salad bowl with extra large fork and spoon, and a number of other items. I wanted my imports to be distinctive and creative. "Could you make samples of these items immediately?"

"Oh, yes, sir!"

"If the work is consistent, I will personally keep your factory busy."

The next evening I returned to a surprise. The items were even better than I'd imagined. The inlaid shells looked like baby mother-of-pearl. I ordered $10,000 worth of stock, beginning with duplicates of the samples, to be ready the following noon. When I returned the next day I said, "You are to keep these samples. I will keep mine to compare with yours. If you ever ship me any of the items that are not of the same quality they will be returned, and you will pay the shipping costs."

"That is fair, sir."

I also visited Hong Kong, where my favorite sport was bargaining with the Chinese and those hard workers from India. They are masters at salesmanship. I checked out merchandise at about a dozen stores. By that time, I had a good idea of the true value of wares. I learned rapidly to make what appeared to be ridiculously low offers on merchandise.

"I cannot accept that price!" the merchant would cry. "You have hurt my feelings!"

"I am truly sorry," I would say, and slowly walk out of the store.

Generally, I would hear, "But, wait, sir! I am going to sell this item to you at your price, but I am going to lose money!" Frequently we continued to haggle.

I purchased a number of magnificent pieces of Chinese furniture and screens inlaid with ivory. I included trunks and various other pieces of furniture, as well as clothing and silks.

In the night clubs, Chinese ladies approach your table and sit next to you. They appear to be considerably under age, and probably are, and they dress in as little as possible. Most are mouth-watering with their long clean hair and big brown eyes. "Me cherry girl. Me go with you, Joe, for only $12 U.S. You will like. I will do very special things to you!" If she thinks you are going to accept her invitation, she will frequently add, "My little sister come along too. She like learn. She fun. She in training! You like, Joe. Only $5 more."

Buy a half million pot plants?

Hong Kong manufactures some of the most realistic plastic flowers and plants I've ever seen. I considered having them manufacture marijuana plants about four feet in height, thinking perhaps they would be nice conversation pieces, especially out on lanais, porches, patios, backyards, and on the roofs of apartments, condos, and office buildings. I figured – let's see, if I imported, say, a half million of them, my cost being around $4 each, I could sell them via mail order, for say $8.00 each. Perhaps $10.00. (I wondered if the DEA would buy them all? I decided to forgo that idea for the time being.)

Hawaiian imports

Upon my return home to Honolulu, I spent time swimming and visiting with my children. I then went to a PTA meeting, and I had conferences with their teachers.

In the days that followed, I visited many store buyers. The buyers were fascinated with the shell inlaid into the wood. I guaranteed the quality would be consistent; if any piece was not perfect, they could return it for immediate credit or refund. The first large order was from prestigious Liberty House. Then orders came in from gift shops at the Royal Hawaiian Hotel and the Kahala Hilton, from Sears Roebuck and the Long's drugstore chain, and from the Post Exchanges at Hickam Air Force Base, Pearl Harbor, and the Marine base at Kaneohe. For the military, Sears, and Long's, my products were of a different design, and without the shell inlay. That way the major stores could charge considerably more for their items, to cover their higher overhead. Orders poured in. I phoned the manufacturer in the Philippines and gave him an order for an additional $20,000. "Mr. Ford, my dear friend. This is the largest order we have ever taken. I will never let you down."

I purchased a two-year-old sky-domed Pontiac station wagon, like new, wholesale. I hired a carpenter to assemble a metal storage shed just behind the swimming pool and to build wooden shelves from floor to ceiling. Then I went to the docks, opened the large crates of Monkey Pod products, and loaded them into the station wagon. I drove into my garage, and unloaded the merchandise onto the new shelves. I had help in polishing the lovely wood, and stored the products in the shed, yet no one seemed to know that I was conducting a roaring business out of our home. I sat by the swimming pool with two phones at my side, and while the children swam, I kept in close contact with the buyers. The product was selling as fast as it arrived, and the factory in the Philippines had to expand. On the back of each piece of wood was a gold seal in the shape of a pineapple. It read: Design & Final Finish in Hawaii by Dave Ford. Hand-crafted in the Philippines.

At the same time I was selling Monkey Pod, I was also buying new condominium apartments, most of them in Waikiki. I'd offer the sellers all cash if they would sell considerably under their retail price. I picked up quite a few, and resold them at market price.

Vietnam, the "perfect storm" of Nixon's untenable drug war

In 1968, as in any other year, whether legally prescribed or self-prescribed, drugs legal and illegal were with us. Reporters in Vietnam estimated marijuana use among servicemen there at 80%. Many of the men were using the barrels of their rifles as marijuana pipes. The government ordered the military to do whatever was necessary to halt the use of pot. After due consideration the brass felt it best not to take the rifles away, so they began arresting the "guilty" soldiers. Only then did it dawn on them that, with four soldiers out of five in the stockade, it was going to be a little hard to fight the war.

Eventually President Nixon did win his battle. Urine samples were coming out negative for marijuana use. The soldiers did quit using marijuana. The administration was ecstatic over their wise policy. But Nixon lost his pot war. Many of the soldiers just switched to heroin! Smack was so inexpensive in Vietnam that a GI could trade a pack of American cigarettes for enough heroin to get high.

The nightmare Nixon failed to foresee was that this country would wind up with thousands of new heroin addicts. The government was obviously deeply concerned about soldiers becoming addicted to heroin, so it gave them free cigarettes – the deadliest drug of all. When the men returned home from the terror of being killed any minute, most of them left behind the desire to use heroin. Now they were just addicted to cigarettes.

Could we have learned a lesson there? We're so embroiled in the hypocrisy and politics, we didn't take notice: stop the use of one drug and another will be used. Nor was it noted that the *banning* of marijuana is what led to the use of dangerous drugs. Surely, the presidential appointees running the War on Drugs are not power-hungry and sanctimonious? But of course, they are. As I read of this insanely destructive policy, I looked forward to what I hoped would be a ray of light amid the gloom, the imminent release of Britain's marijuana report.

The Baroness Wooton Report, 1969

With millions of Americans and Britons continuing to use grass, and none reported to be in lunatic asylums, it was time for another study. The Baroness Wooton Report cited Great Britain's most eminent drug authorities. *The report revealed marijuana to be a relatively harmless drug that did not lead to crime, dependency, or anti-social behavior.*[21] The U.S. Government response: silence. Don't confuse us with facts. Our minds are made up.

"Tell me what you are doing to me!"

One evening, I stopped at the Royal Hawaiian Hotel for a beer, and an attractive blonde lady sitting next to me caught my eye. She was superbly dressed in black dress, high heels, pearls, and fine jewelry – unusual for relaxed Hawaii. We started chatting and I learned that she was a professor at the University of Hawaii, and her name was Brenda. She had already had a couple of drinks; she was feeling them, and ready to play. I phoned the nanny and asked her to put the children to bed at their regular time.

Almost without my realizing it, it was 10:30. We decided to go to a hotel for the night. She was such an elegant lady that I wanted to take her somewhere very special. I recalled Mrs. Paterson, a friendly lady from Scotland who owned and rented out luxurious cottages on the ocean at the foot of Diamond Head. Mrs. Paterson and I had swum together in front of her superb property many times. Her spectacular oceanfront cottages were frequently booked by heads of state. I realized it was late, but decided to phone her to see if she might rent us a cottage. "Come on over, Mr. Ford." She was almost whispering. "Just please be very quiet. My guests have all retired for the night. I'll leave the key under the mat of bungalow number 5."

We drove quietly down her long, steep driveway to bungalow 5, retrieved the key, and literally tip-toed in. The king-sized bed was turned down, there was an orchid on the table and the sweet aroma of a gardenia on the pillow. Even a bottle of wine by the bed – sweet old Mrs. Paterson! Brenda turned on some soft music. It was now midnight. Soon, we were in bed.

"Dave, please tell me what you are doing to me."

"I'm making love to you, Brenda."

"No, Dave. Tell me what you are truly doing to me".

"I'm *truly* making love to you, Brenda."

"No, you're not. *Tell* me what you are *doing* to *me!*"

I began to wish we had only smoked grass and left the liquor alone. Bewildered, I was trying to think of something more creative when Brenda screamed out in the loudest shriek I ever heard, *"You're FUCKING me!* Say it David!" She repeated it, this time even louder, as she was having an orgasm, "OH, GOD, I'm C -O- M- I- N- G... ARE YOU EVER FUCKING ME! I LOVE IT! OOOOHHHH, AAHHHH!"

I wasn't surprised when seconds later there was a violent pounding on the door. I grabbed my pants and gingerly opened the door to find an outraged, shaking Mrs. Paterson in her nightgown. "Mr. Ford. This has never happened before. Would you kindly be out of here in 10 minutes?"

"Of course, Mrs. Paterson. I'm terribly sorry. Please send the bill to my home."

Not speaking, I drove Brenda back to the Royal Hawaiian Hotel. I climbed out of the car and opened her door. As she got out of the car, she said, "Here's my card with my phone number on it. When can I see you again?"

"Never. Good night, Brenda," I sputtered as firmly as my embarrassment and anger would allow. I went home, kissed the youngsters who were sound asleep, and retired to a blessedly silent bedroom.

It seemed like a good idea to climb out of a window!

The following week while I was bodysurfing I noticed a pleasing redhead catching the same wave, just a few feet away. We ended up on the beach, chatting. She recognized me from television, and that was a help in breaking the ice. "I've only been over here for a year. As you can no doubt tell, I'm German. I would enjoy cooking you a good German meal. Would you like that?" I nodded. She gave me her address, and set the time for noon on Friday. She was only 22.

On Friday at noon I was at her apartment with a bouquet of anthuriums and a bottle of wine. She welcomed me and pointed to the table. Two places were set, candles were already lit, and an enticing aroma wafted from the little kitchen. I don't recall the German dishes that Helga served, but they were delicious.

After lunch, Helga excused herself. In a few minutes she returned in a white negligee. She gave me a big hug and a juicy kiss. What's a guy to do? I picked her up and carried her over to her bed. We were soon making uncivilized love.

Later, as we were relaxing, I glanced out the window and saw a car with an obviously military paint job parked across the street, with a man sitting behind the wheel. I didn't think much about it until we were about to begin making love again, and I noticed that the guy was looking directly toward Helga's apartment. "Helga, is it my imagination, or is there a man watching your apartment?"

"Ja, he's my husband. He's with the military police at Hickam. He's jealous, and wants to catch a man who will admit he has been in bed with me. He says it would be thrilling and sexual for him. To me, it is very exciting. He doesn't do that much for me, but it turns me on to be able to sneak men in and out of here. Oh, do it to me again, now! This time put it anywhere!"

Instead, I leaped out of bed. This time I put it in my pants. I don't think it took more than 30 seconds to get my clothes on. A cop! A *military* cop! Hell, I thought, that guy has a loaded weapon, and could easily kill me!

Helga said, "Go out the front door. I'll tell him you were a vacuum salesman." But I'd spotted a rear window and it was there that I made my ungraceful exit. Helga looked disappointed as I almost dove through the open window after noting it was five feet to the ground. I peeked around the corner of the building. Her husband was still in his car, chewing gum rapidly. I would have felt far safer had he been smoking a joint – almost a guarantee of a person not being hostile. My car was between him and the apartment, so I decided on a flanking maneuver. I walked around the block and headed straight for my car, not looking at their apartment or his car. With shaking legs, I drove jerkily away.

Hawaii, the land of Aloha and loving ladies

My next romantic adventure was more sedate. June worked for one of my former sponsors. She was Japanese, and enchanting. Her soft coal-black hair flowed to her smooth hips. After my recent dramas, I made it a point to tell her that I had recently divorced, and was not interested in a romantic commitment; I just wanted to have fun for a time. "Thank you for being so forthright, Dave. Let's have some fun, shall we?"

We went to dinner on the lanai of the Halekalani Hotel, located on the ocean in Waikiki. Tiki torches surrounded us. The moon was full. The stars shone like large uncut diamonds, while live Hawaiian music serenaded us. I asked June what she would like for dessert.

"Close your eyes, Dave. I have already ordered a special dessert." June took my hand and placed something in it. "Open your eyes now, my new friend." It was a key. She smiled and said, "I don't have to be at work until 9 a.m. The key is to my apartment. Could you drop by now and then around seven?"

I used that privilege a number of times. The freedom for me of being divorced felt like being a teen-ager again. June had many special qualities. One in particular heightened our play: she loved grass. She used pot for PMS, relaxing, and eliminating job stress. June said, "I used to get so uptight on the job I'd have a drink or two to relax, but I didn't like the space it put me into – I'd get melancholy. A couple of puffs of pot and the stress would dissolve, and I'd be all smiles. I especially adore it while making love."

After several times using that magic key, June said, "Dave, I don't think of anything other than you when I've had a few puffs and I'm in your arms. I used to have a speck of a drinking problem until I switched from alcohol to a couple of joints a week. I also tried everything to quit smoking cigarettes. That's the worst task I ever had. With grass I was able to quit smoking those nasty things. Now I'm happier than I've ever been. With pot, who needs cigarettes or hangovers? Not us, Davie!"

We got into the habit of surprising each other with choice foods, and we had some fine picnics in bed. A delicious lunch, a short nap, and more lovemaking while Frank Sinatra sang for us from the stereo.

One night I awoke alone at home, around midnight. For some reason a feeling of jealousy hit me. I realized I was being immature. June and I didn't have an exclusive relationship – but telling myself that didn't stop me from being jealous. The nanny was asleep in her room; the children were safe. I dressed rapidly and headed straight for June's apartment in Waikiki.

Her lights were on. When I reached her front door, I put my ear against it – and heard a man's voice. I carefully opened her door with my key and slipped silently into her little kitchen. Pot smoke was heavy in the air. I recognized the man's voice. It was our mutual friend, Fred, who had his own orchestra. They were just smoking, rapping, and giggling.

Then Fred said, "It was nice visiting with you, June. Sorry Dave wasn't here. Just thought I'd take a chance that you guys would be here, and drop by with some Chinese food. I'd best get home or my wife will be upset."

I couldn't leave now without being detected! There was a louvered bi-fold door near me next to the kitchen – a closet. I opened it slowly, slipped inside, and closed the doors. Through the louvers I could see Fred approaching with a dish of food in his hand. I froze like a store-window mannequin.

Fred opened the louvered doors. As he took his jacket off a hanger he looked right into my face. I couldn't believe what he did next. Totally nonchalant, he said, "Would you like some beef egg foo yong?" I took the plate. Fred shook his head, closed the closet doors, and left without saying a word to June.

As soon as June was in bed, I slipped out of her apartment. The next morning, Fred phoned. "Dave, please tell me you were in June's closet last night." I told him the story and begged him not to ever tell June. He said, "I promise. Damn, I feel better. Halfway home I was thinking about it, and I almost decided to quit smoking grass!"

Something about Mari – Jane

One afternoon, I took Sandy and David to a photography shop to have our photos taken for a Christmas card. While there we met a little redhead with a delectable smile. Her name was Mari. Within a week Mari and I were dating. She had three children, each of whom I liked. She too was divorced. This little lady was the Martha Stewart of lovemaking: whatever she did in bed could not have been more perfect.

We dated for about a year. I had shied like a nervous horse that time Lulubelle brought up the subject of marriage, but now for the first time since my divorce from Theo I began to consider seriously the possibility of re-marrying. I began to feel it would be good for the children and for me. Mari was one of the few ladies I brought home to meet the children. They liked each other. Sandy was now six years old and David eight. I knew Mari could be a great "mom" for them, as she was for her children.

Mari would have some help with the children. A few months before I had retained Patty Sue, at 26 only a few years younger than Mari, to be our nanny and housekeeper. She was living in maid's quarters I'd recently added to the property, and was working a few hours a week on her master's degree in education at the University of Hawaii. If she stayed on, she could be the children's "big sister."

Caught in the act by my son!

It was a typical sunny Hawaiian afternoon with the trade winds gently fanning the islands. Around noon I phoned Mari and invited her to come over for lunch, a swim, and a smoke. Patty Sue was at the University and the kids were at school, so we had the place to ourselves. After a couple of puffs of grass, Mari and I were having a swim, going down the water-slide into the pool, playing tag, and doing all the playful things kids and lovers do.

Mari and I would have again been swimming or sunning at poolside by the time the kids got home, but for some reason school let out early that day. David probably would have come through the kitchen door and fixed himself a snack as usual, but for some reason the kitchen door was locked. Unable to get in that way, David quite sensibly entered through whatever door he could find that was unlocked. He chose the next closest door, the one that led directly from the pool to the master bedroom. If that door had been locked, David would just have gone around to the front door, but for some reason Dad hadn't thought to lock it.

Rather than being out by the pool innocently sunning, Mari and I were in the bedroom enthusiastically screwing. You know that feeling when you suddenly know you're not alone? I looked over my shoulder and there stood David in the corner of the bedroom, staring at us! When our eyes met, he made a rapid exit, and I panicked. Oh my God, I thought. At least we were screwing, and in the missionary position! I leapt out of bed, pulled on my shorts and nervously went out to the living room.

There was David lying on his stomach with elbows raised, chin in hands, calmly watching television. It's hard to believe now that I could have been so uncreative, but I stammered, "Son, I was just massaging Mari."

He looked up at me. "Sure, Dad" he said, with an eyebrow raised. We both left it at that.

Mari was dressed, and again being the almost "straight" little mother she was. "Good afternoon, David. How was school?" David rolled his eyes and continued watching television. Both she and I were trying

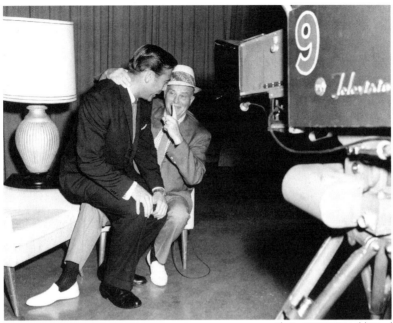

Photo: KGMB-TV publicity dept.

Edgar Bergen, world-famous ventriloquist and father of Candice Bergen, created Charlie McCarthy and Mortimer Snerd. Those unforgettable dummies now live in the Smithsonian in Washington D.C. – maybe I'll wind up there with them!

I had the fun of appearing in Hawaii Five-O a couple of times. In the episode "90 Second War," Jack Lord played both "Steve McGarrett" and his evil double, and I played a French bank guard. I got to shoot the bad guy!

Lovely Patty Sue came into our lives at age 25 – at first, just to help Mari with the kids while I built an importing business and an advertising agency.

Patty Sue and Sandy were good buddies.

PERSONALITY

Where is DAVE FORD?

What has become of the witty, amusing host of "HOLLYWOOD'S GREATEST MOVIES?" Is there no longer room in television for a man of his talent?

With the many ho-hum, so-so, and downright bad programs we TV viewers are asked to stomach, we wonder whither went the good movies and the man whose warmth, wit and sincerity kept us tuned to Channel 9.

Dave was happy to fill us in on what he has been up to recently. It is a far cry from television. . .or maybe it isn't.

Dave told us he has been quite successful at several enterprises into which he has dipped his hand-real estate, advertising, importing and selling.

"Our company imports monkey pod articles inlaid with capiz shell, and a few other things," he said.

Dave was no mean salesman in his TV days, as a matter of fact, and he has a flock of warm letters from sponsors to prove it.

His philosophy of salesmanship is an integral part of his philosophy of television production.

"People watch television to be entertained," he said. "It's as simple as that. People realize that they have to accept commercials to pay for the entertainment, but who enjoys a movie interrupted by an offensive hard sell?

By making commercials enjoyable you accomplish both entertaining and selling in a way that is not offensive. I have always stood behind the products I've advertised. I wouldn't sell cigaretts on TV, for example."

Dave's show, which ran for three years, 1964 to 1967, was televised at 8 o'clock Saturday night and again Sunday morning. It polled a consistent 79 percent rating on the Neilsen scale.

Movies like "For Whom the Bell Tolls" and "Some Like it Hot," were Dave's choices, but he is better remembered for his post-movie interviews with such celebrities as Bing Crosby, Jonathan Winters, Billie Graham, Liberace, Milton Berle and Dame Margot Fonteyn.

So what happened?

"The station was unable to continue the show on prime time," Dave said, "and I was asked to accept on the show a number of movies I had previously rejected. My method was to select the best, highest rated 52 films out of about 200. I felt the show would not live up to its name of HOLLYWOOD'S GREATEST MOVIES. It is not necessarily the station's fault either. Movies are becoming increasingly costly for television. So I went off the air."

Since then, he has been living comfortably in his Waialae-Golf course home with his son, David Guy, 10, and daughter, Sandra Ann, 7, who are both TV performers in their own right, having been seen in various TV commercials.

Does he have hopes of returning to the TV screen?

"I would like to go back," he said candidly. "I miss my first love, TV production. The rewards of creative work are immeasurable, and in spite of the fact that I have been doing financially better in other fields, I would like to go back to do something creative. I am still asked to sign autographs and people still ask me, 'When are you going back on TV?'

That's a good question, fans. When?

13 / TV TIME

Once a year TV Time featured someone they considered one of Hawaii's outstanding people. I was honored to be chosen in 1969.

desperately to believe he didn't know what we had really been doing, but knowing better!

As the weeks passed, I was becoming more serious about Mari and was considering asking her to marry me. The only problem was that Sandy and David were not enchanted with the idea of two more sisters and another brother.

Mari and Patty Sue were becoming good friends. Patty Sue did little dating, mainly remaining around the house when she wasn't at the University. She was inspired with the children. She helped them with their school work, played games with them, and took candid photos while they played. She joined in our swims, playing Marco Polo and other pool games. She worked at her cooking skills, and she was never afraid to do physical work.

About this time, Jack Lord had recently begun his long-running television series, *Hawaii Five-O*. I even appeared in a couple of the episodes. Amazingly enough, at that time I was better known than Jack Lord, but on that series there was only one star.

One episode supposedly took place in France. I played a bank guard. Jack was playing his usual role as McGarrett, and doubling as a villain that was impersonating McGarrett. In a scene in which he was playing the impostor, I ran toward him and pulled my gun to shoot him. "Cut!" yelled Jack.

He walked up to me and thrust his scowling face into mine. From three inches away, he demanded, "Who's the star of this show, you or me?" I didn't feel it was the proper time to joke and say, "Me?" so I just bit my lip.

"Don't ever go past your mark again, OK?"

"OK, Jack", I said. On the next take I hit my mark *exactly*.

Soon after, I was invited to attend the Honolulu Press Club's Annual Roast. (When you're invited it generally means that you will be a target, or involved in the roast in some way.) I invited Mari, and we decided to ask Patty Sue to join us. The roast was held at the Dome at the Hilton Hawaiian Village Hotel.

There were 600 people in the audience, and one of the guests was Jack Lord. During a portion of the evening's outstanding entertainment, the 21-piece orchestra did a number with the entire chorus singing, "Jack *Lord* thinks he's Dave *Ford!*" I loved it, but I doubt Jack did.

Mari and I enjoyed the whole show, but about three quarters of the way through, Patty Sue excused herself, and didn't come back. We couldn't figure it out. Later she explained that she felt like a third wheel – and also that she felt a little envious of Mari and me being so close. She was 26, I was 42. Patty Sue could have been a national pin-up. I was flattered, but not romantically attracted. Mari had numerous artistic talents, not to mention a figure any man would sit up and beg for.

● ● ●

I was about to take another trip to Asia, to buy new products. I was going to ask Mari to join me, but then I thought it would be marvelous to take my son, who had recently turned nine. Mari was a wonderful sport, and encouraged the trip with David.

He and I went first to Hong Kong where we had suits made that were identical, along with white long-sleeved shirts and ties. I was so proud of David. He shook hands with people, and had a smile that made everyone want to know him. He liked people, and they liked him. While there I bought a silver diamond-studded wrist watch for Mari. I purchased a number of new items of Chinese furniture, paintings, and other works of art. In Taiwan, I took David to a poor man's Disney World; and while there, we purchased tableware and some jewels.

We next flew to Tokyo and stayed at the Okura Hotel. The manager was so impressed with David that he had us join him at his personal table for dinner. He presented his beautiful nine-year-old daughter, who was learning to speak English.

Travel is an adventure, but it's always good to return home. It was especially delightful to see Sandy's big smiling brown eyes, and to see Mari and Patty Sue. Sandy was taking hula lessons and doing exceptionally well. Mari loved the watch, and Sandy sort of liked her authentic Japanese doll.

Nixon meets a robot; I marry one!

A few days after our return from Japan I was contacted by the head
of Torro Corporation of America, a subsidiary of a toy
manufacturer based in New Zealand. He wanted me to handle
their advertising. I accepted, and shortly thereafter I had a robot
constructed, and named it Torro. We painted it silver, with a cheerful
face on the head, and installed a two-foot radio antenna. A microphone
and speaker changed a human voice into one that sounded like a robot.
Lights powered by batteries flashed as Torro walked and talked. We
used expandable heating ducts for the legs and arms so that it would fit
almost any size man. I say "man," because in those days of chauvinism
I didn't imagine a woman wearing the outfit, which weighed 42 pounds,
and was hot and uncomfortable inside. For extra impact, I hired a man
six-foot-four to be Torro.

Torro became a star in parades and at shopping centers. He showed
up at hospitals and anywhere children congregated. We got so many
inquiries that Torro was invited to appear on television, and was even
interviewed. People calling in to radio and television stations asked,
"What is this Torro thing? What does it represent? Is there a live person
inside, or is it totally mechanical?" Torro's photo appeared on the outside
of the company's toy boxes and he increased sales.

In June of 1969, I learned with only four hours' notice that President
Nixon was going to appear at Hickam Air Force Base. It was a refueling
stop for Air Force One, which was to take him to Midway Island to
meet with the Vietnamese to work out a peaceful settlement of the
Vietnam War. I hurriedly had a heavy red cardboard sign made: "GOOD

LUCK, MR. PRESIDENT! – from the kids." I phoned my "robot" and told him to stand by to be picked up within an hour. Mari was at work and couldn't join us, so I asked Patty Sue to pile the children in the station wagon and we headed for Hickam, with one stop to pick up our "robot."

When I knocked on his apartment door, he stuck his head out and said, "I been thinking it over, and I'm not going to be inside that thing. No, sir! Not when the President of the United States is going to be there."

I begged him, offering more money, but he refused. Patty Sue, all of five-foot two-and-a-half and a mere 112 pounds, said, "I'll be Torro!"

"You can't be," I said. "The outfit weighs over 40 pounds."

"If you won't let me do it, you'll miss the biggest opportunity yet for free publicity for Torro toys. Come on, Dave, you're the only one I know that can turn a nightmare into a wet dream!"

I couldn't be inside the robot because I had to figure how to get it in contact with the President, and in front of the national news media. Reluctantly, I took Patty Sue up on her offer.

When we arrived at Hickam, Sandy and I helped Patty Sue into the robot outfit. Suddenly our once imposing Torro appeared to be a midget. When the microphone was connected I asked Torro if "he" could hear me. A tiny "Yes, master" came out of our once-six-foot-four, no-longer-baritone robot.

I spotted Boy Scouts preparing to march in a welcome parade for the President. I went over and spoke with their leader – loud enough that the Scouts could hear me. "How would you like Torro to lead your parade in welcoming the President?" Young voices begged their leader, "Yeah! We want Torro!" He acquiesced. I led Torro behind the ropes where the President would be shaking hands with the local dignitaries. Little Torro could well have used a robot seeing-eye dog, but did remarkably well. I gave the leading Boy Scouts in the parade the big good-luck sign to carry. Torro led the parade past a dozen television cameras and motion-picture cameras, representing the world's press.

As the President approached, I retrieved the sign and moved behind the ropes with the other bystanders, just behind little Torro. I yelled out, "Mr. President, Torro wants to shake your hand!" The President obligingly shook hands with our robot! I couldn't have bought that kind of international publicity for $50,000. The sign cost $12.

When the parade was over I extricated Patty Sue from Torro's head and body. Not one word of complaint from our little Torro, only, "Did I do OK?" I was impressed with this lady.

The next day I wrote to the White House and asked to buy copies of the photos of Torro and the President. I figured that surely some had been taken for the Secret Service.

Despite how much Mari and I cared for each other, we both had been coming to realize that our future together was not bright. It was clear that my children were truly fond of Mari, but just as clear that they didn't want any more siblings, and I suspected that Mari's children felt the same.

At about six the Friday evening after our encounter with President Nixon, Patty Sue came over to the lanai, where I was unpacking Monkey Pod products. She was dressed to kill, and had just had her hair done. "Just wanted to say good night. I'm going out on a date. I'll be back before midnight." She'd already cleared this time off with me.

It was a typically balmy tropical evening, with the coconut trees rustling in the gentle trade winds. The plumeria was in full bloom and its perfume permeated the air. As Patty Sue walked past the pool, I looked down and noticed that my legs were running towards her. Then I saw my arms pushing her into the swimming pool!

Quite understandably she came up raving. "You've ruined my evening! Now I can't go out on my date!" It's hard to explain my bizarre impulse. I think that in a somewhat perverse way it was a response to the cumulative effect of all of the fun things Patty Sue had created for our little family, and to her trouper-level performance as Torro for the Presidential coverage – and to what she had said after the Press Club banquet, that she found herself a bit jealous that I was with Mari. As I helped her out of the pool I realized that I also loved this little critter. I helped her dry off, and apologized for my dismal actions. I think she figured it out; she began laughing, and no longer had a mad-on.

A few days later I told Mari of my feelings for Patty Sue. She was wonderful. "I like Patty Sue, and I can see that with all of our children it would be a difficult challenge, at best, for us to be a permanent fixture. I wish you the best of luck." There was a thoroughbred if ever there was one. I knew I would always have a very special love for Mari. And I do.

In the weeks that followed, I dated Patty Sue, and was happily surprised, as I think she was also, that we enjoyed many of the same things. Camping, hiking, swimming, watching good movies on TV, and spending quiet nights at home, as well as going to some of the elegant

Christmas card from our friend Don Ho and his family. For a time our daughter Sandy danced with his show.

Photo: The White House

Our advertising agency constructed a robot and named it after the client, toymaker Torro Corporation. In 1969, President Nixon was on his way to Midway Island to try to negotiate a peace agreement with Vietnam. I saw an opportunity to get some free publicity – but the imposing 6'4" man who'd been wearing the 42-pound robot attire backed out just when we needed him most. Little Patty Sue, 5'3" and 113 pounds, said "I'll be Torro!" – and she was, in front of international media coverage.

When I shouted, "Mr. President, Torro wants to shake your hand!" Nixon obligingly reached into the crowd and shook hands with Patty Sue. I was right behind her, holding up a sign that cost $12 – and got Torro publicity worth thousands. Patty Sue being such a trouper started me thinking about her in a whole new way.

parties in Honolulu. Most important of all, the kids truly cared for her.

Like most people in Hawaii, Patty Sue enjoyed grass. After the children were asleep we would sit and have a puff or two of pot, and tell stories about our lives. The pain of losing Hazel was very slowly diminishing. Getting to know Patty Sue better and better helped with that. She was caring and fun. In the first week of July I got up my courage and asked Patty Sue to marry me. (I believe that was after she told me that, if I didn't, she was leaving.) She accepted. We decided to be married on Christmas Day, when her parents could come from New Hampshire. She mentioned that her girlfriend said that I would be "a good catch." I hoped that I would be.

July 8, 1969, a large manila envelope arrived. The return address: The White House, Washington, D.C. I ripped it open, and there was an eight-by-ten glossy color photo of Torro shaking hands with President Nixon, and me right behind her with a big grin on my face, holding up the sign, "GOOD LUCK MR. PRESIDENT! – from the kids."

I decided to buy a four-place Cessna Cardinal that I located on the island of Kauai. It had only 305 hours total time on it, and had been hangared since it was new. The day after I bought it I invited Patty Sue and the children to meet me at the general-aviation terminal of Honolulu International, where the small aircraft were tied down.

When they arrived, I was standing by an old plane whose paint was peeling off. "Isn't it a beauty! Let's go flying!" I said with enthusiasm. They were good sports and tried to look exuberant, but it was hard for them to hide their dismay. "OK, Dad," said Sandy, "but this plane looks ill." When I confessed and showed them the right plane they were much happier. We went flying.

In the weeks that followed, Patty Sue and I flew to Hawaii's various islands, frequently taking the children with us. One such trip was to Maui. The sugar cane field we landed in at Kaanapali is now crowded with hotels and a busy airport is now located on the other side of the island, where only commercial planes are allowed to land; but in 1969 it was still a cane field, and a paradise. We camped on the sand and swam in the warm blue ocean. We watched whales playing hide and seek, and dolphins visited us. Patty Sue was wearing a fetching yellow bathing suit, trimmed in black. Sandy was now eight, and darling. She was happy. She wrestled with Patty Sue in the sand, and tried to pants her!

Christmas Day, 1969, Patty Sue and I were married at the Episcopal Church of the Holy Nativity in Honolulu. She was a beautiful bride.

My fourth airplane, this lovely Cessna Cardinal, waited for us while our family camped by the ocean. We were thrilled to watch dolphins and whales – who appeared to enjoy watching us too!

My gorgeous friend Mari greeted David and me with leis when we returned from a trip to Asia. He and I were wearing the identical suits we had tailored for us in Hong Kong. I almost married Mari.

The children were perfect, and Patty Sue's parents were marvelous, making the children and me feel a part of their family right away. Patty Sue's little brother Billy, who was nine, was ring bearer. My best man was my old buddy John S. Carroll; an amazing guy – an attorney, state representative, and National Guard pilot, as well as a pilot for Hawaiian Airlines. The managers of the Kahala Hilton and the Hilton Hawaiian Village each presented us with two complimentary nights in their honeymoon suites. Bottles of champagne, fruit, and hors-d'oeuvres were waiting for us in the rooms. I was fascinated by the drapes that opened or closed with the flip of a switch – perfect for people who don't like to leave bed for such a mundane task. I later copied the concept in my home in Sonoma.

Sandy's sex education begins

It was gratifying, and a loving gift, that right after we were married, David and Sandy decided to call Patty Sue "Mom." We located a marvelous lady to care for the children. Joan had been a nun for 20 years, had recently left the convent, and was exceedingly qualified to work with and teach youngsters.

A week after Joan's arrival, Patty Sue decided to have a tea party in order to get acquainted with the ladies in the neighborhood. Most were wives of executives, lawyers, and doctors. The ladies were in the midst of their very formal tea party when Sandy burst into the living room from playing outside with some of the neighbor boys. "Hey, Mom!" she yelled out, "What's 'fuck' mean?" Patty Sue told me afterward that, between our ex-nun and the neighbor ladies, the sound of chins hitting the floor was almost deafening.

She took Sandy by the hand into another room and said, "Sandy, we don't use that word. The proper word is 'sexual intercourse.' I'll explain it to you later when the company is gone, OK, honey?"

"OK, Mom!" Unabashed as usual, Sandy ran back outside to play.

Ten minutes later she again burst in while the ladies were sipping tea. "Hey, Mom, what's that fancy word for 'fuck'?" At that point Patty Sue felt rather faint. One of the ladies helped her to sit down and handed her a cup of tea. Shortly thereafter the ladies departed.

To help Patty Sue recuperate from that sex-education calamity, I invited her to go sailing on a catamaran. It was a typical balmy Hawaiian afternoon. We sailed from Waikiki Beach, about two miles out to sea. We then lowered the sail, enjoyed the sun, and just drifted with the gentle trade winds. Out of the quiet there came a sound like a submarine about to surface from a great depth. Suddenly, a whale at least 30 feet long shot up out of the ocean. It was so close to our boat that we almost capsized. It was magnificent. Patty Sue, with her melodious laugh, said, "Thar she blows!"

I said, "Really?"

The honeymoon

With the children in good hands, we departed for a honeymoon in Europe. We visited England, France, Italy, Holland, and Denmark. Patty Sue's father was born in Denmark. In those countries, people are surprisingly more open about sex and their bodies than we are here in the U.S. Strolling around Copenhagen, we stopped to look at a display of dolls in the window of a department store. There was a boy doll and girl doll; they had no clothes on, and they were "anatomically correct." Two girls about eight years old had their little noses pressed against the window. Did they stare at the dolls? No. They ignored them. They were admiring a teddy bear.

Just as the acceptance of nudity defused the sexual charge for those little girls, re-legalizing marijuana for adults would evaporate the forbidden-fruit thrill of illicit use. It has already done so in the Netherlands, where criminal penalties were repealed in 1978. Decriminalization neutralized youthful rebellion against authority, and caused marijuana use to level out. It also separated hard drugs from pot. In Amsterdam's "coffee shops" only grass and hashish – and coffee – are available.

Since then, hard-drug use has *not* increased – a perfect example of pot *not* being a gateway drug, or the use of hard drugs *would* have increased. Compare that to the U.S., where hard-drug use is on the rise.

It can't be said frequently enough: *Marijuana must be removed from the Schedule I list that equates it with heroin.* It *will* eventually be legalized for adults. But when?

How the media support and fan the War on Drugs

In 1970, those of us in Hawaii were largely unaware of the War on Drugs that was causing terror on the mainland. In Hawaii, we commonly smoked grass out in the open, and we weren't harassed by police officers.

On the mainland, though, the government had begun massaging the news media to sway public opinion. At the request of the White House,

TV producers began including drug propaganda in such shows as *Andy Griffith, The Mod Squad, The FBI, The Name of the Game, Mission Impossible* (perfect name for the drug war), *General Hospital, Mannix, Love American Style,* and our own *Hawaii Five-O.* Scripts were being tailored to exaggerate the danger of illegal drugs. They routinely overlooked the frequent abuse of legal drugs such as Vicodin, Valium, Percodan, Ritalin, and hundreds of others listed in the Physician's Desk Reference whose toxicity can cause death. The worst, of course, were alcohol and nicotine. Illegal drugs caused problems, of course, but most of these came from the illegality rather than from the drugs themselves. If people were addicted to alcohol they were referred to treatment. If they were addicted to an illegal drug, or became psychologically dependent on non-physically addictive marijuana, they often ended up in prison. The majority are in prison for possession only. Many teens were using grass, but teen heroin use was practically unknown. Facts and consequences were irrelevant, however. If it bleeds, it leads.

Time magazine didn't miss that formula. In March of 1970, its editors learned of a 12-year-old boy who was a heroin addict, (a drug czar's wet dream). The magazine ran a story with the headline "Kids and Heroin: The Adolescent Epidemic." *Time* wrote, "The tragedy is that Ralphie is not special. Heroin, long considered the affliction of the criminal, the derelict, the debauched, is increasingly attacking America's children." The story didn't stop there. It went on to say that the number of teenage addicts in New York "may mushroom fantastically to 100,000 this summer. Many experts" – our drug czar and his drinking buddies perhaps? – "believe that disaster looms large." *Time* couldn't resist trotting out that old chestnut, the stepping-stone theory: "If a young person smokes marijuana on more than 10 occasions, the chances are one in five that he will go on to more dangerous drugs."

Devotees of the gateway theory must have giggled gleefully. We were being told that marijuana is a stepping stone to hard drugs, even though scientific studies have consistently proved otherwise.

Parts of the country were already becoming like police states. I began to realize this was not so much a drug war as a propaganda war that had gotten out of control. Lynch-mob mentality was taking over. Nixon was giving more power to police to search homes and conduct wiretaps, and people were going to prison for possessing small amounts of illegal drugs. The public was sucked into the media hysteria. This fevered propaganda frightened Americans into backing the most expensive and deceitful war in the history of the world. It was uptight Richard Nixon, more than anyone else, who needed to smoke grass.

It was exciting to hear that two of the world's most exhaustive marijuana reports were being released in 1970. Perhaps those studies would finally persuade the media to exonerate pot.

The Canadian LeDain Commission Report, 1970

The LeDain Commission's report on cannabis was perhaps the most extensive of all studies to date. This was an international inquiry. Members of the panel received information from the U.S. They traveled to European countries, interviewing hundreds of young people, as well as doctors and hospital staffs. Adult marijuana users were also interviewed: teachers, journalists, business executives, pilots, scientists, politicians, lawyers, and bankers, among others.[22]

The Commission asked why so many young people smoke marijuana in the United States. Two answers were frequently repeated:

- The widespread radio and television advertising of mind-affecting drugs.[23]
- The widespread use of stimulants, depressants, and tranquilizers by their parents.[24]

Young people frequently contrasted the effects of marijuana and alcohol and described marijuana as a drug of peace, "a drug that reduces tendencies to aggression while suggesting that alcohol produces hostile, aggressive behavior."[25]

This commission concluded:

- Marijuana is *not* an addicting drug. Physical dependence on marijuana has not been demonstrated.[26]
- Users do not develop tolerance in the classical sense – the kind of tolerance that leads to increases in dosage.[27]
- If users stay high for several days in a row the drug experience loses much of its freshness and clarity and, consequently, they prefer intermittent use.[28]
- In some cases it was reported that psychological dependence was present. This kind of dependency occurs regularly with respect to such things as TV, music, books, religion, sex, money, favorite foods, hobbies, sports, games, and, often, other persons. Some degree of

psychological dependence is, in this sense, a general and normal psychological condition.[29]
- The usual consequence of overdose is sleep.[30]
- No deaths due directly to smoking or eating marijuana have been documented.[31]
- The stepping-stone theory that marijuana use leads to heroin use is stated but given little credence. Alcohol and barbiturates rather than marijuana have most frequently preceded heroin use.[32]
- No evidence exists that marijuana smoking leads to lung cancer.[33]

In place of the *pretense* that the alcohol, caffeine, and nicotine one generation uses are not drugs while the marijuana its children use is evil, the report recommended that each drug be judged on its merits: "The extent to which any particular drug use is to be deemed to be undesirable will depend upon its relative potential for harm, both personal, and social."[34] The commission summed it all up by saying that it is a grave error to indulge in deliberate distortion or exaggeration concerning the alleged dangers of a particular drug, or to base a program of drug education upon a strategy of fear.[35]

The U.S. Government's apparent response: Don't confuse us with facts. Our minds are made up. I don't recall one newspaper story on the positive results of this exhaustive study. They have instead reported extensively on the false negative studies.

By the late 1970s, with the help of NORML's public education program, the majority of Americans favored marijuana decriminalization. It was a position taken by notable organizations such as the American Medical Association, the American Bar Association, the National Council of Churches, and B'nai B'rith – and by notable people such as Ann Landers, William F. Buckley, Jr., and Art Linkletter.

The Jamaican Study, 1970

The National Institute of Mental Health conducted a study of marijuana use by Jamaicans, who smoked a type that is much stronger than that commonly available in the U.S. The study concluded that marijuana did not cause either amotivational syndrome or mental illness. Many marijuana smokers were the children and *grandchildren* of people who also smoked marijuana. Many of these individuals were probably exposed to marijuana before birth, as well as during their whole adult lives, but no evidence was found of either chromosomal abnormalities or increased incidence of birth defects. The study said marijuana was a relatively harmless intoxicant.

Recommendation: No criminal penalties for marijuana use.[36]

The U.S. Government's presumed response: Those Jamaicans were probably stoned when they did their research. If they just drank their rum we might believe them. Alcohol is good. Don't confuse us with more facts. Our minds are made up.

The federal government and its DEA have charged that marijuana has a high potential for abuse, similar to heroin's, and that even minute levels of THC in industrial hemp pose a threat to public health. (Translation: *Hemp and marijuana are a threat to major corporations. Politics happens.*) They have also asserted that medicinal marijuana is *opposed by all major health and medical organizations.* I wonder if the AMA was surprised to learn it isn't a major medical organization.

Flying our plane to Washington, D.C.

In mid-1971 our family traveled to the mainland. I wanted to buy a newer Cardinal, with the larger 180-horsepower engine, and I located one that was almost new: a beautiful red and white bird. We flew it from San Francisco to Portland, Oregon, to visit sister Carol and her family, then took off for New Hampshire to visit Patty Sue's family. They lived on Squam Lake, where ten years later Katharine Hepburn, Henry Fonda, and his daughter Jane filmed *On Golden Pond.* By that time, our little ring bearer, Patty Sue's brother Billy, was 21, and he ran the speedboat to take Henry Fonda out to the set each day. Those who saw the movie may recall the postal carrier who delivered mail with a speedboat. When she was a teenager, Patty Sue had that job during summer vacation.

Patty Sue finds our stolen Leeteg

Back in my Dave Ford Motors days, I had read James A. Michener's book, *Rascals in Paradise* and been intrigued by his chapter on Edgar Leeteg, "the American Gauguin." Leeteg created masterpieces on black velvet. Some of his paintings were bringing as much as $20,000, even back in the '60's. I wanted to own a Leeteg, but figured they were a bit rich for my blood – until the day a Mr. Jay Edison walked onto the car lot.

He seemed particularly keen on a year-old Cadillac. At last he came into my office, unrolled a black velvet painting of a beautiful young Tahitian girl, and said, "This is an original Leeteg. I'll trade you for that gray Cadillac." I was eager to acquire the painting, but felt I had to be sure about its authenticity. Edison had no objection to my getting an expert opinion.

I phoned the Barney Davis Art Gallery in Honolulu, and arranged for Barney to examine the painting. I was delighted with his evaluation. "It's an original, and it's a good one. It has some very minor damage that could easily be repaired. I can recommend the names of several artists who are qualified to make the repairs."

"Is it worth a trade for a year-old Cadillac?"

"You bet."

Edison and I made the trade, but I was so eager to see the Leeteg on the wall of my home that I didn't take the time to get it repaired. It moved with me from one home to the next for 12 years before I finally dug out that list of artists and called one of them. John examined it carefully, and told me, "It's a fine work. The time it spent rolled up caused some damage that will require a bit of touchup. I can do that within a few weeks. I'll phone you when it's ready to pick up."

A month passed with no word from him, so I phoned. His wife answered. When I asked about the painting, she replied tersely, "John died three weeks ago. He never had your painting. I'm sorry." *Click.*

John *had* had our painting, and I had no intention of losing it. I was sincerely sorry to hear about his death, but when his wife hung up so abruptly Patty Sue and I both concluded she did have the painting, knew she had it, and intended to keep it. We decided to visit her home and try to obtain a truthful answer.

No one was home. I decided to have a closer look, and I found an unlocked window. I climbed in, Patty Sue right behind me. We shared a flashlight, checking cupboards and the garage, where John's studio was located. No painting. While I was groping around the studio, Patty Sue was checking other rooms. "I found it!" she said, laughing. "It's in their bedroom closet." There it was, hidden behind some dresses. We snatched it and made a clean getaway.

I don't know whether John's wife ever figured out what we'd done but we never heard from her. (What was she going to say? "Did you steal back that painting I never had?") Eventually another artist restored the Leeteg for $700. I love the painting and may never sell it; it hangs in my Sonoma home today.

To celebrate, we went to Victoria Station. A nice restaurant, constructed of old railroad cars, with decorations in a railway motif. It featured fine steaks and an all-you-can-eat salad bar.

When we found a slot in the restaurant's dimly lit parking lot, we decided to pause for a puff of high-quality grass. Without pot, life is generally fine, but our minds often wander. With the grass we were totally focused on each other that night. Our bodies purred. We held and slowly kissed. Between the grass and the happy exercise, we were now ravenous. I was still high when we were attacking our salads, and I playfully stabbed at a little cherry tomato with my fork. It shot over to the next table. After a wave and smile, all was forgiven. See how violent you get with pot?

I was approached by Rodney Inaba, son of a mammoth Hawaii land developer, Norman Inaba. "Dave, we would like to commission you to write and produce a motion picture showing the tremendous amounts of money being invested on the Big Island of Hawaii. Would you consider it?"

I knew of their large corporation. Not only was Inaba one of Hawaii's largest subdivision developers, but they also owned Great Hawaiian Realty and Great Hawaiian Financial, with 100 employees. "Sounds interesting," I said.

He continued, "We have a beautiful subdivision. After roads are installed, there will be 1,500 lots, most with views of the ocean. We want a motion picture we can present in Honolulu hotels to tourists and locals we've invited to be our guests for dinner. They'll see the movie, and hear a presentation about the Big Island. Then we'll invite them to join us on a tour to inspect our beautiful Royal Gardens subdivision. It is located in the Kalapana area. My father has authorized me to make you a generous financial offer in exchange for a great deal of creative work."

He went on: "What we want is to have you manage our Waikiki sales office, to give dinner presentations in some of the Waikiki hotels, and to be Director of Research and Public Relations for our company. We'll show the motion picture at these dinners, but we would like you there personally to lend your prestige and to give a presentation on financial leverage. Then you can invite the guests to join you on a tour of the Big Island, and in particular to visit the Royal Gardens subdivision. If that isn't enough of a challenge, we'd like you to narrate the bus tour on the Big Island each Sunday. We're prepared to make it worth your while by offering you two and a half percent of gross sales. In addition, we'll pay you a thousand dollars a month. What do you say?"

"It sounds fascinating," I said. I estimated that I could make at least a couple of hundred thousand dollars a year. The following Saturday I flew Rodney to the Big Island, and we visited all their subdivisions. I was impressed. Lots in the Royal Gardens subdivision were to be priced at $7,500 for an acre. Each lot was an acre or larger. Other than unit one, they all faced on paved roads, and as Rodney had said, most had ocean views. I had learned in dealing with businessmen in Japan that their integrity was faultless. I'd made numerous deals in Japan, sealed with nothing more than a handshake, and they'd never let me down. I was convinced that the two-and-a-half percent of the gross sales would pay off handsomely.

Producing a commercial motion picture – assisted by pot

A little happy grass primed my creativity. I soon came up with an idea and went to work. If I could get Nani, the lovely widow of Kui Lee, I would write the script around her. She agreed to be in the film, and to sing a couple of Kui's songs.

The title of the motion picture was *Nani*. I worked night and day and in three weeks completed the script, with location scenes, music – the works. A professional camera crew shot the film. The lush, majestic Big Island is known for its active volcanoes, so the film opened with a volcanic blast of lava fountaining hundreds of feet into the air. It then dissolved into a magnificent waterfall: breathtaking Akaka Falls on the Hilo side of the island.

Before we began shooting, I contacted Aloha Airlines and explained what we were up to. I told them that we *could* be using Aloha Airlines each week for a group tour to the Big Island, and that I could create a sequence in the movie showing their aircraft, if they would give us a $5,000 credit against future ticket sales. They agreed. I saved money by using my own plane for the aerial photography, and completed the entire 22-minute motion picture in three months for $5,000. With the credit from Aloha, the finished film cost the Inaba family virtually nothing.

On June 7, 1972, the film premiered before 150 guests at a dinner presentation at the Waikiki Yacht Club. Present were the officials of Great Hawaiian Realty and Great Hawaiian Financial and many of the employees in their sales and clerical staffs.

"Nani *the best thing done on the Big Island"*

Columnist Eddie Sherman was also a guest at that first dinner. Sherman ran a daily gossip column that in Hawaii was as popular as Dear Abby's advice to the lovelorn. His reaction was most gratifying. In the *Sunday Star-Bulletin & Advertiser* of June 11, 1972, he wrote under the heading *Honolulu Newsstand:* "Some are calling Dave Ford's *Nani* film the best thing done on the Big Island. Points out the tremendous development that's taken place there and what's planned for the future. Great Hawaiian Realty uses this movie for promotional purposes."

I had never worked harder in my life, or had more success. I spent long hours preparing and delivering dinner presentations to go along with the movie. We took prospects to the Big Island each Sunday on Aloha Airlines, and because most of the passengers were our guests, the airline offered me the use of the aircraft's announcement system to do a running narration of the points of interest along the route. I was happy to do it. Once in Hilo, we had an air-conditioned tour bus waiting.

We stopped at an anthurium farm, where the passengers had a chance to get out and inspect tangerine trees that grew right out of old lava, and each woman was presented with a dozen freshly cut anthuriums. We stopped at a noted park where deluxe plate lunches were provided for our guests. Then on to Royal Gardens, which indeed looked royal. On the lush site were mango, lama, guava, kukui, ohia, coconut, breadfruit, and Christmas berry trees that once supported a large Hawaiian settlement. (That is, until the missionaries and sailors killed them off with chicken pox and measles. The Hawaiians had no immunity. The sailors threw in syphilis. No doubt missionaries also contributed their diseases, while they stole the Hawaiians' land.)

We were taking in between $200,000 and $500,000 in lot sales each week. Many of those remunerative weeks involved 14-hour days for me. I suggested to Rodney and his father Norman that if we constructed a model home in Royal Gardens, customers would see the possibilities more clearly and our sales would increase. They didn't agree, so I had a model home built and paid for it myself. Sales boomed when we used the home as part of the presentation, and I could see that my two and a half percent of the gross would more than pay for the home construction.

I constantly built up the image of the company, and in particular its creator, Norman Inaba. The company newspaper published...

A RELUCTANT INVESTOR'S LAMENT

I hesitate to make a list
Of all the countless deals I've missed;
Bonanzas that were in my grip –
I watched them through my fingers slip;
The windfalls I should have bought
Were lost because I overthought;
I thought of this, I thought of that,
I could have sworn I smelled a rat,
And while I thought things over twice,
Norman grabbed them at the price.
It seems I always hesitate,
Then make my mind up much too late.
A very cautious man am I,
And that is why I never buy.

While oceanfronts, with vibrant waves, and a rather
magnificent look,
Were priced at just a buck a foot,
I wouldn't even make a bid,
But Norman did – yes, Norman did!
When Waikiki was the place to buy,
I thought the climate much too dry;
'Invest on the Big Island – that's the spot!'
My sixth sense warned me I should not.
A very prudent man am I,
And that is why I never buy.

When Royal Gardens was selling units 3 and 4,
I was sure something'd happen, and there'd be
no more.
How Waikiki and the Big Island grew!
Kauai, Maui, and Molokai, too!
When Norman culled those sprawling farms,
And welcomed deals with open arms
A corner here, 1800 acres there,
Compounding values year by year,
I chose to think, and as I thought,
Norman bought the deals I should have bought!
The golden chances I had then,
Are lost and will not come again.
Today I cannot be enticed
For everything's so overpriced.

The deals of yesteryear are dead,
        The market's soft – and so's my head!

Last night I had a fearful dream.
        I know I wakened with a scream:
Some Indians approached my bed –
        For trinkets on the barrelhead,
(In dollar bills worth twenty-four;
        And nothing less and nothing more)
They'd sell Manhattan Isle to me.
        The most I'd go was twenty-three.
The redmen scowled: "Not on a bet!"
        And sold to Peter Minuet.
At times a teardrop drowns my eye,
        For deals I had, but did not buy;
And now life's saddest words I pen –
        "If only I'd invested then!"

Totally sold on Royal Gardens

I was so enthusiastic about Royal Gardens subdivision that I purchased seven lots myself. I prompted the company to increase prices from $7,500, to $9,000, and then a few months later to $12,500, and finally to $16,000. This I felt made a fine profit for the original buyers, and the price was extremely reasonable compared to other subdivision lots of equal size and proximity to the ocean. On Saturdays I was often asked to give a staff seminar on "Closing Sales."

Dollar signs floated in my eyes as the day approached that I'd receive my two-and-a-half percent of the gross sales to date – already several million dollars. I estimated that the Inabas' gross return on the million dollars Norman had invested years ago would be about $16 million.

Payday arrived. Rodney invited me into his father's lavish office. It wasn't every day that employees were invited into Norman Inaba's domain. I felt as though I was being ushered into the Oval Office.

Norman greeted me with a hearty handshake. "Sit down, Dave. It's a privilege to have you with us. You've done great things for our company. And the movie you made for us is the talk of the islands. You really know your business. And please know, the tremendous number of hours you have invested with us will never be forgotten." (Such recognition from such a big man – *I* was impressed.) Rodney was nodding in agreement with all that his father was saying. Norman continued, "You

THE SUNDAY STAR-BULLETIN & ADVERTISER

June 11, 1972

eddie sherman...

Honolulu newsstand

DAVE FORD

Some are calling **Dave Ford's** "**Nani**" film the best thing done on the Big Island. Points out the tremendous development that's taken place there and what's planned for the future. Great Haw'n Realty uses this movie for promotional purposes.

Sunday Star-Bulletin & Advertiser, June 11, 1972
Columnist Eddie Sherman covered the premiere of Nani, the film I created to promote Great Hawaiian Realty's projects on the Big Island of Hawaii. A little happy grass primed creativity, and I completed the writing in three weeks. Without that help, it would have taken several times that long.

I was sometimes putting in fourteen hours a day promoting Great Hawaiian Realty.

know, Dave, we have over 100 employees with Great Hawaiian Realty and Great Hawaiian Financial, and sales increased when the model home was used. It's really a family corporation, so many of our relatives are working with us here, and almost all of our employees are Japanese. You're one of the few exceptions." I smiled and nodded.

"Dave, the family is upset that we offered you two-and-a-half percent of the gross sales on Royal Gardens." (How exciting, they'd decided to pay me more!) "So, rather than having my family lose face by writing such a large check to a haole, we've decided to pay you one half of one percent. You understand we never had any agreement in writing, don't you?"

I could feel the blood drain from my face and the hair stand up on the back of my neck. I almost laughed out loud for being such a fool as to work without a written contract. I had liked Norman. I had thought he was a man of character. As he began to write a check, I turned around and left his office.

My biggest regret was that so much of the time I'd put into this project I could have spent with my family.

I had lent Rodney $50,000 to use as a down payment on a hotel. When the note was due Rodney said, "Why don't you just write it off?" I made it clear that if he didn't have a check for me within three days he'd find himself in court. He paid.

Pot luck – included in the "Who's Who of Hawaii"

One personal bright spot at that time was the news that I had been included in the 1972 edition of Hawaii's equivalent of *Who's Who*. The 667-page book was called *Men and Women of Hawaii*, and cited their contributions. The foreword was written by Chinn Ho, an amazing man who earned special recognition as president of Capital Investment Co. of Hawaii, the developer of the Ilikai Hotel and Makaha Valley. He had been chairman of the board of Gannett Pacific Inc., which published the *Honolulu Star-Bulletin* newspaper as well as two daily newspapers on Guam. I feel that, along with Henry J. Kaiser, Chinn Ho was one of the most outstanding men of Hawaii. Following is a portion of his foreword to *Men and Women of Hawaii*.

> This book does more than present the leaders of Hawaii. In its own way it tells much of the story of Hawaii and reflects within its pages a chart of progressive endeavor along with many channel markers

which clearly show the way for the state to maintain its momentum in providing a better life for its peoples. Hawaii goes into this new decade with a recent history of movement which demonstrates an unusual talent and tolerance for change... Revealed in these pages also is a remarkable determination for self-improvement. The results, in terms of standard of living and increased opportunities, have far exceeded the hopes of most. Our biographies were active participants in these landmarks of change. Many were and are, its architects.

He might truthfully have added, "...and David R. Ford wouldn't be in this book had he not frequently shared with us the creative gifts he got from using cannabis !"

Meeting "the Howard Hughes
of the South Pacific"

My high-profile efforts on behalf of Royal Gardens led to a contact from the president of Amalgamated Land Company, which owned land in the New Hebrides, an island chain 1,100 miles from Australia, and sold it through their Honolulu offices. "Mr. Ford, our company's principals have seen *Nani* and think that it's superb. We want you to make a similar movie for us. We would like you to go to the New Hebrides, look it over, and see if you like it. If you do, and you elect to produce the movie, we'll pay you $20,000 and all expenses. In two days we can have a round-trip first-class ticket ready for you, with no cost or obligation on your part. You'll meet with Gene Peacock, who is a fine man, and one of the largest land developers in the South Pacific." After talking it over with Patty Sue, I decided to check it out.

When the plane landed in Port Vila, the enchanting capital of the New Hebrides, British policemen clad in starched white shirts, shorts, and knee socks boarded the aircraft and blocked the exit. One thundered in a parade-ground voice, "We do not want hippie-type people in the New Hebrides. If this description fits you, be prepared to depart these islands on the next outbound plane." He strutted down the aisle, and stopped a few rows ahead of me, at the seat of a neat, well-groomed young man with clean waist-length hair in a neat braid.

"Do you plan to disembark this plane?" the officer demanded.

"Yes, sir" came the mellow reply.

"Are you a hippie?"

"No, sir. I just like my hair long."

"You're not leaving this plane with that hair! If you want to leave the plane, you're getting a haircut right now. Do you understand?"

"Yes, sir."

Without another word, the policeman took out a pair of scissors and cut off the braid at the scalp!

He then shouted, "If anyone is carrying drugs, hand them over now, or you will end up in our prison." I was glad I'd left my grass at home.

He went on to lay down a code of conduct. "There is to be absolutely no fraternizing with the natives. That means no talking, no giving them rides in cars. They make one dollar a day picking copra. They are not to be spoiled. Do you understand?" Everyone nodded.

"And keep in mind there are rare cases of cannibalism in these islands."

That demonstration should have been enough to make me take the next flight out, but the lush green islands had enchanted me before the aircraft's wheels ever touched the ground. Looking out the window, I imagined that I was seeing what Hawaii looked like a hundred years ago. Transparent, unpolluted water, where one could see a hundred feet down, and miles of coral sand beaches. It was here that author James Michener conceived his *Tales of the South Pacific*. At the time of my visit to the New Hebrides, it was overseen jointly by the British and the French, in a "condominium" government.

I was directed to a new Toyota that was waiting in my name outside the terminal. There was a note on the dashboard saying, "Welcome, Dave. Drive to the Le Lagoon Hotel in town. There is a deluxe room waiting for you. Sign for all food and beverages. This trip is to cost you nothing. I want you to have a true feel of these islands. You will find an open Inter-Island airline ticket to Espiritu Santo in your room. After you have spent all the time you wish in Vila, please come to my home. Aloha, until we meet. Gene Peacock."

This man was a legend. I had heard that he had a mansion overlooking the ocean, and lived the fantasy life of *Playboy* publisher Hugh Hefner. I looked forward to meeting my benefactor.

After checking into the hotel, I bought an English-French dictionary to help me communicate with the local residents. The beauty of the island was intoxicating. I wanted a piece of it before missionaries arrived and stole it as they did in Hawaii. I was directed to a Frenchman named Jacques Farey, who I was told might sell some 200 acres of prime level land overlooking the Tauguma River that could be subdivided. With the help of the dictionary, I managed to make him an offer on his property. Shortly after dawn the following day I boarded Air Melanesia, and flew to Espiritu Santo.

I rented a Jeep and drove around, admiring this paradise. I met another Frenchman who wanted to sell 510 acres of rich almost-level land 200 yards above the ocean. The top soil was 18 feet deep, and it was so rich that I saw fenceposts that had sprouted roots and grown! (I couldn't help but think what fine medical-quality grass could be grown here. Maybe just a quarter of an acre?) The magnificent jungle was woven like lace among the trees. I gave him a $500 cash deposit.

"Are the natives friendly?"

As I was driving back toward town I saw an islander carrying a girl about 12 years old in his arms. He was dripping wet with sweat, and it was obvious that the child's leg was badly fractured. She was crying out in agony, so I stopped and asked him to get into the Jeep. "I cannot. I thank you, but you get in bad trouble if give ride. I have walk four miles. I make to hospital."

I opened the door and insisted they get in. Reluctantly, he complied. She moaned. "I fall out coconut tree." I drove them to the hospital and waited while her leg was set, then drove them back.

There was nothing that I would call a road up the mountain, but there was a narrow, rough trail. With the four-wheel drive engaged we finally made it to their village. It turned out that he was the chief of these people, and he insisted that I remain for food. I was invited to a luau in my honor, and to sit next to him. When it was time to leave, he gave me a hug. "You are brave, beautiful man!"

I continued on the dirt track to the Lokalee Beach Hotel, which was located 38 miles due east of Santo. The "road" was more like a trail, and the Jeep's compass came in handy more than once, when I wasn't certain whether I was on the road or not. In the dense jungle, darkness came early; it was only 5 p.m. but already almost dark. Now, the shadows of the trees 100 feet high began to look like animals closing in. Suddenly, in front of the Jeep and on both sides, there appeared a dozen islanders in loincloths. They were holding cane knives with three-foot blades. Their faces were painted in various unfamiliar designs. Oh Lord, I thought, please don't let me die like this. This is not the way I wish to be eaten.

Am I going to be eaten?

I was alarmed as the natives began closing in on me. Were these cannibals? I had no weapon. I'd already thought of a name for the movie that I wanted to make. The title I had in mind was *The Last Paradise*. Now I began to think of *The Last Supper,* starring me in the title role. I decided to try a bluff, so I jauntily waved and slowly got out of the Jeep with my camera in hand. I beckoned for them to come closer. Acting a bit confused, they obliged. I lifted my camera and pointed to my big smile that was close to turning into a scream. I gestured for them to smile. No smiles. I clicked the shutter, recalling that I hadn't loaded the film. I waved a "thank you", climbed back into the Jeep and floorboarded it.

An hour later I finally found the hotel. It was just like something one would expect to see in a South Pacific movie: slow-turning ceiling fans, tapa cloth attached to walls; outrigger canoes drawn up on the beach, and an expansive bar offering tropical drinks. I learned that the eaters of one's own kind I had encountered were not cannibals after all, but friendly curious natives, probably headed for a tribal celebration, and that they generally carried cane knives to cut their way through the jungle.

The service and hospitality at the hotel were heartwarming. The ocean was crystal clear, teeming with tropical fish of every color. It was eerie seeing a hundred feet or more straight down. There were many varieties of fish I didn't recognize – and apparently I wasn't the only one. I was told that the local residents each kept four or five cats. If they didn't recognize the type of fish they'd caught, before eating it they generously gave a piece to one of the cats. If the cat died, they elected not to eat fish that night.

● ● ●

It was time to meet Gene Peacock. I drove to his palatial residence, located on a plateau that overlooked Port Vila. The houseboy who admitted me showed me to a large cool room and asked me to wait. Lovely young native ladies wearing colorful sarongs followed us into the room and began offering me food and drink, so the waiting was not painful. Abruptly, a large carved door opened. There stood a man in his early 50s who looked like Clark Gable, his arms outstretched in a gesture of welcome. "Dave Ford! You son-of-a-gun! Why, you're the same Dave Ford that practically stole my year-old Cadillac from me when you were in the car business. I should have known!"

My golly, I'd met this man before. "Gene Peacock! I had no idea you were that shrewd seller who wanted retail for your Cadillac!" We embraced like long-lost brothers. "Gene, before we go any further I want to tell you –" Gene interrupted.

"You want to tell me about the two pieces of land you purchased. Forget it. I knew about the sales an hour later. They were great buys. I should have picked 'em up myself, a year ago. Congratulations!"

"Gene, I want to write you a check right now for the round trip here, and pay all the expenses I've signed for."

Gene laughed and waved me off. "All I ask is that you go ahead and write and produce the movie. We'll pay for it jointly, you and I." He snapped his fingers. "Hey! Why don't you sell your land out of our offices, and we'll *all* make some money. I suspect I may be able to help you get it subdivided rather quickly."

What a guy! "It's a deal, Gene. I'm planning on departing tomorrow. I've already changed my return first-class ticket to a regular peon ticket, with your account being credited for the total cost."

Gene smiled. "I know about your reservations to leave. I have business in Fiji, and took the liberty of changing your seat back to first-class, the one next to mine. See you at the airport tomorrow, Dave." We bear-hugged each other again.

The next morning Gene and I met at the airport. Given his prestige, I wasn't surprised at all when guards just waved us through the security check. As soon as our plane was airborne, Gene ordered us Bloody Marys. After the second one, he reached over and said, "Let me shake your hand, and welcome you to the multi-millionaires' club. I can see no way you can avoid netting at least four million dollars on your two subdivisions!" Shaking this fine man's hand was one of the richest rushes I ever experienced.

"Ford's Fun Tour"

After getting home and playing with the children for a couple of days, Patty Sue and I went to a hotel and spent most of the weekend making love. She was eager to see the land I'd purchased, and was enthusiastic and supportive while I worked on the script for *The Last Paradise,* which was coming along swiftly.

Busted

I also created a travel brochure. Patty Sue and I had purchased an interest in the Kahala Travel Agency, and now started an advertising campaign for a tour to the New Hebrides, which we called "A 14-day tour to the New Hebrides, The Last Paradise." Our ad copy continued, "You're invited to join Ford's Fun Tour, departing September 14, 1971, for $760." Gene Peacock and his Amalgamated Land Company collaborated on this campaign because many of his clients wanted to see their land. The trip included stops in Tahiti, Noumea, and New Caledonia, and plenty of sightseeing in the New Hebrides.

Everything went like clockwork – until our departure from Noumea to the New Hebrides.

As I was boarding the plane, two police officers grabbed me, one by each arm. "You David R. Ford?"

"Yes. Is there a problem?" (I got the idea there was.)

"You are wanted in the Commandant's office."

"Please, I'm heading a tour group. I can't miss this flight."

"You *are* going to miss the plane, Mr. Ford. You are *not* wanted in the New Hebrides! Our chief will give you the details."

As they marched me to the commandant's office, I begged, "Please give me a moment to speak with my wife." Patty Sue was brought in and I told her I would get the problem resolved as soon as possible. "Please tell our tour members I've got temporary business in Noumea and they'll be going on to the New Hebrides without me. *Please* contact the British Embassy for help as soon as you land.

Patty Sue was a great sport. "See you soon, darling," she said.

I asked the commandant if he would explain the problem. "We were sorry to do this to you without any warning, Mr. Ford, but we received a wire from the British and French Embassies in the New Hebrides which stated that you made contact with a native on your last visit, and you are no longer welcome in the New Hebrides."

Six hours of humiliation, and concern for Patty Sue and our tour group, passed sluggishly. After telephoning the New Hebrides, sending wires, speaking over direct radio connection, and fervently promising never to speak with an islander again, I was allowed to continue with our tour. After six hours of little more reassurance than Patty Sue's smiling countenance and nonchalant behavior, our passengers never knew that they almost completed their excursion minus one tour director. For them, at least, Ford's Fun Tour lived up to its name.

While we were in the New Hebrides I paid off the balances I owed on the two parcels of land, and ordered surveys, aerial photos, and subdivision plans.

Trying to buy a ship

Back in Hawaii, I completed the script for *The Last Paradise* and sent it on its way to Gene. On September 15, 1972, Patty Sue joined me on a two-week trip to the Far East. We needed to wind up our import business, and I wanted to take Patty Sue to the places I'd been on earlier trips. (Some of them!)

After enjoying the Osaka Hotel and touring many areas of Japan, we decided to take the *S.S. President Cleveland* back to Hawaii, on what was to be the swan song of this classic luxury liner. The President of American President Lines was aboard for this nostalgic voyage. The ship was 610 feet long and carried 511 first-class passengers. It was in fine shape, and was being retired after 25 years' service only because its subsidy from the Federal Maritime Administration had expired. It pained me when I overheard that this magnificent vessel was going to be sold for scrap. When I learned that the scrap price was only $640,000, an idea started buzzing around in my head. I asked the ship's captain to introduce me to APL's president, whose name was Richardson, I believe. He graciously asked me to join him and Mr. Richardson at the Captain's table for dinner that evening.

At that point in the voyage we happened to get caught in Typhoon Ida. The ship rolled badly, and Patty Sue was among many who were seasick. I was able to make it to the Captain's table for dinner, but just barely. I had an idea that if I offered, say, an additional $40,000 they would sell the ship to me instead of scrapping it. My idea was to turn it into a floating hotel, anchored off Magic Island in Honolulu. The ship could be completely self-contained, producing its own fresh drinking water from salt water, and its own electricity. Mr. Richardson was pleased that the ship might "live again" in Hawaii, and of course was not reluctant to accept an additional $40,000.

I told Mr. Richardson that it was my belief that the ship would be an attraction in Hawaii, especially at night, with her lights gleaming across the water, and that I was certain we could show a profit if we rented out the staterooms at about half the price of local hotel rooms. I was also sure that most of the finest local shops, such as Liberty House, I Magnin, Andrade, and The Royal Hawaiian Gift Shops, would rent retail space. I also raised the possibility that we could anchor outside the three-mile limit, and offer a bit of gambling. Mr. Richardson was impressed with my ideas.

I told him I would like him to meet my wife. I mentioned that she was seasick, and would probably find the aromas of the dining salon a bit more than she could handle. He suggested we meet on the leeward side of the boat deck. I went down to our stateroom, and found little Patty Sue looking a bit green. I suggested that some fresh air would help her to feel better. Gamely, she agreed to try, and we headed for the starboard lifeboats, where Mr. Richardson was waiting for us.

"Darling, I'd like you to meet Mr. Richardson, President of the American President Lines."

As Patty Sue reached out to shake hands, the seasickness hit her again and she threw up. Mr. Richardson ducked deftly, and quipped, "I'm thankful that I don't affect all the ladies that way!"

Unfortunately, I hadn't brought along any grass. A few hits of pot would have ended the seasickness. Imagine how noble it would have been to pass out joints to the dozens of seasick passengers!

Would Hawaii's Governor John Burns help us?

The day after we arrived in Honolulu, I recalled something Governor John Burns had said to me after I interviewed him several years before. Echoing Wayne Newton's words almost exactly, he'd said "If there is ever anything I can do for you, Dave, just let me know." This was it. I made an appointment. In his office I briefed him on my idea of a floating hotel.

His response wasn't all I'd hoped it to be. "The idea is outstanding, but the hotels are very well organized. I must tell you that you'll have the entire hotel industry against you. Your chances are about zero." I asked if he didn't feel that having the ship in Honolulu would be such an attraction that he might consider interceding with the hotel industry. "No, as much as I would like to help you, I can't get involved." The idea of a donation for his re-election entered my mind. I decided against it.

About this time word came that the New Hebrides was involved in a struggle for independence, which ultimately resulted in the birth of the nation of Vanuatu. Officials of the new government informed me that I now had the opportunity to *lease* from them my own land, the land for which I had already paid in full. The alternative was to lose it altogether. I declined to sign any papers that surrendered my freehold title.

Darned if I was going to lease my own land! I just let it go and wrote the loss off on my tax return. And Governor Burns, who had offered, "If there is ever anything I can do for you..."? All he did was shake my hand goodbye. No land. No ship. Ah well. One can't take such setbacks seriously, or one might turn to drugs!

Speaking of drugs, we were pleased to note a new marijuana study was about to be released. Ever hopeful, I thought, "If it's positive, surely this time the media won't be controlled by the federal government, and some positive reporting will be published."

National Commission on Marihuana and Drug Abuse, 1972

President Nixon and Congress had given the National Commission on Marihuana and Drug Abuse, also known as the Schaffer Commission, a $1 million budget to determine whether marijuana is a dangerous drug. Included in its membership of 12 were four physicians, two lawyers, and four members of Congress.

After two years of investigation, the commission concluded: Marijuana does not cause violent, aggressive behavior; does not lead to the use of harder drugs; does not constitute a major public health problem; does not lead to chromosomal or brain damage; and does not cause crime, insanity, or sexual promiscuity. Pot does not lead to physical dependency and withdrawal, even after long-term high-dose use, nor to amotivational syndrome. Marijuana is not a stepping stone to other drugs. Marijuana policy had become more damaging to American society than marijuana itself. The commission's recommendation: Eliminate state and federal criminal penalties for pot possession and use.

This recommendation was endorsed by the American Medical Association, the American Bar Association, the American Public Health Association, the National Council of Churches, the National Education Association[37], and the New York Academy of Medicine.[38]

President Nixon rejected the findings of his own commission. As usual, the government had been interested only in a negative report. Government's apparent response: "We prefer to wait for the results of the study by our good friend, Senator James Eastland. His results will show that the Shaffer Commission's investigation was senseless. Don't confuse us with facts. We must continue spending money to convince Americans we're winning the War on Drugs."

It was easy for them to be satisfied with their preference. Senator Eastland allowed only people already opposed to pot to be on his committee. They reported, among other falsehoods, that marijuana diminished people's ability to resist homosexual advances, that it made them more susceptible to communist propaganda, that if you smoked pot just once a week you were constantly high, that marijuana had already led many college students into heroin addiction, and that pot users neglected personal hygiene![39]

The Dutch Baan Commission, 1972

In the same year, the Dutch Baan Commission largely agreed with the Shaffer report: "Cannabis does not produce... physical dependence. The physiological effects of the use of cannabis are of a relatively harmless nature."[40]

Moving to the Big Island and Royal Gardens

At this time, I was still working for the Inabas – and had sold *myself* on the Big Island. The more I thought about it, the more appealing the idea became to move to the model home I was building in the Royal Gardens development on the island of Hawaii. Patty Sue and the children began living on the Big Island while the home was under construction during the kids' summer vacation, 1972. I remained in Honolulu to finish up some projects and lease out the Honolulu home, flying to the Big Island each weekend to join them.

A Hawaiian lady answered the ad to lease the Honolulu home. As I showed her the home, I was concerned that she wouldn't be able to afford the $2,200 per month I was asking. She felt my hesitation. "My husband died a year ago. He had the franchise for the Encyclopedia Britannica in every country in the world except the United States. I'll receive a check for $100,000 every year for the rest of my life. I have an 11-year-old granddaughter, and my maid that will live with us, as well as my mother. Will that be all right?"

"You bet," I told her, and we signed a lease agreement right on the hood of her car. They moved in the next day, and I soon rented out the Japanese-style guest cottage to someone else for $800 a month.

"I have just the maid for you!"

A week later I dropped by unannounced to see that all was in order. A tall black maid in full uniform, and with large breasts, answered the door. She was wearing a very short black skirt with a little white apron, and black five-inch high-heeled shoes. Something about the way the uniform fit made me muse that she just might be a he. My tenant, Mrs. Kealoha, yelled out from back in the kitchen, "Who is it, darling?"

"It's the owner of the house," said the maid in a deep voice.

"Invite him back here!" came the reply. Mrs. Kealoha and four of her friends were sitting at our hardwood kitchen bar, snorting lines of cocaine. Such guts this lady had! She didn't even know I smoke grass. "Have a toot, honey!" she said to me.

The 11-year-old granddaughter said, "Mister, your car seems to be blocking the driveway. '*It*' wants to know if it's OK to move it."

"It" was the maid. I told Mrs. Kealoha that if I ever caught them using cocaine again, they would have to move immediately. "This is the first time we've ever used drugs! Please don't throw us out."

I didn't want to go through the hassle of having to lease the home out again. I repeated, "No drugs, OK?" Mrs. Kealoha seemed hurt. "Some of the nicest police officers come to my parties. They never complain if a weenie bit of drugs are used."

"I do," I said. "Good night."

As I was leaving, the maid walked out to the car and opened the door for me. "I'm really a good girl, sir. I don't do drugs, or anything naughty. But if you'd just drive us over by the golf course, I'd like to give you a blow job." I just shook my head and said, "Good night," and departed, wondering what the hell I had done, renting the house that had been our home to those nuts.

Our Kahala home is cremated

The following week I was at my office in Honolulu when I got an alarming phone call. "Mr. Ford, this is the Kahala fire chief. Your home is on fire. I think you'll want to get over there as soon as possible."

I sped to the house. From a half mile away I could see tongues of fire reaching hundreds of feet into the sky. Five fire trucks were blocking the entrance to the elite subdivision, thick hoses were strung across the roads, and police were waving away all traffic. As soon as an officer recognized me, he said, "I'm sorry for your loss, Dave. Go right past the barricades." The entire house was engulfed in flames. My immediate concern was that no one was inside.

Miraculously, the grandmother just happened to have been moved to a nursing home the night before. (Until then, she had been on oxygen in the room next to where the fire started!) When I arrived, the others were also nowhere to be seen. Afterward, the fire chief informed me that his crew had concluded that the 11-year-old granddaughter was smoking grass with her girlfriend in a small "club house" that David had constructed behind the house, when no one else was at home, and that the girls had accidentally set the house on fire. We never heard from the tenants again.

The insurance settlement was big enough that I was able to pay for an addition of several hundred square feet... but somehow it was no longer the home we'd raised the children in.

For me, the move to the home in Royal Gardens subdivision was refreshing. We awoke in the morning with the aroma of plumeria blossoms, gardenia, and lilikoi. The home was tastefully furnished and decorated. Patty Sue was convinced I would never enjoy being away from constant business challenges, but I did – I felt like a pioneer – I loved it! Chopping wood for the fireplace reminded me of when I was a boy at Stinson Beach. Our lot was one and a third acres. I had planted 50 papaya trees below the home prior to its construction, and five alongside each of the two lanais. After a few months, in the morning we were able to reach out from a dining table on the lanai, and pick papayas for breakfast. And reaching a little farther I could pick the buds off one of a few pot plants I planted near the house under tropical growth. Whenever we had guests, we had some choice grass to offer them.

Ours was the only home in the 1,500-acre subdivision then, and it was as if the clock had been turned back to the time when the original Hawaiians lived in Royal Gardens. The children attended the Pahoa Intermediate and High School 12 miles away.

When David was 13, every school day he drove himself and Sandy down to the bus stop in the convertible, left the car there, and on their return from school drove home. He was a fine driver, but until he was of age to get a license, he drove only within the subdivision.

Frequently, Patty Sue and I would put our bicycles in the Jeep. We'd drive down the steep hill, and then ride our bikes to the world-famous Kaimu (also known as Kalapana) Black Sand Beach, only three miles away. We'd swim, read, have a picnic lunch, and sometimes take a nap under a coconut tree. Other times we'd ride our bikes eight miles to where the Chain of Craters road ended, and have a picnic lunch. Getting there was always a bit of a push, because a strong, steady wind was in our faces the whole way. The reward came on the return trip, when the wind would blow us all the way back to the Royal Gardens entrance. What a rush!

Sometimes Patty Sue and I would take the convertible up the paved road to the top of our steep rolling hill, point the car towards the ocean, stop to take a couple of hits of happy-grass, then coast the whole three miles of the rising and dipping road. We'd get up to 85 miles an hour. It beat any roller-coaster ride; and it was so much fun that sometimes we'd drive back up the hill and do it again.

With the plane it took only 11 minutes to get to Hilo where we did most of our shopping. (We kept a car in the plane's hangar in Hilo.) Driving, it took 45 minutes. When Sandy and David returned from school, we'd play baseball or cards in the evening after they completed their school work. The children found a cave near our home where they enjoyed playing.

To encourage the children not to smoke cigarettes, I offered each of them $1,000 if they wouldn't smoke a cigarette until they were 18. I was certain if they didn't smoke till then, they probably would never smoke that deadly addictive nicotine.

At night we frequently barbecued steaks and ate dinner around the circular fireplace, with candlelight or an old-fashioned gas lamp. The children would fill us in on what had happened at school that day. Then, chore time. This actually became a kind of game, because we didn't have electricity to the house yet. Our power came from a generator that with the push of a button in the kitchen would run for 45 minutes at a time. During that time we bustled through our assigned jobs. One youngster would vacuum the floors while the other ironed clothes, and we'd have the washing machine or the dishwasher running. The race would be to finish our tasks before the generator quit.

One of our greatest rewards living in the paradise of Kalapana was the welcome the local residents gave us. They frequently brought us fresh fish or opii (delicious little shellfish), and invited us to local luaus, featuring a pig steamed in a pit of hot rocks. Poi would be served with lau-lau and other Hawaiian delicacies. We'd drive in to colorful Pahoa village, 12 miles away. When we purchased ice cream they wrapped it in many pieces of newspaper so that it would stay frozen for the ride back to Royal Gardens.

Here, we were just residents. I was not recognized as a local celebrity. It was fun not to be stopped in the streets, as I was in Honolulu and on the other islands. Here it was fun to be – just Dave. I was having a wondrous time.

What I should have taken into consideration was that my little family wasn't taking a welcome extended break from decades spent in a very active business life. I was having the most relaxing time of my life – and they were getting bored. Even though we often went to Hilo to shop or enjoy a movie, Patty Sue and the children missed our Honolulu home with the swimming pool, and the "rich life." After three and a half years in Royal Gardens, Patty Sue decided to sell real estate from an office in Hilo. I was concerned about her driving home alone, sometimes rather late at night. I suggested we both go for our broker's licenses, and open our own real estate office there. I wasn't eager to go back to work, other than perhaps investing in land, but I was reluctant to spend so much time apart from Patty Sue every day.

Into real estate

Patty Sue and I studied together for our broker's licenses at magnificent Kaimu Black Sand Beach, and we continued our picnics there after we took the demanding test and awaited the results. About 30 days after taking the grueling license exam, Patty Sue left me at the beach to go grocery shopping in Pahoa, and to pick up our mail. I had just come in from bodysurfing when I saw her running toward me over the hot black sand. She was yelling, and holding something over her pretty head. I couldn't hear her over the roar of the surf, but finally she was close enough that I could read her pleasing lips. "We passed. We both passed!"

A couple of weeks later we located a perfect office on Banyan Drive, in Hilo's Hotel Row. The family worked together repainting and remodeling it. Wall-to-wall burnt-orange carpeting was installed. We put in new furnishings, including drapes, a sofa, and a coffee table in the reception area. Desks and phones and filing cabinets for 10 brokers and agents completed the job, and our company opened in mid-1975.

Our Royal Gardens home almost demolished by 7.4 earthquake

We purchased a small studio apartment in an oceanfront condominium for times we had an early-morning client, as was the case on November 29, 1975. The whole family stayed at the condo the night before, Sandy and David snuggled into sleeping bags on the floor. Before dawn a violent shaking all but threw us out of bed. The television set crashed to the floor and dishes smashed onto the stove. The building was swaying, and in our sixth floor apartment the movement was sickening. Holding on to the walls, I opened the front door and looked over the railing at the swimming pool. Water was sloshing out. Screams could be heard as residents stumbled down the long flights of stairs, not daring to chance the elevator.

Police loudspeakers were shrieking "Evacuate all buildings! This is a tsunami alert!" A tsunami is often called a tidal wave. It's caused by an undersea earthquake or volcanic eruption. We dressed rapidly and drove to high ground, listening intently to Civil Defense on the radio. "Keep away from the ocean! Go to high ground!"

Just 15 years before, 61 people had been killed by a 100-foot-high wall of water that raced to the shore at 500 miles an hour. A curious feature of tidal waves is that coastal water levels drop sharply before that first big wave hits. Many of the deaths in 1960 resulted from people going down to the ocean to see what the ocean floor had to offer when the water receded. Fish and other sea life were left floundering and helpless – as helpless as the humans who unknowingly gambled with death, and moments later lost. When the tsunami struck, it piled devastation onto the damage done by the underwater earthquake that triggered it. 537 buildings were destroyed. Cost: Over $23 million in damage.

This time Hilo was spared the destruction of a tidal wave, but some of the earthquake damage was striking. When we returned to our apartment we learned that in the middle of the earthquake one of the tenants in our building had rushed down the stairs, staggered to his car as the concrete floor swayed with the quake's gyrations – and didn't realize until he had driven into Hilo town that he was naked. I soon learned how fortunate we were that we had not been in the Royal Gardens home.

Civil Defense spoke again over the radios: "It has been reported that the magnitude of the earthquake was 7.4 on the Richter scale. The epicenter was located in the Kalapana area."

Kalapana! I prayed that our home had been spared. The next day I returned to Royal Gardens. The wild ocean had surged across the highway, tossing boulders over it like pebbles and opening large cracks in the highway. The bases of coconut trees along the beaches were now several feet under water. Boulders the size of washing machines blocked the driveway of our house. Had we been home it would have been impossible to get away – if we could have gotten out of the house at all! The entire house had slipped toward the ocean, and was now within a perilous four feet of a vertical 40-foot embankment. The home's foundation had collapsed.

The doors of the home were jammed closed, so I climbed in a window. The floors were buckled. Fine china was smashed on the kitchen floor. Vases, plants, and bowls were shattered. Broken glass was everywhere. Paintings were scattered on the floor. Dressers and kitchen drawers were open, their contents spilled onto the tilted floors. The gas line was broken. Had we been home, and lit a match, we could have been blown through the roof in an exploding ball of fire.

The next challenge was to find a home big enough for the kids in Hilo, and to begin repairing this cherished home – which lacked earthquake insurance.

We located a comfortably furnished home in Hilo, and found a contractor to jack up the Royal Gardens home and construct a new foundation. I took the destruction of our idyllic retreat as an omen: It was time for Patty Sue and the children to be exposed to more city life... but I still looked forward to returning to my paradise one day.

A River takes our company by storm

In the next year our staff grew to 17 salespeople and a secretary. One morning during a sales meeting, I glanced out the front window and saw a young man with his nose pressed to the glass, studying the photos of our listed properties. He was a rugged individual with a pigtail almost to his waist, a large mustache, a week's beard, and smiling red eyes. I asked him if there was anything we could do for him.

"My mom was in real estate on the mainland. I just found your window fascinating. Thought I'd have a look to see what you have here. It's more than most offices."

"Had you thought of going into real estate yourself? We could use a bright guy like you," I said.

"If I got a license, would you hire me?"

"I would. What's your name?"

"River."

"That's a cool name, River. What do you do for a living?"

"I'm a carpenter and a grower." In the Hawaii of the '70's, it was a sign of honesty to admit to being a "grower" – a term that always referred to pot rather than pineapples! Most people today are afraid to admit that they even smoke grass, let alone grow it. The government has taught us that lying is the safest policy. River would be an asset to our company. After only a few minutes he displayed further trust by adding, "Would you care to see where I live?"

"I would," and waved to knowledgeable Patty Sue to continue with the sales meeting.

What River had constructed was actually a tree house, with windows of stained glass in various colors, crystals and glass chimes hanging by strings, and a wonderful winding staircase. River had displayed imagination, creativity, and ingenuity in building this place. I glanced around his property for some grass, but didn't see any. River smiled.

1976 Sandy and David, happy teenagers and good buddies.

My dear dad was still a good driver at 96.

With 14-year-old beauty Sandy, ready to play in the snow on a sunny May day in Hawaii! At the 13,300-foot summit of Mauna Kea we sledded down the snow on metal sheeting.

Beautiful Sandy at 17, showing off her new hat for Dad.

"Try looking in the trees."

Up in the branches all around were five-gallon plastic bags, containing healthy plants with some beautiful buds. He smiled again. "Tough to see them from helicopters." He rolled up a joint, lit it, and handed it to me. I took a toke. "Nice," I said. He rolled a couple more joints and stuck them into my shirt pocket.

Now that an earthquake had evicted me from Eden, and my little family was happily back in civilization, I took a long look at the "real world." I realized I wasn't enjoying running a real estate office, even sharing that job with Patty Sue, and that I missed working in television.

Back on television

On April 25, 1976, the Big Island newspaper, the *Hawaii Tribune-Herald*, ran a story that read:

> LIVE TV SERIES FROM HILO TO DEBUT
> The first TV series from a network affiliate, CBS, will be broadcast live from Hilo, on Sunday, May 2, 3:30 to 4 p.m. on Channel 9.
> The show, *The Voice of Hawaii*, is scheduled to air every Sunday as a public service, without commercials. Big Island resident Dave Ford has been named producer and host of the 30-minute show, by Cec Heftel, president of Heftel Broadcasting, who is making the show possible.
> As Ford explained, *The Voice of Hawaii* will feature experts in their fields presenting their views on current Big Island issues. In coming weeks, we'll meet and hear the views of those people who are making the news on the Big Island, in Honolulu, and nationally.

The story continued with a complimentary description of my past TV work. We telecast *The Voice of Hawaii* live from the Hilo Lagoon Hotel.

David became a professional TV cameraman and did a superb job. I felt that it aided *The Voice of Hawaii* to have its own cameraperson, someone who understood the types of camera angles I wanted, close-ups of those being interviewed, etc. It gave the show a consistent feel it would have lacked with possibly someone different behind the camera for each show. I wanted the best. And I felt no one could do a better job than David. He excelled in almost everything he did. He has the ability to size up a new challenge quietly and then do a professional job.

Smoking pot on live television

One of the many intriguing people I had the pleasure of interviewing was the fine actor James McArthur, co-star of *Hawaii Five-O*. Another was the distinguished Honolulu attorney, Hyman Greenstein, who headed NORML in Hawaii. I had interviewed him years before, when he ran for Governor of Hawaii in 1962.

Before this second interview, Greenstein asked that I bring along some good pot, and said that we were going to smoke it on live television. I told him I'd be delighted to do that, so long as he would represent me at no cost if we got busted. "Guaranteed, Dave."

After presenting Greenstein's background, I said something to the effect of "Just to poke a little hole in the huge balloon of lies about marijuana – that it has no medical value, that it causes violence, and that people who smoke it act weird or out of control – Mr. Greenstein and I are going to smoke some fine Hawaiian grass right now, out of his pipe. If you would care to come on down to the Hilo Lagoon and follow the scent, you'll be convinced we're smoking the real thing." With that, we lit up.

We discussed how the government, despite the many positive findings that have shown that cannabis is medicine, has said since 1937 that there hasn't been enough *time* to study the long-term effects of marijuana. We made it clear to our audience that for more than 100 years, no drug in or out of the United States has been more thoroughly researched and investigated than cannabis That every non-partisan scientific study has established the opposite of what government propaganda claims. That marijuana prohibition has seduced millions of well-intentioned Americans into supporting actions that undermine all of their basic values: truth, individual freedom, and limited government.

We discussed how wrong it was for convicted pot growers to receive prison sentences longer than those given to many murderers. 15 or 20 people came in to the studio while we were on the air, and they did more smiling than we did. Not one police officer appeared, then or at our doorsteps later. I would be very wary about smoking pot on live TV today, given the risks – although I probably would do it.

I received at least a dozen letters from viewers. All were positive, and included such messages as: "I was shocked to see marijuana smoked on television. However, I thank you. It definitely got our attention!" "It opened my family's eyes, for the first time realizing that marijuana is indeed medicine, and that one could talk intelligently while high on pot." "I had heard from government reports it was only used by 'potheads' to get high, act weird, or become violent! You caused my family to question our government, who apparently has been giving us false propaganda about a plant that we now understand also offers true medical value."

The year 1976 passed quickly. The Royal Gardens home was rebuilt, stronger than ever. I rented it to a carpenter, who assured me he would keep it in top shape. He was scheduled to move in within the month.

At Dave Ford Real Estate (we used my name for the business only because the name was recognized throughout the islands) Patty Sue worked just as hard as I did. We were a dedicated team.

Once we offered a $5,000 cash bonus to the salesperson making the most sales in three months. One Monday morning, shortly after the offer, we were in the midst of our usual sales meeting when a young man in a sharp sports coat and tie walked in. A nice-looking chap with semi-short hair, a groomed mustache, and a broad smile. He stood and watched as I conducted the meeting. I paused and asked if we could help him. "Is that sales job still available? I got my license."

"Actually," I said, "we're not hiring at this time. But Mahalo for asking."

"Hold on," he said. "You offered me a job!"

"When did I offer you a job?"

"About a year ago. I was looking in your window at pictures. You came out and talked to me, and I took you up to see my shack, and you complimented me on my grass!" That got howls of laughter from the staff. I believe all of them were quality pot users, as most of Hawaii was.

I looked at him more closely, and started revising my mental picture. "River?" I asked.

"Yes, it's me, River."

I burst out laughing. "Ladies and gentlemen, I want you to meet our newest staff member, River. Welcome, River!" I hung his neatly framed license on the wall, brought him up to date on the $5,000 bonus offer, complimented him on his haircut and new clothes – and then suggested he dress and wear his hair as he used to. Who would interact with the many growers in the area better than our own River?

"Right on, Dave. Praise the Lord. You won't be sorry!"

River won the $5,000 prize.

Bing Crosby asked his daughter, "Would you like Dave to go back to Hollywood with us?" She said "Yes!" ...but I got no further than the plane — where I almost got Bing to admit his use of cannabis.

Me, smoking pot live on CBS TV? Attorney Hyman Greenstein, pipe in hand, invited me to show the audience that people act normally while high on grass. We talked about medical cannabis. This show got lots of attention and positive letters — and no harassment from the police.

Local businesses look forward to each marijuana harvest

Hilo businesses thrived when the marijuana harvest came in. New cars and pickup trucks were bought. Beauty parlors had waiting lists. Clothing store owners were jubilant. Real estate companies were also jumping. And all of us were laughing. (With the availability of good grass we laughed a lot.)

Just after the harvest, a couple who had seen a piece of property with our sign on it came into our office wanting to buy it. He wasn't remarkable, but she had a chest that was... startling. When it was clear that our discussion was leading to a deal, I asked if they wanted to pay cash or finance the land. The little lady with the big chest asked to use the restroom. When she reappeared, she was almost flat-chested, and she held $20,000 cash in her hands.

Growers were liking us and trusting our company. Many of them weren't treated with respect by some of the older realty companies – although I didn't know of any company that didn't accept their money when it was offered.

We found growers to be among the nicest, most mellow people we had ever met. Most were Christians and treated their children like objects of gold. They rarely swore, they rarely drank liquor, and most were into eating health foods. Many were vegetarians. There was seldom conflict with the growers. They had respect for their land, their God, and their neighbors. Few, if any, became rich; but they were happy doing the hard work that is required to produce a good harvest. They lived simply, took pride in the quality of their product, much of which was sent to mainland cancer patients. Typically, their biggest splurge was to purchase a four-wheel pickup truck with a stereo. I've noticed something else: Some of the finest growers and medical-marijuana activists are women. Without women actively involved in the reform of marijuana laws, we wouldn't be as far as we are today. As my friend River would say, "Praise the Lord for the ladies!"

16

It was "Cheech and Chong medicine"!

One evening our family went to the Mountain View theater, which is on the way to the Volcano House, about five miles south of Hilo. The movie was *Up in Smoke* with Cheech and Chong. Former drug czar Barry McCaffrey once called marijuana "Cheech and Chong medicine." His reference was sarcastic, but there was truth in it. Grass is the best medicine there is for relaxing, forgetting the cares of the world, eliminating stress, and enjoying easy laughter, which is itself, proverbially, the best medicine. In the theater, joints were being passed around with the same thoughtfulness as were the bags of popcorn. One could have gotten high just from the second-hand smoke. The audience was happy, and laughing so loudly it was at times difficult to hear the movie. It was one big happy gathering.

Invited to a party thrown by marijuana growers

Patty Sue was missing her family and friends in New Hampshire, and decided to go visit them. During her absence, some of the largest marijuana growers on the Island invited me to a special harvest party at the Pahoa Inn, in quaint Pahoa Village. The "Thanksgiving" was a gathering of the best-known growers in Hawaii. To my knowledge I was the only non-grower invited, but we had helped many growers to purchase land, and they wanted to show their appreciation.

The night of the party, I drove past the Pahoa Inn twice because a uniformed police officer was out front. The third time, as I drove past slowly, he waved me over. "Dave, you're invited. It's cool. I'm here only because I've been hired on my own time to keep people out who weren't invited. Have fun!" I did. Each grower had several ounces of the finest grass buds on the tables for any of the guests to touch, smell, and smoke. It was a delightful evening.

Growers trusted me to fly them over areas where they lived. They wanted to see if their "gardens" were visible from the air. There was always an ounce of the finest buds under the passenger seat of the plane after they left. It's a privilege to be trusted. To me, love, loyalty, and trust are the most meaningful qualities in life.

When we went on picnics in Hawaii's marvelous beach parks, it was rare not to see people openly light up and pass joints around. In the years I lived in Hawaii, I saw hundreds of couples smoking on the beach, holding hands and running into the shallow water to play like kids. Grass lets out the child in each of us. One twilight evening at a nude beach I saw a young lady smoking a joint and listening to music coming from a portable stereo. After a few minutes, she picked up a bundle from the sand next to her and shook it out. She was holding several yards of blue silk in her hands. She danced, waving and twirling the silk through the air around her as the sinking sun silhouetted her lovely young body.

In over 50 years of smoking grass, and being around others who use it, I have yet to see a single person become mean or hostile from using cannabis *only*. I've seen too much family violence after alcohol use, but I've never observed it when parents only smoked marijuana. Cannabis should not be mixed with alcohol, because the alcohol will take over. Pot-smoking motorists are sometimes charged with Driving Under the Influence (DUI) – but in almost every case other drugs such as alcohol are present. I know of only one sensible use of pot in connection with other drugs. Some people use grass to mellow out and be able to go to sleep after using cocaine or other "upper" type drugs – but I see it as sensible only because these people are using cannabis as a medicine.

Our salesman advertises good pot-growing land in High Times

It was no big thing when one of our fine salesmen, Terry Shoneberg, ran an ad in *High Times* magazine for some good land our company had for sale. The ad was an indication of how open the attitudes toward grass were in Hawaii during the mid- to late 1970s. Terry was aware of the medical value of cannabis and of the large exports of Hawaiian pot to mainland patients. When users of cannabis call it "sacred herb," they're referring to its use as medicine.

THE GOLD RUSH IS ON!

Yes, Hawaii's gold rush is not only in its "smoke" but in its land on the Big Island, which has become internationally known for its sacred herb. Fantastic land values are still available, but for how long?

For as low as $750 down and $50 a month you can own two or three acres in beautiful Puna, Hawaii. This land has soil and trees and wonderful climate. No credit needed. Owner will finance with no questions asked. Excellent way to start your credit.

Hawaii is America's last paradise, and an investment here can't lose. Think what land prices can do if legalization occurs! My name is Terry Shoneberg. I am a licensed real estate salesman, and promise honest competent service, and total confidentiality on your purchase. So whether you have $1,000, or $100,000 to invest, I want to be your man in Hawaii."

[There was a perforated line to tear off the bottom and send it to Terry.]

"Yes, Terry, I am very interested in an investment in paradise. Please send me information about specific properties now on the market. I have $_____ to invest, and can handle $_____ a month."

Terry Shoneberg, salesman, *Dave Ford Real Estate*. Star Rt. Box 26-a. Keauu, Hawaii.

The ad response was good. (Today, Terry is a successful, conservative, middle-aged real estate broker in Hilo.)

For more creativity, how about Brother Roger Christie, who heads The Hawaii Cannabis Ministry? Their doctrine is "*We use cannabis religiously.*"

● ● ●

It was now 1977. David was 18, Sandy 16, and they were both doing well at Hilo High School. Sandy was on the swimming team, David on the track team, and both were avid members of teams racing outrigger canoes in Hilo Bay. You'll recall that several years before I had offered each of them $1,000 cash if they wouldn't smoke cigarettes until they were 18. David got paid off in full. Two years later, Sandy faced me with a small quandary: she'd smoked a joint with friends of hers; had she met the terms of my offer? I resolved my dilemma by paying her $500 – which made David unhappy. He felt she should have gotten nothing. I understood his thinking. My goal, however, had been to keep them from becoming addicted to death-causing nicotine. As she had not smoked a *nicotine* cigarette, I felt that to pay her $500 was fair.

To my knowledge, neither of them has ever smoked nicotine.

In that same year, I was looking forward to the results of the Australian Government's study on grass.

Commission of the Australian Government, 1977

"One of the most striking facts concerning cannabis is that its toxicity is low compared with that of *any* other drugs... No major health effects have manifested themselves in the community."[41]

And the U.S. Government's apparent response? "Those studies from other countries don't mean a thing. Don't confuse us with even more facts, our minds are made up. This is a dangerous drug like heroin. We know we can count on you to approve more billions of dollars to fight it and put more potheads in prison."

A morose divorce

Patty Sue was really into her business, much as I had been at her age. I was 44 when we moved to Royal Gardens, and ready and pleased to be semi-retired. I was thrilled just to wait around for the properties that we'd invested in to be developed as soon as the utilities reached them (and to sit out on the lanai overlooking the ocean, reading a book and sometimes taking a hit or two of grass.) Patty Sue, on the other hand, was not yet 30, and eager to try her wings in other areas. In addition to real estate, she wanted to buy and operate a restaurant and bar. That was one business I didn't want to be involved in; unless you're on the register in the bar, be prepared to take a loss.

I loved Patty Sue and I was confident she loved me; she'd frequently told me that if anything ever happened to me, or if we parted, she'd die. Then she began hanging out with a young lady who seemed to feel that I was holding Patty Sue back. Patty Sue lost interest in our real estate business, and for the first time she told me that it wasn't fair that the company carried my name. Had she objected when the company name first came up I would have been happy to call it Patty Sue Real Estate, Ford & Ford Real Estate, Pot Growers Real Estate, or anything she liked. I had only felt that my name being well known would aid the business.

I was confused and couldn't understand what she wanted. In retrospect I can see I should have given her the business and retired. It took me a while to realize that lack of communication between partners, not telling each other of their needs, is a sure way to rupture a relationship. I can understand now how she felt.

Shortly thereafter she wanted a divorce. I was stunned. So were the children who loved her (and still do). She moved out, and I was too crazed to go after her and try to find out the real reason she wanted out. She was represented by a little turd who decided to give *me* the business. There were rumors that he screwed many of his clients. I'm just guessing they were all women. He screwed the husbands in a different way. He tied up all of my bank accounts and properties, including the home in Honolulu, which was constructed when Patty Sue was 16 and lived in New Hampshire.

Not only was I morose, it was exceedingly difficult to do business, and I no longer had any interest in it. Sadly, Patty Sue and I parted in divorce in 1978. I felt that she was a little girl who decided to "run away from home to be on her own." She was reaching for that elusive rainbow of hitting it big financially on her own.

I will always have a very special love for Patty Sue. Today we are good friends, and she has been a true comrade to the children. A few years ago, she and a partner created a picturesque restaurant and bar in Hilo. Patty Sue invited me to dine there, and I had a very pleasant evening. Apparently, though, she decided the restaurant business was not for her after all. Since 2002, she's been back in real estate, and doing very well. I am truly happy for her.

In the midst of the divorce I ran into an opportunity to purchase a magnificent piece of property consisting of over an acre of land, with an ocean view. On the property was a home that had been framed but not finished. It was in Alokea Plantation, a new residential area 400 feet above Hilo. I went to the manager of Central Pacific Bank, a Mr. Taketa, and told him of my divorce plight, with all of my assets tied up. I told him that I needed $70,000 immediately and had no collateral to offer. He called over his chief bank teller. "Ella, prepare a signature note and a check in the amount of $70,000 for Mr. Ford. He is an honest man. He will repay us when he can." It was refreshing to meet a true old-time banker who would lend on a person's integrity, rather than his collateral.

Feds okay marijuana for patients with medical necessity, 1978

In 1978, a "medical necessity" defense was recognized, and the federal government was compelled to allow some patients access to medical marijuana. It created the Investigation New Drug (IND) compassionate access program. IND allowed some qualified patients to receive medical marijuana from the government. (In 1992 the Bush administration closed it to new participants after it received numerous applications from dying AIDS patients.) *Today, surviving patients still receive medical marijuana in the form of 300 rolled king-sized cigarettes per month from the federal government.* That amounts to seven pounds or more per year per patient. If it were true that pot is so dangerous a drug that it should not even be prescribed by a medical doctor, would the government be supplying it to sick and dying patients? I've smoked one of those government-supplied "medical-quality" joints. Seeds were included along with leaf. The quality was so poor that I coughed uncontrollably – and still the herb has demonstrable medical value! I have to wonder: who's smoking the buds? Shame on the government.

When glaucoma patient Robert Randall died on June 7, 2001, the medical-marijuana movement lost one of its heroes. He made medical history when he persuaded a federal court that his use of marijuana to treat his glaucoma was a medical necessity. No other medications worked for him. Doctors had predicted that he would be blind in five years. Smoking medical marijuana kept Robert's glaucoma at bay until his death, with no negative side-effects. Glaucoma medications such as pilocarpine manufactured by pharmaceutical companies, have side effects that include skin rashes, kidney stones, gastric ulcers, drug fevers, abrupt mood swings, hypertension, respiratory or cardiac failure, and even death.[42] If you or a member of your family suffered from glaucoma, which medication would you prefer?

Flying the "magic carpet"

One day I had just returned from flying a couple around over their property when a fellow approached with a rug rolled up over his shoulder. "I wonder if you might help me," he said. "My grandmother left me this beautiful Persian rug. I'm moving to Honolulu, but I don't want to ship this rug as freight on the airlines. Would you consider flying me and this rug to Honolulu, for say $300, and a fine ounce of the kind?" ("The kind" is yet another name for happy grass.) With so much of my money tied up in the divorce, any cash would be welcome. It was a beautiful day, and I could be back in a few hours, so I agreed. After landing at Honolulu International Airport, I was taxiing to the fuel pumps when a police officer signaled to me to park where he pointed. I complied. The passenger rapidly departed with the Persian rug, after handing me a large envelope.

I asked the officer what was happening. "They're shooting a television sequence. I'm off duty, just hired to keep traffic away from the hangar."

"OK, thanks," I said. I fueled the aircraft and went into the office to pay. There, lying down on the office sofa, where I usually stretched out while my plane was being serviced, was actor Tom Selleck reading a script. He saw me with my flight jacket on, gave me a salute, and said, "How's it, Captain!"

I waved, said, "Great." We small-talked for a few minutes while I paid my bill and filed a flight plan. After getting a weather report from the FAA, I took off. In the air I checked the envelope. There was an ounce of grass, and *five* hundred-dollar bills. Two hundred bucks extra? Nice tip! What a nice guy.

When I was back in Hilo, closing the hangar door, a friend strolled over and asked, "Did you give George and his carpet a ride to Honolulu?"

"You bet," I said.

He laughed and said, "I guess he didn't mention that he'd rolled up 10 pounds of marijuana in the carpet."

Damn, I thought, that was naughty. No wonder he disappeared so quickly when he saw the cop – probably wetting his pants as he ran! If he'd been busted, I'd have lost my plane, for openers. That $500 no longer seemed so generous.

I had the pleasure of becoming friends with one of Hawaii's most respected psychologists, Dr. Jacqueline Brittain. Jacqueline was a gourmet cook and enjoyed preparing meals over a campfire. Sometimes we'd fly to Hana, Maui, and camp there. Hana is that piece of paradise where Charles Lindbergh chose to die and be buried. He oversaw the making of his own pine coffin, and was buried 30 feet deep under rocks, so that no one would disturb his burial site. His widow Anne Morrow Lindbergh, author of *Gift from the Sea,* resided in Hana until her death.

Dad with cancer, afraid of marijuana

When Dad was 82 he had to have surgery for colon cancer. I flew over from Hawaii to be with him. His appetite waned. He was nauseous. He was in pain. I recommended grass. Alas, 60 years of propaganda putting marijuana in the same category as heroin, with no medical value, was too much for him to overcome. He turned it down.

A new love and a nightmare re-run

I had been dating a cherished friend, Lynn, for some time – over a year. It's not easy to trust enough to love again after a divorce; but the companionship was a kind of balm for my heart.

It was January, 1979, and I had just turned 51. Frequently I found myself working late at the office; going over the day's business, and writing newspaper and radio commercials. When one is lonely, or feeling sorry for himself, he frequently works late. It was around eight one evening when one of the salesladies walked in. "Can I speak with you, Dave?"

It was Jana, a bright, beautiful, 25-year-old lady who had worked for our company for eight months. In the evenings she worked as hostess at the restaurant across the street. "Certainly, Jana. Please sit down."

Jana looked straight at me with marvelous, sparkling sapphire eyes. Her golden wavy chestnut hair fell just below her shoulders. "Would you date me?" she asked. I was blown away. I made it a point of policy not to date the ladies who worked for the company; and besides, Jana was half my age. "No, Jana, I wouldn't date you."

"Why not?"

"Because you're living with Peter. I don't date ladies who are with other men. And why would you be interested in robbing the grave?"

She replied: "Come on, you're not *that* old! And anyway, Peter and I have developed into platonic friends. We share a house. It doesn't even have hot water. We're good friends, but that's it. Please date me!"

"Why would you want to date me, Jana?"

"You put your arm around your sales staff, and sometimes ruffle their hair, like you really care for them. I like the way it feels when you put your arm around me and ruffle my hair."

I'd never dreamed of dating Jana, but I heard myself saying, "Jana, if you tell Peter that I might take you out, and he doesn't have objections, I'll consider dating you."

The next day she told me Peter had said it was OK with him. I began going to the office earlier than usual in order to have a cup of coffee with Jana. "I'm not into a permanent relationship just now," I said.

"That's OK," Jana replied, smiling.

We chatted about real estate, and I gave her a few tips on closing sales. We talked about her father's oil business, and about her singing, poetry writing, and painting. We went out to dinner a few times. After a couple of weeks I found myself drawn to this lady. She reminded me of a young deer that was playful, reserved, sensitive, and vulnerable.

One evening I invited her to my home for dinner. She arrived a bit tipsy. We had a fun meal with David. (Sandy was now living with her boyfriend.) We watched television for a while, and she finally asked if I was going to invite her to stay for the night. I did. She was darling, and I must say I was concerned that she meant more to me than I was ready for. If she was late for our morning coffee at the office, my legs felt weak. That hadn't happened since Hazel. I told her about my love for Hazel, and her tragic end. I said that had caused me the most pain I had ever endured, and after all these years I still hadn't gotten over it.

Jana was hungry to be held. She enjoyed wine, liquor, and smoking grass. With alcohol she was frequently depressed; with grass *only* she was upbeat and happy. I told her several times that booze and pot shouldn't be mixed, that alcohol overshadows grass. "You don't have that feeling that orgasms stretch out forever when you mix alcohol and grass. The tendency is to have a heavy foot on the gas pedal and to be reckless, the same as if you were on alcohol only."

Jana wrote funny, sexy, romantic little notes, painted pictures, and wrote poetry. She nicknamed me Yum, and called herself Jana Banana. We were physically attracted, and that attraction continued to grow, yet I was still concerned about her drinking. She said, "Don't worry about it. I like wine, but I can quit any time that I wish. Foolish Yum! Don't worry about my drinking. Just worry about my loving!"

One note that Jana wrote to me read:

> Yum (My name for you....ah you!)
> God, I hope it's been so nicely crazy, relaxing lazy... hugs and dazy! Feeling intense... and completely content! Immensely scared, calmed with eyes shared, small gestures of stroking hair... Makes me want to guard my heart. You frighten me with your love, or is it mine to Yum? Ah yes, dream Yum, the flight of a beautiful bird too swiftly passes. Awesome and so quickly a memory. I love your memory... and yet may the wings of the Yum fly continually in my path.
> Love, *Jana.*

Jana wanted us to see a rock group on Maui, and I invited Sandy and her boyfriend to join us. Jana and I had dated for only a couple of months, but she wanted to move into my house – if all worked out, to be married. I was falling hard for her, and I was afraid to tell her that I was in love with her. It was moving too fast. I couldn't believe that she could actually love a person so much older. I decided that I would tell her that night in the Maui Sheraton hotel that I was in love with her – something I hadn't said in a long time.

We went to the rock concert. It was a rush to share something unique

Patty Sue and I with R. J. Kinny, Captain of the President Cleveland on its last voyage. This was the ship that, as a teen, I had dreamed of one day buying. I made an offer during this trip.

Dearest Jana, just 25 years old.

that is so special in another person's life. My heart was dancing as we held hands. I felt like a teenager, moving with the music, and watching Jana's magnificent blue eyes sparkling as her pretty head and feet moved in time with the beat.

Back at the Sheraton after the concert, we strolled out by the pool. We agreed it was right to give Sandy and her boyfriend some privacy before we retired.

We were stretched out in lounge chairs. The moon was full, the stars were glistening, and the gentle trade winds caressed us. My head was spinning. I felt much like the time that I asked Hazel to marry me. Should I or should I not ask her? There was something fragile about Jana that reminded me of Hazel. Perhaps that's what attracted me to her.

Sandy and her boyfriend came by and asked if they could spend the night sleeping on our lanai, as he didn't have any money. I said, "Sure!" and invited them to join us for dinner. I'd have bought them a room for the night, but I feared that if I were alone with Jana, I might rush to tell her that I was in love with her. Having Sandy and her boyfriend join us for the night gave me an excuse to wait just a little longer. Jana was intelligent, talented, and yet very much a child. Perhaps that's what pulled me to her – the opportunity to be a child again, with a woman-child. That part of her reminded me of dear Hazel....

A couple of nights later, in my desk I found a poem written on a paper napkin.

> *Legs crisscrossed.*
> *Linen fresh.*
> > *Sheets fair, sweat and hair entwined.*
> > *Lips, tongues, imploring, exploring.*
> *Pulsating... grasping, gasping,*
> > *Dancing skin*
> > *In time with rhythms within... without,*
> *Kissing, wishing,*
> *Ever closer.*
> > *Absorbing all of you, David!*
> *PS. I love it!"*

A few days later she casually handed me a poem with a beautifully painted red and yellow hibiscus on the side. I had it framed.

Hello friend, holding you close.
A fantasy come true.
   Talk on pillows,
   Kisses soft.
Questions unspoken in our eyes... and
Sometimes embracing loves gone by...
   Overcoming.
   Tender moments,
   Wings on flight.
Freedom in you, such loving care.
Thank you for any moments we share.
Love, Jana"

I felt that Jana had to know that she was someone very special in my life. I was so happy being with her and she with me. She was fiercely independent, but I managed to present her with a new briefcase, as hers was badly worn. She also needed new shoes, and I was looking for an occasion to buy her a pair.

It was May 9, 1979, the day before Sandy's 18th birthday. She wanted a little party at home, and she wanted me to invite Lynn. Dear Lynn had been with me during the painful divorce, and Sandy felt very close to her. At the office that day, I found a moment to draw Jana aside, and told her about Sandy's request.

"That's OK. I understand – and I'd just as soon not be there with Lynn." Lynn worked at our office too, although I'd known her before she came to work for us. Jana knew that Lynn and I had been lovers. "Anyway, I have Peter's gun, so don't worry about me. And the dog is there – he'll protect me!" Peter was in the hospital with an ear infection, and I didn't really want her to be alone at their little cottage, 12 miles away, without a phone, but she was unconcerned. "Know that I'm just fine. I'll see you at the office for coffee in the morning, Yum!"

I slipped out of the office for a little while, and bought Jana a new pair of shoes. I would give them to her when we met at the office the next morning, before the rest of the sales crew arrived.

Our little gathering for Sandy ended around 9 p.m. Lynn departed, and I retired. I found a note under my pillow. There was a clever pencil drawing of seven boxes that actually appeared to be in three dimensions. At the top it read: "Pick a box..." In one of the boxes it said, "I love you!" Under the drawing it read: "Does it scare you? Have a good night. PS. I'm working on my sweetness, forgive my weirdness." For Sandy, she'd left a birthday card she'd created, showing a moon bright over the ocean. The inside read, "Happy Birthday – Shine on forever, Sandy. Aloha, you sweetie. *Jana.*"

The next morning I left home early, eagerly looking forward to that special quiet time with Jana, and an opportunity to give her the new shoes. She wasn't at the office. I dashed across the street to the restaurant. She was probably there rapping with friends. When I couldn't locate Jana I asked for the manager. "We fired her last night for being intoxicated again. When she left the building she sideswiped a car. I have no idea where she is. Sorry."

I ran to my car and sped out to her house. She must feel terrible, I thought. Her dog was in the yard. I went to the front door with the new pair of shoes in my hand. It was open. Thank goodness. There she was, sitting in a rocking chair. "Jana, you frightened me! Why weren't you at the office, like always?"

No answer. On the floor next to her chair were several empty bottles of wine. "Jana, baby, you've been drinking. Don't worry about losing that job at the restaurant. If you feel you need a part-time job, we'll find one for you. But you're due for a sale on a house any day now. It's time to wake up and come to the office, Jana Banana!"

I shook her shoulder. Then I saw the gun in her lap. I placed my hand on her exquisite face. She was cold. She was dead.

The blood had drained from my head, and I felt as though I was going to pass out. "Jana... what have you done to yourself?" I jumped into my car and headed for a phone. Then I turned around and went back to her house. She's not dead, I told myself. This nightmare can't be. I dreamed it. I ran inside the house again, but there was no mistake.

I began crying uncontrollably, and babbling to her. This time there was no question in my mind. Jana had killed herself. I drove to the closest telephone and dialed 911. Then I phoned Sandy at home. I hysterically told her what happened. "Daddy, I love you. Don't cry. I love you, daddy. Come home!" Lynn lived only a few miles from Jana. I was too emotionally devastated to see her. And I felt guilty. Could Jana have killed herself because I had invited Lynn to Sandy's birthday gathering? I didn't know. All I knew was that my body felt dead. It was like Hazel all over again.

There was a steady Hilo rain as my car moved toward home. I recall not turning on the windshield wipers; it seemed as though the raindrops were my tears on the windshield. Sandy gave me a hug when I emerged from the car like a sleepwalker. Sandy has empathy, and I never loved her more than at that moment. She said the things I desperately needed to hear. I was so upset I don't know what I would have done without Sandy's caring voice. I was numb.

Patty Sue heard the news and came to the house to comfort me. She said, "Dave, I spoke to Peter, Jana's former boyfriend. He told me that Jana had an inoperable brain tumor and that she didn't have long to live." I thanked Patty Sue – and I never asked Peter to confirm that conversation, in case she'd made up the story to help me feel better. What I do know is that Jana was frequently depressed when she drank alcohol. Had she only smoked some grass, with no alcohol, I feel that she would be alive today.

The office staff and some of Jana's friends held a memorial service for her in tranquil Liliokalani Gardens, a lovely park on Hilo Bay. We threw leis to the outgoing tide. The sky was blue and the trade winds gentle: it was visual poetry. Jana would have approved.

There is nothing more painful than finding, dead, someone you love, or seeing her die. It's then more than ever that you need to feel the love of friends or family, because a part of *you* has also died. Handguns must be kept out of the hands of children, and those who are unstable, or there should be locks on all guns. Two of the dearest people in my life have died from handguns.

For months after the death of Jana I was useless at the office. I didn't trust myself to fly the plane. I quit smoking grass, even though muscle spasms in my back were waking me up during the night. I wasn't eating and I lost 15 pounds. The memories of Hazel's suicide returned to haunt me. When someone you love kills herself, guilt consumes you. If only I had said this, or done that....

Eventually, I began smoking grass again, so I regained my appetite and the lost weight. Grass also helped reduce the numbness and heartsickness. I still couldn't concentrate on business, but I realized that I never had wanted to return to a full-time career. David was just 20, and had already gotten his broker's license. He was one of the youngest (and brightest) men in Hawaii to have passed the state examination. I turned the business over to him. He ran it for about six months, then decided that real estate was not satisfying for him either. We closed the office. He enjoys physical work, so he opened a gardening service and has done well.

The Voice of Hawaii *goes silent*

August 26, 1979 *The Hawaii Tribune-Herald* carried a large photo, captioned "Last local show, *Voice of Hawaii*, moderated by Hilo's Dave Ford, will be televised for the final time today." The story began:

> ### *VOICE* STILLED TODAY
> *Voice of Hawaii*, the Big Island's only locally produced, network-affiliated television show, will be aired for the last time today, according to Dave Ford, producer and host of the Sunday afternoon interview show."

The story then went into details of the show.

My friends, especially Jacqueline Brittain, and another irresistible friend, Elisabeth Drews, helped me out of the doldrums. I began flying again. I had forgotten how flying gave me a feeling of well-being.

National Academy of Sciences Report, 1982

It was my hope that the study by the National Academy of Sciences that was about to be released would turn the government and its DEA around. Perhaps *this* time they would rethink their bloodthirsty and false campaign against cannabis and hemp.

According to the distinguished, non-political National Academy of Sciences: "Over the past 40 years, marijuana has been accused of causing an array of antisocial effects, including: in the 1930s, provoking crime and violence; in the early 1950s, leading to heroin addiction; and in the late 1950s, making people passive, lowering motivation and productivity, and destroying the American work ethic in young people. Although belief in these effects persists among many people, they have *not* been substantiated by scientific evidence."[43]

The government's probable conclusion, based on their reaction: "Don't confuse us with facts. Our minds are made up. (Darn. The public may start to believe authentic scientific studies rather than our brainwashing.)"

Planning a resort

By 1982, my divorce from Patty Sue was behind me, and my assets unfrozen. Even without the land development in the New Hebrides, I didn't have any financial worries at that time. I had acquired 34 magnificent oceanfront acres in Kapa'ahu, located just three miles from the world-famous Kalapana Black Sand Beach. I had also just paid off another 2.13 acres on the ocean, with its own black sand beach, lagoon, stream, coconut trees, and "queen's bath," a swimming-pool size tidepool. That property was already designated in the General Plan as the last resort region on the Big Island.

I enthusiastically looked forward to furthering my plans to develop the 34 acres into a garden of Eden. A hundred grass "shacks," a lagoon, a long-house for dances and parties, an amphitheater, and a recording studio were in the planning stage. My plan was that musicians from the world over would come to this unique retreat for rest and relaxation, and to record their music – and write off their travel expenses on their tax returns. Local residents would be invited to watch rehearsals free of charge in the amphitheater, which would also feature first-run movies under the stars. Several times a year we would feature outstanding talent from each of the Hawaiian Islands, for events like the Merry Monarch festival. I would interview celebrities on video that would be released to the television stations. This would offer free publicity for the personalities and for the resort.

In Hawaiian, Kalapana means "sunny place," and it is. A large portion of the 34 acres would be dedicated to an international healing center. Each cottage would have its own barbecue pit, with papaya, tangerine, and banana trees, and plumeria, red ginger, and orchids surrounding it. Landscaping would feature trees, flowers, and other plants indigenous to the area. A Hawaiian-designed restaurant would overlook the oceanfront, and at night floodlights would shine on the waves breaking against the glistening shore, where the rocks look like black diamonds. There would be a museum of Hawaiian artifacts, and gift shops featuring handicrafts of the Hawaiian people. Along Highway 130, where the property ended, we planned to build a tropically-designed gas station and grocery store. There would be a landscaped parking lot close to the highway, and quiet electric golf carts would deliver guests to their cottages. Estimated return: gross, $190,000 a month.

The next months were mellow, flying almost every day, and as much as possible over the beauty of Kalapana. Mist from clouds almost invariably caused the plane to be encircled on the ocean by a color-drenched rainbow. (Hawaii could well have been named the Rainbow Islands.)

In 1982, I purchased a home in Keakaha. This area is only a few miles out of Hilo, yet there is about a third less rain. The home was on the ocean, and the land there is extraordinary. There were many coconut trees and every tropical flower and plant imaginable, a blue lagoon, and the ocean. Next door was an eight-story condominium apartment building with a swimming pool. I leased out the house, planning to keep this property for five to 10 years and then build an apartment building on it, reserving the penthouse for my own use.

Marijuana propaganda causes death

For exercise, I began painting the house while I enjoyed that ocean panorama. I wanted a wider view of the ocean but the tropical jungle has a way of vigorously reclaiming its domain. One late morning in 1986 while taking a break from painting, I began hacking some of the vines with a machete. "How about some help there?" said a voice from behind me. It belonged to a young fellow with shaggy blond hair whom I guessed to be in his mid twenties. He wore a T-shirt, cut-off Levi's, and rubber sandals. "I'm a good worker. I enjoy hard work, I need a job, and I'll work cheap."

"What kind of wages are you looking for?" I asked. "Seven dollars an hour. I can do some carpentry work and painting. If you don't think I'm worth seven dollars an hour, give me a try and check me out. If you're not happy at the end of the day, you owe me nothing. Is that fair?"

"You bet it is. When would you like to begin?" He took the machete from my hand. "Right now. The name's Bobbie."

"I'm Dave Ford."

"I know," said Bobbie, grinning.

Bobbie started full-bore. I stood fascinated watching him slash his way toward the ocean. He moved at least three times as fast as I had been working, and I was put in mind of a marathon runner who starts out at the head of the pack but drops out of the race in about two miles. The temperature was in the mid-eighties. I envied Bobbie with his youthful enthusiasm and energy, but felt at that rapid pace he'd never make it through the day. I went back to painting the trim. Bobbie never did slack his pace. He stopped twice for water, and went right back to work.

I'd never seen anyone work more consistently hard. At 5 p.m. Bobbie returned to the house. He had a joint hanging from his lips. "Nice work, Bobbie. It that your reward for a good day's work?"

"Heck, no. I been smoking a few joints all day. That keeps me working. I can daydream, but the arms keep trucking."

I was amazed. I had read of Africans working in the diamond mines smoking grass to keep up a fast pace, but I had had my doubts. When I smoke, it's the end of the day. It totally relaxes me, and I have a great sleep. In Hawaii I did see many people laboring while they smoked, though. "I have to admit, Bobbie, after a few hours at that fast pace, I figured you might be on speed."

"Naw. This is the only drug I do. I'm planning on getting married, and I want a couple of kids. Most o' them other drugs aren't good for your body. I'll stick to grass. Can I start at seven in the morning, Dave?"

"You can start as early as you like," I said, "but I won't be here till around nine."

The next morning when I arrived Bobbie had already accomplished what appeared to be a half day's work. One could already see almost a third more ocean view. "Morning, Bobbie. Lookin' good!"

"I been chopping away, thinking one day I'm getting married, and we're gonna have a handsome son, and him and me are going fishing."

"Right on, Bobbie." I said.

A few days later when Bobbie arrived for work, for the first time he looked sad. "What's happening, Bobbie?" I asked. "Damn, I just read a book, I think it's called *Marijuana Alert*. It says grass kills your brain cells, and affects a guy's sex hormones, as much as if a guy was castrated! Ya might not be able to father a baby, no matter how much you want one. I'll never smoke grass again."

"Bobbie, you can't believe everything you read," I said.

"I do when Nancy Reagan endorses the book," he said. "She's gotta know!"

I didn't know the book at the time, so I didn't say anything more. I dearly wish I had. Bobbie did an average day's work, but it was as if the Duracell battery was finally running down. It was strange not to see a joint in his hand. At the end of the day he asked for his check. "I'm going to Kona. My girl moved there, and I'll get some work nearer to her. It's been nice working for ya." We had a beer, chatted for a time, and then Bobbie said, "Aloha. I'll come back and check out the job and see how you did without me!"

I missed Bobbie. About a week later a friend told me Bobbie was dead. Not wanting to smoke pot anymore, he tried heroin. Of course that was not a bright thing to do, but tragically there are a lot of Bobbies out there. Some young people will try a hard drug after reading government propaganda that marijuana is more dangerous than cocaine or heroin. Those who trust the government feel that heroin can't be worse than marijuana. The friend said, "I heard that the guy with Bobbie showed him how to inject himself. Bobbie apparently did it, and was dead minutes later." Tears came to my eyes. How could the federal government be so cruel when they know that, compared to alcohol and cigarettes, pot is all but harmless? Bobbie was just 28 when he died in 1986 – a year older than our David.

The Reagan/Bush administration was exerting heavy pressure to eradicate marijuana throughout the 50 states. Hawaii's "Green Harvest" began in earnest. Helicopters flying 50 feet over Big Island homes landed in yards to pull up plants. The fear they caused children, parents, and animals didn't deter the DEA from the carnage of those innocent herbs. What the campaign did accomplish was to cause the price of marijuana to skyrocket. The saddest form of police power became visible. Growers and the smoking public became frightened. The majority, who had been carefree and open about smoking cannabis, retreated into the closet. Many began drinking alcohol and using other dangerous drugs. One can only speculate how many pot-only users switched to dangerous drugs due to propaganda or a fear of urine testing, as Bobbie did, and, as Bobbie did, died as a result. I felt it was time to read *Marijuana Alert*.

Marijuana Alert *scares many away from pot; was it worth it?*

With the new millennium, one would think that the Federal Government and its prohibitionist followers would stop the never-ending false propaganda against grass. But that seems to be an addiction it can't let go of. There's little doubt that the book *Marijuana Alert* is still the bible of the California Narcotics Officers' Association, County Sheriffs of Colorado, Inc., the DEA, PRIDE (Parents' Resource Institute for Drug Education), and the Partnership for a Drug Free America (PDFA).

Dozens of anti-marijuana books are available. For over 60 years, the federal government has created a ready market for negative writing on the subject – and sadly, too many adults still buy into the misinformation. Yet, few kids do! Propaganda campaigns against drugs manage only to popularize the drugs they attack. I cannot emphasize enough that prohibition serves as a lure to young people who are ready and willing to take almost any challenge. If they're frightened away from marijuana, some of them are certain to try other drugs, like heroin, speed, and Ecstasy.

Recycling 65-year-old propaganda

After reading *Marijuana Alert*[44], I was frustrated and incensed. Here was a writer who had every opportunity to provide both sides of the marijuana debate, yet chose only to recycle all the long-debunked falsehoods about cannabis. I vowed to expose the many unproved marijuana accusations in this book.

Peggy Mann was no doubt a loving, sincere mother who simply unraveled when she found her daughter Jennifer smoking pot. Over the years, like the rest of us, she had been blitzed with frightening pseudo-facts about the disastrous effects of marijuana. I can't blame her for being frightened, but I do blame her for letting her fear rather than the facts shape her opinions once she did her research. And I blame her for setting off a public reaction just as regrettable and widespread as the response to the movie *Reefer Madness*.

Reefer Madness *reborn*

Mann had access to current scientific studies, including those that described the proven therapeutic uses of cannabis for patients suffering from the debilitating, nauseating, emetic effects of chemotherapy. She must have read about how marijuana eases the muscle spasms of people in wheelchairs and relieves symptoms of glaucoma, often preventing blindness; how grass restores appetite in anorexia, cancer, and AIDS patients; how it reduces chronic pain. Yet she chose to ignore the facts and adopt a totally negative approach. *Marijuana Alert* replicated *Reefer Madness* with a vengeance.

Just as the public was beginning to realize that marijuana was relatively harmless, Mann drove parents frantic. They were terrified that marijuana would drive their children into shocking behavior, that they would drop out of school and spend large parts of their lives in mental institutions.

Even more than I oppose teenagers' use of pot, unless recommended in writing by a physician, I deplore the use of the legal drugs alcohol and nicotine, at least until users are of legal age and understand that those drugs can cause death. It only makes sense to tell the truth, however, offering both sides of the debate. By frightening parents and their children needlessly, authors like Peggy Mann create an atmosphere in which many young people do turn to alcohol and other drugs far more damaging than grass.

Marijuana Alert – *fact or fiction?*

From the beginning, *Marijuana Alert* plays fast and loose with the truth. The foreword by former First Lady Nancy Reagan says that *Marijuana Alert* is a true story.

It isn't. Rather, it is a one-sided story – more fiction than fact – put together from sources who derive money from the government, and other sources that repeat the negative findings about pot reported by unscientific "studies" rather than the positive findings of legitimate research. Most of the negative findings have not been duplicated by reputable researchers. Representing them as genuine is unethical science, and using them to determine government action is unethical policymaking.

Marijuana Alert can frighten the lightest marijuana user. Author Peggy Mann points out that millions of Americans believe grass is far less harmful than tobacco cigarettes or alcohol.[45] Those millions of Americans are correct, but may find their view undermined by Mann's relentless rehashing of what's now aptly called "junk science."

Mann's inaccuracies pose as truth for the nation, and have fooled not only Nancy Reagan but *Reader's Digest*, which reprinted excerpts from the book and Mann's other *Reefer Madness*-type articles, spreading marijuana panic further.

The potency myth

Mann's obsession with marijuana's current higher potency compared to that of years past consumes 19 pages. She asserts that the higher potency devastates the body organs and brain. Let's set the record straight: If a particular strain of marijuana is more potent, then the pot smoker uses less of it, just as a person drinking 151-proof rum drinks less than if it were 86-proof vodka. If it takes less smoke to get the same high, then there's less irritation to the throat and lungs. It's for this reason that higher potency is actually *recommended* for those using marijuana as medicine. A vaporizer eliminates all smoke and tar; only the vapor is inhaled.

Marijuana users don't need more and more pot

Mann stresses the negative effects of tolerance and dependence. The implication is frightening – if we believe her, the marijuana user must constantly have more and more of the drug. We hear that even if marijuana were legalized, the chronic pot smoker would still need stronger and stronger pot to get high.[46]

Let's return to the facts: Tolerance refers to the gradual adaptation of the body to the effects of a drug in such a way that more and more is needed to achieve the same effect. A person who smokes day after day might develop a tolerance for THC, but very few marijuana smokers ever do this unless it's for serious medical conditions. Then, the user receives the medical benefit, but no longer feels the high. Social pot users know that when they put two or three days between each session of smoking pot the effect is like starting anew.

Keep in mind that pot does not contain deadly nicotine or any other addictive ingredient. Marijuana is simply not physically addictive, and users do not feel compelled to become abusers. Contrast this truth with the experience of nicotine users. Cigarette smokers are driven to inhale their drug approximately every half hour, or experience painful withdrawal. The majority of marijuana smokers, on the other hand, are like the majority of alcohol users, who generally have a few drinks a week and do not abuse the drug. Most drinkers get a pleasant feeling from their martini or two and don't feel any need or desire to increase their consumption. Clearly, and tragically, too many drinkers are physically addicted to alcohol, but it's easy to forget that they're a minority. Ninety percent of alcohol drinkers are not addicted to alcohol – and the same is true of the users of many *other* drugs, legal and illegal.

Pot users generally take two or three puffs, and they are high. People who have a couple of drinks feel a nice buzz. Most let it go at that.

Reverse tolerance

Rather than find they need more and more cannabis, many experienced pot users report "reverse tolerance": they smoke less, yet derive the same high. They have learned what to expect from the herb, and "lean into it."

Fetal Alcohol Syndrome charged

Marijuana Alert claims that a study demonstrated that grass-smoking during pregnancy is more strongly associated with adverse fetal outcomes than two or more drinks of alcohol, or a pack or more of cigarettes a day.[47]

Contrary to Mann's assertions, marijuana is not associated with fetal alcohol syndrome. A 1982 study cited by Mann has been refuted by Dr. Susan J. Astley of the University of Washington. Her study found no link between marijuana exposure and the birth defects attributed to fetal alcohol syndrome.[48]

Monkey business

Marijuana Alert says there is a certain pride in being an addict.[49] The book is so scary that at times it frightened even me – because of the false alarm it sounds. Usually, though, I found myself laughing at the one-sided, pathetic, and biased information reported by Peggy Mann. It just isn't so.

Much is made of a possible link between pot smoking and Amotivational Syndrome. One of Mann's "scientists" asserted that when adolescents used pot, the quality of their long-range goals often changed. She used as an example one youngster who planned to attend law school. After smoking grass he decided to become a guitar player in a rock group, even though he played no instrument. Another pot smoker, made aware of his impaired memory, felt he didn't need his memory because he decided he wasn't going to college anyway.[50]

There's little question that many young people who lack motivation smoke a lot of pot and accomplish little. No authenticated research indicates that marijuana causes them to be that way. Heavy pot smoking is likely to be a *symptom* of a lack of motivation rather than a *cause* of it.

Marijuana Alert goes into frightening detail about the effects of marijuana on adolescent rhesus monkeys, clearly expecting readers to infer that the results obtained from studies of monkeys apply to humans as well. What do we actually learn from these studies?

Mann reports that the testosterone level of a THC-injected male rhesus "teenager" dropped to that of a castrated animal.[51] That's enough to scare any father of a teenage son (he might even quit pot himself) but is it a legitimate worry? University of Iowa researchers were unable to find evidence of marijuana use inhibiting or altering male or female hormones. Six other studies contradicted the one Mann cited. What they found was that chronic use of marijuana didn't affect concentrations of any of those hormones.[52]

Marijuana Alert also says that pot-smoking monkeys hit and bite other monkeys, and under high stress could wound or even kill a cage mate. [53] (So that's why that lady bit me on the neck!) Not one unbiased scientific study in over 100 years has ever shown that cannabis causes human violence.

The book also cites a study that psychiatrist Robert Heath of Tulane University's School of Medicine conducted in the early 1970s, which purported to show that marijuana kills brain cells in rhesus monkeys, and reasoned that these findings could be extrapolated to humans.[54]

Conclusions that marijuana injures the brain and reproductive systems of humans are based on defective research in the first place, however, generally conducted by excitable government-paid opponents of cannabis.

The Heath study is a case in point. In 1980, after six years of requests for an accurate accounting of the Heath rhesus monkey report, *Playboy* magazine and NORML sued the government under the Freedom of Information Act. When they won their case, they learned that the monkeys had been strapped into chairs and pumped with numerous marijuana joints *during five minutes of oxygen deprivation.* It's long been known that oxygen deprivation causes brain damage and the death of brain cells. The Heath monkey experiment was a study of asphyxiation, not marijuana use. Independent researchers agreed that the findings of the Heath experiment were without value.

False alarm

Marijuana Alert has frightened many away from marijuana, just as Peggy Mann intended. Her book changed the way Americans think about cannabis. Our children go through phases of experimenting – it's natural. Most well-adjusted parents do the same. We do our best to teach kids common sense and to give them a value system that will sustain them through the really risky experiments – like alcohol, sex, daredevil stunts, driving fast, and so on. If we're smart, we also teach them how to handle drugs if, in spite of what we say, they elect to experiment anyway. Recognizing that even the best kids won't obey us all the time, and finding ways to minimize the damage their experiments do is simply intelligent harm reduction. If we can see marijuana experimentation as just one more phase, decidedly less risky than others that kids will try, then we can trust our kids to make good decisions. Unfortunately, Peggy Mann frightened parents so much that many now allow their children to drink alcohol in the illusion that they are choosing the lesser evil.

Savvy news people know that the representations of Mann's "scientific evidence" in *Marijuana Alert* and in her articles on the devastating effects of marijuana are not true. If you expose this evidence to the light of honest research by impartial medical doctors and scientists who are not paid by the federal government to come up with pseudo-scientific claptrap about marijuana, you get a different artillery of facts to use against this drug war.

A humorous man vs. the humorless Mann

Mann describes with outrage a small incident that wiser hearts will find funny. President Reagan held a drug-war briefing that featured the agency heads paid to present the marijuana propaganda the government wants us to hear. Mann mentions that the wife of one of the VIPs overheard a reporter say during Reagan's summation, "I'll be glad when he stops the BS and I can get out and smoke a joint!"[55]

I've met teenagers who were so frightened by Peggy Mann's book, which their parents demanded that they read, and by her *Reader's Digest* articles, that they quit pot. They switched to alcohol, cigarettes, crack, Ecstasy, methamphetamine, LSD, cocaine, heroin, glue, or combinations of these. Mann grievously harmed the very teenagers she purported to help by omitting the fact that marijuana is less harmful than any of these substances. She re-ignited a hysterical panic about marijuana. *Reader's Digest* is also to be condemned for not consulting an authority such as Dr. Lester Grinspoon, MD, of Harvard Medical School, now retired, to check on the flawed scientific conclusions Mann foisted on her readers.

Marijuana Alert frightens the public with tales of young people sent to psychiatrists or psychiatric hospitals because of the debilitating effects of marijuana. The hospitals, she claims, reported that the patients were withdrawn and displayed a Pandora's box of psychiatric disorders, including indolence, withdrawal, anxiety and apprehension, depersonalization, derealization, suicidal thinking, fear and agitation flashbacks, narcissism, paranoia, decreasing cognitive and intellectual function, gradual decline of emotional life, increased irritability, panic attacks, racing heart, sweating, palpitations, blackouts, and symptoms of senility. The book mentions that most of these required sedation of the patient. Some psychiatrists and psychiatric hospitals make their living with scary diagnoses, while researchers who come up with positive pot findings frequently find their grants discontinued.

Mann's book also asserts that, although a person drinking alcohol eventually sobers up, a young person smoking marijuana twice a week does not get "sober."[56] Mann states that people might drink quite heavily for twenty to thirty years without alterations to the brain, but using moderate or heavy pot, even for a short time, causes brain damage. Such untrue information has been reported in magazines, in newspapers, on television, and by the DEA and the Drug Abuse Resistance Education (DARE) program presented by police departments to young students.

(DARE has since been shown to be ineffective for grade-school students.)

David E. Smith, M.D., of the Haight Ashbury Free Clinic in San Francisco reported he had not observed any cases of "cannabis psychosis" among the 35,000 marijuana users that had attended the clinic.[57] There will always be a few pot users who are unstable to begin with, and those pot smokers would have experienced similar problems with alcohol or any drug – and often with*out* any drug.

Generally, the effects of grass include the feeling of time slowed down, increased awareness, sensitivity to touch, increased appetite and enjoyment of food, and easy laughter. Some people have temporary difficulty concentrating during the time they are smoking, (short-term memory loss) because so many ideas, sparkling colors, or music flow into the mind. On the other hand, the presence of free-flowing ideas can be an asset to the creative person.

I have interacted with thousands of pot smokers, and fewer than one percent of them ever had a problem. Those who did say it was gone as soon as they "came down" from the high. Frightening young people with largely untrue threats of lasting symptoms will only cause distrust when the truth is learned. It's far better to present both the negative *and* positive sides of any drug.

Another example of Mann's misinformation from her "experts" refers to driving skills: "It's like operating with a faulty speedometer. The marijuana-intoxicated driver *thinks* he is traveling only forty miles per hour, when in fact he is doing eighty or ninety."[58] Another example of Mann's lack of cannabis knowledge. No one should drive under the influence of any drug. Pot smokers, however, with time "slowed down", drive *slower*, not faster. They generally keep watch on their speedometers so as not to drive too slowly.

The real problem

The real problem is usually the panic reaction of parents who learn that their child is smoking pot. If their only experience with marijuana comes from reading such books as *Marijuana Alert*, they may overreact with shock and feel that their child should be hospitalized or arrested. As if either of those experiences wouldn't be enough by itself to give the child (and the parents) a panic attack! If you speak with victims of cancer, AIDS, multiple sclerosis, glaucoma and other illnesses, there will be no question in your mind that many find marijuana far more beneficial than many prescribed medications. Mann scoffs at the idea that marijuana has any positive use. Her chapter 13 in *Marijuana Alert*, "Marijuana as *Medicine?*" speaks to her prejudice, aversion, and lack of understanding regarding the proven medical benefits of marijuana. Marijuana is not the problem. *Marijuana Alert* is the problem.

Concerned parents need a book that will tell what, if any, dangers are *actually* associated with cannabis. Instead, PRIDE (Parents' Resource Institute for Drug Education) *still* recommends *Marijuana Alert* by Peggy Mann, and equally untrustworthy books such as *Parents, Peers, and Pot*, by Marsha Manatt, and *Keep Off The Grass*, by Gabriel G. Nahas. Reefer madness lives on, presenting and re-presenting as fact "information" that has been scientifically disproved.

Eruption!

January 3, 1983, 7:05 a.m. I was lying comfortably in bed at the Alokea Plantation home in Hilo, watching *Good Morning, America,* when the phone rang. It was the NBC television affiliate calling from Honolulu. "Dave, there's a pretty awesome eruption in progress from Kilauea's east rift zone. We can have a cameraman at your hangar by 8:30. Are you available to fly?"

"I'll be there. How bad is it?" I asked.

"Hard to say at the moment. It began at 12:31 a.m. and is fountaining more than a thousand feet in the air."

My plane was always fueled and ready to fly. By the time I showered, filed a flight plan, and got to the airport, it was 8:20. As I pulled the plane out of the hangar I could see Ray Lovall, the cameraman, running toward me, lugging his heavy equipment. After the preflight inspection, we loaded his gear. We strapped in, and the engine sprang to life. I grabbed the mike and pressed the transmit button. "Hilo ground control, Cardinal three zero five niner niner request taxi for takeoff."

"Five niner niner, cleared to runway eight. Wind, zero eight zero at five knots."

It was a cloudy morning with showers from the northeast. At the end of the runway I ran up the engines, checked the magnetos, and switched to the tower frequency. "Hilo tower, Cardinal five niner niner ready for takeoff runway eight."

A clear, confident voice boomed back, "Five niner niner cleared for takeoff." I requested 3,500 feet of altitude to climb over the clouds, and a frequency change to radar vectoring as there was already heavy traffic heading for the eruption site.

Within 20 minutes the clouds parted, revealing a scene that could have come out of Star Trek, or perhaps hell. It was as if Madam Pele, the fire goddess, was spewing red-hot cinders the size of bricks a thousand feet into the air.

"Get as low as you can, Dave, I'd rather not have to use the telephoto lens any more than necessary; you know how it amplifies any movement," said Ray. Lower. Right. Monitoring traffic, I obtained clearance to lower our altitude to 2,000 feet. With the terrain about 1,000 feet we were only 1,000 feet above ground level, and about as close to the Dragon Lady as I cared to get. The turbulence was horrific and pieces of burning cinder were flung close to the aircraft. What a sight! While Ray shot footage, I fought the controls to keep the plane level. We could feel the heat inside the plane. It was exciting, but I was glad when Ray told me he had enough footage, and we could get back on the ground.

That night some of that footage appeared on both local and national television. I received a phone call from *USA Today* for an update on the eruption. It appeared that this was the Big One, one that might continue for years.

My telephone answering machine was taking calls 24 hours a day. I had to turn off the ringer at night to get any rest at all. Nearly every morning when I checked the messages, there were at least a half-dozen requests from people who wanted to fly over the eruption site. Because I never use marijuana when I'm flying, I didn't smoke grass for weeks. I had no withdrawal symptoms, by the way.

"A bad birth"

One night a lady doctor phoned from Honolulu. She wanted the plane to herself: no other passengers on her flight over the eruption site. I said that would be fine, and we went on to agree that a night flight would be especially dramatic. At the hangar she noticed me admiring her. She was very attractive, with long blonde hair and deep blue eyes. She appeared to be in her mid-thirties. I had never seen such white smooth skin. "You're probably curious why I didn't want any other passengers in the plane. And now you notice my appearance. My white skin. Am I correct, Mr. Ford?"

"The name's Dave. And yes, I am curious." In a soft, even voice she said, "I've always wanted to see an eruption. This is a very special night for me and I didn't wish to be distracted by other passengers. You see, I'm dying. I have leukemia, and about a month to live. I just wanted to have this time without others talking or laughing."

I felt like wrapping my arms around her and holding her tight. I didn't. I just said, "I'm terribly sorry. My Cardinal is going to give you the most exciting ride of your life, doctor."

We flew for about an hour. I showed her the city lights, and magnificent Mauna Kea silhouetted by the moon. "If you count from its base on the ocean floor, Mauna Kea is the highest mountain in the world, rising 32,000 feet. Over 13,000 of those feet are above sea level. In winter, if you set up a good telescope at Hilo Bay you could see people skiing on the slopes of Mauna Kea, then lower the telescope and watch surfers riding waves in the warm Pacific ocean.

She nodded, and smiled at my obvious pride in my home island. She said, "Your island grows fine cannabis."

"Yes, it does," I replied. "Have you tried it, doctor?"

"I have. It superbly eases the fear of dying and is one of the world's safest medicines."

We headed for the eruption site. Red lava was gushing out of the growing cinder cone. The doctor's face was ashen. "How do you feel, doctor?" I asked.

"It's certainly a thrill of a lifetime, and I'm OK. But it reminds me of a bad birth."

When we landed, I asked if she minded if I gave her a hug. She was a fine hugger, and we both had tears in our eyes. I drove her to the main terminal for her last-ever flight back to Honolulu.

As I drove home, the sights we'd seen replayed in my mind's eye. The rivers of lava glowing angrily in the dark and moving slowly down the mountain were frightening. They looked like rivers of blood that were all too ready to give Royal Gardens a transfusion. Shortly after arriving home I fell into a deep sleep. I dreamed I was flying three passengers directly over the eruption when the engine quit. The 2,000-degree heat of the lava drew the plane like a magnet into the volcano's bloody mouth. When the plane plunged into the lava and exploded, I awoke with a scream. Thereafter, I restricted flights to daytime only. Whenever time permitted and seats were vacant I invited Sandy, David, and my daughter-in-law, David's bride Cathy, to join the flights.

Royal Gardens becomes the target of the fire goddess

On a flight two months after the eruption began it became obvious to me that the innocent Royal Gardens subdivision was now prey to the devastating, insatiable hunger of the Fire Goddess. Most Royal Gardens residents were happy to help each other move their belongings off the hill and out of harm's way. Half of the subdivision's estimated 150 residents were cramming housewares into cars and trucks. Pele was a glutton. By March 4, two of the homes had been destroyed and a lava flow that had been moving all night lumbered through the thick rain forest toward more homes. Pele was burying everything in her path with a 30-foot wall of lava. The thunder of propane tanks exploding from the heat of the lava was eerie and terrifying; rocks, chunks of lava, and pieces of houses and even septic tanks skyrocketed, as though we were on a battlefield. At any minute I expected to be hit in the face by an airborne turd.

I drove back to our Royal Gardens house with a gallon of red paint. With the help of an eight-foot ladder I climbed to the roof and painted in three-foot letters "HOT LOT SALE," and added our Hilo phone number. The national news media took an aerial photo of the house, and the picture appeared not only on the front page of the *Honolulu Star-Bulletin*, but also on television in most of the world. I received a call from New Zealand, where one of my cousins had seen the picture.

A voyage; meeting "smoking" ladies

By May I felt the need to retreat from the continuing gluttony of the fire goddess. An esteemed friend of mine, Patti Oliver, saw the distress I was experiencing in the loss of this magic area that I loved, the losses of friends' and clients' homes, and of dozens of lots, including mine. Patti booked me on a Mediterranean cruise starting in Venice.

I flew to Los Angeles, and then nonstop to London. After a restful night there, I flew on to Venice. What a spectacular city! I had almost no time for sightseeing, but I was amazed by St. Thomas' Square, the canals, and the romantic gondolas. (I was reminded of a joke about a young lady who won five gold medals in the Olympic swimming competition. When asked where she learned to swim so fast, she answered, "I was a prostitute in Venice.") After only a few hours I boarded the luxury ship, the *Sea Princess*, for a three-week adventure. After settling into my stateroom, which I shared with a doctor, the ship weighed anchor and headed on a southeasterly course for Itea, Greece. On the second day we rippled through the Adriatic Sea, passing within 12 miles of the Isle of Corfu.

There was a tour group of registered nurses on board, several of whom were seated at our dining table. One of them, an attractive auburn-haired lady named Irene, had smiling green eyes. Later that night we danced and chatted. The next day, we visited the ancient sanctuary of Apollo at Delphi together and saw the amphitheater, the best preserved of the ancient Greek theaters.

Many nurses smoke pot for sex, and recommend it as medicine

The second night out, Irene invited me to her stateroom. I arrived with a bottle of champagne. "Thanks for the champagne", said Irene, "but I'm not much of a drinker. I hate hangovers. How is your schedule, Dave? Are you obligated to anyone?"

"No, I'm alone," I said; "I'll just phone my roommate, so he won't report me overboard." A few minutes later Irene emerged in a black baby-doll outfit, revealing some previously hidden charms.

"Would you care to join me in a little smoke, rather than the champagne?" Irene asked. "You bet", I said; "Do many nurses smoke pot?"

"Lots of us do." She went on to say, "Some of us, if we trust a patient who is overwhelmed with nausea from chemotherapy, we'll give him a joint." She described cannabis as "a bang-up medicine" for nausea and dozens of other ailments, and said that "One day it will be recognized as a true miracle drug." She also said that she has recommended it to women friends who haven't yet experienced an orgasm. At one point she looked especially thoughtful. "When I was a teen my brother and I used to shoot birds with his BB gun. After smoking a few joints with him I didn't want to kill anymore; I put myself in the place of those poor helpless birds. It's a medicine of peace."

I nodded in agreement. "I've been doing an enormous amount of flying recently," I said, "so it's been about three months since I've smoked. This will be great."

"Are you an airline pilot?" she asked.

"No, I fly just for business and pleasure," I said.

"The grass is from Thailand," said Irene. "I think you'll like it." She was now on her hands and knees at her bedside compartment. "I know there's a zipper baggie in here somewhere..."

Her back was toward me; she had apparently forgotten to put on her panties, and it was like admiring a beautiful valentine. "Take your time," I said.

"Got it!" She sat down next to me, lit up, and took a toke. The smoke was mellow. We each took a couple of hits.

Within a few minutes I felt the warm tingling glow enveloping every part of my body. It settled in my groin, because marijuana amplifies what you're doing at the time. Irene lit two candles and I turned off the lights. "Dave, my whole body is purring. How do you feel?" I slowly took her into my arms and kissed her on the mouth. Then I kissed her closed eyes and stroked her face. I felt as though we were melting together. Her skin was so soft, and the grass was doing a fine job of heightening sensations. Her skin now felt like silk. Those staterooms are so small, where can one go but onto the bed?

Within a half-hour we were making marvelous animal sounds as we made love, and then we cuddled in perfect contentment. She whispered into my ear, "Friends of mine, also nurses, have said that reciprocal oral sex becomes something pure, more beautiful, and intriguing when using grass. Trepidation melts away and relaxation takes over."

She was right.

Hours later we showered together in the narrow shower stall, then slept in the slender bed. Sometime in the night we made love again. The next night I left the champagne in my stateroom and brought along some Hawaiian smoke.

On the evening of May 18, the *Sea Princess* left Itea, sailing past Konnthiakos and headed now toward the Messina Strait and Naples. About 10 p.m. the captain of the ship turned out her lights so the passengers could see the glow of the erupting volcano, Mt. Etna, on the island of Sicily.

When we disembarked in Naples the next morning, Irene and I both wanted to see the ruins of Pompeii, where 20,000 people had been buried in pumice stone and ashes in 79 AD. Today, much has been dug out to reveal a surprisingly modern ghost town. Pompeii was equipped with piped water – charcoal-filtered, no less – and featured an open marketplace, community baths, houses of prostitution, and artful paintings. Frescoes buried for nearly two millennia were found in almost perfect condition. In the garden of one of the homes archaeologists found ancient seeds that later germinated; today, those plants are flourishing in that garden, as their ancestors did thousands of years ago.

Irene left the ship in Naples, where she would spend time with relatives before returning to the States. We hugged goodbye, in a warm conclusion to our classic shipboard romance. Before she left, Irene had introduced me to various other nurses, and apparently had given me an admirable recommendation. I got lucky with three of them, and they all smoked pot.

Judy was an RN who worked in a urologist's office. We were walking topside admiring the full moon when she confirmed what I had heard many times from couples. (And it works for me.) She said, "Cannabis opens blood vessels in all the right places! It even shows up in the eyes – the telltale red-eye. That's blood going to the capillaries. When it goes to the groin, happy things take place." She added that "Some 25 million men suffer from erection 'letdown' at one time or another. With cannabis, sexual vitality and stamina are greatly increased." She made an intriguingly accurate prediction: "I'll bet pharmaceutical companies will bring out an expensive manufactured sexual stimulant. However, it will be hard, pardon the play on words, for them to beat pot."

I laughed. "Would you care to give me an opportunity to test the validity of your insight?" I asked, producing a joint.

Judy joined my laughter, then took my hand. In minutes we were in her cabin, proving her right.

Dr. Pessler only wanted to pinch an Italian lady's bottom

My stateroom companion, Dr. Gordon Pessler, confided that all his adult life he'd had a compulsion to pinch the bottom of a lovely Italian lady. "History informs us it's the way of life in Italy, Dave, and that the women love it." He sighed, "But I don't have the courage. I guess that's why I'm not married..." He looked very wistful, and then I began to see resolve in his eyes. "Dave, I've seen you roll some joints. I haven't smoked pot since I was a teenager. I was beaten by my stepdad, and I became violent. There were times I wanted to kill him. Then a friend turned me on to pot. It was the first time that I remember laughing. I no longer wanted to kill my stepfather, or even hit him. Pot may have saved his life, and mine. Do you think that it might give me the nudge that I need to accomplish my fantasy?"

"Let's find out," I replied as I lit a joint, took a couple of puffs and handed it to him. In a few minutes he was all smiles. I enjoyed egging him on. "Gordon, I think it's a splendid idea. Let me be your witness, and help you find an Italian beauty."

We went ashore, and kept our eyes peeled as we strolled along the busy avenues of Naples. Suddenly Gordon elbowed me. "There's the one! Isn't she a pip, Dave? I'm getting an erection already," said the doctor. I was getting excited myself. She was in her mid-twenties, in a low-cut silk dress. Her breasts seemed ready to pop out – much like Gordon's eyes. "I could never do this back home..." I could see he was still hesitating, and gave him a slight elbow toward her. Damned if he didn't give her a really good pinch right on her luscious bottom. We waited for her demure smile and squeal of delight. Instead, her beet-red face whirled around, and she slapped the doctor across the chops. It was at that fateful moment that we both recognized her as a passenger on our ship! Dr. Pessler practically licked her hand, apologizing.

Back on board, I met auburn-haired Helen. She was a sexy tease. She was beautiful, tall, about five-foot nine, with long legs, sensuous lips, perfect teeth, and a regal dress sense, which included fine jewelry. Her penetrating eyes were encouraging. I guessed her to be about thirty-six. There was a dance party scheduled for that night. She did whisper in my ear "My friend is leaving the ship in Egypt, as he has to get back to business." As we danced, one of her firm thighs moved between mine. It didn't take a brain surgeon to suspect a new adventure on the horizon! A long twenty-four hours passed with no lovemaking. Perhaps we both needed a rest, I rationalized.

It was May 21 when we cleared the Naples harbor and the Messina Strait, and set a southeasterly course toward Alexandria, Egypt. When we visited the museum in Cairo, the pyramids, and the Sphinx, I felt we were cruising back into the Golden Age of history. Inside the Great Pyramid, Helen and I climbed 180 steps up the worn, narrow passageway to the burial chamber of the Pharaoh Khufu. There was almost no light at all, and Helen said she was frightened and wanted me right behind her. I was pleased to oblige. I was as close as one could get to that lovely swaying bottom as it moved tantalizingly upward. I controlled my instinctive urge to give that mouthwatering target a soft bite.

When we were finally back in sunlight and fresh air, Helen rested while I went for a ride on a camel. I couldn't help remembering the days that doctors actually endorsed Camel cigarettes – and the old joke advertisement that "Two out of three doctors who've used camels state they prefer *women!*" For some time I wondered about that third doctor.

We were told that some camel drivers, once they get you out in the desert, don't bring you back unless you give them an extra tip of five or ten dollars. A young man approached me with his camel and offered a "good ride, sir, for only five dollars." I said, "I'll go with you, but I don't want to get hit up for more money when we're out in the desert, OK?"

"Oh, sir," he said, "I would never do such a thing. Certainly not to an American! You see, sir, my camel's name is America. It is embroidered right on his saddle blanket." So it was.

"Let's go," I said.

He had the camel kneel, and I climbed onto the smelly beast, while he tried to spit at me. The camel driver led it away from the Pyramids and gave it a slap. The animal took off as if it had been goosed. We were soon about a quarter of a mile away from the Pyramids. The young man followed, running surprisingly well in the sand. When he was alongside me he said, "Do you like it out here, sir?"

"It's very nice", I said, "but it is hot. I think it's time to return."

"Oh, yes sir. I agree with you completely. And for another ten dollars we shall return."

I had bought a souvenir camel whip, and happened to have it with me. I hoped the camel was like a horse. I hit the critter on its behind. It made a strange noise as if it were shifting gears, then ran full throttle back to its base, leaving its master alone in the desert. "America" decided this rider was not a sucker, and knelt down. Helen had been watching. As I climbed off the critter, she was holding her sides laughing.

As the sun set that evening, hundreds of us sat under the stars to observe the light show. Enormous floodlights lit up the pyramids in gold and blue hues. Giant stereo speakers, hidden next to the pyramids, played angelic music, and then we heard the voices of centuries past, telling the history of the pyramids. As total darkness enveloped us, camels and their riders rode silently off into the night. One of them was close enough that I could see the blanket on which the rider sat. On it was embroidered, "America"!

Too soon the voyage ended. Helen was lots of fun – but also a great tease. I'm sorry to report that we didn't "connect" during the voyage. As we were clearing customs in Los Angeles, I reached for my passport and a joint slipped from my pocket and fell to the floor. Helen nonchalantly reached down and picked it up, and discreetly placed it in my hand. She departed for her home in the Los Angeles area, and I caught a flight to Hawaii. We became good friends, and she visited me often in Hawaii – where she went far beyond teasing.

More Hawaiian adventures include double eruptions

By the end of 1983 lava flows had destroyed 15 homes in Royal Gardens, and 330 one-acre lots were covered with fresh lava five to 15 feet deep. No one had died – no one has ever been killed by an eruption in Hawaii. In 1984, the bizarre occurred: Two separate eruptions were in progress at the same time, which hadn't happened for 65 years. In addition to the Kilauea eruption continuing to eat up the Kalapana area, Mauna Loa's northeast rift began erupting, threatening the town of Hilo itself, and coming within a few miles of my home in Alokea Plantation. I spent more time in the air, helping passengers check on their homes and flying television camera crews over the eruption sites, than selling real estate, which I was no longer interested in, unless it was my own.

Helen was an executive with a large firm in Los Angeles. For fun and relaxation she moonlighted as a professional belly dancer, dancing in Las Vegas as well as in Southern California. She was a creative lover. On more than one visit she transformed the wardrobe closet in the master bedroom into an "Arabian tent," with silks hanging from the walls and over a mattress, and candles that perfumed the air. I dressed as a sheik and wore dark glasses. She emerged in full belly-dancing costume. Sometimes I would undress her while she danced. Since high school days I had fantasized about a belly dancer dancing unclad; Helen fulfilled that fantasy. It was *great*. On a vacation trip to Germany we stayed in a chateau resort in Rottach-Egern, in the Bavarian Alps. There she danced at our hotel's talent night (with costume on). We enjoyed the philosophy "Live as if you'll live forever. Yet, live as if you'll die tomorrow."

In March of 1984 I was contacted by a reporter from the *Star* tabloid, found next to the *Inquirer* in every supermarket checkout lane. Usually, I don't give information to tabloids; but the reporter said they were going to do a story on our eruptions, a page and a half long with four or five color photos. Would I please give her some information by naming at least one of the people affected. I relented, so long as she promised to keep the story accurate. It appeared in the March 27 issue, and turned out to be fairly accurate, although sensationalized of course. The headline was a page and a half wide with color photos of the eruption, and of two houses being ignited:

FAMILIES TELL WHY THEY REFUSE TO GIVE UP LIFE IN FIERY SHADOW OF DEADLY VOLCANO

They are known as volcano people – the tough, defiant, stick-it-out loners who refuse to leave their homes, even though the fiery fingers of death move closer to them with each new eruption.

She is known as Madame Pele, the legendary volcano goddess who, many believe, is determined to drive them out and reclaim her land. The battle between man and myth is being waged on Mauna Loa, the massive peak on the island of Hawaii and the site of Kilauea, one of the world's most active volcanoes.

It has erupted no fewer than 16 times since January, 1983, spewing out a river of white-hot lava that runs ever closer to the homes in Royal Gardens, a settlement on the side of the mountain.

But despite living with the nightmare prospect of everything they own being wiped out in seconds by the volcano, the residents refuse to leave. Carol Wright's home is just 100 feet from where the lava flow stopped in the most recent eruption in February.

Even Hawaiian TV personality, David Ford, 56, who lost two plots of land, doesn't think the goddess is deliberately trying to drive the residents out. "I don't think Madame Pele is seeking revenge against those of us who built on her slopes," he said. "I think she is working to increase the size of her island."

A handsome eruption: our grandson is born

October 12, 1985, a great joy erupted: our handsome grandson Scott was born. I couldn't have been happier. I felt a special closeness with him when he was just weeks old. I hoped we would be very special buddies. I was grateful that semi-retirement gave me time to spend with him. Even so, I wanted to be with him much more often than I actually could. David and Cathy were working long days, as I had when David and Sandy were little. The sad thing about being a grandparent is that it makes you wish you'd had as much free time to spend with your own children.

Early the following year I brought my parents over to visit their great grandson. They were thrilled. Dad was so proud to have a photo of the four generations of Fords. On Scott's first birthday, I gave him a rocking horse and a $1,000 certificate of deposit. On his birthday card was a little boy riding a horse, and I added this message:

> This horsey looks like yours, young man. Grandfather wishes you unlimited happy rides. So ride 'em, cowboy!
>
> You're just beginning life's great adventure. Like the cowboys, you will find yourself riding mountains and valleys. Seek the trail with the best view. When you look for the best in yourself and others, you will usually find it.
>
> Your parents love you very much. Respect them. Be loyal to them. Love them. Wishing you a good ride, cowboy, for another hundred years!
>
> Love you,
> Grandfather

It was a great thrill for me to have this wonderful child join the family. Grandparents hope they can have the opportunity to impart love, friendship, and wisdom that can make the working portion of life's trip easier, more rewarding and fun for the child. My little grandson joined his mom and dad on some flights in the Cessna Cardinal over the eruption. He certainly seemed to enjoy it. I dreamed of the day he might want "grampa" to teach him to become a pilot, and to take him on trips to other parts of the world – certainly to see his relatives in New Zealand, for starters.

Lady pot smokers are the finest lovers

One evening in August, 1985, I joined a Parents Without Partners party at a private home. On the dance floor my eyes met those of a vivacious gray-eyed smiling lady with short curly brown hair, in her early 40s. She was wearing jeans that showed off a pair of lovely legs and more. She was dancing with a guy who was moving her around as if she were a truck; for once, I was watching a dancer who was even worse than I! She looked at me with an expression that said, "I'm available to be rescued." I tapped her partner's shoulder and cut in. She smiled, and when the truck driver was lost in our wake, she said, "Thanks. I feel good vibes, Dave." (Hmm. That reminded me I needed to pick up more batteries for my home vibrators.) We glided around the dance floor with one of her lovely legs between mine.

We began dating. She also treasured grass. It encouraged us to talk, and also amplified our jokes and stories – and of course, our lovemaking. She was an exceedingly huggy little teddy bear, and so I began calling her "Teddy Bear." We both loved going camping, and we made love at many secluded Hawaiian beaches, not to mention her home and mine. At Christmas she presented me with a scrapbook filled with photos she had taken, and a six-page poem, a marvelously thoughtful gift that must have taken a great deal of time to create. I greatly appreciated it. Here's a part of it:

A Special Friendship
A warm August evening at a singles party they met,
The Western Band played... the best entertainment yet.
Conversation came easy but dancing was the best,
They nestled together as though in a warm nest.
An intruder gave her a hard time on the dance floor,
She asked for protection and she got even more.

They exchanged phone numbers without an embrace,
But glances throughout the evening made their hearts race.
She managed to slip away and get out of sight,
It was a long lonely drive to get home that night.
The party was great and she wondered if he would call,
She dreamed of the smiling handsome man who was tall.
A few days later he did call... an invitation to dinner.
He would cook at his home... Oh, he must be a winner!
Excitement flowed through her as she got the directions,
She found it in the daylight... the best of suggestions.
Panic overtook her, he had a big beautiful house.
Wondering if she could trust him or was he a louse.
Nervous.. Uncomfortable... wondering where she was being led,
Hoping he wouldn't wine and dine, then drag her off to bed.
Dinner time came and he greeted her at the door,
Looking so cheerful... getting ready couldn't be a chore.
Dinner was quite wonderful... a true delight,
Fun to watch him cook and have it come out right.
First lesson she learned was it was okay to let him cook,
To sit back and relax... let him do his thing, without a book.
Any other time she would have jumped in to assist,
But his kind words to relax... she couldn't resist.
Tension mounted at last for her... things had to be said.
Thoughts of not being good enough went through her head.
Being threatened by his worldly possessions and wealth,
Made her say – I'm going to be me – no airs – just good health.
Since that time she puts money in the back of her mind,
And thinks of him as he is – so wonderful and kind.
The beautiful flowers so dear, from his heart to hers,
Could never be made up by having gems and furs.
Conversation went well and they were finally at ease,
Not having to put on false pretenses to please.
They talked and then touched – trotted off to the back room,
Oh what a real shock... the mirrors on the ceiling hit her with a
boom!
Discomfort set in to see her body in the light,
Pleasure came to see his next to hers, holding tight.
The caressing, the warmth, the holding, the touching, the
kiss,
Became a wonderful exciting feeling she did miss.

The horrible thought occurred to her of what he must think,
This gal doesn't really like me, she only wants a mink.
And then there was an immediate feeling of trust,
Scared though, wondering what he'd think of her lust.
When they departed each other's company with a hug,
She had high hopes to hear again from this love bug.
Day did pass without a word – she asked people about him,
There was a lot of gossip and rumors placing him on a limb.
He was the rich playboy of the little town of Hilo,
Supposedly having every gal in his bedroom – friend or foe.
The advice was a warning to stay clear and not see him again.
She made her own decision on which she felt she could depend.
Days later he did call – giving her heart a little rush.
Thinking of the last time... it brought on a pink blush.
She frequently questioned his manner of being so kind.
Yet she gracefully accepted the invitation to be wined and dined.
So wonderful to relax with a real person without a suggestion.
All the faults and handicaps seemed to be accepted without
question.
A delightful understanding friendship started to develop fast,
Even with good feelings, there was always doubt it wouldn't last.

That spirited and benevolent poem went on for six pages! Teddy Bear and I are still true friends, and frequently phone each other. She has a great son, Steve, who is one fine salesman and now a loving father and consummate husband.

Royal Gardens and Kalapana area overrun by hot lava

By 1986 every property I owned on the Hilo side of the Big Island except my home in Alokea Plantation was all new land. Or, to put it another way, it was all covered with lava, devoured by that lady with the ravenous appetite. Queen's Bath, that sanctuary of tranquility where we once swam, was now covered with thousands of cubic yards of crackling, flaming lava, transforming a paradise into a temporary purgatory. When the eruptions ended, those idyllic 34 oceanfront acres, which I once dreamed would be a restful haven, were a wasteland.

For some reason I wish I could figure out, my daughter-in-law Cathy and I have never quite found a way to get along with each other. That saddened me because of the strain it put on my son David, dividing his loyalties between his wife and his poor old pop. It saddens me to this day because it has made it virtually impossible for me to spend the time I'd

A friend and I were camping at a secluded Hawaiian beach. While she was taking a shower she noticed I had my camera, and was kind enough to strike a saucy pose for me. (Sorry, guys. She insisted on anonymity!)

Four generations of Fords. David married attractive Cathy, and soon there was a handsome baby, Scott. Great-grandfather Ford was clearly awestruck.

My dear friend "Teddy Bear" sunning by the pool at the Akolea Plantation home in Hilo. (Maybe she's the reason my dad's mouth was hanging open!)

have dearly loved to spend with my grandson. Invitations to take Scott to New Zealand to see the home of his great grandfather, and to visit his relatives, went unanswered. When David and Cathy divorced ten years ago I despaired of ever bonding with Scott as I badly wanted to.

Moving back to the mainland after 30 years

Sister Margo was living in Palo Alto, California. Margee was an extremely talented and creative jewelry artist, poet, and painter, as well as a loving mother. I bought a mobile home for her, not only so she could have a home of her own, but also so she could live near our parents. They were in a beautiful mobile home park in lovely Sonoma, California, in the wine country north of San Francisco.

My stepmother was now 85, and had the dreaded Alzheimer's. Dad, at 95, was her caregiver. Mom had been so bright as an accountant, a fabulous cook, and beloved friend. Now, she was a different person. She would drive into town and get lost. Dad found her putting napkins into the toaster and clothes into the oven. When she became incontinent, Dad reluctantly put her into a convalescent home – an oxymoron, if there ever was one.

I felt it was time to "be there" for Dad and Mom. The distance between Cathy and me limited the time I could spend with Scott, removing one of the biggest motivations I had to stay in Hawaii. I would miss my children, my grandson, and many of my friends, but it was time to say Aloha.

I sold the Alokea Plantation home in Hilo and the home in Honolulu. Selling the airplane was painful, like getting rid of a faithful dog. It was my fifth airplane since I was 23, and my favorite. I moved to Sonoma in June of 1987, ending just over thirty years of living in paradise. Moving in with Dad in their mobile home was a wonderful opportunity to really get to know him, and to help him in every way possible. I knew how much he missed Mom. He was the sweetest guy in the world. At 95 he'd still never lost his enthusiasm for life or his sense of humor. He frequently dressed for dinner and wore a tie. "Why do you wear the tie for dinner, Pop?" He answered, "It keeps me from getting food on my shirt!"

Dad wanted me to enjoy going to church with him, so one Sunday morning I did join him. We attended the First Congregational Church in Sonoma, where he and Mom had gone for years. Dad nudged me to join him in taking Communion. He knew I enjoyed an occasional glass of Sonoma's famous wines, and as I sipped from the cup of red wine that he passed me, he looked at me and nodded his head. "*It's good wine, isn't it, Son!*" I think he thought that if I liked the wine I'd accompany him again. I also think he thought he was whispering. I believe everyone in the congregation heard him. They all loved him, though, and he loved every one of them, especially the minister, The Rev. David McCracken, whom he considered his "second son."

I needed a car and ended up buying a new Cadillac Coupe DeVille. Dad loved it. He was still a competent driver and enjoyed tooling around town in it. It was a pleasure to take him to the little picturesque town square in Sonoma and on picnics to the Russian River.

Cannabis: geriatric wonder drug?

One day when I visited Mom she was coherent. She said, "Son, many of the people here are considered senile because they slur their words and act depressed and have memory loss. But a lot of them are alcoholics. Some tell me how they'd fall down when they were drinking. I've seen them with the hidden bottles their friends bring them. And most of them have been drinking for years." For the older populations the first drug of choice is alcohol. The second is Valium. When the two are ingested to numb the pain in an already depressed person, the body responds with increased depression. And an older, depressed alcoholic runs the highest risk of suicide.

A 1998 Mayo Clinic study reported that 41 percent of persons age sixty-five and older who enrolled in the clinic's alcoholism treatment program first showed symptoms of alcoholism after age sixty. Clearly, for them alcohol became a problem when it was mixed with age.

Could cannabis come to the rescue? I foresee the day when cannabis will be as acceptable to the public as aspirin is. Name a botanical that might overcome depression, increase appetite and well-being, and produce a smiling, mellow senior citizen without chronic pain! But – <u>Caution</u>: Marijuana causes easy laughter! Four in 10 nursing-home residents who are known to be in pain get little or no relief from their suffering.[59] Imagine how those "caged" patients would act about an hour after their doctor-approved "brownies" were passed out! Valium and other tranquilizers, sleeping pills, alcohol, and lots of other medications would be in serious jeopardy. These drugs provide a major portion of the revenue of the hundred-billion-dollar pharmaceutical industry, which advertises that it wants to help seniors (stockholding seniors). Not only does cannabis not cause depression or self-destruction,

Sonoma Valley, California   The Sonoma Index-Tribune   Friday, January 29, 1993 – A17

VALLEY LIFE

Man of a thousand stories

From chatting with celebrities, to fleeing volcanoes – Dave Ford has done it all

By Dennis Wheeler
INDEX-TRIBUNE STAFF WRITER

Dave Ford has plenty of stories to cram into the autobiography he's writing.

There are all those celebrities he's interviewed, for instance – Bing Crosby, Tiny Tim, Billy Graham, Dame Margo Fonteyn, Liberace, Sophie Tucker, Jonathan Winters and Edgar Bergen.

Or the time a Hawaiian priest blessed the house he owns in Hawaii to save it from the lava rolling toward it from a volcano – and the blessing apparently worked.

Or the three days when he broke a world's record in diving by participating in a sensory deprivation experiment.

Or the time during the Persian Gulf War when he spent four days at a Buddhist monastery in Southeast Asia with 450 monks, who were appalled at the carnage being rained upon Iraq by the Americans.

Nowadays, Ford calls Sonoma his full-time home (although even this month he jaunted off to Hawaii for a few weeks).

"I just love it here," he said contentedly.

Currently Ford, 65, is writing his book and dabbling in a few other entrepreneurial pursuits. He lives in a lavish, 3,400-square-foot home he helped design, located on the northeast edge of Sonoma overlooking a vineyard. There's a pool out back, paintings of his Hawaiian property, and a staircase lined with large photos of him hobnobbing with all those stars. And the unique mailbox out front is made of the diving helmet in which he broke that world's record.

Twice married and divorced, Ford has two grown children, Sandra and David, who live in Hawaii. His "sweetheart," he says fondly, is local accountant Carol Sue Werner.

FORD WAS BORN in the Marin County town of Ross. But after his parents divorced he attended 32 different elementary schools, many of them on the East Coast, before returning to graduate from San Rafael High School. Even at the tender age of 13, however, he was producing a radio show over the school's intercom, and later he worked at a local radio station, producing a highly rated show called "Junior Jamboree" between stints as a freelance Santa Claus and Easter Bunny.

In 1948 he won the Hearst newspaper chain's forensics contest, competing against 100,000 other students. Then it was off to the College of Marin, then selling encyclopedias in Los Angeles, remodel-

age of 22 and journeying to Alaska "where I sold insulation to Eskimos," and finally returning to California where he sold cars.

His love affair with Hawaii began, he recalls cheerfully, on "a cold, frosty morning in February of 1957. My hands were blue, and there was frost on the ground, and a car drove up with five Hawaiians in it, playing ukeleles. I asked them how the weather was in Hawaii – and then I gave two weeks' notice. My wife and I bought a Cadillac convertible, we filled it up with our stuff, and took it on a steamship to Hawaii."

IT WAS IN 1959 that he volunteered for a bizarre experiment in sensory deprivation, coordinated by the University of Hawaii. He spent 76 hours in a diving suit underwater, eventually hallucinating and having to stop the experiment when the air compressor failed – although he managed to set an underwater endurance record.

Around the same time he also worked for another car dealership, founded "Dave Ford Motors," and eventually worked for a builder for whom he started doing "zany-type commercials" on television.

His big break in television came, however, when he worked for the CBS affiliate in Hawaii, hosting a show called "Hollywood's Greatest Movies," which was often followed by his interviews with big-name celebrities. Another big draw (the show raked in ratings of 79 percent) were his slapstick comedy and the commercials he wrote himself. Sometimes he even built intricate sets that matched those in the movies, then skillfully spliced them into the film so it appeared the sponsors were doing their commercials right in the midst of the action.

Ford became so well-known himself, he recalls with a laugh, that he once was interviewing Charlton Heston when they were besieged by autograph-hounds – who wanted Ford's signature, not the actor's. "He just laughed and asked me how it feels to be a big frog in a small pond – and I said it feels great!"

And when actor Jack Lord later started his own TV show, "Hawaii Five-O," local pundits quipped at a roast, "Jack Lord thinks he's Dave Ford!"

Meanwhile, through most of the '60s, Ford continued interviewing stars – including Cab Calloway, Richard Widmark, Donald O'Connor, Eva Gabor, Wayne Newton, and Harry James. "To me it was fun and a challenge," he said. He still has a photo of himself imitating Charlie McCarthy on Edgar

> **“** I asked them how the weather was in Hawaii – and then I gave two weeks' notice.
>
> — Dave Ford **”**

DAVE FORD PAUSES on the staircase lined with photos of his many interviews with celebrities. (Index-Tribune photo by Windsor Green)

handstand on the railing of his hotel balcony.

In 1968, however, Ford quit to satisfy his yen for travel, and he started an import business, touring the globe. He shot a promotional movie called "Nani," founded his own real estate firm in 1975, and returned to television in the mid-'70s with a talk-show, "The Voice of Hawaii."

He moved to Sonoma in 1987 to help care for his parents, longtime Sonoma residents Ernest and Mary Ford, who are now deceased (a sister, Margo Crawford, still lives here).

Ford kept his holdings in Hawaii, however, and was devastated in 1990 when an estimated $1 million worth of his property fell to the implacable lava flows from the Kilauea volcano. He had hoped to build a resort called "The Last Paradise" there, but

molten stone, he had to concede it could now be called "The Lost Paradise."

Ford's nearby home barely escaped destruction – perhaps because he called in a "kahuna," or Hawaiian priest, to bless the house and protect it from Madame Pele, the Hawaiian goddess of fire. The lava came within 50 feet and encircled the building but left it unscathed – and to this day, Ford has to hike across an eerie lunar landscape to reach the isolated house, which has its own self-contained electricity and water supply.

Ironically, "volcano insurance" wasn't available before the eruption, but it is now – so Ford says with a laugh he may ask the kahuna to come back and curse the house so he can collect insurance on it.

If it works, after all, that'll be just one more anec-

The Sonoma Index-Tribune, January 29, 1993

I returned to the mainland to be with Dad and Mom, but couldn't stay out of the public eye completely. The Sonoma Index-Tribune did a feature article... that didn't include many of the most entertaining stories in this book!

it's an order of magnitude less expensive – or would be if prohibition weren't driving the price up.

Have you ever read of someone committing suicide after smoking grass? Have you ever read of a group smoking pot and then holding up a bank? (They'd probably start laughing on the way to the heist and decide to have a snack instead.) Have you ever seen anyone lying in the gutter with a joint in his hand? Have you ever read of a kid bringing a gun to school and shooting students and teachers when the only drug he used was pot? Have you ever heard a pot user talking about a preemptive strike against anyone – or any country? You won't. (Perhaps that is why the feds are against happy grass. You don't want to hurt or kill anything.)

It's past time to start examining the truth. The above tragedies *do* happen with alcohol and some FDA-approved drugs. But not with cannabis.

Cannabis as psychotherapy for prisoners – including terrorists?

I also foresee a day when violent, sullen, or hostile prisoners are given marijuana during their session with a prison psychiatrist. Marijuana is an herbal "truth serum." It makes it easier to express oneself and it stimulates a *desire to communicate*. It makes the smoker relax. Hostility melts. A prisoner given pot would be more open to psychotherapy, and to genuine rehabilitation.

Instead of torturing al-Qaeda, Taliban, and other terrorist prisoners, as some have astonishingly recommended, we could give them an opportunity to provide useful information after offering them a peaceful drug, cannabis. Hatred is contagious, but so is compassion.

As conditions are today, most prisoners receive no therapy, and are more hostile, resentful, and violent on release than when first incarcerated. To prevent recidivism, it is critical that when the prisoner returns to society, he feels he was helped. The system must be changed so that instead of receiving punishment, prisoners receive treatment for the problem that caused them to be in prison. A prison should be a "hospital" to help, rather than a "penitentiary" to humiliate them. Today, a prison is not a "correctional" facility. If we can't do better, we should call it what it is: a "punishment" facility.

Hawaii state representative John S. Carroll shows courage

State Representative John S. Carroll (R–12th District, Hawaii) had the courage to say he felt that any imprisonment for possession of marijuana was too punitive. "Just to even go to jail for one day is not right." (I've known John since grade school, and he doesn't smoke grass. What he said, after careful investigation of the herb, took bravery.)

Dad becomes a best friend

I cherished being with Dad, but the mobile home was a bit confining. I wanted to have my own home constructed, and hoped that Dad would like to share it. My sister Carol's esteemed friend, and mine, Anita Haywood, told me of a new development on the east side of Sonoma where 17 homes were soon to be constructed. It was only minutes from the sparkling clean, proud, and quaint little Sonoma plaza. Thanks to Anita, I purchased a beautiful lot that backed up to Sebastiani's Vineyard. It was perfect. I felt if I couldn't see the ocean, at least I would enjoy the exquisite vineyard. I began drawing the floor plans, which included a large bedroom and bath for Dad. I would have an architect have the plans make sense structurally. It was a coincidence that I chose the same architect who did the design for the Sebastiani mansion located on the hill above us. I had had the pleasure of a visit or two from Anita while she was in Hawaii a year before. We had gone for hikes, and I enjoyed flying her over the eruption sites, and on to Kona, where she departed for the mainland. She and her former husband, Peter, created the Haywood Winery in Sonoma.

Meeting an artistic lady friend in Sonoma

Shortly after arriving in Sonoma I visited the Chamber of Commerce to pick up a local map. I couldn't help but notice a very attractive lady there before me. She was about five-foot-seven, with black hair in a pageboy style and big, radiant brown eyes. Her hair shimmered from the windows' sunlight, and I couldn't look away. She too was there for a map. I asked where she was from. "Florida. Actually I've been here for about a year, but I still don't know all of the interesting places to see." I introduced myself. "Would you have time to show a stranger what you've found enticing here in the Valley of the Moon?"

"Sure. My name's Anne. I'm an artist. I can show you the art galleries, and some of my work if you'd like." I guessed Anne to be in her mid-thirties. We stopped at a gallery that featured her work. Modern stylish faces of people, with emphasis on the eyes that seemed to be staring right into your soul. Her art was unique. "Do you have more paintings than are here?"

"I do, at my home. Would you like to check them out?"

"I would, but may I first have the pleasure of taking you to lunch?"

"I was on my way to lunch when we met. I'd be delighted," smiled Anne. We took my car.

I phoned Dad to let him know I wouldn't be home for lunch. I mentioned to him that I'd just met a charming lady, and had invited her to lunch.

"Atta boy!" he chuckled. "You have fun, now. Take your time and don't rush home. I'm just fine, son. I'll take my nap. I love you, son."

"I love you too, Dad. See ya later."

After lunch we went to Anne's home, which was also her studio – one very large room. Apparently it had once been a store. In the corner was a king-size bed with various colored pillows artistically arranged. I again marveled at her paintings. A very talented artist. She chuckled. "I noticed you checked out my bed. You like my bed better than my paintings?"

"Your paintings are outstanding," I said, a bit embarrassed. After more chatting I told her about Dad and Mom. I felt safe in asking if she might know the availability of some local grass.

She laughed. "When one has lived in Hawaii, who would want anything else? I hear it's the best. But trust me," she said; "this area is not known only for its grapes!" She continued: "I happen to have a pipe all ready to do its thing. Actually, after a few hits of smoke is when I really get creative in my paintings. It's as if a curtain lifts in my mind. It leads me to creativity that I wouldn't normally have thought of."

A look of regret crossed her face. "The only problem is I have a client coming by, and I really need to do a bit more work on his face." She laughed. "His face needs all the help it can get!" She considered for a moment. "I'm sure he'll give me a lift back to my car. If it would be OK with your dad, would you like to come back here later? I'm a fairly good cook, and I'd like to have you for dinner."

"I'd love it," I said. "I'd like to have *you* for dinner, too."

She chuckled. "What's your most favorite meal?" she asked.

"I love steak, baked potato with lots of butter, and any vegetable. But please don't get anything special for me. I'd be happy just for your company." As we shook hands goodbye, our eyes met. Bingo! I was certain the evening was going to be fun.

When I left Anne, I went to visit Mom. Dad went twice a day, to feed her so he could be certain she ate. Though there were times when she remembered me, frequently she thought I was one of the doctors. It was very depressing.

That evening I cooked dinner for Dad, and told him about my invitation to Anne's for supper. "Good boy! You have fun. You deserve an evening out. You spend most of your time with me."

"I enjoy spending time with you, Pop," I said, and kissed him on the forehead. No matter how depressed he might be over Mom, no one would ever know it. He was amazing, and I was delighted to have this opportunity to be with him.

He reassured me, "And don't worry about me. I'll leave the door unlocked, but if for some reason you don't come home tonight, I'll be just fine." What a guy! I showered, stopped at the store for a bottle of wine and some flowers, and was on my way.

Anne was wearing a black body suit that displayed her attractive figure. As I handed her the bottle and flowers, she took the flowers in one hand and the bottle in the other, and gave me a friendly bear hug. I was wearing a silk aloha shirt which let me feel her warm firm breasts and hard nipples.

"How did it work out with your client?" I asked.

"Super. He likes it, and will pick it up tomorrow. Thank you for the wine, and the flowers – they smell yummy. Please sit down and make yourself at home."

She brought out the pipe, lit it, took a hit, and passed it to me. After a few seconds of holding her breath, she exhaled, and said, "This stuff is getting so expensive, sometimes I even put a paper bag over my head. But I didn't want to freak you out."

"A worthy idea. Let's do it!" I said. Anne produced a large paper bag from a Safeway supermarket, and we took a second hit. I had to laugh as I helped her slide the bag over her pretty head. There was a muffled, "Is this the first time you've had to put a bag over a lady's head, Dave?"

"Come to think of it, there was that one time... naaah, actually this *is* the first time," I said. When it was my turn she got even, and howled louder than I had. It was sweet smoke, not Hawaiian for sure, but nice. I was beginning to feel that floating, warm glow. As I removed the paper bag, she said. "That should encourage your appetite and taste buds." She put a thick steak into the broiler. She had a salad on the table, and peas ready to go into the microwave.

There were a dozen large candles lit around the room, and incense burning. "You shouldn't have gone to all that trouble to fix such a fine meal, but I really appreciate it. The studio is cozy. I like candles a lot." Anne smiled and nodded, "How do you like your steak?"

"Medium rare, or even rare, would be perfect. How about you?"

"I like my meat really rare. I was a cannibal in a past life. Do you like garlic on your steak? I hope so, cause there's lots of garlic on it, and in the salad too. I know I should have asked you, but you looked like a garlic man."

"You're right."

"That's probably 'cause you're a cannibal too," said Anne.

"Yes, I am," I admitted, grinning.

"That's good. I like cannibals," she chirped, with a raised eyebrow. Dinner was a delight, fine food properly cooked and seasoned.

I had no idea if I would be invited for the night; but just in case, I had my overnight bag in the car. Anne brought out the pipe again. "After-dinner smoke?" she purred.

"I really don't smoke when I'm going to drive. But thanks, anyway. The dinner was primo."

"Would your dad mind if you spent the night?"

"No, he wouldn't."

"Then it's settled," she said.

"Not quite," I said. "I'll stay on two conditions."

"And what are they?" Anne looked puzzled.

"First, you let me do the dishes. I have a rule: the person who cooks the meal doesn't do the dishes. Second, you try some Hawaiian smoke."

"I believe I can live with those conditions," she said. Anne worked on her painting while I did the dishes.

"OK, Dave. I'm all set for some Hawaiian smoke. I've never had any."

"I'll be right back," I said.

When I returned from the car with my overnight bag, the lights were out, the bedding was folded down, and Elvis was singing *Love Me Tender* from the stereo. She appeared in the doorway wearing a beach towel that barely covered her thighs and ample breasts. "I hope you don't mind my white body. I don't like the sun."

"You're beautiful," I said.

"What do you have there?" she asked.

"It's a water pipe."

"Why a water pipe?" asked Anne.

"It cools the smoke," I told her. "And to eliminate any actual smoke, vaporizers are now available. They heat the cannabis to just under 400 degrees. All that you inhale then is the vapor."

Anne climbed in bed, pulling the covers up to her neck. I said, "Would you care to check the aroma of these buds, and load the pipe while I change into something more appropriate? I feel overdressed." I handed her the pipe.

When she put the buds to her nose, she moaned, "Ummm. They're delicious. You certainly *are* overdressed," she said with a mischievous smile.

I slipped out of the room, hung up my clothes, put on a robe, and returned. Anne displayed a warm inviting smile. She beckoned with a slender index finger. Only one candle was lit now. I slid into bed as Anne lit the pipe. "I already took a hit. It's sweet and mellow. I want more!" said Anne. We both drew in the sweet mild smoke. After two puffs, we both felt the warm tingling body glow, encouraging us to melt together.

As she moved closer, I reached to put my arm around her, and noticed that the towel had magically vanished, but my focus was on her eyes. "Anne, God put gold glitter in your beautiful big brown eyes." We took our time and slowly kissed and explored each other's bodies with our fingertips. "Your skin is soft as cream, Anne," I whispered. And it was. Her hair had that clean sweet female smell which is so exciting.

She was spectacularly uninhibited. We made love several times. I'm not certain that we ever did sleep, yet in the morning we were full of energy, and happy as two children who had won a wondrous exciting game. As we showered together, I couldn't help but believe that lovemaking gets better all the time.

Anne guided me back toward the bed and I was about to plead for mercy when she turned and grinned at me impishly. "You've earned a good breakfast," she said "We're going to have ham and eggs, and a side order of grits, and we've got plenty of milk." We both did full justice to the meal.

We parted with the understanding that Anne would join Dad and me for dinner at his place that evening. I knew he would enjoy meeting her. I explained his hearing problem – that sometimes he'll pretend to hear and understand when he really can't, by saying things like "wonderful," "good", "uh huh." I gave her an example: One day my son, David, phoned from Hawaii to say hi to his grandfather and me. He told Dad that his wife Cathy had recently been struck by lightning and knocked out for a few moments. Dad responded, "Wonderful!"

Anne and Dad got along famously. Dad found good in every person he met. With his sense of humor, immaculate dress, and his respect for ladies, I never met one that didn't genuinely care for him. Anne and Dad visited while I broiled chicken covered with Hawaiian-style sweet-and-sour sauce, and put the finishing touches on the baked potatoes and steamed broccoli. For dessert, Dad's favorite: apple pie a la mode. Anne left around nine.

● ● ●

Dad's angina was causing him some serious chest pain. He had been taking nitroglycerin pills for about two years, but the pain persisted. I took him to the Sonoma Valley Hospital for a full workup, as ordered by his internist, Dr. Douglas Campbell, and made sure they included every conceivable test to diagnose the problem. Dad was in the hospital for three days.

Each time I visited him he had a big smile and a hug for me. He asked about Mom, and I told him I was seeing her twice a day and feeding her. "So don't you worry about anything, Pop. Did they come up with the results of all those tests?"

"Yes. They said there is nothing the matter with me." He was really very straight, and I'm certain he said the following for my amusement. "Did they think I came here to seduce a few nurses? What more could one expect? It's Friday the 13th!"

I laughed. It *was* Friday the 13th. The first day I visited him, he said, "Give Anne my love." The next day Anne visited him, as did my friend Anita Haywood, and Elisabeth, who had recently moved from Hawaii to the East Bay. At the end of the third day's visit, he said, "Be sure to give my love to *all* the ladies!"

● ● ●

In early 1988 we broke ground for the new home. I spent several hours each day making certain that it came together as per the blueprints and specifications. Dad enjoyed visiting the construction site, too; it's always exciting watching a building come to life.

Anne and I had been having a great time, frequently at her studio-home, occasionally on a trip somewhere, often including a stay at an inn in a romantic location. On day trips, sometimes Sis Margo would join us, and we took Dad to some fun places for picnics, or to the charming Russian River, where so many years ago I'd been a lifeguard. Or we'd picnic at picturesque Spring Lake, with a beautiful backdrop of willow and redwood trees. There's a swimming lagoon and a dock where one can rent various types of boats, only twenty minutes from Sonoma. A couple of times while relaxing by the lake I noticed college students passing joints around with their friends. One fellow looked my way one Sunday afternoon and then I heard them laugh. They were probably saying, "That old guy has no idea what we're smoking!" I was tempted to say, "Hey! Don't be so stingy with that joint!" With Dad there, however, I didn't feel that would be cool. Or, as those students might say, coolio!

During the 14 months that I lived with Dad, we spent several evenings a week just visiting and getting to really know each other. He became my closest friend. He knew I smoked grass, but he never mentioned it. Out of respect for him I didn't smoke in his home. I'm sure he would have looked the other way, but I wouldn't do anything that might offend him. Many of his friends were heavy cigarette smokers and drank too much liquor. Many of them died from the toxicity, but that was socially acceptable and legal. I understood: it's perfectly acceptable to die from alcohol complications, but not to have a safe high from grass.

One evening Anne, with a joint in her pretty hand, smiled and said, "I'm glad to see that lots of college students I've talked to have learned about the dangers of crack addiction and other dangerous drugs and many have switched to pot. If the government was honest, it would be glad."

"You're right, Anne," I said.

The new home was completed in September of 1988 – just as Anne left to take up an offer to teach art at a Florida college, a job she had applied for prior to our meeting, and one she greatly desired. It was with reluctance and a heavy heart that I kissed her goodbye and watched her drive away in her car loaded with paintings.

First high school reunion – forty years later

Elisabeth, with her long blonde hair and gray eyes, had originally come from Vienna, and has never lost her intriguing accent. She had lived in Hawaii and then moved to Palo Alto, about 75 miles south of Sonoma. She joined me to attend my first San Rafael High School reunion in 40 years. My best friend and "adopted brother" since high school, Glenn "Vern" Hughes, traveled up from Los Angeles, and brought along his beautiful 20-year-old daughter, Jennifer. He'd never lost his great sense of humor. Throughout the reunion, he introduced his daughter to everyone as his wife, and she went along with the joke. He received many envious smiles as he acted avidly in love with her. I also had the thrill of dancing with the first girl I'd ever made love to. Remember me hiding from her father in the family's wine vat? Janice was there with her husband. He was a great sport, and encouraged her and me to dance.

When I moved to my new home, Sis Margo moved in with Dad. As soon as Dad was released from the hospital we all went together to see Mom. Dad was frail but spry. He leaned over and gave her a hug. When he saw her rapid decline from just a few days earlier, he asked, "Mom, do you know who I am?"

She looked him right in the eye, and said, "Don't *you* know who you are?"

"Good one, Mom!" I said. We usually didn't know if she really knew who we were, and I quit asking her after I got too many wrong answers. More than anyone else, she recognized Dad. He'd say, "Mom, you'll be home soon, and everything will be fine. We'll go for picnics with Dave and Margo, and we'll have fine times, just like the good old days." With eyes staring into space, she'd smile. When he turned his head away, I noted tears running down his cheeks. We all knew this was her last stop. Still, she never forgot to kiss him goodbye. She would tilt her head up from the wheelchair and pucker her lips, like a baby bird about to be fed. His love for her and his love and zest for life were still present, but I began to notice that whenever he gave people a hug or a handshake goodbye, he did it as though it might be the last time he would ever see them. When he shook hands, he would place his other hand over theirs. Wouldn't it be lovely if we all, always, possessed those feelings? I spent as much time with Dad as possible.

At Christmas I threw an open house party, mainly because it was Dad's 97th birthday. I asked a new friend I'd recently met at a party, Trudy King, to be my hostess, and she was perfect. Dad was all decked out in a navy-blue suit and white shirt, with a Christmas bow tie in green and red. Almost every one of the 80 or 90 guests knew him, as many of the folks that I invited were his friends from the park, and he had a great time. I wanted to show him off to my friends, too, so the party was nicely mixed with older and younger people, and included my neat new neighbors. I've never had greater neighbors, and parents, than here. They frequently invited their neighbors to join them for

My best friend – my "brother" – Glenn "Vern" Hughes, enjoying our 40th high school reunion with my companion Elisabeth

"Ready to go to the party, daddy?" When our comedian Sandy was four she said, "Daddy, I don't know if I like that hair that grows out of your nose and turns into a mustache." Does she still look a little dubious here?

parties. When liquor wasn't being served, their children were frequently present, polite and respectful to the adults. It was a delightful evening.

The new year arrived rapidly. Dad loved my new home, but he decided to remain at the mobile home park, where he had many friends. He visited often though, driving his own car. He said, "I think I might decide to live to be 100!"

"You can do it, Pop!" I said. There is nothing finer than living to a ripe age, so long as you have quality of life. And Dad had it. He retained his marvelous sense of humor and his enthusiasm for life, and he was still a sharp dresser. I was proud of my Pop. He could easily make that 100 mark; I was certain of it. I was pleased too that Dr. Campbell and family lived across the street. I felt that if Dad really needed him, I could run across the street, grab him, and take him to Dad, and that caring doctor would come, black bag in hand.

Death doesn't take a holiday

On the evening of March 8, 1989, I joined Dad on one of his twice-a-day visits to Mom, as I often did. He carried on his loving routine of feeding her, chatting as if the conversation weren't one-sided, and hugging her. The next morning around 9 a.m. Margo phoned from his home. "I think you better come on over here. Something's wrong with Dad." I didn't bother to ask what was wrong; I just got over there as fast as I could. As I walked in Margo said, "Dad's dead."

I didn't believe it. Dead? How could he be? We had just seen each other and visited Mom the evening before. I ran into his bedroom. There he was lying on his bed. His cheeks were pink, as always. I put my hand on his head. He was warm. I tried to get a pulse. There wasn't one. I ran to the phone and dialed 911. Then I returned to him. Kissed him on the forehead. "Dad, please be alive. I love you. Don't go away." I stroked his face and opened one of his eyes. It was glassy. I began mouth-to-mouth resuscitation.

The 911 crew arrived, and rushed in to do their job. After an anguished time, one of the men said, "I'm sorry. It's too late. He's gone." I was empty. I felt he had finally admitted to himself that Mom would never come home, and that it was time to go.

Sister Margo was OK. I went home as soon as Dad was taken away. I phoned my children and our sister Carol in Oregon. I called my friend Jacqueline in Hawaii. Jacqueline was always there when she was needed. Sandy flew in from Hilton Head Island in South Carolina, and was a great comfort, as were Carol and her husband Harold. Jacqueline arrived with several boxes of red anthuriums, orchids, birds of paradise – all of the tropical Hawaiian flowers that Dad had loved.

A single large white anthurium in one of the boxes captured my eye when Jacqueline was doing the flower arrangements. The memorial took place at the First Congregational Church in Sonoma, where the Rev. David McCracken, Dad's "second son," conducted a beautiful service. My eyes kept being drawn to that single white anthurium; it seemed like an angel that had come to meet Dad's spirit. The church pews were filled, and many members stood to eulogize this man who had loved so many people. We brought Mom in a wheelchair. Sis Carol and I held her, and told her several times that Dad had passed away. She only stared.

I began visiting Mom twice a day. I hugged her and fed her as Dad had done. I told her how much Dad and all of us loved her, and what a wonderful Mom she was. On May 15, Mother's Day, 1989, I was getting ready to go visit her when the convalescent center phoned to tell me she had died during the early hours of the morning, less than 10 weeks after Dad's passing. We held a memorial service for her, and then sat down to discuss their wishes. I wanted to do it while Sandy was still visiting. Dad and Mom had told us that they wished to be buried at sea. The cost was $300 to $500, which was reasonable, but the disinterested attitude of the fisherman was painful. "We're here to fish, not deliver ashes." A new plan was in order.

Burying dad and mom at sea, illegally

Sandy and I decided there was no better time than the present. I taped Mom's and Dad's boxes of ashes together and placed them in a double paper bag. On top of the boxes of ashes, to weigh them down and provide some innocent-looking camouflage we placed a six-pack of beer. We took the ferry from scenic Larkspur to San Francisco on a lovely calm Sunday afternoon. The boat happened to be the *Sonoma* – so appropriate. The perfect weather drew all the passengers topside, and the observation deck was crowded. We passed close to San Quentin Prison, where I'd met Bogart and Bacall years before, and soon we were out in the bay. As San Francisco crept closer I was reminded of the many times that Dad had driven our car onto the ferryboat in Sausalito to go to San Francisco, before the Golden Gate Bridge was completed, and I remembered how much he loved the bridge.

It was more than frowned upon to throw anything over the side of the boat (especially your Mom and Dad); it was illegal. The bridge loomed over us to starboard, and Sandy and I made our way to the port rail. I opened a can of beer and pretended to drink from it. As we were passing the center of the bridge, I yelled out, "Look! There's the Golden Gate Bridge!" Not the most creative attention-getter I'd ever crafted, without the help of a puff of pot, but it worked. As all the passengers stared at the elegant bridge with its ruddy towers soaring toward the heavens, I said quietly, "We love you, Mom and Dad. Rest in peace," and I dropped the bag into the bay. It was comforting to have my precious daughter with me.

"Humans and animals have always sought intoxication"

In one of many efforts to forget the loss of Mom and Dad I went to the library and picked out a book that had just been published, *Intoxication; Life in Pursuit of Artificial Paradise* by Dr. Ronald Siegel, pharmacologist with the School of Medicine, University of California at Los Angeles. Dr. Siegel is among the growing group of experts who have concluded that animals, including humans, have always sought intoxication, and that the quest for altered consciousness is a force as natural as the drive for water, food, or sex. They call it the *fourth drive*.[60]

For proof, these experts point to the animal world – from birds to cats, from elephants to jaguars, animals all seek out mind-altering plants[61] – and to a human history filled with drug use – from Sumerians who slurped up alcohol 5,000 years ago to South American Indians who have chewed coca leaves for thousands of years. Filipinos and others in the islands of the South Pacific drink *kava,* an intoxicating mixture made from the root of the pepper plant *(Piper methysticum).*[62] Every country has some acceptable way for its citizens to get high. Our country has chosen alcohol, caffeine, and nicotine. Politicians, with ever-growing contributions, protect those industries while users fall dead.

The eruption never stops

The beautiful properties consumed by molten lava refused to satisfy the hunger of the fire goddess, Madam Pele. All of noble Kalapana was being covered. In May, 1990, the lava crept closer to the Star of the Sea Catholic church, and the congregation moved the church off the site just in time, in two days working 24 hours a day. On May 18, President Bush declared Kalapana a federal disaster area. My jewel of oceanfront land with its own velvety black sand beach, lagoon, stream, and coconut trees was now in imminent peril. It was located across the street from colorful Walter Yamaguchi's Kalapana Store and Drive Inn. On June 6, the store was destroyed by lava. Just hours later so was my last piece of paradise. I received a letter from Civil Defense Director Harry Kim, confirming the destruction of my sun-drenched, moon-kissed 2.13 acres of Eden. He mentioned that it had been his boyhood dream to own that piece of land. Now, we shared the loss of the dream that once was one of the most beautiful spots in the Hawaiian islands. By the end of June, the eruption had claimed 165 homes and other structures, and had caused at least $70 million in damage.

May 10, 1990. Sonoma county's largest daily newspaper, The Santa Rosa *Press Democrat*, featured a front-page story by correspondent Dennis Wheeler. There was a color photo of me standing before a four-by-eight mural in my den of what had been the world-famous Kalapana Black Sand Beach. Today that beach is an ocean of smoldering rock. The headline read:

> LAVA TURNS 'LAST PARADISE' INTO 'LOST CAUSE'
> Sonoma – Dave Ford's posh Sonoma home and his impressive list of achievements suggest a man who is out of the ordinary, but his latest distinction is one he could do without.
>
> Ford, a businessman and former talk show host who currently lives in Sonoma, may have lost more land to the volcanic eruptions than any other private property owner in Hawaii. To date, he estimates, $1 million of his property has fallen to the lava flows from the Kilauea volcano on Hawaii's southeast coast.

The story continued for three columns.

Going to Southeast Asia – and possible death

My old buddy Vern Hughes was Director of Government & Community Relations for the Port of Los Angeles. He was also Executive Chairman of the Mayor's Council for Sister Cities, under Mayor Tom Bradley. Vern had received an invitation from the Consul General of the Republic of Indonesia to visit in January of 1991, and he invited me to join him on the trip. I agreed to meet him in Los Angeles on December 30. When I arrived, Vern introduced me to Mayor Bradley, whom we would next see at the Conference of Sister Cities in Jakarta, LA's sister city, a few weeks later.

The next evening at one of the New Year's Eve parties, I talked with a Deputy District Attorney of Los Angeles, and brought up the subject of marijuana versus alcohol. I was curious to know his opinions, and freely admitted my having smoked grass off and on for almost fifty years. I told him it enhanced my creativity, relieved my back muscle spasms, was fun, a relaxant, and a sexual plus. His feeling was that marijuana is a minor drug compared to alcohol, "but it's illegal." I acknowledged that obvious point, but pointed out the hypocrisy of keeping that "minor drug compared to alcohol" illegal, while fine liquor was flowing all around us. Since I don't care for hangovers, I went outside and took a couple of hits off a joint.

Vern and I left Los Angeles International Airport for Jakarta at 8:10 p.m. on January 3, 1991. A few miles out of Honolulu, it seemed that the majority of passengers, mostly foreigners, and the flight attendants began chain-smoking.

Me, in a monastery?

On January 6, 1991, we left Jakarta for Thailand. In Bangkok the weather was similar to Indonesia's: oppressive. Vern said, "I know a Thai monk who now lives in New York, but maintains ties to his life here. How would you like to spend four or five days in a monastery?"

"It would be a new experience. Let's do it," I said, words that dear Hazel frequently used. We took a bus for the 20-mile trip from Bangkok. Above the windshield was an area about four feet wide, covered with glass. Behind the glass was white cotton. Pressed into the cotton was a centipede the size of a healthy crab, as well as a tarantula and a scorpion that was six inches long. I suspected they weren't being advertised for sale as souvenirs. More probably they were intended as an aid to nonverbal communication in an emergency: if one assaulted you, before you fell unconscious you might have time to scream and point to its twin imbedded in the cotton. The thought made my skin crawl.

At the monastery we were welcomed like family. Visitors were a treat they rarely experienced. One of the monks asked me if I would care to teach English reading, and I was happy to oblige. I used an English children's story book, "The Three Bears." The little monks, some as young as five years old, would sound out the words as I slowly read them. When they failed to understand the meaning of a word I was asked, "Make us do it again!" I was reminded of the time I was their age, learning to tie my shoes. I was rewarded with "Thank you, Mr. Dave."

Vern and I were each assigned to share the living space of one of the monks. Their quarters consisted of cubicles about 12 feet square, enclosed by screening. The "beds" were pieces of ply-board about 30 inches wide. No mattresses. No blankets. No pillows. I was assigned to bunk with 23-year-old Nari.

We retired about 10 p.m. and were scheduled to rise at dawn. Owing to the tremendous humidity and heat, I was sleeping in my undershorts. It must have been around 1 a.m. when I awoke with a start. Something was crawling on my body; I could feel too many feet walking across my chest. Lying in pitch dark, I was virtually paralyzed, fearing this... thing... would inject me with some deadly venom. Surrounded by 450 monks, I didn't think it would be appropriate to scream; and besides, that might startle the beast – the *last* thing I wanted to do. Was it a scorpion? A centipede? It edged toward my left ear, and then changed directions, crawling slowly toward my stomach. Thank Buddha, I had underwear on. But there was no light; I couldn't see the thing, and that was increasingly unnerving. After about five minutes I called out in the lowest voice possible, "Nari. Nari. It's me, David. Can you hear me?" The only answer was snoring. By now I was drenched in sweat from raw terror.

With the first rays of daybreak, I was able to make out the thing that was now crawling from my knee to my left thigh. It appeared to be a four-inch cockroach. I knocked it off me so hard that it hit Nari in the face, waking him up. He picked it up. "It only bug. No hurt. No bite. Sleep." I fell thankfully into a deep sleep for about an hour.

8:30 a.m. January 17, 1991. I was preparing an English reading lesson when Nari approached me. He had tears in his eyes. He looked at the ground as he spoke, "David. You kill innocent people?"

Realizing at once that the long-impending Gulf War must have started, I answered with a guilty-sounding, "No."

"Please. You come," he said.

There were 25 monks watching an antiquated 12-inch black-and-white television set. The sky appeared almost black with bombs exploding from aircraft, lighting up the sky as if it was the Fourth of July. Nari turned to me and said, with pain in his voice, "David. You say you no like kill people."

"That is true, Nari. I feel all killing is wrong."

"Your President do what you want him do?"

"No, Nari, it's the other way around," I answered feebly. Most of the young monks were openly crying.

I felt ill. My energy had been low for days, and I was having an increasingly hard time keeping up with my fast-paced, high-energy traveling companion and best friend, Vern. Perhaps it was the food. Perhaps it was the war; I had dreaded this conflict. I realized that Saddam Hussein was a grisly leader. If President Bush wanted to murder Hussein, why didn't he do it through covert action rather than killing thousands of innocent people? Our country, with its weapons of mass destruction, was like the San Francisco 49ers playing against a kindergarten team. One had to wonder, what is the *real* reason that we want to control Iraq? Life is so precious; it's horrifying to think of it ending – violently, abruptly – for so many people. I had no doubt that in minutes hundreds, perhaps thousands, would be dead or dying. And, of course, there was the possibility of our own young people in the military losing their lives, and for what? And if they didn't die, they could pick up some foreign disease, or be exposed to poison gas. Was this war for oil?

Can we name a country that we've been to war with that later didn't join us as a trading partner? So why kill to begin with? What are we teaching our young people? That violence can solve problems quickly? That's the mentality of street gangs. I felt an urge to leave the monastery, so Vern and I headed back to Jakarta, where I made plans for my return to Sonoma.

I feel a poison dart aimed at my back

I was walking alone down a narrow road in Jakarta after our return from the monastery, and feeling ill, when a burly man approached me. "What your name? Where you from?" were familiar questions.

"David. USA."

He held what appeared to be a hand-carved cane. "You buy?" He mentioned a price equivalent to $30.

"No, thank you," I said.

He continued following me. He pulled the cane apart. It was a blowgun. He produced a metal dart and slipped it into the barrel of the blow gun. "You have boy?"

"Yes, I have boy," I said.

"Boy kill birds – or other things – with this," he said.

"No, thank you. My boy no like kill anything."

"My wife out to here." He put his hands out in front of his stomach to indicate advanced pregnancy. He quoted a reduced price, $25.

"You are good salesman, but I no buy. Thank you. Where you from?" I asked.

"Borneo. We hunters. We know how kill with poison dart. Make good blowguns." He put the blowgun to his lips and puffed. I saw nothing come out of the blowgun. I kept walking. Fifty feet down the road I came to a tree about four inches wide. In the center was the dart from the blowgun!

Now he confronted me. "I need money. You give me money *now!*" Had I not been feeling so ill, I might have been thinking more clearly. I should have just given him the money for his wife, and told him to keep the blowgun for his own son.

I wasn't that together. I said, "Thank you. But I do not want blowgun." I abruptly turned right, toward a hotel.

"Dirty murdering American! You will be sorry!" My back was toward him, and it felt like a bull's-eye that was about to be scored. I walked another 10 paces, waiting to feel the point of a poison dart. I felt nothing but nausea. I slowly turned around. He was gone.

How it feels to be the ugly American

I returned to our hotel. "Ol' buddy," I said to Vern, "I feel lousy, and can't seem to shake it. I'm going to head to Sonoma tomorrow. I know you have to stay here for Mayor Bradley. Could I have a key made to your home? I left my jacket there."

"Of course," said Vern, "But you'll miss one heck of a party. It's likely that you're just not used to the food." He handed me the key.

I walked down the street to where I had seen a man with a key-duplicating machine. "How much cost to make key?" I asked. He quoted me a price comparable to 25 cents U.S. "Good. Please make now," I said.

As he placed the key in a clamp and started the little motor that honed out the ridges of the key, he yelled out something. All I understood was "American."

Slowly a crowd of at least 10 young men gathered around me. The key maker finished his work – but he placed both Vern's key and my copy in his pocket. I held out the money.

He ignored the cash in my hand. "You American?" One of the young men had a bicycle chain in his hand. As he looked at me he started to swing it in circles.

I lied. "Canadian," I said.

Before I could stop him, one of the young men reached into my inside jacket, and snatched my passport. He waved it over his head. "American!" he shouted. The menacing crowd grew.

A large man I guessed to be in his mid-40s held out something from his pocket and shouted angrily. The crowd backed off. He came to where I was, and placed a beefy hand around my upper arm. He then said something to the key maker, who yelled at him. With a tight hold on my arm, he said to me, "Give the man two American dollars at once." I complied. The keys were tossed on the ground. I picked them up.

With authority, my captor shouted something to the man who held my passport. The man spat at me and yelled, "Murderer! Bush mad dog! You go home Yankee, and kill him!" He then thrust my passport at the man holding my arm, who slipped it into his pocket. He spoke close to my ear. "I was educated in the United States," he said "I am with the police. I have told them I am taking you to police headquarters. Keep your back to the wall and your hand on your wallet."

He now had my arm bent up behind my back. He yelled something I couldn't understand. He began pushing me down the street. I tried to pull away from him. He bent my arm so hard it hurt badly. I yelled out. The crowd pulled back to give him room, and cheered him on! They were swearing at me. One yelled out, "To you American dogs, courage is murdering helpless human beings!" The police officer pushed me roughly toward a Mercedes with police insignia. A man from the crowd opened the back door for him. The officer propelled me in so hard that I went head-first onto the leather seat. He slammed the door shut. As he started the car, he locked all four doors. "What hotel are you at?"

"The Sari Pan Pacific," I said.

"You are most fortunate that I was where I was. You had better remain inside your hotel. When do you leave Jakarta?"

"I'm going back to the States tomorrow," I said.

"Have the front desk call a cab for you. They'll arrange a friendly driver. Do not take an airport bus."

"I thank you from the bottom of my heart," I said. "Can I pay you?"

"No. Who knows? One day I may be back in the U.S., and you might do the same for me."

"You bet! And thank you, my brother," I said. As I got out of the car, he handed me my passport.

When I finally arrived home in Sonoma, I was exhausted. It was comforting to see my friendly neighbors and Trudy and sister Margo again.

Our sojourn in the monastery was an adventure for me, but apparently had a more lasting effect on Vern, who had been into philosophy since high school. He became an ordained Buddhist minister, and today he teaches Theravada Buddhism classes and performs weddings at Thousand Oaks, California. (Incidentally, he doesn't use cannabis.)

● ● ●

By early April of 1991, Hawaii had written off the home in Royal Gardens because it was surrounded and isolated by lava. The eruption had continued non-stop for eight years, and there was no sign it would stop. I then wrote the home off with the IRS – or tried to. The IRS gave me the finger. One of my neighbor friends, hearing about my problem, told me that her CPA was outstanding, and introduced me to Carol Sue Werner, a petite blue-eyed blond. Carol Sue and I talked for only a minute before she said, "I can work you in during lunch tomorrow, and we can talk about your problem. Is that OK with your schedule?"

"I prefer a little more privacy when I talk taxes," I said. "How about a salad for lunch at my home tomorrow?"

"Fine, I'll see you at 12:30 at your home." We exchanged business cards, and she was gone. Over lunch at my home the following day, Carol Sue made a fast study of my overall tax situation, and it was obvious she had a keen eye for facts and their implications. I retained her to represent me with the IRS.

Diagnosed with cancer; marijuana becomes my medicine

My hopes that coming home would cure my ills were dashed in mid-June, when my doctor told me that I had cancer, located near the prostate gland. The surgeon, Dr. Elboim, recommended I have the tumor removed as soon as possible. I didn't want surgery if I could avoid it, but after a second opinion I accepted the test results and the proposed treatment.

I checked into the Sonoma Valley Hospital for surgery on June 20, 1991. Afterward, the pain was excruciating. The nurses were injecting me with morphine every hour to control it. It felt as though my skin was crawling. When I went home, I was on two Vicodin painkillers every four hours, but at times the pain was so intense that I started to pass out. Carol Sue frequently came over and gave me a massage, cooked meals, and provided TLC. I found myself intrigued with this lady. I cared deeply for Trudy King; but Trudy wanted permanency and I didn't. I felt that I was holding her back. It was painful giving Trudy up. It was also painful to learn that I had cancer and to recover from the surgery.

After regaining some strength, I felt a strong desire to visit my children and my grandson in Hawaii. Carol Sue joined me on the trip. I was apprehensive about my health; I didn't know whether I could stand more surgeries or whether I even had a future. Carol Sue always had a smile, and would say such things as "I'm almost as tall as you are." (I'm a little over six feet tall and she's 5' 2".)

On July 26, the children joined us at a secluded beach on the Kona side of the Big Island of Hawaii, where we were camping. Swimming, camping, and visiting with the children and grandson eased the pain for me; and Carol Sue was very taken with the little one. She and I spent several days in that exotic paradise, where the sunsets were like melting gold. The water was warm and gentle; the waves friendly and soothing. Riding over bumps was very painful, though. A premonition told me that the surgeries were not over.

On August 21, back in Sonoma, I was admitted to the hospital for a another operation. Again, I was in serious pain after the surgery, and unable to sleep; the morphine doesn't always do its job.

This time, though, I had come prepared. Still connected to the IV and to a urinary catheter, I struggled out of bed and almost collapsed from weakness. I made it to the closet where my jacket hung, and after a bit of fumbling pulled out a joint. I hauled the IV tower into the bathroom with me. By now I was dizzy; sweat dripped from my face, and pain and nausea almost overwhelmed me. I thought I was going to pass out but I was afraid to press the call button on the wall.

I lit the joint and took a puff. Good Lord, I thought, how embarrassing if I pass out in here and they find me with a joint in my hand! I was scared stiff: would they call the police? I took another hit. Then the miracle came to pass. Peace enveloped me. I stopped sweating. My body relaxed. The pain faded and I felt drowsy. My trip back to bed was easy and almost painless. I fell into a deep, restorative sleep, and awoke three hours later as a food tray was placed before me. I ate ravenously.

All the hospital medications were helpful. They were also toxic and addictive. Again I was released from the hospital and returned to my own bed. The grass was in some ways better for easing the pain and relaxing my muscles then those prescribed painkillers. I now understood why the Chinese, thousands of years ago, used marijuana as an anesthetic for major surgeries. They mixed the resin of the cannabis plant with wine, administered it to the patient, and within an hour they were able to begin cutting. In the months following I had four more surgeries, and I continued to medicate myself with marijuana. I still have an unfilled prescription for Vicodin.

In New Zealand baby lambs are better known as lamb chops!

In case the cancer couldn't be stopped, I wanted to make sure David met his New Zealand relatives. I was living one day at a time, enjoying each sunrise, and I also hungered for a closer relationship with my son. I invited him to join me on a three-week visit to New Zealand. We left on February 11, 1992. It was my second visit to the country. I wanted David to see for himself where his grandfather had lived as a boy; to enjoy, as his granddad had, the magnificent white sand beaches that stretched for hundreds of miles around these very special islands; and to revel in the sight of the lush rolling hills, trimmed as neat as golf courses by sheep and lambs. It's a beautiful country – seventy million sheep can't be wrong!

One evening early in our visit my cousin Ken said, "I'm going to kill a lamb for dinner."

"Isn't it hard to kill those cute baby lambs?" I asked.

Ken replied, "I don't see them as cute baby lambs. I see them as lamp chops!"

It was a fine visit with loving cousins. David and I hiked Mt. Maunganui, in Tauranga. We visited the Karangahake gold fields, and crossed the Owharoa Falls of the Ohinemuri River on a flimsy-looking suspension bridge, about three feet wide and at least a hundred feet above boiling rapids and jagged rocks, held up by a single tenuous little cable. It swayed crazily with the wind. When David and I were halfway across, Ken's wife Nola, with a well-developed sense of rough Kiwi humor, began jumping up and down on the makeshift bridge. David and I crouched and held on to the cables, and tried vainly to laugh.

As we toured the island, I fell into conversation with people and asked questions.

> Question to a police officer: "Why does one read of so few people being shot in New Zealand?"
> Answer: "Handguns are illegal, and the police don't carry weapons unless they're chasing a criminal that is known to be armed. The criminal types that do have handguns know that if they shoot a police officer, our police department will never give up going after them. Rifles

are allowed with a permit for special uses. However, bullets must be kept in a different area of the home."

Question: "Don't you have something comparable to a National Rifle Association?"

Answer: "A what?!"

Question to a magistrate: "Why is there no death penalty in New Zealand?"

Answer: "Many years ago there was a hanging. We learned too late that one of the men whom we hanged was innocent. We also learned that the death penalty is not a deterrent to murder."

Question to a nurse: "What are some of the ways AIDS is controlled?"

Answer: "We do constant education. Also, when we realized several years ago that one of the ways AIDS is spread is through the use of dirty needles, the law was changed so adults may now purchase syringes without a doctor's prescription."

Question to a waitress: "Why is there no tipping in New Zealand, and how do you feel about that?"

Answer: "We receive a fair wage, usually $9 or $10 an hour. Most of us would consider a tip a handout, humiliating." (I understand that some tourists, and now a few local residents, will tip anyway. As usual, too many tourists screw up a good thing.)

Question to a cab driver: "Is prostitution legal in New Zealand?"

Answer: "No, but if it's known that the 'house' is engaged in safe sex, the police look the other way. We're hoping that in the next few years it will be legalized. In that way, the women can be protected, educated, and regularly tested."

Question to a half-dozen residents: "Is marijuana close to being legal in New Zealand?"

Answer: "No, but it will happen. A lot of people smoke it, and it's known to be far less harmful than alcohol."

I was asked, "No one in America gets killed over pot, do they?" I had to reply, "Unfortunately, all too often: ordinary people are terrified –

and some innocents are killed – when police crash through their front doors in midnight drug raids. Sick and dying patients are prevented from using the only medicine that works for them. Young kids are shot in turf wars between gangs. So *many* deaths!"

Still in pain

Back home again, I visited my caring surgeon for a checkup. After examining me, he told me that the cancer had returned and that I needed another operation. In a conversation with my revered friend Trudy, she gave me the names of a couple who had had cancer and were cured by a radical change in their nutrition. That sounded weird but I soon learned otherwise. What I read decided me that I needed to take charge of my cancer and my life. I had been brought up with the training that dairy products, eggs, and meat would keep us healthy for life. Right? Wrong. I was searching for alternate methods to stop the cancer, and I learned that the old adage is true, "You are what you eat." (A scary thought sometimes!)

Weight gain, cancer, and other diseases corrected by diet change?

If you've ever had a weight problem it can easily be corrected. We've been programmed by billions of dollars in advertising to eat the wrong foods. Fad dieting does not work. Are you going to drink Slim-Fast for the rest of your life? It may be nourishing, but it would soon be boring. It's not difficult to be trim for the rest of your life, the easy, non-dieting way. Have you ever known a true vegetarian who was fat? The trick is to eat foods that are *not* fattening. Then you will keep those extra pounds off permanently.

Not only have we been denied the truth with respect to marijuana, we have also been denied proven information on how we can frequently be cured of cancer, heart disease, diabetes, and other degenerative diseases. *Detoxifying the whole body and changing the diet are the basis of the treatment,* a change that is simple and inexpensive.

We were taught in school that the "Four Basic Food Groups" include meats and dairy products, which we should eat every day. We were educated for this myth by the powerful National Dairy Council ("Got Milk?"), McDonald's, cattlemen's associations, and others, who provided the posters for schools. Almost all of us bought the propaganda. The results are obesity, constipation, high blood pressure, and more.[63]

The teeth of carnivores are designed to tear apart raw meat, but human teeth are mostly flat for grinding grains and vegetables. Had I not eaten junk food for years, I'm certain I wouldn't have had cancer to begin with. Most of us don't act on such information; but let's give it a try. (Close your mouth if you're still with me.) Osteoporosis, an illness that results in porous, fragile bones, is practically unknown among African women who frequently bear as many as 10 children, sometimes in the fields where they are working. They return to work minutes after the baby is born, and they *don't* drink milk to replace the calcium that the baby's getting. *Unprocessed vegetables contain sufficient calcium and protein to keep mother and child healthy.*

The alleged need for all that protein is based on research dealing largely with the nutritional needs of rats. At birth, rats require 10 times the amount of protein that a human baby does. In humans, an overabundance of protein washes calcium from the body into the kidneys, leaving calcium-deficient bones and an increased risk of kidney stones.[64]

How teen pregnancies could be reduced

Fat in the diet can affect hormones, and the hormones estrogen and testosterone are involved in reproduction and sexual functions. It was enlightening to learn from *The McDougall Plan* how a rich diet that emphasizes fats causes youngsters to develop sexually about four years earlier than those raised on a low-fat diet. Girls on low-fat diets reach menarche and begin menstrual periods at about 16 years. Those on fat-rich diets often begin at age 12 or earlier; and for them, menopause begins about four years later. Boys on fat-rich diets also reach puberty earlier. Until Japanese girls switched to an American diet of rich foods, they began menstrual periods at an average age of 16.5 on a diet consisting largely of rice and vegetables, compared to American girls at 12.5 years of age on rich foods.[65]

A mournful discovery

My Sis Margo and I frequently exchanged dinner invitations. Margo's gourmet cooking included roast beef, steaks, heavy gravies, and baked potatoes with lots of sour cream and bacon bits – all the foods I used to eat and love. As I got away from rich foods and into the vegetarian way, I was losing my taste for such meals. I invited Margo to my home for dinners, trying to convert her to vegetarianism. I gave her a copy of *The McDougall Plan* and a set of McDougall's audio tapes.

Margee wouldn't budge. She continued to pour several teaspoons of sugar into her coffee, to nibble on Danish, and to prepare meals where meat and fats were the main feature. I ran down her major health problems: "Sis, you have diabetes, you recently had your gall bladder removed, you have high blood pressure. Most of the problems you've had – headaches, stuffy nose, hypertension, kidney stones, tooth decay, constipation, obesity – have all been due to eating rich foods. Isn't it time to quit?"

Margee answered, "I sure do love you, Dave. Thanks for trying to help, but it's just not my cup of tea."

On December 3, 1993, Margee phoned me: "Dave, I have the flu. I feel rotten!" I shopped for her and phoned her twice a day to check on her. On the morning of December 7th I phoned her several times without getting an answer, so I decided to go over. I got to her mobile home around 11 a.m. The front door was unlocked. I didn't want to awake her if she was asleep so I went in quietly. The house was cold. I noticed an empty gallon milk jug and a bottle of chocolate syrup on the kitchen counter. Still no sight or sound of her. She was probably asleep under her electric blanket. I went into her bedroom. She wasn't there. Perhaps she had felt better and gone out for a walk. I casually stuck my head into her bathroom. There she was, sitting on the toilet, leaning up against the wall. "Sorry, Margee. I thought you weren't home. ...Are you OK?" No answer. I ventured in. She didn't move. I touched her arm. It was cold. She was dead.

We held a memorial service at the mobile home for her. Dozens of friends attended, as well as Margee's children, Scott, Brian, and Noori. (Brian may one day be a nationally recognized author, Noori is a poet, and Scott is a builder.) I hope the next funeral that I have to attend will be my own. The death certificate stated that she died from diabetic coma. A week earlier, Margee had turned 66. There was little question that the wrong foods caused her tragic death. Wrong diet causes hundreds of thousands of unnecessary deaths each year.

Hoping to save my children from the "proper" food

I've always been deeply concerned about my children's eating habits. I feel responsible for educating them on the American diet that we were exposed to as children. I sent *The McDougall Plan* and a set of his tapes to each of them. My son has allergies, which leave him with a chronically stuffy nose. I'm convinced his allergies developed from the incorrect diet I brought him up on. With my dad's colon cancer, and my cancer,

I felt it was imperative that those whom I love watch their diets carefully. I wanted none of my family to experience what my father and I and Margee went through. (That includes you, dear reader.)

● ● ●

In early January, 1993, it was cold and wet here in Sonoma. Carol Sue asked what I would like to do for my birthday. I said, "I'd like to be in Hawaii, visiting my children and my grandson." A few days later Carol Sue presented me with two-round trip tickets to Hawaii, a wonderful 65th birthday gift. As always, it was beautiful when we arrived in Kona. A large friendly turtle kept us company when we went swimming the next day; and while food was cooking we sat on the golden sand, smoked a joint, and enjoyed the grandeur of a Hawaiian sunset.

David, Cathy, Scotty, and Sandy joined us at the beach for two days of camping. It was the best time yet with my seven-year-old grandson, who was already learning to surf. When I started to talk about healthy nutrition, Cathy said: "We don't have to eat what *you* eat." I decided to back off suggesting diet changes, even though almost every friend I've lost has died from illness caused by alcohol, nicotine, or incorrect diet.

In May, Carol Sue and I made another trip to Hawaii. The eruption had slowed and moved away from Royal Gardens subdivision, at least temporarily. It was my hope that this would be the end of it. I had elected to refurbish the Kalapana home, and lease it to a courageous young couple who felt they could outrun an eruption should there be another one in this immediate area.

Lava had flowed across the highway, isolating the house. A four-wheel-drive vehicle could make the crossing, but not a truck big enough to carry the building materials, so I engaged a helicopter to ferry the building materials to the house from where the highway was blocked by lava. At four in the afternoon a shiny green 12-wheeler truck arrived, and its crew unloaded wide white sheets of metal roofing and other materials.

Carol Sue and I had decided it would be fun to set up camp right on the highway, next to the materials. We ate dinner and soon afterward retired under a blue tarp that protected us from a light rain. The sounds of footsteps and voices woke me around 2 a.m. I stuck my head out from under the tarp and saw that a truck was now parked next to the building materials, and three men were gazing at them. One said, "Man, we could use *all* this stuff!"

I crawled out from under the tarp and said, "Can I help you load it?"

The guy yelped, "Goddam, they have a watchman!" and they jumped into their truck and split, peeling rubber. I dozed until around six, when David appeared in his pickup. He was a tremendous help, strapping together the metal roofing material for the helicopter. Carol Sue and I and some helpers spent four days working up at the site. We painted the house, and manicured and replanted the grounds while the men installed the new roof.

On June 4 there was to be a total eclipse of the moon at 12:15 a.m. People flew in from all over the world to view it. We were back in Kona, camping at a secluded beach with the best possible view. We had a couple of hits off a joint and waited. There was not a cloud in the sky, and the show was breathtaking. We watched the brightest moon we had ever seen against a background of stars like diamonds on black velvet. Gradually, one edge of the brilliant disc darkened; then the darkness slowly crept across the whole face of the moon. An hour later the moon had been reborn to its full glory.

We left for San Francisco the next day. While I was returning the rental car at Kona International, I chatted with a lady returning to South Australia, where she was a corrections officer in a prison.

"What is the feeling about marijuana in Australia?" I asked.

"In South Australia, it's been essentially legal for the past five years."

"How come?" I asked excitedly.

"Well, they were finally convinced that marijuana causes far fewer problems than alcohol."

Innocent mother shot in neck and killed by SWAT team

Marijuana does cause serious problems – or rather prohibition of it does. Later that year, in Everett, Washington, a police SWAT team killed Robin Pratt in a "no-knock" raid conducted to serve an arrest warrant on her husband. The husband was released after the allegations on which the arrest warrant was based turned out to be false – freed to return home and try to pick up the pieces of a life shattered by the War on Drugs. The *Seattle Times* summarized the raid this way:

> SWAT members threw a 50-pound battering ram through a sliding-glass door that landed near Pratt's six-year-old daughter and five-year old niece. As deputy Anthony Aston rounded a corner to the Pratts' bedroom, he encountered Robin Pratt. SWAT members were yelling,

'Get down,' and she started to crouch to her knees. She looked up at Aston and said, 'Please don't hurt my children.' Aston had his gun pointed at her and he fired, shooting her in the neck. She was then handcuffed, lying face-down. According to attorney John Muenster, she was alive another one to two minutes but could not speak because her throat had been destroyed by the bullet.[66]

The DEA decides it likes my home

I left for Hawaii August 6, 1994, hoping to see my children and grandson, and planning to prepare the Royal Gardens property for renting out – again. The former tenants had been spooked by the real possibility of more eruptions. The house had been vacant six months by then. A neighbor there had informed me that squatters were moving into vacant houses in the area. The road to the subdivision was again covered with lava and closed to the public but David learned it would soon be opened to four-wheel drive vehicles. I stayed with David for the first few weeks. He was building a new home, doing practically everything himself. I was proud of his construction ability along with his other talents.

On September 20, 1994, I received a letter from the Drug Enforcement Administration of the United States Department of Justice.

> Dear Mr. Ford:
>
> Your property located in the Royal Gardens subdivision in the County of Hawaii is being utilized at the present time to cultivate and facilitate the cultivation of marijuana.
>
> Unknown persons have taken residence on the above-mentioned property with your knowledge and are believed to be responsible for the cultivation of this marijuana. It is the intention of the Drug Enforcement Administration to seize this property under federal law.
>
> If you have any questions regarding this matter, you should contact your attorney.
>
> Sincerely,
> Joseph Parra
> Resident Agent in Charge

I was convinced that the DEA was attempting to steal my property. (I was reassured, of course, by seeing that they had called me *Dear* Mr. Ford.) There are hundreds of vacant acres in the area around Royal Gardens where pot could be grown; only an idiot would knowingly allow anyone to grow pot on his property. I didn't contact my attorney. I didn't have an attorney. I tried repeatedly to contact the sincere Mr. Parra in Honolulu. A week after I received the letter, I finally reached DEA Investigator Robert Aiu.

I convinced him there was no way that I could have known someone was growing anything on my land. He said he would back off and not seize the property.

I asked him if he had that authority.

His answer: "I'm the Seizer."

I could not resist asking, "Like Julius?"

He didn't laugh but he did back off, and I sighed with relief.

I had a good visit with David and my eight-year-old grandson, Scott. On October 3, I rented a four-wheel drive pickup, bought food and cleaning supplies for the house, and headed for Royal Gardens. The once magnificent Kalapana Black Sand Beach, the Kalapana Drive-in, and the oceanfront properties I'd had such beautiful plans for were now covered with five to twenty feet of lava. Even as I mourned the loss of my dreams, I was awestruck by the sight, much as it must have been thousands of years ago, before waves and weather had transformed the rough stone into soft beaches, and life in its myriad irresistible forms had given it a gentler beauty.

The "road" wandered over chunks of lava. Soon, I could see our white home up on its perch, overlooking the ocean. In spite of the appalling road, the ocean view was so outstanding I knew there would be no problem renting this three-bedroom, two-bath home for $500 a month. One of the first things I did after arriving was to check the land for illicit cultivation. There was not one pot plant to be seen. Surely, the DEA wouldn't say that there was, just so it could seize the property? Other than dusty windows and empty liquor bottles on the floor, the house looked good. I set to with a will, washing all the windows inside and out, cleaning the kitchen, bathrooms, and lanais, stopping more than once to admire the new white metal roof. The paint was fresh, and that and all the other work that had been done made this special home look new again. It was a thrill to see it coming back to life.

Fire!

It was now around 4:30 in the afternoon, and I hadn't stopped to eat lunch. I had brought along a propane camp stove because no utilities were connected, and I decided to treat myself to French fries with ketchup, and eat them with a salad and a papaya. After pouring the oil into the pot to heat, I went into the living room and stretched out on one of the sofas. I began to read the book, *A Call For Hawaiian Sovereignty*, and I fell asleep. I awoke startled by what sounded like an explosion. The glass patio doors had shattered! The room was filled with smoke. My eyes were burning. The lanai was aflame. I crawled out of the house and forced my terrified legs to run to the workshop below the house into the carport where I always kept two fire extinguishers.

I ran back to the house and pointed the extinguisher at the flame. Nothing came out! I grabbed the other one. Same thing. They had obviously expired. I heard the sound of a helicopter. I ran to the street above the house and waved for the helicopter to land. Running to the craft, I asked the pilot to radio the Hilo control tower and ask them to call the fire department in Pahoa village. "Please ask them to get a helicopter up here with a bucket, and dump water on the lanai. Tell them it will take too long to get a fire truck up here."

He pushed his microphone button and made repeated calls to Hilo. No voice came from the speaker. "I can't get a response here, but I can as soon as I take off and get some altitude."

"Thanks," I said. "Please hurry." Within seconds he was airborne. There was another explosion. The propane tank, I was sure. The fire was already beginning to eat its way into the living room.

The wind was picking up. Searching the horizon for the fire helicopter was futile. Smoke and flames were rising into the evening sky, and tears were running down my face. I didn't know whether it was from the smoke or seeing my beloved home beginning to die. Now the entire living room was in flames. The sounds were grotesque. The home was perishing, groaning, as if it were in agony, yet trying to stay alive until help arrived. I felt so helpless.

No helicopter. No fire truck. The new metal on the roof began twisting. The smell of burning paint, wood, and carpet became ever stronger. Almost an hour had passed. It was now nearly dark. Finally, I saw headlights on the road a mile below. The entire house was now in flames. When the fire truck finally made it up the steep hill, the home that we had lived in, loved in, played in, feasted in, was now a smoldering corpse. I was numb. The fire chief looked at me with sympathy in his eyes. He shook his head, and said, "Sorry. There was no helicopter available." They poured water from their truck onto the corpse. I slowly nodded a silent goodbye to a home and place that I had loved for 22 years.

William Foster sentenced to 93 years for growing his medicine

While recuperating from the tragedy of losing the Royal Gardens home to fire, I read of the far worse tragedy of William Foster, a 38-year-old, highly paid computer programmer in Tulsa, Oklahoma. For years he had suffered from crippling rheumatoid arthritis. Pain had become so intolerable that his doctor prescribed highly addictive analgesics like Percodan and Percocet. Their side effects – intense nausea and moodiness – were almost as disabling as the pain.

Then Foster heard about the medical benefits of smoking cannabis. Others who suffered from chronic pain told him that smoking grass not only relieved their agony but boosted them out of the depression that so often accompanies chronic illness. Desperate to get back to work and to fathering his two children, Foster planted about 70 cannabis seeds in a locked part of his basement, hoping to end up with 12 or 13 ounces of medicine.

Instead he wound up with a 93-year prison sentence. Foster lost his career, his wife, his life savings, and his freedom.

Perversely, politicians use the drug war's collateral damage to justify its intensification of punishment. It reminds me of that infamous line from the war in Vietnam: "We had to destroy the village in order to save it." Ironically, fear of appearing "soft on drugs" and lacking sympathy for victims of drug abuse compels innumerable politicians, like Oklahoma's Governor Frank Keating, to support a policy of grim cruelty. The War on Drugs has put thousands of innocent, suffering Americans like Foster in prison, and discouraged thousands of others suffering from cancer and chronic pain from using a benign, nonaddictive herb as medicine for their bodies and their spirits.

In our "rehabilitation centers" many prisoners guilty only of disagreeing with the government about the best treatment for their illnesses are gang-raped. Innumerable inmates have committed suicide, or have been murdered while Uncle Sam "took care of them." In their despair, many turn to heroin and the other hard drugs available in federal and state prisons. When the government can't keep drugs and violence out of a controlled environment like a prison, can any intelligent person think it will be more successful "on the outside"? That we'll have an America that's both peaceful and drug-free? That belief is as realistic as saying that we've never executed an innocent person.

The bitterly sad story of William Foster and many like him convinced me it was time I did something with all that research I'd conducted over the years. Over the next few years I became engrossed in writing *Marijuana: Not Guilty As Charged.*

Medical marijuana legalized in California and Arizona

During my lifetime, I've had face-to-face encounters with thousands of people who have used marijuana medically, socially, and to enhance creativity and loving sex. In 1996, the voters in both California and Arizona finally saw through more than 60 years of malicious propaganda against cannabis and approved it for medical purposes. In California, 56 percent statewide voted for the Compassionate Use Act of 1996, far more than voted to re-elect Bill Clinton. (In our Sonoma County, the figure for decriminalization was even higher: an emphatic 70 percent.) The passage of these landmark initiatives provoked the wrath of the Clinton Administration. The DEA immediately began harassing doctors, threatening any who recommended marijuana to ease suffering with loss of their licenses to prescribe a large number of common medications – and thus, effectively, loss of their right to practice medicine.

Arizona legislators claimed that the 65 percent of Arizonans who voted for the Drug Medicalization, Prevention, and Control Act were somehow "duped" into voting for medical marijuana, and repealed the measure. A referendum in 1998 restored the law, which was greatly needed by the ill and dying. Unfortunately, details on the amount of medicinal marijuana and its distribution were not specified, and that lack has caused years of wrangling in court.

My caring and wise primary physician was already aware of my use of medical marijuana. On December 12, 1996, he wrote: "David R. Ford is my patient. He suffers from back muscle spasms from former injuries. Marijuana stops the spasms. I recommend that he continue to use it for that condition. Documentation related to this may be found in his chart." It was dated and signed. (I would include his name, but I don't think he's up to having several thousand new patients!)

Writing Marijuana: Not Guilty As Charged

In the course of writing *Marijuana: Not Guilty As Charged* I heard the true-life stories of hundreds of people who have used pot for medicine, relaxation, sexual enhancement, and simply for fun. Many of those narratives are in that book. Except for times I was in surgery for cancer, I devoted most of five years to writing it. The book includes the myths and outright government lies about a relatively harmless herb, cannabis, and its nonintoxicating cousin, hemp. It includes dozens of pages that document the experiences of medical and social users of marijuana. It includes the history of marijuana and explains how the Federal Government created a systematic campaign of deception that began in the 1930s. It tells why marijuana was placed in the same category as heroin: "too dangerous to prescribe, and with no medical value." You'll want to read the book to learn more. (It's distributed exclusively by Bookworld Companies and is available in most bookstores, from DavidRFord.com, or at Amazon.com.)

By the time an author completes a book, he or she has invested thousands of hours. In addition to writing and rewriting the text, there's a strong obligation to provide references that validate what the author has written. Doing exhaustive research, working on reference notes and the index, and working with editors and the designers of the book and its jacket are all part of the challenge. Toward the end it feels like giving birth. (I'm certain my brain now has stretch marks.)

When I wrote *Marijuana: Not Guilty As Charged,* I included what I felt were the most salient myths concocted by the Federal Government and its covey of anti-marijuana prohibitionists. As pages about these myths poured out of me, I realized that an entire book could be assembled on this one subject. A few months after my book became available nationally, I was delighted to see the publication of *Marijuana Myths, Marijuana Facts: A Review of the Scientific Evidence.* This extremely valuable book is written by two of America's most eminent scientists, John P. Morgan, MD, and Lynn Zimmer, Ph.D. Dr. Morgan is Professor of Pharmacology at City University of New York Medical School. Dr. Zimmer is Associate Professor of Sociology at Queens College, City University of New York.

This abundantly referenced work should be within reach of every member of Congress. In fact, everyone who wants to know the truth behind every marijuana myth should have this book. It's published by the Lindesmith Center Drug Policy Foundation, now called the Drug

MARIJUANA

Not Guilty As Charged

DAVID R. FORD

Foreword by
**Tod H.
Mikuriya, M.D.**

**"Marijuana, in its
natural form, is
one of the safest
therapeutically
active
substances
known to man."**

—Francis L.Young, DEA's
(Drug Enforcement
Administration's) own
administrative law
judge, 1988

The front jacket of Marijuana: Not Guilty As Charged

CURRENT AFFAIRS $24.95

Marijuana—Learn why it should never have been illegal! A powerful and courageous book that everyone—parents; those in government, law enforcement, and
medicine; the media; nonusers and users of marijuana—needs to read. Learn
from honest research, not false government propaganda, about marijuana's

- Virtual harmlessness compared to other drugs
- Validated medical benefits
- International studies that confirm it is not a "gateway drug"
- Not being addictive, any more than TV, sports or the Internet
- Never causing one recorded toxicity-related death
- *Unavailability*, which causes the use of more dangerous drugs

*David Ford brilliantly conducts us on a tour through the "Malice in Blunderland" of
American marijuana policy. Based on authoritative documents, news clippings and
personal stories, he presents tales of viciousness, hypocrisy and ignorance facilitated
by self-serving special interest groups.*

TOD MIKURIYA, M.D., Head of marijuana research for the
National Institute of Mental Health in the late 1960s

When I wrote Wasted *(McGraw-Hill), the story of my son's drug addiction, I thought
marijuana was a stepping-stone to heavier drugs. I'm now convinced that pot had
nothing to do with it.* Marijuana: Not Guilty As Charged *is a valuable and honest
book—a "must read" for anyone who wants to know the truth. David Ford also presents ample evidence that marijuana is medicine. It's a compelling book, and it often
reads like a spicy novel.*

WILLIAM CHAPIN, Author

The author offers a **$50,000 cash reward** to anyone who can
scientifically prove that marijuana is not medicine. A portion of
the profits from the sale of this thought-provoking book will be
contributed to the National Organization for the Reform of
Marijuana Laws (NORML).

**Marijuana: Not Guilty As Charged
will be a reference book sought
internationally. A valuable gift that you
will be recommending to your friends.**

ISBN 0-9655932-5-8

9 790965 593259

The back jacket of Marijuana: Not Guilty As Charged.

Policy Alliance (DPA), a drug policy research institute that seeks to stimulate more informed analysis and discussion of drugs, and sober drug-control policies. The center was founded and is headed by the brilliant Ethan A. Nadelmann, Ph.D. Dr. Nadelmann is one of the world's most respected educators on U.S. and international drug control policies.

A special love, and encouragement to publish

One of my most ardent supporters when I was writing *Marijuana: Not Guilty As Charged* was a dear and beautiful lady, Eleanor Nazarek, a former teacher who had taught and loved thousands of children. Eleanor retired in 1991 as assistant principal of Santa Rosa High School in California. And now she was dying of cancer.

With notes and letters and gifts of encouragement, Eleanor spurred me on to follow my dream: the hope of educating the public to the truth about marijuana and its medical value.

In October, 1996, just a month before medical marijuana was legalized in California, and only two months before her death, Eleanor astonished me. She insisted on getting out of her bed of pain to introduce my speech to 100 seniors at Oakmont, a retirement community in Sonoma. It was intensely touching. My book was not yet published, and I believe she wanted to give me the opportunity to talk about it now, in case she was not alive when it was. I was overwhelmed at the positive reception, and I'm sure much of it was due to the exquisite introduction Eleanor gave me. She was so frail that she had to hold onto the podium for support; it was obvious that she was near death. I was both touched and elated at how open-minded those seniors were, and how compassionate toward Eleanor. These folks are aware of the government's and big business's political interest in preventing the national re-legalization of medical marijuana.

For seven months, even with her prescribed medications for nausea, pain, depression, appetite, and sleep, Eleanor's suffering did not cease. She frequently found sleep unattainable. As a former cancer patient myself, I suggested she try marijuana. "It would be difficult, Dave," she explained. "For so many years I've taught children what I had been taught – that marijuana is a dangerous drug and has no medical value."

The effects of the chemotherapy caused such terrible nausea that Eleanor frequently threw up her medications. Her weight dropped from 135 pounds to less than 75. I finally convinced this dear 72-year-old, law-abiding lady to try marijuana. After two puffs and five minutes,

Eleanor fell into a peaceful sleep. I sat by her bedside for two hours. Then her beautiful blue eyes opened. She looked up, smiled, and said, "I'm hungry! That marijuana did all the things those five capsules were supposed to do."

It was then that Eleanor decided to introduce me to the group at Oakmont. I felt that she was just being the loving teacher that she'd always been, encouraging me to write about a subject that was clearly close to my heart. Then, within a week of her death, she said, "Dave, your book has a very important and honest message. Get your book out there. Marijuana is indeed medicine."

Sadly, however, Eleanor discovered that medicine too late to save herself from the brutal effects of cancer and chemotherapy. The day after Christmas, Eleanor died from starvation. She hadn't been able to eat for more than a month.

As she had requested, I spoke at her memorial service on January 18. The church was packed with hundreds of friends and former students. Like all of us, Eleanor had wanted to believe our government – and that belief had starved her to death.

Medical marijuana honesty from The New England Journal of Medicine

The prestigious *New England Journal of Medicine* has been published since 1812 by the Massachusetts Medical Society. It has played a major role in debates over health policy. Following are insights from Jerome P. Kassirer, M.D., the journal's editor-in-chief, writing in 1997.

The advanced stages of many illnesses and their treatments are often accompanied by intractable nausea, vomiting, or pain. Thousands of patients with cancer, AIDS, and other diseases report they have obtained striking relief from these devastating symptoms by *smoking marijuana.*

The alleviation of distress can be so striking that some patients and their families have been willing to risk a jail term to obtain or grow the marijuana. Despite the desperation of these patients, within weeks after voters in Arizona and California approved propositions allowing physicians in their states to prescribe marijuana for medial indications, federal officials, including the President, the Secretary of Health and Human Services, and the Attorney General sprang into action. At a news conference, Health and Human Services Secretary Donna E. Shalala gave an organ recital of the parts of the body that she asserted could be harmed by marijuana, and warned of the evils of its spreading use. Attorney General Janet Reno announced that physicians in any state who prescribed the drug could lose the privilege of writing prescriptions, be excluded from Medicare and Medicaid reimbursement, and even be prosecuted for a federal crime...

I believe that a federal policy that prohibits physicians from alleviating suffering by prescribing marijuana for seriously ill patients is misguided, heavy-handed, and inhumane... It is also hypocritical to forbid physicians to prescribe marijuana while permitting them to use morphine and meperidine to relieve extreme apnea [difficulty breathing] and pain. With both these drugs, the difference between the dose that relieves symptoms and the dose that hastens death is very narrow; by contrast, there is no risk of death from smoking marijuana... *What really counts for the therapy with this kind of safety margin is whether a seriously ill patient feels relief as a result of the intervention, not whether a controlled trial "proves" its efficacy.*[67] [Emphasis added.]

After interacting with thousands of medical-marijuana patients, I have no doubt in my mind that cannabis *is* medicine. It's pitiful and despicable that the National Institute of Drug Abuse (NIDA) is the government's "hit man." With virtually unlimited government funds it has been able to support some government-paid researchers who were able to provide the hypothetical "dreadful results" of cannabis only by including such measures as injecting THC (marijuana's psychoactive ingredient) straight into the veins, brains, or abdominal cavities of animals. Only with experiments of questionable relevance, and only with questionable ethics, was NIDA able to show that THC produced a medley of biological effects that have *never* shown up (and never will) in *human* marijuana users: infertility, brain damage, immune-system impairment, and physical addiction.[68] Does the federal government encourage such nonsensical "research"? You be the judge. In 1982, NIDA's budget was about $3 million. By 1987 it was $15 million and by 2003 it was $967,898,000![69]

NIDA does sometime use humans as test subjects, comparing long-term heavy marijuana users with infrequent users or non-users. Many of the heavy users have multiple problems that preceded their use of marijuana. As a result, these studies may identify adverse characteristics in users that are actually due to factors other than marijuana use. NIDA and other government agencies then disseminate negative findings to

A20 – Friday, July 17, 1998

The Sonoma Index-Tribune

Religion

A look at medical marijuana

Reflections

David McCracken
Pastor, First Congregational Church, Sonoma

A couple of months ago, a couple came in to see me. The husband is a pastor of an evangelical church in the county. His wife has been diagnosed with multiple sclero-sis and has experienced a rapid deterioration in the use of her legs and arms, along with an increase of pain and muscle spasms.

Throughout her life, she has been highly sensi-tive to both prescription and over-the counter medications. She has had severe side effects and two life-threatening reactions which put her in the hospital. The only medication she has tried which relieves the muscle spasms and pain without side effects is marijuana.

Yet, the medications that produced these adverse reactions in her and in many others have been FDA approved, while marijuana, an effective, non-addictive drug with few, if any, unpleasant side effects, remains illegal and stigmatized.

In recent years, I have stood by the bedside of several people who were dying of cancer who would echo these same thoughts and feelings. It was marijuana which brought them relief, thereby enabling them to face their own death with digni-ty.

Marijuana has been repeatedly proven to help control muscle spasms in people with cerebral palsy and multiple sclerosis, reduce nausea and vomiting for cancer patients undergoing chemotherapy, reduce suffering for AIDS patients, reduce eye pressure for glaucoma patients, decrease anxiety and depression, reduce the pain and discomfort associated with premenstrual syn-drome, and ease withdrawal from alcohol, cocaine and nicotine cigarettes.

If a doctor and patient come to a mutual agree-ment on the use of marijuana for that patient, to ease their suffering and pain, the doctor should have the same right to write out a prescription for marijuana that can be taken to the local druggist as with any other prescribed drug. It's as simple as that.

Two years ago this November, voters in Califor-nia and Arizona each passed a proposition whose message clearly indicated that, despite years of government hysteria, a growing number of Ameri-cans are affirming marijuana as legitimate medi-cine. Yet the government continues to bear down hard on physicians, patients, growers, and distrib-utors, causing the price of marijuana to remain exorbitantly high and out of reach for many seri-ously ill people who could greatly benefit from it.

As members of the faith community, we are called upon to help bring relief to the sick and suf-fering around us. One of the ways we can do this is to educate ourselves on the use of marijuana for medicinal purposes. I would like to suggest the possibility of a town meeting at the Sonoma Com-munity Center or meetings in local churches and synagogues to learn for ourselves the value of marijuana among patients who are extremely ill and/or dying.

David Ford has written, "As a people, we are all connected; we are all one. Care and honesty should prevail, rather than false hysterical press releases. Anti-marijuana crusaders, including leg-islators, must be challenged to report the facts honestly. So, too, must some of the media. Chances are these people would open their minds to the medical magic of marijuana if a family member was suffering from AIDS or cancer." ("Marijuana: Not Guilty as Charged," by David R. Ford, Good Press, P. O. Box 1771, Sonoma, CA 95476)

This is not an easy issue to deal with. We have been conditioned for so long to believe that mari-juana is an evil drug. Through honest education and lots of personal struggle, I have no doubt that we can turn this whole issue around and thereby become a channel for helping to relieve suffering and pain for many of our sisters and brothers in our society. We will also be reaching out to people in our local communities, such as this minister and his wife who came in to my study, in love and compassion. Let's be about it!

The Sonoma Index-Tribune, July 17, 1998.

The highly respected pastor of the First Congregational Church in Sonoma, David McCracken, described his experiences sitting at the bedsides of dying cancer victims and other patients, of the adverse reactions they had to FDA-approved drugs, and of the relief that cannabis gave them. He generously quoted from Marijuana: Not Guilty As Charged, *"Chances are that [legislators] would open their minds to the medical magic of marijuana if a family member was suffering from AIDS or cancer."*

Congress, the media, and the public through official reports, press releases, and drug "education" pamphlets. Animal studies are used and cited as evidence of biological harm to marijuana users, even when researchers have consistently found *no* such harm in humans.[70]

Drug czar blowing smoke

Former drug czar and Secretary of Education William Bennett was a two-pack-a-day cigarette addict. (For him to pontificate on drugs inverted an old saying – for once it was the kettle calling the *pot* black!) When asked about marijuana and other drugs, Bennett said: "This is a deadly and poisonous activity. People should be imprisoned for long periods of time for doing it."[71]

In 1997, then drug czar Barry McCaffrey, on behalf of the federal government, commissioned the Institute of Medicine (IOM), an arm of the National Academy of Sciences, to conduct a $1 million study on marijuana. The results were reported on March 17, 1999. The government's hope was that the study would demonstrate that pot is dangerous and has no medical value. Boohoo, that was not to be.

The New York Times said:

> The report, the most comprehensive analysis to date of the medical literature about marijuana, said there was no evidence that giving the drug to sick people would increase illicit use... Nor is marijuana a "gateway drug" that prompts patients to use harder drugs like cocaine and heroin.

The report itself said:

> We acknowledge that there is no clear alternative for people suffering from chronic conditions that might be relieved by smoking marijuana, such as pain or AIDS wasting, ...[72]

Earlier, the *Press Democrat* spoke more sharply:

> ANTI-DRUG CAMPAIGN TELLS LIES TO OUR KIDS
> ...Ads are produced by the *Partnership for a Drug-Free America* – the best-funded and -connected propaganda machine in America today...
> The slickness and pervasiveness of the campaign conceals one flaw: The message is a bald-faced lie.

...Honesty demands that the silent dad in the PDFA ad admit to his son that he smoked a good deal of pot when he was young, and still occasionally lights up at parties and has turned out just fine.

Instead, the PDFA insists on using our tax dollars to lie to your kids... If the PDFA had a shred of integrity, its ads would be battling alcohol and tobacco, America's two most injurious drugs and the two most popular among teens...

Many heroin users are able to use their drugs and conduct functional lives. What makes heroin users' lives so crazy is that their dependence on an illegal drug forces them to enter a criminal underworld.

The PDFA ignores these subtleties. Most of the 22 million Americans who've tried it (cocaine) have had no trouble walking away from it. And pot? No one has ever overdosed.[73]

Perhaps after such findings in a report commissioned by his imperial majesty the drug czar himself, the government would back off its persecution of those who produce what is probably the world's least harmful medicine? Unfortunately not.

Todd McCormick, "the Luther Burbank of medical marijuana"

Beginning at age two, Todd McCormick had a series of tumors known as histiocytosis X. His condition was treated as malignant cancer nine times before he was 10 years old. The youngster endured major surgeries, chemotherapy, and radiation, leaving his young body deformed and in pain. Unlikely as it seems, cannabis was a great help in reducing his pain, creating appetite, and helping him to sleep.

I wrote to Todd's courageous mother, Anne, to ask her how it happened that she was savvy enough to understand that cannabis might ease her son's almost constant agony. Here is her answer:

Todd was born on 10-07-70 at 7:10 p.m. at St Joseph's Hospital, which is on Peace Street in Providence, RI. I think fate was trying to tell us something right from the start. In 1979, I watched helplessly as my nine-year-old child – though being kept alive – lost all quality of life. Though the chemotherapy drugs kept him alive, they eroded his health at an alarming rate. After seven years of his heart-wrenching suffering, I happened to pick up a copy of *Good Housekeeping* in the hospital waiting room. I read the following: "As research proceeds, scientists are finding that the major active ingredient in marijuana – tetrahydrocannabinol, or THC – may be highly valuable in treating such conditions as glaucoma, asthma, and even terminal cancer."

I have no problem with telling people of Todd's early marijuana use. In 1979, even Jimmy Carter was calling for an end to marijuana prohibition as we know it. State legislatures across the country were passing medical-marijuana legislation; Rhode Island's passed unanimously in 1980. The federal government had just started the Investigational New Drug (IND) program for medical marijuana, and Nancy Reagan's shrill hysterics were still five years in the future. There was significantly more common sense in play at that time than we've seen in the past 18 years. I tried cannabis on Todd. It quelled the nausea, eased the pain, and increased his appetite. As he ate, he became stronger, more active. He wanted to go outside and play! As he played, he became more fit. His muscles grew, his circulation improved, the color returned to his cheeks. The doctors and modern technology saved his life, but marijuana restored his health.

What happens when you give medical marijuana to a desperately ill nine-year-old boy? He grows up to be a pacifist, a vegetarian, a non-drinker of alcohol, and militantly anti-tobacco. He shuns synthetic (pharmaceutical) drugs. He leads a "green" lifestyle, cares about the environment and abhors political corruption. He might even grow up duped into believing that he actually does live in a "free" country and can make his own choices as long as those choices do not intrude on the rights of non-consenting others.

Each and every one of us must JUST SAY NO to this unbridled abuse of power, waste of precious resources, and infliction of unspeakable crimes upon the American people and the United States Constitution.

I've had the pleasure of knowing this courageous young man. He is witty, brilliant, and exceedingly knowledgeable in many areas – in particular, medical marijuana. Todd spent time in Amsterdam where he learned that there are more than 30,000 variations of the medical cannabis plant. His goal, by researching thousands of cannabis plants, was to locate *specific strains* that would improve treatment of particular illnesses. He is a master medical-marijuana horticulturist. His publisher and backer was Peter McWilliams, who provided a financial advance so that Todd would have the necessary funds to rent a property and analyze the plants. The goal was for Todd to write a book offering the world *specific species of cannabis to aid specific ailments*.

Todd reminds me of Luther Burbank, the famous horticulturist who lived in Santa Rosa, California. Burbank conducted plant-breeding experiments that brought him world renown. His objective was to improve the quality of plants and thereby increase the world's food supply, and he did.

Todd McCormick's goal was to narrow the strains and improve the quality of medical marijuana. His "farm" was raided July 29, 1997, by agents of the DEA and the Los Angeles Sheriff's Narcotics Bureau. Fifty flak-jacketed men arrived with guns drawn to arrest one pacifist. Todd surrendered to the court on January 3, 2000. Rather than face a 10-year mandatory-minimum sentence (possibly life) and a $4 million fine, McCormick accepted five years in federal prison on a reduced charge. He had been arrested on "conspiracy" charges. (A conspiracy to provide better treatment for the sick and dying is criminal?)

McCormick didn't investigate all 30,000 species; he had time for only 4,000 before his facility was raided. Each plant had been labeled with its botanical history and was awaiting sale to a medical-cannabis outlet. The government claimed that the identification tags on plants, many of which were only inches tall, were used to show the *"intended buyer of the plant"!* Bail was set at an outrageous $500,000 – more than that usually set for murderers, rapists, and child molesters. Thousands of Americans were appreciative of McCormick's research, and outraged at his arrest. One of those was his loving mother, Anne McCormick. She had seen how marijuana had aided her son while no other medicine, including Marinol, the synthetic pot capsule, had. The talented actor Woody Harrelson, also a marijuana and hemp reformer, generously put up the $500,000 bond.

On May 15, 1998, Bill Maher devoted his entire show, *Politically Incorrect,* to medical marijuana, and Todd was there to defend the herb. The show brilliantly lampooned America's bizarre drug politics.

Todd McCormick was not given the opportunity to complete his research and write the definitive book on certain strains that would best treat glaucoma, loss of appetite, nausea, muscle spasms, chronic pain, and more. He did, however, complete the book, *"How to Grow Medical Marijuana."* (Look for it at Amazon.com.)

MADD wants alcohol part of anti-drug ad campaign

Even though alcohol is a drug whose abuse often causes death and violence, the National Beer Wholesalers and other groups do anything they can to prevent alcohol from being included in anti-drug advertising.

In 1999, Mothers Against Drunk Driving (MADD) lobbied Congress to include alcohol and underage drinking in a national advertising campaign aimed at reducing drug use. MADD held a press conference in Washington D.C. to counter what it said were efforts by the National Beer Wholesalers Association, the Partnership for a Drug-Free America, and "friends of the alcohol industry in Congress" to exclude alcohol from the billion-dollar ad campaign. "Alcohol is an illicit drug for Americans under the legal minimum drinking age of 21," said Karolyn Nunnallee, national president of MADD. "It is very sad that the Partnership for a Drug-Free America appears interested in only a partly drug-free America for youth."[74]

Amazing courage from author William Chapin

Even Pulitzer-Prize nominee William Chapin was not aware that marijuana is *not* a "gateway drug."

Just before *Marijuana: Not Guilty As Charged* was printed, I read *Wasted,* the outstanding author William Chapin's heartrending book about his son's drug addiction. *Wasted* was nominated for a Pulitzer Prize. I was disturbed when in it he said that marijuana had led his son to hard drugs. I sent him a copy of my manuscript, never thinking I would get anything but a bland thank-you note.

His generous reply was overwhelming and altruistic. He jeopardized sales of his own book with his recommendation of mine. His words are printed on the back jacket of *Marijuana: Not Guilty As Charged.*

> *When I wrote Wasted (McGraw-Hill), the story of my son's drug addiction, I thought marijuana was a stepping stone to heavier drugs. I'm now convinced that pot had nothing to do with it. Marijuana: Not Guilty As Charged is a valuable and honest book – a "must read" for anyone who wants to know the truth. David Ford also presents ample evidence that marijuana is medicine. It's a compelling book, and it often reads like a spicy novel.*
>
> *— William Chapin, Author*

The foreword to *Marijuana: Not Guilty As Charged,* was written by one of the world's foremost authorities on medical marijuana, Todd H. Mikuriya, M.D. Dr. Mikuriya had headed marijuana research for the National Institute of Mental Health, and his foreword is a scathing denunciation of the federal government – almost worth the price of the book by itself.

Dr. Mikuriya says that marijuana works in three ways with prescribed medications:

- As a substitute for a more harmful drug, altogether or in part
- To decrease the use of another drug, to minimize undesirable effects
- To suppress the side effects of another drug in order to permit its use for beneficial effects

Insurance pays for my ripped-off medical-marijuana plants

In the first week of May, 1997, I planted six medical-quality cannabis plants in the backyard of my home. (I was tired of spending $400 for an ounce of questionable quality or adulterated medicine.) Even though I spent hours tending the plants, two "passed away." In the first week of September I could see that the plants were ready to become my medication. On September 8 I picked up my new pruning shears to harvest the buds and headed out to the garden. The plants were gone! Disappointment and anger engulfed me. I ran into the house and phoned the Sonoma police. Within minutes a police car pulled up in front of the house. Police Captain Robert Wedell and an officer appeared at the front door. I first showed them my written doctor's recommendation for my use of medical marijuana, then gave them the facts. They were polite.

As soon as I waved goodbye, I phoned State Farm Insurance Company, which in due course paid for the loss.

Solution to patients' plants being stolen

There must be a state-approved distribution system. If *medical* marijuana were legalized nationally, cost would drop from $400 an ounce to, I estimate, $35 to $50 an ounce, more if the government taxed it. It would no longer be necessary for patients to grow their own, and thieving would stop. (It would also stop cartels from growing and selling black-market cannabis. They use the profits to manufacture speed, which is more lucrative.) The government says it cares about our health. If that were true it would allow pharmacies to sell physician-prescribed medical-quality cannabis. Quality growers would be respected, not imprisoned.

Do international book distributors smoke pot?

My national/international book distributor invited me to the Chicago Book Exposition. He had had the front jacket of *Marijuana: Not Guilty As Charged* blown up to two by three feet, with a spotlight on it. There were thousands of people there from all over the world. A myriad distributors were dazzling visitors with free gifts of books, cloth carrying bags, letter openers, watches, pen sets, and much more. Book buyers and nationally recognized authors were there, along with book reviewers and radio and television reporters. Radio station representatives from all over the United States and Canada asked if they could phone me and some of the other authors for telephone interviews. I was tremendously excited to see that my book was receiving as much attention as the books of the best-selling authors. There were magazine editors and writers, all looking for stories. Book buyers from the world over were present to purchase books for their stores, nationwide and internationally; and I was excited to see orders for my book going to Germany and other countries.

It was a thrill to meet so many people interested in cannabis use, both medical and social. Of course it was delightful to sign books, shake hands, and answer questions about grass. Dozens of people, including authors, related how cannabis expands creativity, increases sensitivity, and provides insight. We sold hundreds of copies of the book. There were parties constantly in progress at the convention center and at The Palmer House Hilton Hotel, where we were staying. A party on the 50th floor of the Sears Tower featured representatives of talk-show hosts like Oprah Winfrey and Montel Williams, scouting for authors to interview. I was amazed at how many distributors and authors from all over the world asked me if I might have a joint on me. Who would guess that a *joint* would be valuable "PR"! I was pleased to note that quite a few guests at the parties avoided alcohol.

Marijuana: Not Guilty As Charged became a national fast seller. I saw to it that $14,000 worth of the books were given to some members of Congress, the media, judges, attorneys, district attorneys, heads of churches, and others who I felt would benefit from knowing the truth about the herb that has never in 5,000 years caused one toxicity-related death. I have been interviewed on more than 100 radio stations in the U.S. and Canada. I did book signings at Barnes & Noble and Borders as well as at smaller book stores, and also spoke at dozens of institutions and events around the country, including the New College of Santa Rosa and Sacramento Reads. I had the pleasure of being invited to speak to pain patients at the Sonoma Valley Hospital, and at retirement communities, business clubs, hemp stores, and even churches. Twice I have spoken at the Million Marijuana March in United Nations Plaza in San Francisco.

Lady gets possible death sentence for using cannabis as medicine

On August 8, 1998, I received a frantic phone call from a lady who had read my book. She had hepatitis C. "Mr. Ford, can you please help me? I'm going to die if I don't receive a liver transplant. To relieve severe pain I smoked a marijuana cigarette three weeks ago. I was recently urine-tested. I came out positive. They told me that I would be tested one more time, and if I came out positive again I would be off the list. I was told, 'That means you will be dead, lady.' They're going to repeat the test. Can you help me?"

I called Keith Stroup. Within an hour he had John P. Morgan, M.D., phone me. Dr. Morgan is an internationally recognized professor of pharmacology at City University of New York, and co-author of *Marijuana Myths, Marijuana Facts: A Review of the Scientific Evidence.* I told him the story and asked, "John, could marijuana in any way cause further liver injury?"

"Absolutely not," said Dr. Morgan. "Had she been drinking alcohol, of course, that would cause further injury."

Allen St. Pierre, the executive director of NORML's educational sister organization, the NORML Foundation, has been equally helpful in such cases. Fortunately, the lady passed the second urine test and remained on the waiting list for a donor.

The saga of Eric, a loveless boy who wanted to kill himself

On June 30, 1998, I was invited to present a talk and book signing at the Barnes & Noble book store in Santa Rosa, California. One of the many people I met that night was a gentlemen named William Larson. Will got my attention when he invited me to inspect his *Private Gardens,* a non-profit patient-care facility. In addition to caring for several patients, Will taught medically qualified patients how to grow, brew, or make their own medicine, under a doctor's supervision.

One of the patients was Eric, a clean-cut, nice-looking lad about 20. Eric's eyes darted around the room and occasionally met mine. He appeared frightened. "I'll be in the garden," he said to the room at large as he left.

Will began telling me about Eric. "He was born to a speed-addicted mother. The terrified child was taken from her and put into a foster home at age three. The foster 'parents' told him how stupid he is, and treated him harshly. Eric ended up being passed on to several other foster homes, where again he was brutalized. One family locked him in closets. Eric was beaten to a pulp, physically and mentally. Years later the abuse by the last foster couple was reported. He was finally removed from their 'care' and sent to a youth detention center; at that time there was no other place for him.

"Eric is bright," Will said, "but with the constant punishment he began thinking all that he was worth was pain, so he turned to self-destruction. By age 14 he was carving words into his arms and burning himself with cigarettes. By 16, he was an alcoholic. In spite of all of his problems, though, he's very intelligent, and he completed high school early. Thinking of what they told him about his mother's drug abuse, Eric, confused, began shooting up speed, and looking for any drug that would make him feel normal – or kill him. He became conflicted with the desire to live – and the desire to die.

"He was then sent to Indio Juvenile Hall in Blythe, California, where drugs were even more readily accessible than on the outside. At 18, as happens to all released prisoners, Eric was discharged into society with no preparation. He fell in with other troubled teens and started drinking to excess again. He and others of his new acquaintances stole a car for a joy ride, and were caught and arrested. In jail he was given food with maggots crawling in it. Somehow he managed to cut major veins in his arms, and en route to the hospital the accompanying jailer told him he'd show Eric how to do the job correctly next time so he would die, and not just mess up his cell with blood.

"With no psychiatric guidance he was released on probation. The only people he knew were drug-addicted homeless kids. He was living on the streets, shooting heroin or any drug that might end his hopelessness. He decided to go to San Francisco with the hope of getting a job. Resting in a San Francisco park, he met an old friend of mine, Dennis Peron.

"Dennis called Eric's probation officer to let him know that Eric was headed for guidance and healing. The probation officer said that, no, Eric was headed for jail, that he had violated his parole. Dennis had no choice. He put Eric on a bus back to Lake Tahoe, where he was again punished. He was also put on high doses of Thorazine and Clonopin. After spending his 19th birthday in jail, he was released three days before Christmas 1998. He found Dennis, who called me, told me Eric's story, and asked if I would accept him in my facility. I decided to meet Eric, but from what Dennis told me I was not hopeful: if Eric continued shooting up, his future would be prison, AIDS, and probably suicide.

"I went to see Eric. He was so heavily medicated on psychiatric drugs that it was impossible to converse with him. Even so, I asked him if he would have Christmas with our 'family,' and, ill though he was, he accepted. After returning him to Dennis, I left my business card with him. The next day Eric called and told me that he was interested in entering our patient group. I called his probation officer, who informed me that Eric would need lots of psychiatric drugs. He felt Eric should be institutionalized.

"I told the probation officer I disagreed, that I am against mind-altering medications that block a person's individuality, that medical marijuana would play a meaningful part in Eric's recovery, and that it would also be helpful in eliminating his thoughts of suicide. I made it clear that what Eric needed was love, not incarceration; and none of those ingredients are available in institutions. He finally agreed; and indeed Eric has responded to love and caring. He has not used alcohol or any drugs other than medical marijuana. He helps me with all sorts of projects."

I'm telling you this story because there are thousands of Erics out there. Most of them are in prison, and only becoming more and more depressed. Other patients have told me they were so heavily medicated on psychiatric drugs that it was impossible for them to interact. "I felt like a zombie," is a phrase I heard often – until, that is, under their doctors' supervision they quit using drugs like Vicodin for pain, Delmane for sleep, Thorazine to keep them calm, and Valium to relax them further. When they switched to marijuana they found they didn't need the other drugs, and were once again able to feel and act normally.

A life cannot be turned around without a caring relationship. If prison wardens and guards were more like Will Larson, far fewer inmates would return to prison.

Peter McWilliams and the death penalty – for using pot

I had just finished reading the American classic, *Ain't Nobody's Business if You Do – The Absurdity of Consensual Crimes in Our Free Country*, by Peter McWilliams, when I learned to my shock that this best-selling author and medical-marijuana patient had died at age 50. He was a victim of cancer and AIDS. The medications prescribed by his doctors were saving his life, when he could keep them down, but they also caused him to vomit uncontrollably – except when he smoked marijuana. Everyone who met him was struck by his optimism and unfailing good cheer in the face of two deadly illnesses. He touched the lives of millions with his books on personal growth and individual freedom, such as *Life 101, Getting Over the Loss of a Loved One*, and *How to Heal Depression*. He financed Todd McCormick's quest for individualizing medical marijuana and his production of a book on that subject. Cannabis had kept McWilliams alive, and he hoped it would do the same for others. McWilliams was a true hero who fought and ultimately gave his life for what he believed in: the right to treat oneself medically without government interference.

Perhaps *because* he was a prominent activist for medical marijuana and living proof of its worth, the federal government prosecuted McWilliams, not just as a user, but as "drug kingpin." He was not allowed to mention his medical use of marijuana in his defense. He was jailed for almost two months, until he could raise $250,000 bail. When his elderly mother pledged her house, the prosecutors informed her that if her son used marijuana, she would *lose* her home. Peter tried Marinol, the synthetic pot capsule. He couldn't keep it down. Unlike marijuana, it did not stop his horrendous vomiting.

On June 14, 2000, Peter McWilliams was found dead in his bathroom, where he had choked to death on his own vomit. The coroner's report, released July 27, said the cause of death was a heart attack. If that's true, Peter's heart gave up when it realized that the closing phrase of the Pledge of Allegiance, "with liberty and justice for all," is a lie. May God forgive the federal government for refusing to recognize that for some patients marijuana is the only medicine that works.

The Million Marijuana March

On May Day, 2000, I invited Will, Eric, an activist friend Nolan, and Nolan's lady friend Zoë, to attend the Million Marijuana March at the United Nations Plaza in San Francisco. Eric's mistreatment while in jail made him fearful of being in the presence of the police, but he was courageous and elected to join us. In addition to being a speaker, I was provided with a table, on which I displayed my books and T-shirts with *Marijuana: Not Guilty As Charged* printed on them.

Eric, Will, and Nolan manned the table and did a superb job. After my speech it began to rain. The books were going to get wet, so we decided to leave early. There were at least a dozen police officers there, and I asked one of them if I could please drive my car through the crowd so we could load our boxes of books and shirts. He replied, "You bet. I've read your book!" The crowd was so thick it seemed impossible to drive into the tightly gathered throng. Three police officers appeared, and with total courtesy they slowly moved the crowd out of the path of the car. We quickly loaded everything, and the officers escorted us out and waved goodbye. Eric, now with a big smile, waved and joined us in thanking the officers.

Eric is still under Will Larson's care, but he is clearly a new, happy, healthy person, with marijuana as his only medicine.

What is the Million Marijuana March about?

On or around May 1st, the Million Marijuana March, organized by Dana Beale, takes place in just about every major city of the world. For the past two years, in northern California it has been held at the most appropriate location of all, the United Nations Plaza in San Francisco. Ordinary people who are for peace and freedom and nationally legalized marijuana gather by the thousands. Nationally recognized activists speak. The major themes are:

- The restoration of hemp agriculture and industry
- A patient's right to medical marijuana
- An end to the arrest and incarceration of pot smokers
- An end to drug testing for marijuana
- Protection of children by regulating the sale of cannabis as is done with alcohol and tobacco

After the event I wrote the following letter to the editor, which appeared in both the Sonoma *Index-Tribune*, and the Santa Rosa *Press Democrat*:

MARCH SHOWED POSITIVE ASPECTS OF MARIJUANA
To the Editor:
    On Saturday, May 1, the Million Marijuana March was held not only at the United Nations Plaza in San Francisco, but also worldwide. The mass rallies and marches were designed to call attention to the fact that marijuana *is* medicine, to release it to the sick and dying and to end the prison state.
    We should be seeking cures, not a war against sick and dying patients. We should stop the federal government's lies against a medical herb that in 5,000 years has not caused one toxicity-related death. (Compare that to the hundreds of thousands of deaths caused annually by the toxicity of alcohol, nicotine products, and drugs that the FDA calls safe.)
    There were some 30 speakers: authors, doctors, attorneys, poets,

caregivers, and disabled Americans. The majority of those who gathered for the event were medical-marijuana patients. The San Francisco Police Department estimated the crowd at between 3,000 and 4,000. Most of those who attended took a few puffs of pot; there was music and dancing, singing and hugging; but not one fight. Imagine the result of that many people drinking alcohol. I offer respect and congratulations to the SFPD: The officers were an example of what police should be in every community and state where marijuana has been medically legalized – respectful, courteous, and helpful. There was not one arrest.

The only sad note was that with pharmaceutical drugs, beer and nicotine products buying so much advertising with the media, there was virtually no coverage for an amazing educational event.

David R. Ford

Sonoma

The Seattle Hempfest, at Myrtle Edwards Park August 18 & 19, 2002, drew more than 150,000 people, and had the same philosophy as the Million Marijuana March. The Seattle gathering was created, hosted, and directed by the brilliant Vivian McPeak, writer, musician, and minister. This free, peaceful assembly promises to draw thousands more people each year, yet the media, with millions of dollars of advertising revenue from alcohol, tobacco, and pharmaceutical companies, did not cover this amazing newsworthy gathering of freedom-loving Americans.

Foster is released after his 93-year sentence is reduced

Earlier I told of the 93-year sentence imposed on William Foster, an Oklahoma medical-marijuana patient. The absurdity and cruelty of the sentence drew national attention. In 1998, an appeals court found that the length of the term "shocks our conscience;" and reduced it to 20 years. By then, Foster had spent four-and-a-half years in prison, enough to open up the possibility of parole. Oklahoma Governor Frank Keating turned down Foster's parole twice, then finally relented. Foster's immoral sentence had gained national attention, aiding his early release; but thousands of unknowns remain in prison for using marijuana as medicine. It was speculated that Keating was willing to approve the third parole request only because he was no longer a potential candidate for President, Attorney General, or drug czar.

William Foster was released April 26, 2001.

A return to the islands

On New Year's Day, 2003, Patty Sue phoned from Hawaii, asking me what I would like for my 75th birthday, which was rushing at me like an oncoming train. I immediately said, "I'd love to find time to zip over to Hawaii and visit Sandy and David." A few days later round-trip tickets arrived. (I guess even a really skillful divorce lawyer can't always destroy the loving feelings two people have shared!)

Patty Sue elected to have a party also. David's unique sense of humor prompted him to suggest she invite some of the lady friends I got to know after our divorce. She did it! Gulp! It was a great party, with many friends there, including my dear friends, Patty Oliver and Dr. Jacqueline Brittain. They were still beautiful. Lynn was off island, alas, but I did get to meet her for a hug before I left.

As I watched David circulate through the party I couldn't help regretting that my grandson Scott wasn't there too, but the distance between his mother and me has made it all but impossible for me to see him over the years. Scott is very bright. He graduated from high school at sixteen, and currently attends the University of Oregon. He's specializing in computer-based design, and hoping to make it his career.

David took me on a hike over miles of lava to locate what once had been that magnificent 2.13 acres of oceanfront property with its own black sand beach, a stream running along side of it, and covered with coconut trees and Hawaiian flowers. Now it was covered with 30 feet high lava. The 34-acre property was the same. Ah, well. If one has good friends, and good health, that's the most important thing in life. It was a loving and memorable week. It's always fun to travel, especially to see loved ones, but it was good to get back home to complete this book!

How time speeds by! David at six years old...

...and at 43, after taking me on a great hike over our lava-covered land. Still my loving and handsome son, March 5, 2003.

Urine testing is all wet

The right of the people to be secure in their persons... against unreasonable searches and seizures, shall not be violated, and no Warrants shall issue, but upon probable cause.
— The Fourth Amendment to the Constitution
of the United States of America

Drug testing is a form of surveillance, albeit a technological one. Nonetheless, it reports on a person's off-duty activities just as surely as if someone had been present and watching. It is George Orwell's Big Brother society come to life.
— Federal Judge H. Lee Sarokin, September 19, 1986

Urine testing for Congress?

Members of Congress have quietly opposed urine testing for themselves. They have said it is "unnecessary, insulting, and undignified." Surely they deserve something special for their unflagging hypocrisy. How about "The Golden Shower Award"?

Invited to debate the nation's largest urine-testing companies

On July 21, 1999, I received a phone call from Michael Meredith, the clinical director and case manager of all Employee Assistance and Substance Abuse Professional assessments conducted by the national drug-testing company, PharmaTox. He invited me to debate the heads of the urine-testing industry at their national convention in Boston September 30 to October 1,1999, on the subject of medical marijuana. The convention was sponsored by Substance Abuse Program Administrators Association. The SAPAA says its mission is "to establish, promote, and communicate the highest standards of quality, integrity, and professionalism in the administration of workplace substance abuse prevention programs through education, training, and the exchange of ideas."

I had long wondered if urine-testing companies rewarded members of Congress for passing legislation that assured there would be ever more urine testing. How could I pass up such an opportunity to get an answer to that question? I couldn't, and didn't. Meredith suggested that I have a couple of cases of my books sent to the convention. Considering the audience, I suspected that only a case would be purchased.

I arrived at Boston's Logan airport at 3:45 p.m. on September 29 and took a taxi to the Marriott Hotel in nearby Peabody. As I checked in I was handed an impressive name tag, which proclaimed: SUBSTANCE ABUSE PROGRAM ADMINISTRATORS ASSOCIATION, and displayed below it, DAVID R. FORD, SPEAKER. It was connected to a purple harness to be worn around the neck. No expense spared here. I put on the harness and left a message for my host letting him know I'd arrived.

My reception: as warm as urine on ice

When I reached my room, the message light on the phone was blinking. Meredith was busy, but would meet me at the welcoming party. After unpacking and freshening up, I headed for the banquet room. SAPAA members were drinking and chatting; I overheard at least one conversation about the public-spirited service they were performing.

I had never met Meredith in person, so I scanned the room for his name tag. After checking a hundred tags, I concluded he wasn't there. No one said hello, no one said welcome. I checked my vest pocket; no, there wasn't a joint sticking out. Shucks, I thought, and I'm the kind of guy that's making them rich. I felt rather abandoned so I went to my room, lit up a joint, and soon was all smiles, thinking tomorrow maybe I'd get a laugh out of them if I offered to let them urine-test me.

Are members of Congress rewarded for increasing urine testing?

That very night I got the answer that lured me to the convention. While sitting in my room smoking that joint, I spotted a brochure on a writing table. It was a welcome addressed to SAPAA members by their president, Matthew Fagnani. It said in part:

Welcome, SAPAA Conference Attendees... A number of SAPAA Board and Association members have visited key governmental regulators and members of Congress... These visits have had a substantial impact on these key governmental and legislative leaders. I am always encouraged by the reception and reaction when visiting the Hill. I take this opportunity to remind our Congressional leaders and regulators that a *great many* of the *regulations* that now exist *were written by leaders of our industry*... I have found this to be of the utmost importance to these critical SAPAA contracts... It is important to consider the footprints SAPAA leaves behind in the halls of legislatures and regulators on both a federal and state level. Our footprints leave a firm and lasting impression... Our voices will be heard, and our membership will be served. [Emphasis added.]

I could almost see the money changing hands.

The next morning I made my way to the main ballroom. At a table just outside, I spoke with one of the women who was handing out literature, and she kindly said she'd be happy to collect the money for copies of *Marijuana: Not Guilty As Charged*. It was almost nine, time for the speakers to go at it.

The stage was well set up, with a microphone for each speaker. The room was filled with some 100 owners and CEOs of the country's major drug-testing companies. I took my place on the stage, and checked the schedule. Yep. There it was on the program: "Hot Topic Session: *Medical Marijuana*."

Nationally recognized speakers resurrect Reefer Madness

Sitting next to me was Katherine Ford (no relation), Director of Communications for the Drug-Free America Foundation, Inc. To her right was George R. Feicht, Master Trainer for the National Institute of Drug Abuse, NIDA. Also at the table was Dr. Michael Peat, who joined LabOne in June 1994 as Senior Vice President, Toxicology. Since 1999 he has served as President, Substance Abuse Testing. Formerly, Peat was VP of Toxicology for Roche Biomedical Laboratories and CompuChem Laboratories. Until 1994, he was a member of NIDA's Drug Testing Advisory Board of the Department of Health and Human Services.

The moderator was Michael Meredith, whom I finally met. Each speaker was given 10 minutes. So that you'll hang in there with me, I'll condense the talks.

First speaker, Katherine Ford:

> We are fighting all Schedule I drug legalization... any marijuana legalization, including so-called medical use. If marijuana were legalized it would have a great impact on your industry. Medical marijuana is a smoke screen to legalize marijuana for recreational use. The Florida initiative says that a third party can recommend medical pot. That means that even your auto mechanic can authorize the use of medical marijuana for athlete's foot, dandruff, a stubbed toe, etc. – which gives you an excuse to get high on the job."

(I came close to lighting up a joint at that point – purely for medical reasons: I needed something to keep from puking.)

Reality check:

Ms. Ford appears to have come unhinged by the horror, widespread in the drug-testing industry, of any re-legalization of pot, even as medicine. The facts: The Florida initiative protects *physicians*, not mechanics, who *recommend*, not "authorize," medicinal marijuana, and specifies penalties for fraudulent certification or use. If someone just wants to get high on his lunch hour legally, he still has to drink alcohol, like urine testers.

Second speaker, George R. Feicht:

> I'm familiar with the Haight-Ashbury area where all of our children were smoking pot, going on to acid, dropping out. With California decriminalization, there was a 50% increase in pot use. Use of a driving simulator showed that those who smoked pot killed everything that was in front of the car! There are almost 500 ingredients in marijuana. Ninety are cancer-producing. We have Marinol, which furnishes the benefits of THC without the garbage of pot. In my community only 450 students out of 1,000 will graduate. And 82% smoked pot."

Reality check:

I wondered whether Mr. Feicht had graduated – and the poor man must have been having a flashback. The Haight-Ashbury scene he was describing was from the 1960s. The facts: In California, since medical marijuana has been frequently in the news, teen use of pot has dropped to seven percent. Nationally it's 10 percent. The California Highway Patrol (CHP) published a study by the California Department of Justice, titled *Marijuana and Alcohol: A Driver Performance Study*. The study was expected to show that pot was more dangerous than alcohol. To the CHP's surprise and embarrassment, results showed that some motorists actually drove more skillfully after smoking marijuana. In 1998, Australia conducted a similar test. Findings were that those under the influence of marijuana were no more likely to have an accident than those who were drug-free. (My own opinion is that no one should drive under the influence of anything.)

Mr. Feicht's statement that there are almost 500 ingredients in marijuana compares with the statement that there are hundreds of ingredients in mother's milk, or coffee. True, but so what? And if there are "90 cancer-causing ingredients in marijuana," why do scientific studies show no record of anyone getting cancer because of cannabis?

Marinol doesn't provide the benefits cannabis provides. When nausea is severe, most patients cannot swallow the Marinol capsule at all, and others cannot keep it down for the up to an hour Marinol needs to start taking effect. One or two puffs of pot stop the nausea and vomiting, generally within two minutes. The cost of cannabis is pennies per puff, and with today's stronger cannabis, one puff frequently does the job; Marinol can cost $2,000 or more a month. Last, if 82% of the students in Mr. Freicht's community use pot, it would appear that Californians for Drug Free Youth is not doing well.

Third speaker, David R. Ford:

In his introduction of me, Meredith said, "David R. Ford is the author of the hardback book *Marijuana: Not Guilty As Charged.* David comes into the lion's den. For the writing of his book he interviewed physicians and more than 300 medical and relaxation users of marijuana. He has been interviewed on more than 100 radio stations in the U.S. and Canada."

I felt more like David taking on Goliath than the prophet Daniel, but maybe Meredith's analogy was apt after all. This surely was the liar's den – uh, lion's den. The other speakers were "singing to the choir." Even though their livelihood was at stake, I found it difficult to believe that those in the audience, who had to know better, were eating up what their "Masters of the Universe" were dishing out.

I'll include only a few excerpts from my speech, mostly things that I have not already addressed, or that could use repeating:

> Alcohol causes more violence and death than all illegal drugs combined. It's the teens' drug of choice, and it's killing them. Millions of teens and adults have switched from relatively harmless pot to alcohol, nicotine products, Ecstasy, speed, heroin, and other dangerous

drugs. Why? Because those are rarely included in urine testing. In California, where marijuana as medicine is frequently in the news, pot use is seven percent among teens, compared to 10 percent nationally.

Impairment testing of those responsible for public safety makes sense, and must replace urine testing, which repeatedly produces results that have nothing to do with performance. Performance testing takes less than a minute, using a video screen and a person moving a cursor. Certainly you are aware of impairment testing; it's understandable why you wouldn't want it implemented. To deny innocent persons jobs, however, or to cause them to lose employment and earned benefits because of smoking a joint two weeks before, is yet another government-sanctioned injustice. Let's work together to stop the hypocrisy and outright government-endorsed lies. Marijuana prohibition was created in response to false charges like these, among hundreds of others:

- Marijuana is the most violence-causing drug in the history of mankind.
- It turns people into criminals.
- Many marijuana users become hopelessly insane.

Trusting the government, politicians, and police, rather than doctors, to tell us what is and what is not medicine would be laughable if it weren't causing deaths. The DEA's own judge, Francis Young, in 1988, after two years of studying thousands of pages on medical marijuana, and interviewing patients and medical doctors from leading universities, stated, *"Marijuana, in its natural form, is one of the safest therapeutically active substances known to man."*

Final speaker, Dr. Michael Peat:

There should be science behind the use of that drug, documented studies of its safety, before its use is approved. I would advocate that if there is a medical use, it be documented. If it is, it is going to be associated with THC (the psychoactive ingredient in pot). And it would have to be an improved delivery system such as Marinol capsules.

If not, it's going to lead to legalization. In Amsterdam today you can buy marijuana in coffee shops. But Europeans are rethinking those decisions. We don't want to make the same mistakes.

Federal law is that marijuana is a Schedule I substance. Therefore its use is illegal. The science behind the medical use of marijuana is still to be proven. I strongly recommend against the passage of any medicinal marijuana regulations.

Reality check:

Dr. Peat's insistence that we lack scientific evidence for marijuana's safety and medical value looks like a serious case of denial. The facts: Dozens of scientific studies have documented marijuana's medical value, including the one published earlier that same year by the Institute of Medicine (IOM), a division of the National Academy of Sciences. The IOM's results reconfirmed marijuana's medical value. Every legitimate, objective national and international study for over 100 years has found that marijuana is not a dangerous drug, and that there should be no criminal penalties for its use.

The Dutch experiment is working and they are not rethinking that decision. Allowing "coffee shops" to sell cannabis has not increased use of hard drugs – a perfect example of pot *not* being a "stepping stone" to hard drugs. The "improved delivery system" he claims we need is already available – and much better than Marinol capsules: Vaporizers get the medicine in cannabis into the bloodstream faster, and eliminate all smoke and tars.

A Schedule I drug is one that is too dangerous to prescribe and has no medical value. It's obvious to any honest, informed person that marijuana does not fulfill *either* of the Schedule I criteria. Marijuana should immediately be reduced to a Schedule III drug. Indeed it should never have been made illegal for adults in the first place, but the least we can do is to stop denying people the medicine they need.

The audience was polite. Each speaker received hefty applause, even I – although when they applauded me I had a feeling that hundreds of toes were crossed. Moderator Meredith then opened the floor to questions from the audience. Most were addressed to me.

I was asked, "How do you think marijuana use as medicine will impact drug testing and prevention programs in this country?"

I replied, " To give us genuine protection from those whose drug use actually compromises safety, we must shift from urine testing to impairment testing. Prevention programs will eventually change when the government stops telling lies about pot, when it is forced to tell us the truth, that marijuana is medicine, that it is far less dangerous than alcohol, nicotine, and other drugs. Marijuana is also nature's tranquilizer. It is not for kids in school, and it is illegal for them, and always has been. Compared to other drugs, however, marijuana is the least harmful.

A woman in the audience asked, "You said alcohol causes more death and violence than all illegal drugs combined. What do you base that statement on?"

My reply: "First, as I already mentioned, in 5,000 years pot has never caused one toxicity death. Can we say that about alcohol? No. I've interviewed dozens of police officers, and asked them, concerning family or spousal violence, 'How many calls have you answered where the only drug used was pot?' Answer: 'I can't think of any.' 'How about alcohol?' Answer: 'At least 90 percent.'"

At one point, after I finished answering a question about what urine testing actually measures, Dr. Peat surprised and delighted me by jumping in and confirming that "it's not THC that remains in the system, but rather an *inactive* metabolite." That metabolite can remain in fat tissue for weeks, like the vitamins A, D, E, and K, producing a "positive" urine test, even though the cannabis user is no more impaired than a person who downed a couple of brews the night before the test.

In the speaker biographies it had mentioned that I'd created a number of business enterprises – and that I had owned airplanes since I was 23. One man in the audience asked, "Being a marijuana smoker, do they actually let you fly a plane?" "I do not fly a plane when I have smoked pot." I considered answering, "Being an alcohol drinker, do they actually let *you* drive a car?" Instead, I just smiled.

The questions went on, still primarily directed at me. It was obvious to me that the audience absorbed nothing positive that I said relating to the unfairness of urine testing, particularly regarding pot users. The proof? Not one person bought a book! Normally, when I talked to an audience of a hundred people, at least thirty or forty of them would buy books. It wasn't the lack of sales that bothered me; what did concern me was that those who thirst for our urine do not have an equal thirst for truth. If I hadn't known already that the War on Drugs is a war on truth, I'd have learned it that day: Medical marijuana was the enemy, and as its ally, I was the enemy too.

Performance testing makes sense; urine testing smells

SAPAA's goal is to retain and expand urine testing. If this drug-war farce continues at all, urine testing, which is primarily designed to catch pot users, must be replaced by impairment testing. Equipment for such tests can report within a minute whether a person is impaired for work – a tremendous savings to employers. More important, it tells employers what they actually need to know, whether you can work safely, right now, rather than whether you had a good time in your off hours, a week ago. Whether you smoked a joint the night before or are taking a pharmaceutical prescribed by your doctor is irrelevant. If the test shows you are impaired, you are impaired! If not, you go ahead and do your job. Employees must demand performance testing, and talk to their unions about refusing urine testing. I foresee a day when employees will rightly refuse urine testing.

Following the stream of urine-testing reasoning

Urine testing was first performed on those working in jobs in which innocent bystanders could be injured or killed by those on drugs, such as military personnel, bus drivers, and airline pilots. These days, millions of civilians are tested, including people who work at desk jobs, and kids in grade school. The industry is driven by billions of dollars in profits. Home urine-testing kits are available for parents who don't mind losing the respect of their children. Threatening children with, "I can test you at any time" encourages children who wish to experiment with drugs to sniff solvents, or pursue other dangerous substances that can cause death, but do not show up in a urine test.

Kids are being taught early on that they are guilty until proven innocent. They must find school lessons on the Constitution and Bill of Rights confusing.

When England and Wales began testing prisoners, use of marijuana decreased but the use of harder drugs, such as heroin, almost doubled, because heroin is out of the system faster than pot and won't show up in the results of urine tests.

In a 1998 study of high-tech industries by the Institute of Industrial Relations, researchers found that "drug testing programs do not succeed in improving productivity. Surprisingly, companies adopting drug-testing programs are found to exhibit lower levels of productivity than their counterparts that do not test. Both pre-employment and random testing of workers are found to be associated with lower levels of productivity." Resentment – colloquially and perhaps more appropriately, being "pissed off" – causes many test subjects to cut back on production when forced to pee on command.

Drug testing does not work. It enhances neither safety nor productivity. It unjustly punishes innocent people who use drugs responsibly. It poisons the relationship between employees and management, and between citizens and their government. It makes a mockery of the United States Constitution.

The Supreme Court creates new prospects for the urine-testing industry

During the month of June, 2002:

- The 9th U.S. District Court ruled that requiring schoolchildren to recite the Pledge of Allegiance was unconstitutional because the words "one nation under God" constitute an impermissible establishment of religion.

- The U.S. Supreme Court ruled that schools are allowed to require students who participate in after-school extracurricular activities to be urine-tested. Urine testing is hypocritical and counterproductive. Now, students in the choir, band, or cheerleading teams must consent to regular drug tests. Most kids who are experimenting with drugs will either drop such programs, which in themselves keep kids off drugs, or they will switch to dangerous drugs that are out of the system by Monday.

Maybe the words that don't belong in the Pledge of Allegiance are "...with liberty and justice for all."

Findings and recommendations

What I've learned in 58 years from thousands of drug users

I've learned that drug prohibition does not work. Never has. Never will. The drug war has produced more injustice, corruption, racism, violence, broken families, and broken politicians' promises than all illegal drugs. Overdose deaths from hard drug use result primarily from drugs that are contaminated, or of unknown strength, and the contamination and unknown strengths are caused by prohibition. If drugs were decriminalized, prescribed by medical doctors for addicted patients who have been unable to kick the habit, such drugs would be uncontaminated and the strength would be carefully calibrated.

Inveterate heroin addicts will not quit heroin willingly, and prison punishment is counterproductive. For those who are truly addicted to hard drugs, there should be programs of medical and psychiatric attention, not prison—where all drugs are available at a price, and where many inmates are beaten, raped, or killed. When released, many previously nonviolent inmates subjected to such horrors return to society with anger and resentment toward our government. It has been shown in Europe that with doctor-approved low maintenance doses, many addiction patients are able to go to work, stop stealing or prostituting themselves for drug money, and support their families. Psychiatric help can wean them off such drugs as heroin.

Designating marijuana a Schedule I drug is disgraceful hypocrisy

Thus even users of heroin, which *is* dangerous and *does not* have medical value, would be much better off if their drug were decriminalized.

Punishing them instead of helping them is simply crazy. But how much crazier is it to punish people for using a drug that *isn't* dangerous and *does* have medical value? Equating marijuana with heroin by lumping them together in Schedule I is disgracefully hypocritical and cruel. If the government seriously intended to "protect us from dangerous drugs," it would "get tough" on the legal drugs that do fit the Schedule I criteria: alcohol and nicotine products, which together cause the deaths of more than 500,000 Americans each year. The deaths caused by all illegal drugs combined are a tiny fraction of that number, and the number of deaths from pot by itself is *zero*.

Marijuana is the least dangerous of all drugs. By arresting marijuana growers and users, the government opens the door to all the other, more easily concealed drugs, such as heroin, speed, Ecstasy, and other designer drugs that are just waiting to be released.

The DEA insists against all the evidence that marijuana is addictive. Really? There are medications to combat addiction to almost every known addictive drug. There is no medication to combat marijuana addiction. Why not? Because cannabis is simply not physically addictive.

The federal government wastes seven to eight *billion* dollars of our tax money each year to keep pot and hemp illegal. The government's intention is to keep the war on medical cannabis going, and to continue imprisoning the ill and dying, along with anyone else found in possession of pot. Without the arrest of more than 700,000 cannabis users each year the drug war would be like a three-legged stool. (If we sat on it, we know where we would land.)

"We're doing it for the kids" is a bald-faced lie

"We're protecting kids from drugs!" Such touching concern is well demonstrated by putting parents in prison, some for more than twenty years, don't you agree? Putting children in foster homes because their parents participated in nonviolent, victimless, consensual crime creates resentment by the parents *and* the children, leading to more drug use, not less. Teens can tell you that it's easier to obtain pot than beer or liquor. Why? Because those drugs are legal, but regulated. Drug dealers do not ask for IDs; they couldn't care less if the customer is 10 years old. They push synthetic "club drugs" and frequently include a free sample of speed or heroin.

TV warning ads increase *teen drug use!*

Hysterically exaggerated anti-drug television ads actually encourage kids to use the targeted drugs. Young people are always ready to take up the challenge, especially when they know they're being lied to. Warning kids not to use a drug they hadn't even heard of is like warning them *not* to see a certain "wild sex movie." Of *course* they're going to try it.

During alcohol prohibition, 12-year-olds were buying booze on street corners and becoming early addicts, like kids are doing today with certain illegal drugs. It seems the only thing we learn from history is that we don't learn from it.

The DEA will say that its efforts have reduced drug use by 50 percent. Not true. After more than 30 years of drug war and $300 billion expended, we have more addiction, more overdoses, and more substance abuse than ever before. Today, illegal drugs are cheaper, purer, and include new designer drugs that are more easily obtainable than ever before. Stop the flow of drugs in one place and it finds another channel. Suppress production of one drug and new ones are manufactured. Destroy the Medellin cartel and the Cali cartel expands to fill the vacuum. Throw the leaders of the Cali cartel in prison, and their lieutenants form decentralized organizations that are harder to combat. They say we must keep fighting the War on Drugs. Do they also feel we should still be fighting the Vietnam War?

In addition, we have the ever-growing criminal black market that always accompanies prohibition. We're not fighting drugs; this is a federal government crime against our own people. You might call it "blowback." Or "friendly fire."

Is it any wonder that teens switch to dangerous drugs? When they are reminded that marijuana is a Schedule I drug along with heroin – shucks, might as well give heroin a try. Heroin is the most physically addictive drug there is, apart from nicotine.

In mid-May, 2002, Drug Czar John Walters admitted that $1.8 billion worth of federal anti-drug ads were having opposite effect on teens. Some adolescents are more likely to use drugs after viewing ads, a federally commissioned report noted. Despite such findings, funding the TV ads will continue at $180 million a year![80]

Walters and the DEA continue to spout that they only go after major traffickers. Really?

In three decades of constantly escalating drug war, there have been more than 15 million marijuana arrests in the U.S., including 734,498 arrests in 2000 alone. About 88% of all marijuana arrests are for possession only, most often for amounts less than two ounces. Many have served long sentences. Right now a half million nonviolent Americans are behind bars on drug charges, compared to 50,000 in 1980. With that kind of carnage, the prohibitionists must surely be close to winning their war – shouldn't they?

When President Richard Nixon launched the War on Drugs in 1971, he said we'd have a drug-free America by 1995. In 1997, President Clinton ordered a five-year plan to halt drugs coming from Mexico. On February 12, 2002, George W. Bush aimed at 25% drug reduction within five years. Drug-use rates remain constant – as does the constant flow of lies.

Marijuana laws and propaganda are based on lies, not science

One of the government's professional prevaricators, DEA Administrator Asa Hutchinson, stepped down early in 2003 but his lies linger on.

On March 14, 2002, speaking before the American Pain Society, Hutchinson said:

"None of the studies on medical marijuana have produced results indicating that patients benefit from its use."

The truth:

The U.S. National Institutes of Health, Department of Health and Human Services (HHS), Workshop on the Medical Utility of Marijuana, 1997, reported: "Smoked marijuana has been shown to lower intraocular eye pressure (IOP) in subjects with normal IOP and patients with glaucoma... Clinical studies and survey data in healthy populations have shown a strong relationship between marijuana use and increased eating... Inhaled marijuana has the potential to reduce chemotherapy-related nausea and vomiting."

Dozens of scientific studies have demonstrated marijuana's value in reducing nausea and vomiting, stimulating appetite, promoting weight gain, and diminishing IOP from glaucoma. There is also evidence that THC reduces muscle spasticity from spinal cord injuries and multiple sclerosis, and diminishes tremors in MS patients. It has also been shown that smoked cannabis provides relief from migraine headaches, depression, seizures, insomnia, and chronic pain. No fewer than 25 scientific medical references supporting the mentioned medical benefits have been identified.[81]

If marijuana has no medical value, as Hutchinson claims, why would a pharmaceutical company copy marijuana, in its synthetic pot capsule Marinol? And why does the federal government's Investigational New Drug (IND) program continue to supply certain patients with marijuana cigarettes each month? And why did the DEA's own chief administrative judge, Francis Young, state in 1988 that marijuana's medical use is "clear beyond any question"?

If we knew nothing about cannabis, and a botanist stumbled across it in some distant rain forest, and researchers discovered its dozens of medical applications, it would soon be hailed as a miracle drug.

In the same speech before the American Pain Society, Hutchinson also claimed:

"We are making significant progress in our fight against drugs. Drug use overall is down by 50 percent in the last 20 years. Cocaine use is down 75 percent in the last 15 years. That is progress."[82]

The truth:

Hutchinson's numbers are about as accurate as Enron's. If you believe them, ask any federal prosecutor, probation officer, or substance abuse counselor. Shucks, ask your youngster! Cocaine use is down somewhat, due only to the high cost. Coke users just switched to methamphetamine, also called "ice," "speed," and "crystal meth."

The DEA's "Green Harvest" operation has been "successful" in eliminating cannabis cultivation on the Big Island of Hawaii, including virtually all of Hawaii's medical-quality marijuana plants – and thus gave a boost for the black market that I'm sure organized crime appreciates greatly.

In his invitation on August 27, 2002, to a summit on crystal meth, acting Big Island Police Chief Lawrence K. Mahuna wrote, "The Big Island has a major, and growing, ice problem. Statistics indicate that the use of crystal methamphetamine is higher here than anywhere else in the nation."

Congratulations, Asa! Until your "success," Hawaii residents favored relatively harmless pot. Now they've switched to a dangerous drug. Are you proud of duplicating Nixon's success in Vietnam, when he caused soldiers to switch from pot to heroin?

Hutchinson continued his lies in a debate with NORML executive director Keith Stroup on CNN's *Crossfire*, Thursday, July 25, 2002:

"I think that we ought to listen to the American Medical Association that believes there is a not a medical benefit for marijuana, for smoking marijuana. And so I think that's the group that we should listen to, and they have not said it is good medicine. We are a compassionate society. We want to provide good medicine. We're authorizing continued studies of any health benefits. Thus far, they're not there and so we have the right policy."

The truth:

When cannabis was prohibited in 1937, the American Medical Association was outraged. Many of its members knew very well that cannabis has numerous medical benefits. Since then, study after study has confirmed pot's medical value, and as each one is announced the DEA just sticks its head farther into the sand.

On *Crossfire* Hutchinson also said – almost certainly counting on viewers to fail to distinguish between *dependence* and *addiction*:

"...225,000 Americans each year are admitted to treatment programs because of marijuana dependence."

The truth:

None of those who enter such treatment programs are addicted to cannabis, because it's simply not physically addictive. Many don't have a dependence problem either; they're there only because the alternative was a prison term. *Most* pot users enrolled in drug treatment programs are poly-drug abusers who also report problems with alcohol, amphetamines, cocaine, tranquilizers, or heroin.[83]

National and international studies paid for by the federal government have constantly shown that cannabis is not physically addictive. One such study: The Federal Narcotics Hospital in Lexington, Kentucky, conducted an investigation. Ten men were kept "high" constantly, with at least one joint every waking hour for 30 days, then abruptly deprived of cannabis entirely. No withdrawal symptoms were evident.[84]

Articles and books that do claim a growing cannabis dependence problem have been written by providers of drug treatment – who are not exactly unbiased![85]

Another Hutchinson lie on the *Crossfire* program: "More teenagers go into treatment for marijuana addiction than any other drug, including alcohol. It is a serious problem in our country."

Parents who have been fed propaganda of marijuana killing brain cells, causing violence, suppressing ambition, and all the other false charges, and who then catch their kids using pot, are quite naturally scared to death – and thus understandably likely to buy the notion that only "rehab" will "save their children."

By this time, the tip of Hutchinson's nose had disappeared behind the opposite edge of the screen, but that didn't stop him from lying again:

"It has health consequences. It is more toxic than tobacco."

The truth:

Research in Jamaica and Greece, funded by the U.S. government, found no physical or mental problems among men who had used marijuana heavily for many years. Numerous studies showed that marijuana did not produce physical dependence and withdrawal, even after long-term, high-dose use.[86]

In 1995, relying on 30 years of scientific research, editors of the internationally respected British medical journal *Lancet* concluded that "the smoking of cannabis, even long term, is not harmful to health."

Saying that pot is more toxic than tobacco is, to be polite, dangerous misrepresentation. To be less polite, it's criminal fraud. Some 430,000 Americans die from the toxic effects of nicotine *each year*. In more than *5,000 years* no one has ever recorded the death of a single person from the toxicity of pot. Talk about "sending the wrong message"! Young people who believe Hutchinson will believe they are safer trying cigarettes than experimenting with pot. Many will become addicted, and a third of those will die from the toxic effect.

Lies upon lies upon lies

With distorted evidence, the drug czar and prohibitionist organizations such as The Partnership for a Drug Free America (PDFA) and Parents' Resource Institute for Drug Education (PRIDE) have frightened teens and parents alike. They have proclaimed, with support from the federal government, such false propaganda as:

> Marijuana wrecks the immune system. It's physically addictive. It's a "gateway" to heroin and other hard drugs. It's carcinogenic, more dangerous than tobacco. It's poison. It kills brain cells. It's 10 times stronger, and therefore more dangerous and addictive, than in the 1960s. [That's to scare parents who grew up in the 1960s.] It causes large breasts to grow on young men. [It didn't take long for disappointed transsexuals to disprove that myth.] It causes genetic deformities. It causes users to be susceptible to communist propaganda. It causes cancerous tumors, it causes short-term memory loss – permanently. It incites rape. It causes death. It incites crime, causes marijuana-related hospital emergencies, and is a major cause of highway accidents. It causes fetal alcohol syndrome, homosexual-

ity, and AIDS. It causes children to join gangs and encourages gun
possession. And it has no medical value.

Not one of the hundreds of such fabrications has *ever* been confirmed
by honest scientific investigation. With the wealth of proven fact available
to them, the drug warriors cannot possibly be honestly ignorant, yet they
continue their constant drumbeat of deceit. The charges above are so
absurd, so preposterous that no one would believe them if they weren't
repeated endlessly. And so they repeat them endlessly, in a campaign
reminiscent of the Big Lie technique used by Hitler's propagandists. Is it
any wonder that millions of parents, police, and even some doctors still
believe the misinformation spread by drug warriors?

Studies show that cannabis is not a major DUI concern

One of the classic hobgoblins conjured up by the drug warriors is the
image of pot-crazed drivers recklessly causing thousands of deaths on the
highways. No one should drive while using any drug, including legal
medications *and* marijuana, but in fact marijuana DUIs are negligible
compared to alcohol DUIs. Almost invariably, when pot is found in the
system of a driver involved in an accident, alcohol is also present.[87]

What does actual research tell us?

- A study conducted by the California Highway Patrol (CHP) in 1986,
  titled *Marijuana and Alcohol: A Driver Performance Study* started
  from the hypothesis that smoking marijuana diminished a person's
  ability to operate a vehicle competently. To the CHP's surprise and
  embarrassment, results showed that some people actually drive more
  skillfully after smoking marijuana.[88]
- Researchers who conducted a study for the Department of
  Transportation in 1993 concluded: Of the many psychoactive drugs,
  licit and illicit, that are available and used by people who subsequently
  drive, marijuana may well be among the least harmful.[89]
- In a 1993 study, researchers compared marijuana's influence on
  driving to the influence of low levels of blood alcohol content (.04%
  BAC, half of the legal limit in many states). Alcohol produced
  significant reductions in driving ability and marijuana produced
  none.[90]
- Studies have also found that subjects tend to drive more cautiously
  after smoking pot. They take fewer risks, drive at slower speeds,
  and maintain a greater distance from other cars.[91]

- In 2002, British scientists found that motorists who smoke a cannabis joint retain more control behind the wheel than those who drink a glass of wine.[92]
- Marijuana has far less impact on psychomotor skills than alcohol and is seldom a causal factor in automobile accidents, according to the findings of recent international studies. Britain's Transport Research Laboratory (TRL) found that drivers under the influence of marijuana performed better behind the wheel than those under the influence of alcohol. A similar study concluded that drivers who used marijuana – unlike those that used alcohol – were aware of their impairment and attempted to compensate for it by driving more cautiously.[93]
- Similar results were reported in 2002 by a South Australian team at the Department of Clinical and Experimental Pharmacology at the University of Adelaide. Their study found that alcohol "overwhelmingly plays the greatest role in road crashes ... [and] conversely, ... marijuana has a negligible impact on culpability." An earlier Australian review of 2,500 injured drivers also found that cannabis had "no significant effect" on drivers' culpability in motor vehicle accidents.[94]

Why few doctors, and no drug companies, recommend cannabis for pain

One question puzzled me for a long time. How can so many physicians, the most thoroughly educated professionals, be unaware of the low risk and high benefits of medical cannabis? Or if they are aware, why don't they recommend its use much more often than they do?

Certainly the truth is right in front of them, in black and white. The respected *Merck Manual of Diagnosis and Therapy*, the most widely used medical text in the world, states:

> Cannabis (marijuana) can be used on an episodic but continuous basis without evidence of social or psychic dysfunction... the chief opposition to the drug rests on a *political*, and *not a toxicological*, foundation. The testing that identifies an inactive metabolite only identifies use. *It has no correlation with dysfunction, and the smoker may be free of effect by the time his urine tests positive.*[95] [Emphasis added.]

When therapeutic drugs are under discussion in medical school, there is no mention of therapeutic marijuana. Doctors have been subjected to the same false pot propaganda and hysteria as the rest of the public.

Pharmaceutical companies, with huge resources at hand and enormous profits to protect, make enormous effort to inform doctors about their products. What defenders of medical marijuana have those resources – and that level of financial incentive?

Doctors have had to learn the medical benefits of pot from their patients' testimony, which they're routinely taught to question. They also fear the government – and for good reason: Even in states that have legalized medical marijuana, it requires real courage for physicians to recommend cannabis to a patient, when officials at the highest levels of the federal government threaten to exclude them from Medicare and Medicaid reimbursement, to rescind their licenses to prescribe government-approved drugs, and thus, practically speaking, the loss of their right to practice their profession, and to prosecute them for federal crimes.

Who are these potheads, and why have they wasted their lives?

Perhaps you remember something I said in the Preface: that I wasn't telling you my story to blow my own horn, but to show you that, far from being a detriment, pot can be a source of creativity, healing, solace, passion, and success. (If you've forgotten, I do understand. After all, that was a lifetime ago!) Along the way I've told you stories of many other men and women I've met whose lives were enhanced by their use of cannabis. There have been many others I haven't met who would tell you the same.

One of thousands of super-successful "potheads" was the world-renowned astronomer, Carl Sagan, professor at Cornell University. Sagan died December 20, 1996, after a two-year battle with a bone-marrow disease. He credited cannabis for inspiration in his lectures and his popular science books, among them *Cosmos, Contact,* and *The Dragons of Eden.* Sagan was perhaps the world's greatest science educator, reaching millions of people through newspapers, magazines, and television broadcasts. His Emmy- and Peabody-award-winning series *Cosmos,* was the most-viewed series in the history of public television, and was watched by more than 500 million people in 60 countries. The accompanying book, *Cosmos,* was on The New York Times bestseller list for 70 weeks and was the best-selling science book ever published in English.

Sagan also credited cannabis for his inspiring essays and scientific insight, as well as for helping him write university commencement speeches, and for improving his sex life. Lester Grinspoon, M.D., professor at Harvard Medical School, now retired, kept the secret of

Sagan's marijuana use until after the death of his friend.

Dr. Grinspoon also smoked, after a rather late start: he didn't try cannabis until he was 44 years old. After years of research he courageously wrote *Marihuana Reconsidered*, and *Marihuana: the Forbidden Medicine*. His son Danny died from leukemia. During bouts of chemotherapy, his constant vomiting ceased after a few puffs of pot, and he asked for a submarine sandwich. Danny died peacefully in 1973.

A few other notable cannabis users who have admitted their use: the Beatles, Paul McCartney, John Lennon, George Harrison, Ringo Starr; trumpet player extraordinaire Louis Armstrong; actor, singer, and prolific songwriter Willie Nelson; crooner Bing Crosby (almost), actor Woody Harrelson; former New Mexico Governor Gary Johnson; Vice President Al Gore; Arizona Governor Bruce Babbitt; U.S. Senator Claiborne Pell; Congressman Newt Gingrich; and President Bill Clinton.

Then there are a few million other well-known, respected Americans who have put pot to their lips, including major motion picture stars. Many still prefer not to be identified. And how about the 83 million other Americans who have smoked pot, and are doing just fine? It's my hope that this book will encourage others to open the closet door and take pride that cannabis increased their health and creativity. I will never "out" anyone. They must make that decision. My goodness, what *would* the government do if, tomorrow, 83 million Americans stood up together and said, "Yeah, I've smoked pot – *and I inhaled!*"

Cannabis is competition to major cartels

Who is behind all the lies told about cannabis and other drugs? Well... who benefits from the lies?

Multibillion-dollar corporations have politicians in their pockets. Marijuana is stiff competition for the products of multibillion-dollar, multinational corporations – and it's not their cup of "tea" because you cannot patent an herb. They have huge vested interests to protect – and huge reserves of money to contribute to individual politicians and political action committees (PACs).

The mass media have found that dramas that demonize drug users and news stories of big drug busts draw big audiences, and huge advertising revenues – including the more than $1 billion from drug companies. When the pharmaceutical companies wield that much clout, we have to ask: Do the media tend to *ignore* the dangers of *legal* drugs, while overblowing the dangers of *illegal* drugs? Pharmaceutical companies themselves mention possible death-causing drug reactions –

to avoid legal action when users die from their TV-advertised drugs

Thousands of marijuana users are incarcerated in privatized money-making prisons that are on the New York Stock Exchange – yet another industry with a financial stake in continued prohibition: Releasing nonviolent pot "criminals" would reduce stockholder profits.

Think of the many medical problems marijuana eases or eliminates: loss of appetite, nausea, vomiting, muscle spasms, premenstrual syndrome (PMS), depression, anxiety, stress, lack of sleep, chronic pain, glaucoma, and more. Now think of the *billions* of dollars spent on synthetic pharmaceuticals to treat the same ills. Would their manufacturers want the government to legalize an herb that you can grow in your back yard, yet that accomplishes much the same relief? Are cigarette companies interested in an herb that is *not* physically addictive? They wouldn't have steady buyers. And how about alcohol companies? Surely, they aren't afraid of pot. Or are they?

Competition from pot haunts alcohol companies

Professor Alfred R. Lindesmith, an Indiana University sociologist, said, "It is of incidental interest that some pot smokers, both old and young, have developed an aversion to alcohol, regarding it as a debasing and degrading drug, a view which is standard among the Hindus of India, where alcohol is strongly taboo for religious reasons. Some of these people were heavy users of alcohol before they tried cannabis and feel that the latter saved them from becoming alcoholics."[96] Others echo Lindesmith's observation. A Denver beer distributor: "Our retailers say they can tell when a big shipment of marijuana hits town. The [beer] sales go down."[97] The manager of a discotheque in Miami, Florida: "Marijuana spells disaster to the liquor trade. If they ever legalize it, the liquor business is dead." He added that if his young patrons could buy marijuana legally, *many* "wouldn't touch liquor."[98]

Is the drug war profitable for those who perpetuate it?

One would expect that after more than 32 years and $300 billion down the urinal, even the most hawkish general in the drug war might think it was time for a cease-fire. On the other hand – if you were on the receiving end of those billions, would you want the drug war to end?

The DEA web site reports that, in 1972, its agents numbered 2,775. By 2003 that number had more than tripled, to 9,629. The feds spend $20 billion a year on their conveniently permanent drug war, with a large portion devoted to keeping you from smoking a joint for your depression

– depression you probably wouldn't have without the war on pot!

Early 20th-Century critic and social activist Randolph Bourne said "War is the health of the state." Certainly the number of government workers whose financial health depends in whole or in part on their War on Drugs is huge: myriads of judges, bailiffs, jailers, parole officers, prison guards, court clerks, prosecutors, customs officers, contractors who construct prisons, wardens that run them, bus drivers that haul both pot users and authentic criminals to them, manufacturers of police cars, helicopters, and body armor, the CIA, the FBI, the DEA, the National Guard, the Coast Guard, ... Drug thugs from the czar down to his lowliest serf depend on the perpetual prosecution of the drug war.

Alcohol, tobacco, and pharmaceutical companies reap huge profits from the sales of their products – but they aren't the only ones. Taxes on these products are very high, and the government rakes in billions. If pot were legalized – even if only for medical use – many users would grow their own. For commercial pot to compete with homegrown, government would have to keep taxes low. Thus government itself has a powerful financial incentive to keep cannabis illegal – and steer potential pot users to alcohol and other drugs.

Is marijuana competition to pharmaceutical companies?

How do pharmaceutical companies view the prospect of legal medical cannabis? Journalist Carl Wagner gave this answer in the Hull *Daily Mail* (United Kingdom) on May 31, 2002:

> LITTLE PROFIT IN CANNABIS CURE
> The truth is that herbal cannabis in natural forms would yield little profit for pharmaceutical corporations, while eliminating in the long term profit-driven patent drugs. Why allow people to use a safe plant for pennies when you can sell them a pill for a pound?

Nothing dramatizes the difference between cannabis and the products of the pharmaceutical giants than Marinol, the synthetic prescription drug that contains marijuana's active ingredient, THC – "pot in a capsule." (Question: Where do you suppose the name Mari – nol came from? Mari – juana, by chance? You bet!)

The following excerpts are from the *Physician's Desk Reference* (PDR) 2003: pp. 3234-3235:

INDICATIONS AND USAGE

Marinol is synthetic delta-9-tetrahydrocannabinol... Delta-9-THC...
A natural occurring component of cannabis sativa [Marijuana]

Marinol... treatment of anorexia associated with weight loss in patients with AIDS.

Nausea and vomiting... metabolites have been detected for more than five weeks... patients should be advised of possible changes in mood... so as to avoid panic... A cannabinoid dose-related 'high.' [Easy laughing, elation, and heightened awareness.]

WARNINGS

Patients receiving treatment with Marinol should be specifically warned not to drive, operate machinery, or engage in any hazardous activity *until* it is established that they are able to tolerate the drug and to perform such tasks safely. [Emphasis added.]

Employers that reject any applicant that smokes marijuana have no problem hiring people who take Marinol – yet the two drugs have the same psychoactive ingredient, and the same psychoactive effects. If Marinol does not automatically invalidate a worker's job performance, neither does organic marijuana.

In fact, there *are* medical differences – and all of them are in marijuana's favor.

Synthetic marijuana compared to the real thing

A pot high lasts for an hour or so, while a Marinol high may last for as long as 12 to 14 hours, and is often so intense one can't do useful work.

Marinol takes about an hour to kick in – an hour that seems endless when you're reeling from pain or nausea.

When Marinol is swallowed, it must proceed through the stomach and into the small intestine before being assimilated into the bloodstream. After absorption, it passes through the liver, where a significant proportion is biotransformed into other chemicals. Due to metabolism by the liver, 90 percent or more of swallowed THC never reaches sites of activity in the body. A recent study showed that, two hours after swallowing 10 to 15 milligrams of Marinol, 84 percent of subjects had no measurable THC in their blood. After six hours, 57 percent still had none. By contrast, two to five milligrams of THC consumed through smoking cannabis reliably produced blood concentrations above the effective level within a few minutes.[99]

Inhaling, whether from a joint or a vaporizer, acts as rapidly as an intravenous injection. Relief from pain and nausea is almost immediate.

Cannabis smokers and vaporizer users can control dosage much more precisely than Marinol users: if one puff doesn't do the job, they can take another – and can easily stop before they become impaired. Incidentally, a vaporizer heats the cannabis to just under 400 degrees. The cannabis does not burn. You inhale only the vapor – no smoke, no tar – and I found that you obtain about twice the medicine from a vaporizer that you do from a joint, so it actually pays for itself. The cost of a vaporizer runs from about $85 to around $350.

And imagine trying to swallow a capsule while gagging from nausea and about to vomit.

Are organic cannabis patients treated fairly?

There are other differences as well. Marinol can cost up to $2,000 a month. On the black market, marijuana is expensive too, but if it were legal, the price would drop by about 90 percent.

Of course, as tens of thousands of Americans have found by bitter experience, the biggest difference between Marinol and marijuana lies in how their users are treated. Users of both drugs are subjected to humiliating, company-required urine tests, but Marinol users are handed a Get Out of Jail Free card, while smokers are routinely forced into drug treatment, fired – or sent to prison.

Marinol users buy their quality-controlled drug from a pharmacist in a reputable drug store. Marijuana users must buy low-quality cannabis on the black market, often from a thug who also deals in dangerous narcotics.

Those who manufacture Marinol are treated as pillars of the community. Those who grow cannabis for the sick and dying are arrested charged, tried, and imprisoned – and not even permitted to tell the jury *why* they grew marijuana. Under present federal law, benevolent intentions are no defense.

The feds don't really mind if you use drugs, so long as they are corporate *synthetic* drugs that contribute to giant profits for the pharmaceutical companies. They persist in the absurd claim that Marinol has medical value and cannabis doesn't. Next they'll be telling us that Vitamin C tablets are OK, but possession of orange juice is a felony.

Pot smokers come from all walks of life – but walk a thorny path

The gross disparity between how Marinol users and medical-cannabis patients are treated is typical of the rank discrimination practiced against *all* marijuana users. When I started this book I planned to contrast the judicial treatment of cannabis users with that of alcohol and nicotine users, and found that this job had already been done by Mikki Norris and her husband Chris Conrad, two internationally recognized authors and lecturers on cannabis and hemp. Chris is the author of *Hemp, Lifeline to the Future and Hemp for Health,* and co-author with Mikki Norris and Virginia Resner of *Shattered Lives: Portraits From America's Drug War.* The latter work is a beautifully produced volume, detailing case after case of average Americans caught in the needless tragedy of the War on Drugs.[100] They did an outstanding comparison, so let's use theirs:

> Cannabis consumers are professionals, working people, artists, musicians, athletes, teachers, and students. They have good relationships with their families, contribute to their communities, pay taxes, desire a safe and healthy environment for their children, and are otherwise law-abiding. They are indistinguishable from their non-smoking peers, yet they are routinely discriminated against because of their decision to use cannabis for medical, spiritual, social, or other personal purposes. The chart below shows some examples of how unfairly they are treated, and it's been going on for too long.

People who consume alcohol or tobacco:	People who smoke or grow cannabis:
Can use and possess alcohol and tobacco in private or often in public without fear of arrest as long as they use it responsibly (and are not minors).	Are subject to criminal penalties, fines, possible arrest, prosecution anywhere, and can be sent to prison for simple possession, regardless of age or responsible use.
Have the right to privacy and to own a home and keep a personal supply on hand to share. Their private property, cash, cars, bank accounts, and assets are legally secure.	May be subjected to asset forfeiture and lose their home or business if cannabis is found. Cash, private property, cars, bank accounts, and assets are constantly at risk.
Can live in public housing safely where people can sit in the front yard to drink, smoke, and socialize without any recrimination.	May be kicked out of public housing if a friend or family member smokes marijuana in their homes, even without their knowledge.
Can drink or have a cigarette if parents. In a divorce, generally given preference over pot smokers for custody of their children, regardless of which is the better parent. Pregnant women keep their children.	May be arrested and lose their children if they use cannabis. Discriminated against in child custody battles. Pregnant women may lose their right to their children if they test positive for marijuana.

People who consume alcohol or tobacco:	People who smoke or grow cannabis:
Can take and keep a job if they use alcohol on their own time. Not screened for alcohol or tobacco as a condition for employment.	Are subjected to drug testing and banned from employment, may lose pensions, and get fired if they test positive for using cannabis, even if it was on their own time.
Can get education and student loans if caught drinking or smoking, even if under age.	Can lose student loans and educational opportunities if arrested for marijuana. Can be expelled from school if found with marijuana, even if adults.
Have freedom of religion to use alcohol as a religious sacrament, even when given to minors.	Are prohibited from using cannabis and face arrest if they use it as a religious sacrament only among adults.

(Note: This chart used by the kind permission of Mikki Norris and Chris Conrad. Please visit their web site, www.equalrights4all.org.)

As is tragically often the case, this insane and cruel mistreatment hits most severely those who are most vulnerable.

Racism in the War on Drugs

The war on marijuana was created and is fueled today by ignorance, arrogance, hypocrisy, politics, greed, power, money, corruption, outright lies – and racism.

Black and Hispanic Americans are far more likely than whites to be chewed up in the voracious jaws of the criminal justice system. African-Americans make up 13 percent of drug users, yet represent 35 percent of arrests for drug possession, 55 percent of convictions, and 74 percent of prison sentences.[101] The drug war has succeeded in imprisoning large segments of our population based on skin color. It's understandable that, given the horrendous punishment being dealt out to minorities, they prefer not to be visible targets of more persecution. It's crucial, however, that members of minorities unite with their brothers and sisters of all colors and become personally involved in the struggle against unjust drug laws. We should also ask friends in the entertainment field to become vocal. If we do that, the War on Drugs – a war on each of us – will end sooner rather than later.

Women used, abused, and incarcerated

Women have been urine-tested without their permission immediately after giving birth. Many who tested positive have been handcuffed to their beds in the recovery room and their babies have been taken from them by government "child protection" agencies. Such sanctions deter pregnant women who use illegal drugs from seeking prenatal care, and thus increase maternal and infant mortality. Those suffering from addiction are far less likely to pursue medical management.

The coercion of prison frequently has the opposite effect of furthering and deepening addiction. When women do go to prison, what has been accomplished? Drugs are readily available in most "correctional" facilities. Women are frequently sexually molested, and diseases are part of that package. Violence is learned. Women's spirits are broken. Anger is created. Children are put into foster homes. Is all of this going to stop illegal drug use? The problem is that the wrong people were, and are, going to prison. It should be the ones who initiated and continue the drug war.

Each year we're told about the thousands of deaths caused by drug "overdoses" – many of which would be prevented if presently illegal drugs were sold in pharmacies as their cousins from the big pharmaceutical companies are. Yet how many news stories report how many thousands of deaths have been caused by police, drug gangs, and organized crime as a *result* of the War on Drugs?

The Higher Education Act punishes the poor

The Higher Education Act cuts off federal financial aid to any student convicted of a drug-related offense, even simple possession of a small amount of grass. Placing obstacles in the way of students' ability to complete their schooling is hardly a fertile approach to the issue of substance abuse. The major drug problem on most campuses is not pot use, but rather alcohol abuse. No one seriously proposes that cancellation of eligibility for financial aid would be a sensible approach to that very sober problem.

The Act fails to distinguish between use and abuse, or between cannabis and amphetamines. A student smoking a joint is no more a gauge of addiction than adolescent drinking is an indicator of alcoholism, yet this ruinous law disallows financial help to students who desperately need the aid, youngsters from low-income families. Offspring of wealthy parents needn't fear losing college opportunities, because their families can afford to pay the tuition themselves – not to mention the legal representation that might well spare them a drug conviction in the first place.

It isn't enough that you're sick or dying...

The Department of Health and Human Services reports that two thirds of all terminal cancer patients do not receive adequate pain medication. This outrage is a direct result of the DEA's pressure on physicians who even *appear* to over-prescribe painkilling drugs.[102] Now U.S. Attorney General John Ashcroft is playing doctor, doing his best to halt assisted suicide in Oregon. He ordered the DEA to seek to suspend or revoke the licenses of physicians who prescribe drugs for assisted suicide, if the doctors follow the wishes of Oregon voters and their own patients. He obviously prefers that terminally ill patients die in agony. We treat our dying animals with more compassion. The federal government made the same threats to doctors who recommended state-approved medical marijuana.

DEA terrorizes sick and dying California cannabis patients – why?

California was the first state to pass the Compassionate Use Act in 1996. Since then, it has become patently obvious that the DEA intends to raid California medical-cannabis patients and facilities relentlessly, as a warning to other states that might be considering reform. Using armed force on innocent people for the purpose of instilling fear in others is a pretty fair definition of the word "terrorism." One case in particular demonstrates that the DEA is more interested in terrorizing us than protecting us from terror:

On October 25, 2001, while California's bridges stood under warnings of possible terrorist attack, 30 armed DEA agents found time to shut down the West Los Angeles Cannabis Resource Center, headed by courageous Scott Imler. Almost a thousand patients, sick and dying of AIDS, cancer, epilepsy, MS, and glaucoma, had written referrals from their doctors, but that didn't stop the DEA. Once again, the federal government terrorized medical-marijuana patients, and sent them out to back alleys to search for inferior medicine. Since the October raid, 19 club members have died and more are slowly dying. Medical-marijuana advocates hung a banner on the facility that read, "Shame on George Bush for the Los Angeles Cannabis Resource Center's D.E.A.th."

The DEA should learn a lesson from Abraham Lincoln, who in 1840 said: "Prohibition makes a crime out of things that are not crimes.... A prohibition law strikes a blow at the very principles upon which our government was founded." San Francisco District Attorney Terence Hallinan agrees with Lincoln. He does not prosecute state medical-cannabis cases.

What's the alternative?

If government can't keep heroin and other drugs out of its own prisons, it's clear that prohibition simply doesn't work. We should repeal it, as we did alcohol prohibition 70 years ago. Until we find the courage to take that step, there is much we can do to ameliorate the misery prohibition causes. Drugs are here to stay, whether legal or illegal. We must learn to live with them as safely as possible. A primary goal should be *harm reduction*.

First on the list of harm-reduction strategies would be *honest* drug education, making people aware in a nonjudgmental way of the *genuine* risks that different drugs pose, so they can choose lower-risk alternatives to the most dangerous drugs, like heroin and nicotine, and minimize the harmful effects of the choices they make. Harm-reduction methods range from *managed use* to *abstinence*. Advising "ravers" who use Ecstasy and similar "party drugs" to have their drugs tested for purity, to use no more than one pill, and to rest and re-hydrate would save lives.

Needle-exchange programs have been proven *not* to increase the use of drugs, and the programs could avert thousands of deaths from diseases like hepatitis and AIDS. Simply removing the prescription requirement for needles and syringes, nationally, would save many lives, at no cost to the taxpayers. The federal government is aware of these facts, yet continues its lethal policies.

In 1996, Arizona passed a law that diverted nonviolent drug offenders into drug treatment and education rather than incarceration. Of the offenders referred to treatment, 75 percent have stayed clean, which has allowed Arizona to use its jail and prison cells to hold serious and violent offenders. California's Proposition 36, passed in 2000, mandates treatment instead of incarceration for first- and second-time nonviolent drug offenders, saving millions of dollars a year.

Money that users and abusers spend to purchase illegal drugs enriches thugs, who then invest the money in other criminal enterprises; money spent on legal drugs goes to honest, taxpaying businesses. Legalizing marijuana, even if other drugs remained illegal, would move an enormous amount of money from the black market to the white market – and if marijuana were sold in pharmacies, most buyers of the herb would have no reason ever to meet dealers in heroin and other potentially fatal drugs.

Who decides? Who should decide?

After the tragedy of September 11, 2001, the government is learning how other countries deal with terrorists, and is now using their methods. It's time that we also study the marijuana policy in other countries such as the Netherlands. If it is found that cannabis use *reduces* the use of hard drugs, and if our country is sincere about "It's for the kids" (and not just to help politicians to get campaign contributions), then let us incorporate those findings and procedures into new marijuana laws.

The Netherlands decriminalized possession and allowed small-scale sales of marijuana beginning in 1976. Yet marijuana use in Holland is at half the rate of use in the U.S.A. It is also lower than in the United Kingdom, which has continued to treat possession as a crime. The UK is now moving toward decriminalization.[103] As of October, 19, 2001, the Netherlands allows pharmacies to fill marijuana prescriptions, which are paid for by the government.[104]

One approach that looks promising is to persuade Congress to leave decisions about medical marijuana to the states.

Our founding fathers feared a powerful federal government and spelled out a strictly limited set of responsibilities in the Constitution. The Tenth Amendment specifically reserved all other responsibilities to the states and the people. Republicans often argue for state's rights, and Democrats style themselves the party of the people. Why have administrations of both parties been so zealous to nullify state laws that liberalize treatment of marijuana users, and deny people's right to make their own decisions?

While running for President, George W. Bush said, regarding medical marijuana, that states' rights trump federal law. I know hundreds of marijuana users who voted for him because he took that stand – and now that he's got the office he's going after providers of medical marijuana.

Today's activists will be tomorrow's heroes

Never doubt that a small group of thoughtful committed people can change the world. Indeed it is the only thing that ever has.
— *Margaret Mead*

Over the years it's been my pleasure to meet hundreds of altruistic activists and authors on this subject. Long hours and years are spent by those who give of themselves to educate the public that there is a better way than putting our parents, sisters, brothers, and children in prison.

Our Founding Fathers were activists. They were scorned by their own country, England, which called them traitors. Today they are our heroes. Frederick Douglass and the other abolitionists were regarded as dangerous radicals. Today they are our heroes. So it will be for today's reformers, who work day in and day out to educate the public that marijuana prohibition is wrong, and that marijuana and hemp should never have been made illegal. These activists and organizations tell thousands of tragic stories about the system that has let our citizens down, including those of the 500,000 nonviolent drug prisoners of this sanctimonious War on Drugs. Even those who escape rape, death, or injury by guards or other prisoners suffer disease, humiliation, and loneliness each day in prison. Families are shattered; children end up on foster care, where many are physically or sexually abused. Promising careers are destroyed, and some former inmates become permanently unemployable. The state loses billions of dollars in tax revenues and our whole society loses the contributions of people who were once hard-working, taxpaying citizens like us.

Bringing such brutality to light is the self-chosen mission of "Grandma" Kay Lee, who discloses prison atrocities at the Florida Department of Corrections, which hundreds of inmates call "the Department of *Corruptions.*" Many of her letters go directly to Governor Jeb Bush. We need more Kay Lees to lay open similar cruelty in other U.S. prisons. All government leaders and all voters are asked to consider a rational approach to ending this war against cannabis and our own people. Help rid the earth of this beast, given birth in a cesspool of hypocrisy.

Too few users are active in the movement to reform marijuana laws

Should we obey corrupt, immoral pot laws that were created by racism and lies?

> *Cowardice asks the question: is it safe? Expediency asks the question: is it politic? Vanity asks the question: is it popular? But conscience asks the question: is it right? And there comes a time when one must take a position that is neither safe, nor politic, nor popular – but one must take it because it is right. One has a moral responsibility to disobey unjust laws. ...An unjust law is a code that is out of harmony with the moral law.*
> — *Dr. Martin Luther King, Jr.*
> *"Letters from a Birmingham Jail" (1963)*

So long as we're not harming someone else, what we use, eat, smoke, drink or do should be none of Uncle Sam's business. It doesn't bother Uncle when we use alcohol and nicotine products; why pot? If you believe that, get involved. Millions of grass users resent the inequity of marijuana prohibition – but of the 83 million Americans who have used cannabis how many have joined organizations who work to change the laws?

There are many outstanding organizations working constantly to educate the public that drug war is not accomplishing what it was intended for, to rid the country of drugs of mass destruction. Also, to incarcerate major drug king pins. (Rarely does the governments' DEA accomplish either. It's much easier, and much less risky, to arrest mellow pot smokers.)

These organizations typically keep their membership information confidential, and request annual dues of only $25 to $35 a year. If each of them had just one million members, tens of millions of dollars a year would be working hard to reform marijuana policy, and I have little doubt that the war on marijuana would end very soon – and that medical marijuana, at least, would be legal nationwide within three years.

I apologize for not mentioning all of the outstanding organizations, and their local groups. Space permits me to describe only the ones I'm personally involved with, yet I have great respect and admiration for each organization working for freedom.

Are you a NORML person?

One of the most vocal organizations advocating marijuana-related reform is the National Organization for the Reform of Marijuana Laws. NORML was founded in 1970 by a courageous young attorney named Keith Stroup, its executive director. The organization has been working steadily since its inception to reform the laws and to pressure the federal government to admit marijuana's medical value. *Yet fewer than ten thousand people are members of NORML!* (Hundreds of those attribute their joining to *High Times* magazine, the Internet, and my book, *Marijuana: Not Guilty As Charged,* which devoted an entire chapter to the subject, "What is NORML?") NORML is primarily an advocacy group; the mission of its sister organization, the NORML Foundation, is citizen education.

In 1972, NORML filed a lawsuit to compel the government to recognize the therapeutic use of cannabis. Finally in 1986 the DEA in effect said: if our own judge can rule on it, OK, sure, we'll have an open mind. The DEA made a crucial mistake: it happened to pick an honest judge, Francis Young. Judge Young spent two years reading thousands of pages on medical cannabis, interviewed medical doctors from leading universities, and numerous patients who made it clear that cannabis was the only medicine that worked for them, when pharmaceutical drugs did not. The judge's conclusion: Marijuana's medical use is "clear beyond any question," and cannabis in its natural form is "one of the safest therapeutically active substances known to man."

NORML, and thousands of sick and dying patients were grateful that the DEA kept their word. Or did it? On December 30, 1989, DEA Administrator John Lawn ordered that marijuana remain listed as a Schedule I narcotic, "having no known medical value." The judge tried his best to cause the DEA to be honest. The DEA must have felt terribly betrayed.

I was jubilant when I read that NORML had brilliantly capitalized on New York Mayor Michael Bloomberg's admission during his campaign, when asked if he had ever smoked pot: "You bet I did. And I enjoyed it." NORML publicized this response widely, in an attempt to persuade Bloomberg to reverse the city's policy of arresting and incarcerating minor pot offenders. Prior to former mayor Rudolph Giuliani's reign of pot terror, fewer than 2,000 pot-possession arrests per year was the norm. With Giuliani, and now Bloomberg, pot-possession arrests have skyrocketed to more than 50,000 a year. Who could know better than Bloomberg that pot is relatively harmless? Yet, by terrorizing New Yorkers, he is causing them to switch to dangerous drugs.

NORML founder and executive director Keith Stroup appeared on several national talk shows. "While we appreciate Mayor Bloomberg's refreshing candor about his own pot smoking, we cannot have two systems of justice: one for the rich and famous, and another for the rest of us." (I'm reminded of a judge who smoked pot at my home one morning – and that same afternoon sentenced other pot users to prison.)

Allen St. Pierre, the NORML Foundation's executive director, kindly sent me a video of some of the many news and TV shows that aired the NORML spot and interviews exposing Bloomberg's use of pot. Most news people and comedians acknowledged the announcement with amusement, or, by playing to what they thought their audiences would like to hear. One has to wonder how many of them smoke pot themselves. One of the most cannabis-wise and gracious was talk show host Gloria Allred, of MSNBC in Los Angeles, who emphasized responsible behavior. The most bigoted was Sean Hannity of *The Hannity & Colmes Show.*

The cannabis-ignorant Hannity said: "Alcohol is less dangerous than marijuana. Pot is a gateway drug. When they try marijuana and then move to crack and heroin and die, I would argue that marijuana contributed to their death."

TV talk-show host Bill O'Reilly, of *The O'Reilly Factor*, stated: "New statistics say that 60% of teenagers in drug rehab right now in America have a primary marijuana diagnosis. And 76% of all Americans started with pot. What say you about that?" Stroup answered the question well.

It's imperative to know the truth. The figures O'Reilly cited came from government-paid researchers whose job is to keep parents frightened. It's understandable that O'Reilly would ask those questions. What he didn't say was that the vast majority of those in marijuana rehab were given the option of incarceration or treatment. Which alternative would you accept?

The fact is that those who are truly in need of treatment programs are poly-drug abusers who also report problems with cocaine, alcohol, amphetamines, tranquilizers, or heroin.[105] Pot users are often said to be "marijuana-dependent" even when they do not meet the standard for dependence; even when, as many social pot users do, they put one or two days between use. Cannabis is not physically addictive. Medical-cannabis users who use the plant *daily* do not feel the high, but only the medical value. O'Reilly's assertion that *76% of all Americans who abuse hard drugs started with pot,* was just the same old DEA smoke and mirrors, a superficially correct statistic that is meaningless when used to try to prop up the long-disproved "gateway theory."

Given that 83 million Americans have used pot, *naturally* a percentage of people who use other drugs had some prior experience with pot.

Every nonpartisan, scientific study, national or international, has discounted the gateway theory. It was created to scare people away from cannabis (and, very possibly, into using alcohol). Alcohol, caffeine, and nicotine do not cause people to use cannabis. Cannabis does not cause people to use heroin, cocaine, or Ecstasy. What *does* cause many people to use dangerous drugs is prohibition of cannabis, and the government's scare campaign about it. In fact pot actually helps people *quit* alcohol, nicotine, and other drugs.[106]

I was pleased to hear Richard Cowan, outstanding activist, former national director of NORML, and current member of the NORML Foundation's board of directors, interviewed on the Phil Donahue Show. His courage enabled him to say that he has used cannabis medically and for relaxation for 27 years. Cowan is editor and publisher of Marijuananews.com.

The Drug Policy Alliance

The Drug Policy Alliance (DPA) is the leading organization working to broaden the public debate on government policy toward *all* drugs, and to promote realistic alternatives to the War on Drugs.

Ethan Nadelmann, the DPA's founder and executive director, received his BA, JD, and PhD from Harvard, and a Masters degree in International Relations from the London School of Economics. He then taught politics and public affairs at Princeton University from 1987 to 1994, where his speaking and writing on drug policy in publications ranging from *Science* and *Foreign Affairs* to *American Heritage* and *National Review* attracted international attention. He also authored the book *Cops Across Borders*, the first scholarly study of the internationalization of U.S. criminal law enforcement. In 1994, Nadelmann founded the Lindesmith Center, a drug policy institute created with the philanthropic support of George Soros.

In 2000, the growing Center merged with another organization to form the Drug Policy Alliance, which advocates drug policies grounded in science, compassion, health, and human rights. Described by *Rolling Stone* as "the point man" for drug-policy reform efforts, Ethan Nadelmann is widely regarded as the outstanding proponent of drug policy reform both in the United States and abroad.[107]

It was the Lindesmith Center that published the outstanding book I recommended in Chapter 19: *Marijuana Myths/Marijuana Facts* examines and exposes, with scientific facts, the 20 fear-provoking myths about cannabis most frequently trotted out by the prohibitionists. With nearly 70 pages of reference notes, the book clearly shows that marijuana's dangers have been grotesquely exaggerated, and that the laws have caused tremendous suffering, especially for the sick and dying. Their book should be mandatory reading for every member of Congress. In fact, everyone who wants to know the truth behind the myths about marijuana should read this book. It's inexpensive and a fast read, at only 163 pages plus reference notes and index.

Common Sense for Drug Policy

Bright Kevin B. Zeese is president of Common Sense for Drug Policy (CSDP), an organization that challenges all aspects of the War on Drugs.

As a young attorney Zeese worked for reform of marijuana and other drug laws as far back as 1978. He has debated DEA Administrator Asa Hutchinson, advised John Stossel of *20/20* for his documentary on drug policy, and helped Walter Cronkite on a documentary he did on drug policy a decade ago. Zeese is an outstanding and knowledgeable speaker and has appeared on numerous national TV and radio programs about the drug war. The Common Sense for Drug Policy web site honestly answers almost any question about drug policy you can imagine, and provides links to other organizations concerned with drug policy.

To the government's assertion that those who use drugs are supporting terrorism, Zeese responds powerfully: "Millions of Americans spend billions of dollars on Ritalin for youth, Prozac and Viagra for adults, and caffeine, nicotine, or alcohol, but none of *these* drug dollars fuel terrorism. Thus, it is not the drugs but the *illegality* of the drugs that creates profits for terror – profits that also fuel organized crime, corruption, and violence around the globe."[108]

The Marijuana Policy Project

The Marijuana Policy Project (MPP), based in Washington D.C., was created in 1995 to change immoral marijuana laws. MPP is headed by hard-working, skillful executive director Robert Kampia. Kampia has appeared on NBC's *Today* with Katie Couric, and on dozens of other national and local TV programs. He's often quoted in major newspapers. Kampia graduated with honors from Penn State University in 1993 with a Bachelor's degree in Engineering Science.

MPP devotes much of its energy to creating and fostering marijuana-related ballot initiatives. It deserves especial appreciation for creating Nevada's high-profile Question 9, which would have legalized the social use of cannabis, for quantities of three ounces or less, only for adults 21 and older. MPP director Rob Kampia said: "By bringing marijuana in off the streets and regulating it, we will be taking marijuana out of the hands of teenagers who currently find marijuana easier to obtain than beer."

MPP members and other proponents of Question 9 spent roughly $2 million on their campaign. The drug czar's office devoted a large part of its $180 million advertising budget for 2002 to a series of frightening, deceptive anti-marijuana ads that began in September. One commercial, shown heavily on network TV, linked marijuana to violence, while another suggested that marijuana is a date-rape drug. (The world's most widely recognized date-rape drug is alcohol.) Drug czar John Walters made two trips to Nevada to blitz the voters with his usual truth-twisting, including once again that hoary old chestnut: "Marijuana is a gateway drug that can destroy lives."

Such falsehoods, along with a heavy Republican turnout, caused the defeat of MPP's Nevada initiative – but the 39% vote in favor was a strong indication that support is growing for an end to marijuana prohibition. In the aftermath, Kampia said, "We knew Question 9 would be an uphill battle."

MPP held its first national conference, in combination with Students for Sensible Drug Policy (SSDP), November 8-10, 2002, in Anaheim, California. I was amazed that more than half of the 400 advocates of cannabis-policy reform who attended were brilliant SSDP college students. Many were studying medicine, law, engineering, and other disciplines at major universities. Students spoke openly about their disappointment in the government not admitting that cannabis has superb medical value, and their outrage that some students have been arrested at protests on behalf of medical marijuana. Rob Kampia and his staff presented a dignified and well-organized conference. SSDP's chief, Shawn Heller, was an outstanding speaker. He declared, "*We* are 'the DARE generation.' Our name was used to perpetuate these laws. 'We have to protect the children.' We are here to tell them, 'Stop using our names!'"

At the conference, I also had the pleasure of meeting the chairman of Common Sense for Drug Policy, Mike Gray, author of *Drug Crazy* and *The China Syndrome*. Gray is a noted speaker and has appeared on CNN and on ABC's *Nightline* to educate the public on our failed War on Drugs. He also writes for *Rolling Stone* about drug issues. I also chatted with Dr. Joycelyn Elders, the former Surgeon General, after her speech, in which she wisely said, "We are not drug free. We are less free." I told her I'd sent her a copy of *Marijuana: Not Guilty As Charged*, and asked her if she had received it. I mentioned that the book described the friction she'd experienced at the White House. She said she hadn't received it, gave me her personal address, and asked me to send her another copy. I asked her, "If I send you another one, will you read it?" She laughed and said, "I promise to read the part about me!" I sent it.

Another conference speaker, film producer Aaron Russo, asked me for a copy of the book, and two T-shirts that he had already heard carried the title, *Marijuana: Not Guilty As Charged*. I delivered them to him. In his talk he was unwavering in his sentiment that California Governor Gray Davis should be removed from office for failing to support the state's medical-marijuana laws. Dozens of policy experts, medical researchers, law-enforcement officials, and student activists shared their feelings about the failed War on Drugs. Dr. Ethan Nadelmann and Dr. Marsha Rosenbaum of the Drug Policy Alliance spoke, and author Mike Males described how he believed drug policy should treat children and teenagers.

The Internet will be a major factor in ending the War on Drugs

Many admirable groups are working to provide drug-war honesty using the Internet. One of the most outstanding is DrugSense/Media Awareness Project's (MAP) information. It provides more than 37,000 drug-related news articles. The web site is the most-surfed drug-policy site in the nation, averaging more than 70,000 hits a day. The DrugSense/MAP web site presents an alternative to government propaganda, the truth regarding the drug war. The site was born out of the vision of Mark Greer, executive director of DrugSense and the Media Awareness Project (MAP) Inc.

Greer has been interviewed on more than 250 radio and television talk shows on issues of drug policy reform. MAP has over 400 "news hawks," almost all volunteers, sending in about 1,000 news articles a month from the U.S., Canada, Western Europe, and Australia. Visit www.drugsense.org.

David Borden, a Princeton University graduate, heads the Drug Reform Coordination Network. That site has grown into a national network of more than 21,000 activists and concerned citizens, including parents, educators, students, lawyers, health care professionals, academics, and others working for drug policy reform. The Drug Reform Coordination Network's purpose is to stop the chaos and violence of the illegal drug trade, and end the bondage of mass incarceration suffered by hundreds of thousands of nonviolent offenders; stem the spread of deadly epidemic disease; secure the right of patients to appropriate medical treatment; restore Constitutional protections; and ensure just treatment under the law for all. DRCNet advocates a public dialogue on the full range of alternatives to current policy, and the implementation of peaceful, public health-based approaches for reducing the suffering caused by drugs and the drug war. See www.drcnet.org.

Jurors have more power than they know

Judges often tell jurors that they are to judge only the facts in the case before them, and not the law – but there is a long-established tradition in both English and American common law called "jury nullification" –

the right of individual jurors to judge the law as well as the defendant. The Founding Fathers believed that the people should be the final arbiters of the law, and that it is in their role as jurors that they exercise their judgment of the law. It takes only one juror holding out for a not-guilty verdict to prevent an unjust conviction. Alcohol prohibition ended partly because ordinary Americans serving on juries exercised their right, in essence, to convict prohibition rather than the defendant. The 18th Amendment was repealed in large part because it was becoming almost impossible to convict nonviolent alcohol users. If enough jurors learn that they have these rights, and use them today to acquit victims of the War on Drugs, medical-marijuana prohibition too will end.

Medical-marijuana patients and caregivers winning jury trials

The Sonoma Alliance for Medical Marijuana (SAMM) is an organization that organizations across the country could well imitate. It works cordially with the police and the district attorney's office. Its members support patients who attempt to take advantage of California's Compassionate Use Act of 1996 and are arrested for growing or possessing medical cannabis, often attending their trials. SAMM does not sell cannabis to patients, but rather refers those who qualify to growers of medical-quality cannabis. It is headed by Ernest "Doc" Knapp, his wife Kumari, and Mary Pat Jacobs, who donate their time.

As a member of SAMM, I attended the trial of two men, Mike Foley and Ken Hayes. The prosecution was attempting to prove that the men were dealers, not healers, and that each should spend five years in prison. They were charged with possession of 899 plants, grown to provide the medical herb for 1,280 patients of a San Francisco medical-cannabis outlet. (I was reminded of physicians who frequently care for more than a thousand patients.) Highly regarded attorney William Panzer represented the men. San Francisco District Attorney Terence Hallinan, who is aware of his city's many AIDS patients, knows that cannabis is good medicine. He testified for the defense, as did Chris Conrad, who is a court-qualified cannabis expert and the author of numerous books on the subject. Both witnesses were outstanding, and Panzer took full advantage of their testimony.

During a lunch break I presented William Panzer with a *Marijuana: Not Guilty As Charged* T-shirt. He smiled and said, "Very appropriate. I may wear this when the jury returns a verdict of not guilty!" I fantasized Bill tearing open his shirt and tie like Clark Kent, — Superman, and displaying the T-shirt. That didn't happen; but I did applaud along with others when, on April 18, 2001, the men were found not guilty.

Shortly after the trial, Sonoma County District Attorney Mike Mullins began working with SAMM openly and sincerely. He reviewed SAMM's research and agreed with our suggestions, and helped make them law for the county. Sonoma County now has the most liberal medical-marijuana guidelines in the nation: Patients may possess up to three pounds of cannabis annually, and growers are allowed 100 square feet of plant canopy and up to 99 plants.

The struggle continues...

> Dissent is the highest form of patriotism.
>
> — *Thomas Jefferson*

Advocates and activists for sane drug policy continue such efforts every day. Sometimes we score exciting victories, and sometimes the forces that have set themselves squarely against justice and compassion gain back lost ground.

Federal court rules that doctors can recommend pot

September 7, 2000: In a decision with sweeping implications for physicians and patients in California, a federal judge ruled that doctors have a constitutional right to recommend pot to their patients, and cannot be disciplined by the government for doing so.[109] The order, by U.S. District Court Judge William Alsup, also prohibits the government from initiating investigations of physicians who have made such recommendations. Alsup wrote that the order applies "even if the doctor anticipates that a patient would use that recommendation to obtain marijuana in violation of federal law."

Nice that freedom of speech has been rediscovered!

The Supreme Court ignores marijuana's confirmed medical value

May 14th, 2001: The U.S. Supreme Court, in a unanimous 8-0 decision, parroted federal law and ignored a vast body of research, and ruled that marijuana has no medical value, and that there can be no medical-necessity defense for its use. (Where states have legalized medical pot, laws protect qualified patients and physicians from prosecution in state courts.)

The efficacy of medical marijuana is confirmed – again

The British government is confirming yet again the healing power of cannabis, as reported by *The Observer* (London) on November 3, 2001:

CANNABIS A MEDICAL MIRACLE – IT'S OFFICIAL

Scientific Tests Of "Wonder Drug" Give Patients New Hope.

Cannabis is a "wonder drug" capable of radically transforming the lives of very sick people, according to the results of the first clinical trials of the drug. Tests sanctioned by the Government are proving far more successful than doctors, patients, and cannabis campaigners ever dared hope. Some of the patients are simply calling it a "miracle."

Taking the drug has allowed: a man previously so crippled with pain that he was impotent to become a father; a woman paralyzed by multiple sclerosis to ride a horse for the first time in years...

Until now claims of the benefits of the plant for certain conditions have been anecdotal. But the preliminary results of the UK government trial, started last year, suggest that 80 percent of those taking part have derived more benefit from cannabis than from any other drug. Many are describing it as "miraculous" ... Scientists now predict that cannabis – first used for medicinal reasons 5,000 years ago – will follow aspirin and penicillin and become a "wonder drug" prescribed for a wide range of conditions... Twenty-three patients suffering from multiple sclerosis and arthritis were recruited for the first trial and given daily doses of cannabis by spraying it under the tongue...

A former paratrooper suffers from a severe spinal condition. The pain was so bad he considered suicide; he found that legal painkillers turned him into a zombie and he couldn't have sex with his wife for five years. But after starting the trial he became a father. His doctor said, "His pain has been sufficiently controlled to engage in sex again." ... He also suffered from uncontrollable spasms. Cannabis has transformed his life.

Jo, the wife of a school chaplain, suffered badly from multiple sclerosis... "It's miraculous, really extraordinary. I've never had any sort of relief of this kind, and I've pretty well tried everything," she said.

"We're getting 80 percent of patients good-quality benefits from cannabis. For some we are getting almost total relief from their pain."[110]

Santa Rosa bust drives patients back to the alleys

May 29, 2002: The DEA raided yet another legitimate medical-marijuana clinic in Santa Rosa, California. That raid forced the clinic's 100 patients to procure cannabis on the black market instead, and subjected the clinic's operators to possible federal prison sentences of five to 60 years.

Santa Cruz bust targets the dying

September 5, 2002: In its most reprehensible bust yet, the DEA shut down the Wo/Men's Alliance for Medical Marijuana in Santa Cruz, California. The disgrace began when agents kicked in the door of what had been a hospice. Organically grown cannabis was given *free* to some 230 patients there with cancer, AIDS, and other serious illness. WAMM's facility was full; the only time it could accept a new patient was when another died. All patients held doctor's recommendations to use cannabis to alleviate symptoms of their ill health. For six years, city, county, and law enforcement officials had worked closely and sympathetically with the Alliance.

The DEA arrested WAMM administrators Mike Corral and his wife, Valerie, on suspicion of possessing marijuana with the intent to distribute, and suspicion of conspiracy. When such ludicrous charges are filed against those who work for free to relieve pain and save lives, what are we to think of the DEA's protestations that it only arrests major drug traffickers?

San Francisco is a winner

November 5, 2002: San Francisco voters passed 63% to 37% a measure placed on the ballot by County Supervisor Mark Leno to allow the city to grow and distribute its own medical cannabis, making San Francisco the first city in the U.S. to provide cannabis for sick and dying patients.

Is beautiful Diane Sawyer cannabis-educated?

December 4, 2002: For years I've admired, and smiled with, ABC TV journalist Diane Sawyer. Her enthusiasm and sparkle make me think of a grown-up Shirley Temple. On December 4, 2002, she interviewed vocalist Whitney Houston. When she invited Whitney's husband, singer Bobby Brown to join them, she pushed hard for confessions of drug use. Bobby was forthright in admitting that he is bipolar and does use marijuana to keep him on an even keel. Sawyer immediately asked why he didn't use one of the prescription anti-depressants. As bright and beautiful as Sawyer is I was disappointed that it appears she is not educated about the medical benefits of cannabis.

Federal judge's gag order backfires

February 12, 2002: On Abraham Lincoln's birthday, the DEA arrested Ed Rosenthal, without a doubt the country's most widely recognized authority on growing cannabis, and the author of more than a dozen books on the subject. He was charged with growing approximately 100 plants, and conspiring to grow more than 1,000 clones so that patients could grow their own, then released on $500,000 bail. (I hope the DEA is not targeting marijuana authors!) Rosenthal had been deputized by the city of Oakland as an officer in the city's program to distribute medical cannabis. He faces 10 years to life if found guilty of – sympathy for the ill and dying.

February 1, 2003: Rosenthal was found guilty, after a trial in which the judge, basing his decision on federal precedents, denied him the right to use the word "medical" in his defense. The only relief was that the jurors found him guilty of growing 100 plants, not 1,000. He faces a minimum of five years in federal prison.

February 5, 2003: The feds' gag order gave them a huge headache four days later, when four of Rosenthal's twelve jurors announced they would have voted for acquittal if they'd known he grew the marijuana for patients, and called on the judge to order a new trial. Under the front-page headline "Jurors say they were duped" the San Francisco Chronicle reported, "Four of the 12 jurors who convicted medical-marijuana advocate Ed Rosenthal of federal cultivation charges stood beside Rosenthal Tuesday and called for a new trial, saying crucial facts had been withheld from them... they felt misled by the judge's refusal to let them hear that Rosenthal's motivation for growing marijuana was to supply medical patients." By any reasonable reading of the Constitution Rosenthal was deprived of due process of law.

February 21, 2003: Ed Rosenthal and the four jurors were featured on a segment of *Dateline NBC* with Stone Phillips. The jurors publicly apologized for finding him guilty. Later in the show, drug czar John Walters once again stated that cannabis has no medical value.

Terminal multiple sclerosis patient meets Congressman

February 22, 2003: The day after Ed Rosenthal's appearance on *Dateline NBC* I received in the mail a grimly pathetic videotape from NORML's Keith Stroup.

The Case of Cheryl Miller: Medical Marijuana Necessity is a documentary by filmmaker Peter Christopher. Cheryl is dying of multiple sclerosis. Her loving husband, Jim, has been taking tender care of his wife for ten years. Her little body is almost stiff now. She can no longer walk and can barely move. She is down to 85 pounds of agony. This is her 17th year with MS.

Jim now carries Cheryl when she's not in her wheelchair or in bed.

Cheryl has been prescribed every MS pharmaceutical drug available. Their toxicity has had negative side effects. Marinol was prescribed, 40 milligrams a day for nine years, at a cost of $25,000 a year. The cost has been picked up by New Jersey taxpayers, via Pharmaceutical Drugs for the Aged and Disabled. Marinol has been helpful, but it takes about an hour to kick in and hasn't helped Cheryl's stiffness, or her sleep. A friend suggested that Cheryl try natural cannabis, something she had never before used. Jim broke the law and obtained some grass. He mixes it with salad oil and feeds it to Cheryl who found that it was twice as helpful as Marinol. It relaxed her muscles, enabling her to move her arms slightly, and to fall into a deep restful sleep. Cannabis also enables her to be able to talk more easily. Without cannabis, Cheryl would prefer death to take her in its arms.

Would Cheryl give up free Marinol, and use cannabis instead, with the chance of Jim going to prison for buying it, if it didn't work better than Marinol? Last year Cheryl made an agonizing trip to Washington D.C. to be a part of Congressman Barney Frank's news conference in support of his bill, HR 2592, the States' Right to Medical Marijuana Act, which NORML has actively supported.

Congressman Barney Frank pushes for states' rights to legalize medical marijuana

2003: Most of the progress in recent years toward a saner attitude about medical marijuana has been made at the local and state levels, but there are occasional rays of hope at the federal level. Representative Barney Frank (D-MA) introduced legislation in the 107th Congress to leave states free to allow the medical use of marijuana, in a bill titled the States' Rights to Medical Marijuana Act, HR 2592. If passed, it would have created an exception to the Controlled Substances Act and the Food, Drug, and Cosmetics Act, allowing states to operate medical-marijuana programs without federal interference. The bill would also have rescheduled marijuana from Schedule I to Schedule II, enabling doctors to prescribe it.

"People who are suffering from severe or terminal illnesses who find a measure of relief from marijuana ought to be able to use it without being treated like criminals," Frank announced. "This bill offers an opportunity for my conservative colleagues to decide if they really want to be consistent on the question of states' rights or if they think the federal government should tell states what to do."

Joining Frank in submitting this bill were Reps. Tammy Baldwin (D-WI), Earl Blumenauer (D-OR), John Conyers (D-MI), Peter DeFazio (D-OR), Jerrold Nadler (D-NY), John Olver (D-MA), Nancy Pelosi (D-CA), Pete Stark (D-CA), and Lynn Woolsey (D-CA). Similar legislation was prepared for introduction in the 108th Congress, and marijuana activists had reasonable hopes that the number of co-sponsors would be much larger.

Congress must pass the States' Rights to Medical Marijuana Act. This act will allow sick and dying patients complying with the laws of states that have legalized medical marijuana to obtain and use the medicine they need without fear that they will be prosecuted by the federal government and put in prison for 10 years or more.

Attorney General John Ashcroft raids firms selling cannabis equipment

February 24, 2003: The DEA began raiding stores that sell materials that many medical-marijuana patients use, in a campaign dubbed "Operation Pipe Dreams" and "Operation Headhunter." Glass pipes were wiped from shelves and shattered. Such attacks on businesses that don't even sell controlled substances are immoral – and futile. People who want to smoke pot instead of drinking alcohol or smoking cigarettes are not going to stop. They will only change to rolling joints in toilet paper, or using traditional briar pipes. (Perhaps I shouldn't give Ashcroft any ideas!) It's understandable that it is far easier to go after mellow people than terrorists, or criminals, who have guns and can retaliate. Water pipes cool the smoke. Vaporizers eliminate smoke and tars entirely. Such items can save lungs, and lives. For dying cancer and AIDS patients, vaporizers provide life-saving natural cannabis medicine. Ashcroft's justifications for these raids make as much sense as if he were to say that he reads Penthouse magazine for the occasional bible references. The tragedy is that those who do sell such merchandise are now facing up to three years in prison, a $250,000 fine, or both. Shape up, John. There are better ways to get money to repay the national debt.

States free inmates to save money

March 9, 2003: The Associated Press reported that, desperate to avert projected deficits, legislatures nationwide have curtailed corrections spending – or are at least considering it – by releasing inmates early, closing prisons, diverting drug offenders to treatment programs and moderating tough sentencing laws. The appetite for building ever more prisons has faded.[111]

Medical-pot users lose in U.S. court

March 11, 2003: In another legal setback for medical marijuana in California, a federal judge says two patients who used locally grown pot with their doctors' approval could face prosecution under federal drug laws. In a ruling made public Monday, U.S. District Judge Martin Jenkins expressed sympathy for the two women, for whom "traditional medicine has utterly failed." But he said the federal ban on marijuana applied to everyone, including patients using drugs that never cross state lines.[112]

Poll puts pot on front burner

March 11, 2003: New York City Councilman Phil Reed (D-Manhattan), who is pushing for legal marijuana, says he wants AIDS patients, cancer sufferers, and others with debilitating diseases to be able to alleviate their pain. Reed's resolution is to get a hearing in the Health Committee next month. It is supported by the New York State Nurses Association, the New York AIDS Coalition, and other groups.[113]

Vermont Senate passes medical-marijuana bill

March 13, 2003: After an intensive lobbying campaign and three committee victories in Vermont this year, the Vermont Senate passed the Marijuana Policy Project's medical-marijuana bill by a convincing 22-7 vote. If enacted, the bill would allow patients and their caregivers to possess and grow marijuana without the fear of arrest. The bill then moved to the Republican-controlled House, which passed a nearly identical bill in 2002 by a vote of 82-59.[114]

Canadian judge stops pot possession trial

March 14, 2003: In Summerside, Prince Edward Island, judge Ralph Thompson stayed charges of marijuana possession against a 19-year-old man, citing an Ontario ruling that said the charge of possession of marijuana is unconstitutional. "Until such time as the law is changed by Parliament, or the higher courts provide a ruling which will enable such an approach, this charge involving simple possession of marijuana will not proceed in this court."[115]

Dutch pharmacies start stocking medical marijuana

March 14, 2003: Under a groundbreaking new law effective March 17, physicians in the Netherlands will be able to prescribe medical marijuana and pharmacies will dispense it to patients as they do other prescription medications. This will make the Netherlands the first country to treat marijuana in the same manner it treats other prescription drugs. In order to establish a stable, quality-controlled supply of the medicine, the Dutch government will shortly begin contracting with medical-marijuana growers, who will be required to meet specific standards covering product quality, as well as security rules designed to prevent diversion into the illegal market.[116]

Cannabis medicine "on sale this year" in Britain

March 22, 2003: The United Kingdom's drugs minister, Bob Ainsworth, announced that the first cannabis-based prescription medicines in more than 30 years will be available in British pharmacies, perhaps before the end of the year. GW Pharmaceuticals, which was licensed to carry out clinical research trials on cannabis, has submitted "an extremely positive" report to the medicines control agency before final approval. The drug company has been testing an under-the-tongue spray in trials involving about 350 patients. The spray has been useful in treating multiple sclerosis, and helps reduce nerve damage pain and sleep disturbance.[117]

Bush to nominate woman prosecutor to head DEA

March 21, 2003: The White House announced that President Bush would nominate Karen P. Tandy, head of the Justice Department's Organized Crime Drug Enforcement Task Force, to head the DEA. If approved, Tandy would replace John B. Brown III, who has been acting agency head since former DEA chief Asa Hutchinson resigned.[118]

Maryland legislature snubs drug czar, okays medical marijuana

March 26, 2003: Ignoring a last-minute intervention by drug czar John Walters, the Maryland Senate voted 29-17 to approve medical-marijuana legislation. The Maryland House of Delegates passed a similar measure last week. Maryland thus becomes the second state to reform its medical-marijuana laws through the legislative process, after Hawaii did so in 2000. All other medical-marijuana measures in recent years have been enacted through the initiative and referendum process.[119]

GOP leaders pressure Maryland governor to veto medical marijuana

April 3, 2003: The Bush administration and other top national Republicans are heavily pressuring Gov. Robert L. Ehrlich Jr. to veto a proposal that would drastically reduce penalties for terminally ill patients who smoke marijuana to ease pain. Former Education Secretary and drug czar William J. Bennett is having trouble getting his phone calls to the governor returned.

John P. Walters, the White House drug policy coordinator said, "It is an outrage that, in this state, the legalizers would come here to try to put additional people in harm's way." Ehrlich, who co-sponsored medical-marijuana legislation in Congress, is unfazed by Walters' warnings. Ehrlich said, "I can take some pressure." In the past, Ehrlich said he watched his brother-in-law die of cancer two years ago. Walters said, "[Maryland] could face lawsuits from those injured by marijuana, such as victims of car accidents caused by users of the drug."

Some Maryland Republicans are outraged that the White House is trying to derail the legislation, calling it a slap at Bush's promise of "compassionate conservatism." "In this war on Iraq, you see all this concern for civilians," said former Republican delegate Donald H. Murphy of Baltimore County. "Why in this War on Drugs doesn't the drug czar have this same concern for the innocent and sick?"[120]

Football star uses cannabis for relaxation and medicine

May, 2003: In an interview in *Playboy* magazine, former All-Pro NFL lineman Mark Stepnoski said he is an active member of NORML. When interviewer Curt Sampson asked him why, Stepnoski replied, "The cost to taxpayers of arresting, prosecuting, and imprisoning people for simple possession is between $7.5 billion and $10 billion annually. Ninety percent of the 724,000 people arrested each year for possession are caught with an ounce or less." With our states thirsting for money for schools, and more, is that the bright way to spend our hard-earned tax dollars?

What must be done

- Just as we repealed alcohol prohibition in 1933, we should decriminalize all cannabis-related activity by adults.
- Until we find the courage and common sense to take that more modest step, we *must* repeal all laws, state and federal, that prohibit the growing and sale of medical marijuana so that those facing pain and death can get the medicine they need. Until then, the federal

government must accept "medical necessity" as a defense, for both patients and those who supply them with medicine.

- Employees must demand impairment testing in place of urine testing.
- Government at all levels must recognize that users of cannabis have the same rights as users of alcohol and nicotine products.
- Voters must cast their ballots for politicians who recognize that cannabis is far less hazardous than alcohol and nicotine, support equal rights for its users, and oppose the war on medical marijuana – and encourage other voters to do the same.
- We must encourage young people to become far more active in voting, calling in to radio talk shows, and writing letters to editors regarding medical marijuana, telling of patients they know who have been helped by cannabis.
- Politicians must understand that parroting the federal government's lies about pot in order to garner votes has become counterproductive, now that the majority of Americans are *for* the legalization of medical cannabis.
- The DEA must immediately reclassify pot from Schedule I to Schedule III, the same category as Marinol.
- Qualified cannabis patients traveling from state to state must be allowed to carry their medicine and not be harassed.
- Cannabis should be sold in drug stores.
- *Quality* medical-cannabis growers should be revered, not criminalized and sent to prison.
- Nonviolent offenders, "prisoners of (drug) war," must be released from jails and prisons, and given full pardons.
- Federal drug warriors such as Attorney General John Ashcroft, former DEA administrator Asa Hutchinson, and drug czar John Walters must try honesty for a change, and acknowledge publicly that cannabis is medicine.
- Citizens should learn about "jury nullification," and when they serve on juries they should exercise their right to free defendants prosecuted under unjust laws.

One final question

If God were to appear tomorrow and stop the chronic pain of millions and the consequences of other illnesses, aided by cannabis, would the government first insist on FDA approval?

And while we ponder that question, my back is in spasms. I'm going to invite a dear lady friend over, turn on my vaporizer, take a puff to stop the spasms, ...and then have some great sex!

References

1   National Organization for the Reform of Marijuana Laws (NORML) press release, 20 August, 2002.

2   "1,400 college deaths yearly tied to alcohol," Santa Rosa *Press Democrat,* 10 April, 2002, p. A10.

3   *San Francisco Chronicle* editorial, 13 February, 2003.

4   Terence Monmaney, "Medications Kill 100,000 Annually, Study Says," *Los Angeles Times*, 14 April, 1998.

5   "New Pain Killer Often Abused," Santa Rosa *Press Democrat,* 5 March, 2001, p.A6.

6   Marsha Rosenbaum, "A Mother's Advice About Drugs," *San Francisco Chronicle* [Open Forum], 7 September 1998, p. A23.

7   Edward M Brecher, "Licit and Illicit Drugs," *Consumer's Union Report* (Boston, 1972), p.414.

8   H. Li, "An Archeological and Historical Account of Cannabis in China," *Economic Botany*, XXVIII (1974), p. 437-8

9   "Marijuana More Dangerous Than Heroin or Cocaine," *Scientific American* (May, 1938).

10 "Mayor's Committee on Marihuana, The Marihuana Problem in the City of New York: Sociological, Medical, Psychological and Pharmaceutical Studies," Lancaster, PA (Jacques Cattel Press, 1944).

11 From the original motion picture *The Burning Question (Reefer Madness)*, produced by George Hirliman (Albert Dezel Production, 1936).

12 75th Congress, Public Law No. 238, 2 August, 1937, reprinted in Solomon, *The Marijuana Papers*, p.53.

13 Brecher, p. 414.

14 Ibid, p. 415.

15 *The Murderers*, Farrar, Strauss & Cadahy, (New York; 1961), p. 38.

16 *Press Democrat,* 3 July, 2002, p. A1.

[17] *USA Weekend*, February 14-16, 2003.

[18] Robin Fields, "Unmarried-partners households in U.S. up 72%," *Press Democrat*, 20 August, 2001, p. A1.

[19] Anjetta McQueen, "U.S. plan of attack against suicide," *Press Democrat*, 3 May, 2001, p. A8.

[20] Deb Riechmann, "Nixon had idea to go nuclear in Vietnam," *Press Democrat,* 1 March, 2002, p. A3.

[21] Her Majesty's Stationary Office, "Advisory Committee on Drug Dependence, *Cannabis"*, (London, 1969).

[22] Brecher, p. 455.

[23] Ibid.

[24] Ibid.

[25] Ibid., p. 457.

[26] Ibid., p. 460.

[27] Ibid.

[28] Ibid.

[29] Ibid.

[30] Ibid.

[31] Ibid.

[32] Ibid.

[33] Ibid., p. 457.

[34] Ibid., p. 459.

[35] Ibid.; p.463.

[36] R. Engs, *Alcohol and other Drugs: Self-Responsibility* (Bloomington, IN, 1987), p.294.

[37] United States Senate, "Marijuana Decriminalization," Hearings Before the Subcommittee to Investigate Juvenile Delinquency of the Committee on the Judiciary, (14 May, 1975), pp. 2-3.

[38] New York Academy of Medicine, Committee on Public Health, "Marihuana and Drug Abuse," *Bulletin of the New* York *Academy of Medicine, XLIX* (1973), pp. 77-80.

[39] John P. Morgan, MD, and Lynn Zimmer, PhD, *Marijuana Myths/Marijuana Facts, a Review of the Scientific Evidence,* (Lindesmith Center, 1997), p. 10.

40 Werkgroep Versovende Middelen, *Background and Risks of Drug Use*, The Hague: Staatsuitgeverij (1972).

41 Senate Standing Committee on Social Welfare, *Drug Problems in Australia – An Intoxicated Society?* (Australian Commonwealth Government Printing Office, 1977).

42 Lester Grinspoon, M.D., and James Bakalar, *Marijuana: The Forbidden Medicine* (New Haven, 1993), p.51.

43 National Research Council, *An Analysis of Marijjuana Policy*, (Washington D.C., 1982).

44 Peggy Mann, *Marijuana Alert,* (New York, 1985).

45 Ibid., pp. 30-31.

46 Mann, p.183.

47 Ibid., pp. 145-146.

48 "Facial Shape and Perennial Exposure to Marijuana, Alcohol, and/or Cocaine," *Pediatrics*, January, 1992, p.67.

49 Mann, p.231.

50 Ibid.

51 Ibid., p. 160.

52 California NORML Reports, April, 1992. (Based on a study originally published in *Drug and Alcohol Dependence*, XXVIII (1991), pp.12-28.

53 Mann, p. 139.

54 Ibid., p. 171.

55 Ibid., p. 4.

56 Ibid., p. 221.

57 Brecher, p.461.

58 Mann, p.272.

59 University researchers, 25 April, 2001, Journal of the American Medical Association, The *Press Democrat*, 27 April, 2001, p. A12.

60 Ronald K. Siegel, Ph.D., *Intoxication; Life in Pursuit of Artificial Paradise,* (New York, 1989), p. 10.

61 Ibid., p. 11.

62 Ibid., pp. 300, 302, 303.

[63] John A McDougall, M.D. & Mary A. McDougall, *The McDougall Plan*, (New Win Publishing, 1983), p.2.

[64] Ibid., p.5.

[65] Y. Kagawa, "Impact of Westernization on the Nutrition of Japanese: Changes in Physique, Cancer, Longevity, and Centenarians," *Prev Med,* VII, (1978), pp. 86-87.

[66] NORML, *Active Resistance*, (Washington, D.C., Summer, 1994), p.7.

[67] "Open Forum," *San Francisco Chronicle*, 30 January, 1997.

[68] Morgan and Zimmer, p. 13.

[69] NIDA web site.

[70] Morgan and Zimmer, pp. 12-14.

[71] ABC news, 7 April, 1995.

[72] *The New York Times*, 18 March, 1999.

[73] Seth Stevenson, "Anti-drug campaign tells lies to our kids," *Press Democrat,* 3 August, 1998, p. A7.

[74] Mothers Against Drunk Driving, 8 June, 1999.

[75] Associated Press, 8 August, 1998.

[76] Richard Glen Boire, Marijuana Law (Berkeley, Calif.: Ronin Publishing, Inc; 1991), 1986 CHP study, p.92.

[77] McDougall & McDougall, p. 76.

[78] British Medical Journal, June, 1996.

[79] Edward M. Shepard, and Thomas J. Clifton, *Drug Testing and Labor Productivity: Estimates Applying a Production Function Model,* Institute of Industrial Relations, Research Paper No. 18, Le Moyne University, Syracuse, NY (1998), p. 1.

[80] The NORML Leaflet, Summer, 2002, p. 2.

[81] Morgan and Zimmer, pp. 168-169.

[82] www.dea.gov, 14 March, 2002.

[83] R.I. Hubbard, et al., *Drug Abuse Treatment: A National Study of Effectiveness*, Chapel Hill, 1989.

[84] R. Gannon, "The Truth About Pot," *Popular Science* 192, May, 1968, pp. 76-79.

[85] S.H. Schnoll and A.N. Daghestani, "Treatment of Marijuana Abuse," *Psychiatric Annals* 16 (1986), pp. 249-54.

86 Morgan and Zimmer, p. 8.

87 www.mpp.org

88 Richard Glen Boire, Esq., *Marijuana Law* (Berkeley, CA, 1992), p. 92.

89 H. Robbe and J. O'Hanlon, *Marijana and Actual Driving Performance*, Washington D.C.: Department of Transportation (1993), p. 107.

90 Ibid.

91 A. Smiley, "Marijuana: On-Road and Driving Simulator Studies," *Alcohol, Drugs and Driving 2*, 1986, pp. 121-34; G.B. Chester, "Cannabis and Road Safety: An Outline of the Research Studies to Examine the Effects of Cannabis on Driving Skills and on Actual Driving Performance," in *Inquiry into the Effects of Drugs (other than Alcohol) on Road Safety in Victoria, Report of the Parliament of Victoria,* (Melbourne, 1995), pp. 67-96; A.B. Dott, *Effect of Marihuna on Risk Acceptance in a Simulated Passing Task,* (Rockville, MD: U.S. Department of Health, Education, and Welfare, 1972).

92 AlterNet (US Web, 6 January, 2003).

93 www.norml.org

94 www.norml.org

95 "The Merck Manual of Diagnosis and Therapy, 1992," Active Resistance, NORML (Washington D.C.), Summer, 1993, p.2.

96 Brecher, p.431,432

97 Ibid., p. 432

98 Ibid. p. 432

99 Morgan and Zimmer, pp. 18-19.

100 www.equalrights4all.org.

101 Neal Peirce Column: "International Condemnation for our 'War on Drugs,'" *Washington Post,* 26 August, 2001.

102 Milton Friedman, "America's Misguided 'War on Drugs'" [Forum], *Press Democrat*, 13 January, 1998, p. B5

103 Center for Drug Research, "Licit and Illicit Drug Use in The Netherlands 1997" (University of Amsterdam, The Netherlands: CEDRO, 1999; Netherlands Ministry of Health, Welfare and Sport; "Drug Policy in the Netherlands: Progress

Report Sept. 1997–Sept. 1999 (The Hague, The Netherlands: Ministry of Health, Welfare, and Sport, November, 1999); U.S. Dept. of Health and Human Services, Substance Abuse and Mental Health Services Administration, National Household Survey on Drug Abuse, 1998, 1999, and 2000 (Washington D.C.: SAMHSA)

[104] Anthony Deutsch, Associated Press, "Dutch Cabinet OKs Pharmacy Pot Measure," as in the *Press Democrat*, 20 October, 2001.

[105] R. L. Hubbard et al, *Drug Abuse Treatment: A National Study of Effectiveness* (Chapel Hill, NC, 1989).

[106] www.norml.org.

[107] www.drugpolicy.org

[108] www.cspd.org.

[109] "Order to Halt Assisted Suicide Blocked," *Press Democrat*, 9 November, 2001, p. A9.

[110] Anthony Browne, Health Editor, *The Observer (UK)*, 3 November, 2001. Details: http://www.mapinc.org/media/315 The Observer's web site: http://www.observer.co.uk.

[111] David Crary, Associated Press, as in the *Columbus (OH) Dispatch*, 9 March, 2003.

[112] Bob Egelko, *San Francisco Chronicle*, 11 March, 2003.

[113] Frankie Edozien, *New York Post*, 11 March, 2003.

[114] Marijuana Policy Project Updates, 13 March, 2003

[115] CBC News Online.

[116] Marijuana Policy Project Updates, 14 March, 2003.

[117] Alan Travis, home affairs editor, *The Guardian* (UK).

[118] The Week Online with DRCNet, Issue #280 (28 March, 2003), a Publication of the Drug Reform Coordination Network.

[119] Ibid.

[120] *Baltimore Sun,* 4 April, 2003.

Index of Celebrities

Index of Other People and Concepts

Index of Organizations

Index of Reports, Publications, and Media Items